Seven Servants

Seven Servants

Four Works
by
Wilfred R. Bion

Jason Aronson, Inc.
New York, N.Y.

ISBN: 0-87668-325-1

Library of Congress Catalog Number: 77-80323

Manufactured in the United States of America

LEARNING FROM EXPERIENCE

●

ELEMENTS OF PSYCHO-ANALYSIS

●

TRANSFORMATIONS

●

ATTENTION AND INTERPRETATION

INTRODUCTION

One of the benefits obtained from reading a book is that the reader can find out something about the subject of which the book treats. This book, for example, purports to be about psycho-analysis. Therefore, if you read it you may find out something about psycho-analysis.

A book has another aspect that tends to be passed unobserved—a fringe benefit that not even the beneficiary realizes. I recently overheard two people debating whether to go to a paper that was to be given by Bion. "Oh, I've heard all his stuff. It's always the same anyway." The speaker I have quoted probably did not realize that he had thus learned something about himself—how much he already knew. That is what I call a fringe benefit. What about my "fringe benefit"?

I likewise learned what I knew already, namely how little I knew and how often I repeated that small amount. It also stimulated, as is often the case, my curiosity about the vast, the infinite, domain of my ignorance. The idea that I should collect and publish these four books in one volume made me wonder what they were about, and that led to my re-reading them.

The result was a revelation.

I may summarize my discoveries briefly thus:

1. I had forgotten how much I had learnt from John Rickman and Melanie Klein.
2. I must have understood what I meant when I wrote it, but I do not understand what it means now. As the poet

replied when asked what he meant by *Sordello,* "Once God and Robert Browning knew; now, only God knows."

3. How much I thought I understood of what I meant, but in fact have only now begun to understand. In other words, some of what I said had an underlying significance that was not apparent when I wrote it.
4. The books were pro- and e-vocative.

What else can I say? Perhaps a warning would not come amiss: All helpful endeavours have a foundation which is, like most foundations, unobserved—the belief that things can be improved. Even psycho-analysis is tainted with ideas of cure that imply a better state. I think it is "better" to know the truth about one's self and the universe in which I exist. But I do not wish to imply that it is "nicer," or "pleasanter." Whether it is "better" is a matter of opinion which each individual has to arrive at for himself: his opinion and *only his.*

The Seven Pillars of Wisdom are:

> I keep six honest serving-men
> They taught me all I knew;
> Their names are What and Why and When
> And How and Where and Who.
> I send them over land and sea,
> I send them east and west;
> But after they have worked for me,
> *I* give them all a rest. *

The missing one completes the seven.

* Rudyard Kipling, "The Elephant's Child," *Just So Verses.*

Seven Servants

LEARNING FROM EXPERIENCE

But the mortallest enemy unto Knowledge, and that which hath done the greatest execution upon truth, hath been a peremptory adhesion unto Authority, and more especially, the establishing of our belief upon the dictates of Antiquity.

—Thomas Browne, *Enquiries into Vulgar and Common Errors: Of Adherence Unto Antiquity*

ACKNOWLEDGMENTS

Some of those to whom I am indebted I know, and to them I can acknowledge my debt. I am aware of others, notably patients, on whose cooperation I have always to depend, but who must remain anonymous. Dr. Elliott Jaques, Mr. R. Money-Kyrle and Dr. H. Segal have helped by reading and criticizing my manuscript. Just what generosity of time and effort this means for practising psycho-analysts can only be appreciated by another practising analyst.

Finally, as always, there is my debt to my wife without whose support I could not attempt to write at all.

INTRODUCTION

1. As the problems raised in this book are fundamental to learning they have a long history of investigation and discussion. In psycho-analytical practice, particularly with patients displaying symptoms of disorders of thought, it becomes clear that psycho-analysis has added a dimension to the problems if not to their solution.

2. This book deals with emotional experiences that are directly related both to theories of knowledge and to clinical psycho-analysis, and that in the most practical manner. The man trained in philosophical method does not usually have the analyst's intimate experience of disturbed thought processes, and even psycho-analysts rarely undertake such cases. I have been fortunate in this respect, but lack the philosopher's training. I have however had the advantage of having undergone an analysis first with John Rickman and then with Melanie Klein.

3. I have experience to record, but how to communicate this experience to others I am in doubt; this book explains why. For a time I thought of concentrating on analysis of trainees. I am confident that psycho-analysts are right in thinking that this is the only really effective method of passing on analytic experience that we have at present; but to limit one's energies to this activity smacks of the esoteric cult. On the other hand, publication of a book, such as this, may seem premature. Nevertheless I believe it may be possible to give some idea of the world that is revealed by the attempt to understand our understanding. If the reader is tempted to go further the object of the book is achieved.

4. I have kept notes and references down to the minimum; they are essential to thinking the thought through rather

than merely reading the book. The book is designed to be read straight through once without checking at parts that might be obscure at first. Some obscurities are due to the impossibility of writing without pre-supposing familiarity with some aspect of a problem that is only worked on later. If the reader will read straight through, these points will become clearer as he proceeds. Unfortunately obscurities also exist because of my inability to make them clearer. The reader may find the effort to clarify these for himself is rewarding and not simply work that has been forced on him because I have not done it myself.

5. It may seem that I am mis-using words with an established meaning, as in my use of the terms function and factors. A critic has pointed out to me that the terms are used ambiguously and the sophisticated reader may be misled by the association of both words with mathematics and philosophy. I have deliberately used them because of the association, and I wish the ambiguity to remain. I want the reader to be reminded of mathematics, philosophy and common usage, because a characteristic of the human mind I am discussing may develop in such a way that it is seen at a later stage to be classifiable under those headings—and others. Nevertheless I am not discussing whatever it is that the function may become; my use of the term is intended to indicate that whether the person observed is performing a mathematical calculation, a walk with a peculiar gait, or an envious act all are for me functions of the personality. If I concern myself with the accuracy of his mathematics it is not because I am interested in his mathematics but because his mathematics, and the accuracy of his performance, are functions of his personality and I want to know what the factors are.

6. If the reader will consider the previous paragraph (5) again he will see that by claiming the use of the term function and wishing it to retain its penumbra of associations I leave it to be supposed that the term will be used by me in accordance with the rules and conventions by which mathematicians and philosophers regulate its use. If I fulfil this expectation I may be thought to use the term

"properly". But if I disappoint the expectation (aroused by the penumbra of associations of which I do not divest it) I may reasonably be said to mis-use the term. It is then open to me, if I agree with the criticism, either explicitly to divest the term of its penumbra of associations, or, to accept the conventions of use implied by its associations.

7. In fact I wish to follow neither course. Suppose I see the man walking. I may say that his walk is a function of his personality and that I find, after investigation, that the factors of this function are his love for a girl and his envy of her friend. Or that the factors in this function are his love for the girl and his envy of her friend. After further investigation I may decide that to his love for the girl is added envy of her friend; or F (his gait) $= L + E$. ($F =$ function, $L =$ love, $E =$ envy). But I may feel that my observations approximate to the Kleinian theory of projective identification and that I can express my opinion of the facts best by saying the function walking is a sign that the patient feels he has taken into him a loved girl with whom he is identified and a rival of whom he is envious but with whom he has also identified himself, and that both objects are controlled by being enclosed in his legs. I shall spare the reader a geometrical figure, expressing this last idea "mathematically"; but will ask him to consider whether in Chapter I the terms "function" and "factor" are mis-used. I understand that the use can confuse but cannot agree that it can be decisively declared to be mis-use. In a later chapter I claim that the use of ideas, and the symbols representing them, is less advanced than the process by which ideas are evolved. For this reason I am prepared to believe I am mis-using an idea, or its symbol, or both, but I am not prepared to agree that there is yet a definitive criterion by which the matter can be decided. In psycho-analytic methodology the criterion cannot be whether a particular usage is right or wrong, meaningful or verifiable, but whether it does, or does not, promote development.

8. I do not suggest that promotion of development provides a criterion without reservation; psycho-analytic theory and practice, in cases where thought shows serious disturbance,

indicate the need for a reformulation of ideas about the origin and nature of thoughts and a parallel reformulation of ideas about the mechanisms by which "thinking" thoughts is achieved. But if it is necessary to change our views about thoughts and the mechanisms of thinking it is likely that the change of views, if it is as significant as I think, will require modification of the way in which we produce "thoughts" and the methods we employ in using them. My method of producing "factor" and "function" (and their fitness to represent a realization) is not necessarily wrong because it is different from methods ordinarily accepted as conformable with the proper production, nature and use of concepts, but my method is not therefore exempted by the critical scrutiny to which I consider all thinking needs to be subjected in the light of psycho-analytic experience.

9. The methods in this book are not definitive. Even when I have been aware that they are inadequate I have often not been able to better them. I have found myself in a similar position to the scientist who continues to employ a theory that he knows to be faulty because a better one has not been discovered to replace it.

Summary of Contents

The following plan of the book may serve as a rough guide:

Chapter 1 embodies a preliminary explanation of two terms.

Chapter 2 is a demarcation of area in which I wish to use the terms as part of my equipment of inquiry.

Chapter 3 commences a stylized description of emotional experiences, realizations, in which I have participated, that form the stimulus for the whole of this book. By "stylized" I mean that it is consciously sophisticated because the falsification that is introduced by such a method of presentation is immeasurably less than the falsification produced by any others, including so called mechanical recordings. These last have the truth that pertains to a photograph, but the making of such a record, despite a superficial accuracy of result, has forced the falsification further back—that is into the session itself. The photograph of the fountain of truth may be well enough, but it is of the fountain after it has been muddied by the photographer and his apparatus; in any case the problem of interpreting the photograph remains. The falsification by the recording is the greater because it gives verisimilitude to what has already been falsified.

Chapter 4 is a brief statement of some of the ideas that are discussed throughout this book.

Chapters 5–11 are a summary description of clinical phenomena related to the subject matter of the book; these are familiar to analysts but couched in terms that are probably more meaningful to analysts trained in Kleinian theories. The description indicates the use to which I put the term alpha-function and contact-barrier and at the end of Chapter

11 I draw attention to the importance of the choice between modifying frustration and evading it.

Chapter 12 commences with a discussion of projective identification and its bearing on the genesis of thought. The subject leads on to the part played by oral and alimentary experience in providing a model for thinking. I draw attention to the serious consequences for development of a mother incapable of reverie.

Chapter 13 deals with problems of recording sessions and the theories used by the analyst, and discusses possibilities that offer an approach to a method of scientific notation in Chapter 14.

Chapters 14–16 introduce the signs L, H, and K, for use in the discussion of the matter of this book.

Chapters 17–18 return to the use of the abstraction "alpha-function" for discussing the genesis of thoughts. The problems of abstraction or generalization and concretization or particularization are then discussed.

Chapter 19 starts the discussion of the use of psycho-analytical models.

Chapter 20 is an investigation of abstraction in which an attempt is made at using abstract signs to elucidate some of the problems of abstraction as they present themselves in analysis.

Chapter 21 introduces the Kleinian theory of interchange between depressive and paranoid-schizoid positions: its relationship to learning and the emotional experience associated with the terms employed in theories of causation is explored.

Chapters 22–23 discuss model making and abstraction in the context of analytical practice.

Chapters 24–27 continue the explanation with particular reference to learning (K link). Chapter 28 is an elaboration of the same theme in minus K (− K).

CHAPTER ONE

1. To CALL AN ACTION by the name of the person of whom it is thought to be typical, to talk, for example, of a Spoonerism as if it were a function of the personality of an individual called Spooner, is quite usual in conversation. I take advantage of this usage to derive a theory of functions that will stand up to more rigorous use than that for which the conversational phrase is employed. I shall suppose that there are factors in the personality that combine to produce stable entities which I call functions of the personality. The meaning that I attach to the terms "factors" and "functions" and the use to which I put them will presently appear, but some preliminary explanation may not be amiss.

2. The statement "A factor in X's personality of which we shall have to take account is his envy of his associates" is one any layman might make and may mean little or much; its value depends on our estimate of the person who makes it and of the weight he attaches to his own words. The force of the statement is affected if I attach to the term "envy" the weight and meaning with which it has been invested by Mrs. Klein.

3. Suppose now another statement: "X's relationship with his associates is typical of a personality in which envy is a factor." This statement expresses the observation of a function, the factors in which are transference and envy. What is observed is not the transference or envy, but something that is a function of transference and envy. It is necessary, as a psycho-analysis proceeds, to deduce new factors from the changes observed in the function and to distinguish different functions.

4. "Function" is the name for the mental activity proper

to a number of factors operating in consort. "Factor" is the name for a mental activity operating in consort with other mental activities to constitute a function. Factors are deducible from observation of the functions of which they, in consort with each other, are a part. They can be theories or the realities the theories represent. They may appear to be commonplaces of ordinary insight; they are not because the word used to name the factor is employed scientifically and therefore more rigorously than is usual in conversational English. Factors are deduced not directly but by observation of functions.

5. The theory of functions makes it easier to match the realization[1] with the deductive system[2] that represents it. Moreover, its use gives flexibility to an analytical theory, that may have to be used in a wide variety of analytical situations, without impairing the permanence and stability of the structure of which it is a part. Furthermore, by virtue of the theory of functions deductive systems possessing a high degree of generalization can be seen to represent observations in the analysis of a particular patient. Since psycho-analytic theory has to be applied to the changes occurring in the personality of the patient this is important. If the analyst observes functions and deduces the related factors from them, the gap between theory and observation can be bridged without the elaboration of new and possibly misguided theories.

6. The function I am about to discuss for its intrinsic importance also serves to illustrate the use to which a theory of functions can be put. I call this function an alpha-function so that I may talk about it without being restricted, as I would be if I used a more meaningful term, by an existing penumbra of associations. By contrast, the meaning of theories that appear as factors must be preserved and employed as rigorously as possible. I assume that the meaning has been made sufficiently clear by the authors and others who have discussed the theories with critical sympathy. The freedom implicit in the use of the term alpha-function and the concentration of precision of expression and employment into all that pertains to the factors,

confers flexibility without impairing structure. The use I make of an existing theory may seem to distort the author's meaning; if I think so I have acknowledged it, but otherwise it is to be assumed that I believe I am interpreting the author's theory correctly.

7. The term alpha-function is, intentionally, devoid of meaning. Before I indicate the area of investigation in which I propose to employ it, I must discuss one of the problems incidental to this investigation. Since the object of this meaningless term is to provide psycho-analytic investigation with a counterpart of the mathematicians variable, an unknown that can be invested with a value when its use has helped to determine what that value is, it is important that it should not be prematurely used to convey meanings, for the premature meanings may be precisely those that it is essential to exclude. Yet the mere fact that the term alpha-function is to be employed in a particular investigation inevitably leads to its reinvestment with meanings derived from the investigations that have already been carried out in that field.[1] Constant vigilance must therefore be exerted to prevent this development or the value of the instrument is impaired at the outset. The area of investigation is approximately that covered by the writings described in my next chapter.

CHAPTER TWO

1. DESCRIBING THE INSTITUTION of the reality principle Freud said, "The increased significance of external reality heightened the significance also of the sense-organs directed towards that outer world, and of the consciousness attached to them; the latter now learned to comprehend the qualities of sense in addition to the qualities of pleasure and pain which hitherto had alone been of interest to it." I emphasize, "the latter now learned to comprehend"; by "the latter" Freud presumably means "the consciousness attached to the sense impressions".[1] The attribution of comprehension to consciousness I discuss later. Of immediate concern is the function of comprehension itself; comprehension of the sense impressions and comprehension of the qualities of pleasure and pain are both investigated in this discussion. I treat sense impressions, pleasure and pain as alike real, thereby discarding the distinction that Freud makes between the "outer-world" and pleasure and pain, as irrelevant to the theme of comprehension. I shall however discuss the bearing of the Pleasure principle and the Reality principle on the choice that a patient can be seen to make between modifying frustration and evading it.

2. The attribution of comprehension to consciousness leads to contradictions which are avoided by accepting, for purposes of the theory I wish to propound, Freud's later conceptualization, "but what part is there left to be played in our scheme of consciousness, which was once so omnipotent and hid all else from view? *Only that of a sense-organ for the perception of psychical qualities*". (Freud's italics.)

3. Continuing the quotation from Freud's Two Principles of Mental Functioning "A special function was instituted

which had periodically to search the other world in order that its data might be already familiar if an urgent inner need should arise; this function was *attention.* Its activity meets the sense impressions half-way instead of awaiting their appearance."[1] Freud did not carry his investigation of attention far, but the term, as he uses it, has a meaning I would investigate as a factor in alpha-function.

4. To continue, "At the same time there was probably introduced a system of notation, whose task was to deposit the results of this periodical activity of consciousness—a part of that which we call memory." Notation and the deposition of the results of attention are also phenomena to be investigated by the aid of the theory of alpha-function.

5. Certain theories of Melanie Klein and her co-workers will be considered; I list them here. They are: Splitting and projective identification[1]; the transition from the paranoid-schizoid to the depressive position and vice-versa;[2] symbol formation and[3] some of my previous work on the development of verbal thought.[4] I shall not discuss them except as factors modified by combination with each other in a function. So much for previous work; I now give an example of the employment of this Theory of Functions in a psycho-analytic investigation of the field covered by the work referred to in this chapter.

CHAPTER THREE

1. An emotional experience occurring in sleep, which I choose for reasons that will presently appear, does not differ from the emotional experience occurring during waking life in that the perceptions of the emotional experience have in both instances to be worked upon by alpha-function before they can be used for dream thoughts.

2. Alpha-function operates on the sense impressions, whatever they are, and the emotions, whatever they are, of which the patient is aware. In so far as alpha-function is successful alpha elements are produced and these elements are suited to storage and the requirements of dream thoughts. If alpha-function is disturbed, and therefore inoperative, the sense impressions of which the patient is aware and the emotions which he is experiencing remain unchanged. I shall call them beta-elements. In contrast with the alpha-elements the beta-elements are not felt to be phenomena,[1] but things in themselves.[2] The emotions likewise are objects of sense. We are thus presented with a state of mind precisely contrasting with that of the scientist who knows he is concerned with phenomena but has not the same certitude that the phenomena have a counterpart of things in themselves.

3. Beta-elements are not amenable to use in dream thoughts but are suited for use in projective identification. They are influential in producing acting out. They are objects that can be evacuated or used for a kind of thinking that depends on manipulation of what are felt to be things in themselves as if to substitute such manipulation for words or ideas. For example a man may murder his parents and so feel free to love because the anti-sexual internal parents are supposed by this act to have been evacuated. Such an act is intended

"to rid the psyche of accretions of stimuli". Beta-elements are stored but differ from alpha-elements in that they are not so much memories as undigested facts, whereas the alpha-elements have been digested by alpha-function and thus made available for thought. It is important to distinguish between memories and undigested facts—beta-elements. (The use of the terms "digested" and "undigested" will be investigated later.)

4. If the patient cannot transform his emotional experience into alpha-elements, he cannot dream. Alpha-function transforms sense impressions into alpha-elements which resemble, and may in fact be identical with, the visual images with which we are familiar in dreams, namely, the elements that Freud regards as yielding their latent content when the analyst has interpreted them. Freud showed that one of the functions of a dream is to preserve sleep. Failure of alpha-function means the patient cannot dream and therefore cannot sleep. As alpha-function makes the sense impressions of the emotional experience available for conscious and dream-thought the patient who cannot dream cannot go to sleep and cannot wake up. Hence the peculiar condition seen clinically when the psychotic patient behaves as if he were in precisely this state.

CHAPTER FOUR

1. The emotional experience must now be considered generally and not only as it occurs in sleep. I shall emphasize what I have said so far by re-writing a popular theory of the nightmare. It used once to be said that a man had a nightmare because he had indigestion and that is why he woke up in a panic. My version is: The sleeping patient is panicked; because he cannot have a nightmare he cannot wake up or go to sleep; he has had mental indigestion ever since.

2. The more general statement of the theory is this: To learn from experience alpha-function must operate on the awareness of the emotional experience; alpha-elements are produced from the impressions of the experience; these are thus made storeable and available for dream thoughts and for unconscious waking thinking. A child having the emotional experience called learning to walk is able by virtue of alpha-function to store this experience. Thoughts that had originally to be conscious become unconscious and so the child can do all the thinking needed for walking without any longer being conscious of any of it. Alpha-function is needed for conscious thinking and reasoning and for the relegation of thinking to the unconscious when it is necessary to disencumber consciousness of the burden of thought by learning a skill.

3. If there are only beta-elements, which cannot be made unconscious, there can be no repression, suppression, or learning. This creates the impression that the patient is incapable of discrimination. He cannot be unaware of any single sensory stimulus: yet such hypersensitivity is not contact with reality.

4. Attacks on alpha-function, stimulated by hate or envy, destroy the possibility of the patient's conscious contact either with himself or another as live objects. Accordingly we hear of inanimate objects, and even of places, when we would normally expect to hear of people. These, though described verbally, are felt by the patient to be present materially and not merely to be represented by their names. This state contrasts with animism in that live objects are endowed with the qualities of death.

CHAPTER FIVE

1. We must now examine enforced splitting associated with a disturbed relationship with the breast or its substitutes. The infant receives milk and other creature comforts from the breast; also love, understanding, solace. Suppose his initiative is obstructed by fear of aggression, his own or another's. If the emotion is strong enough it inhibits the infant's impulse to obtain sustenance.

Love in infant or mother or both increases rather than decreases the obstruction partly because love is inseparable from envy[1] of the object so loved, partly because it is felt to arouse envy and jealousy in a third object that is excluded. The part played by love may escape notice because envy, rivalry and hate obscure it, although hate would not exist if love were not present. Violence of emotion compels reinforcement of the obstruction because violence is not distinguished from destructiveness and subsequent guilt and depression. Fear of death through starvation of essentials compels resumption of sucking. A split between material and psychical satisfaction develops.

2. Fear, hate and envy are so feared that steps are taken to destroy awareness of all feelings, although that is indistinguishable from taking life itself.[1] If a sense of reality, too great to be swamped by emotions, forces the infant to resume feeding, intolerance of envy and hate in a situation which stimulates love and gratitude leads to a splitting that differs from splitting carried out to prevent depression. It differs from splitting impelled by sadistic impulses in that its object and effect is to enable the infant to obtain what later in life would be called material comforts without acknowledging the existence of a live object on which these benefits depend.

Envy aroused by a breast that provides love, understanding, experience and wisdom, poses a problem that is solved by destruction of alpha-function. This makes breast and infant appear inanimate with consequent guiltiness, fear of suicide and fear of murder, past, present and impending. The need for love, understanding and mental development is now deflected, since it cannot be satisfied, into the search for material comforts. Since the desires for material comforts are reinforced the craving for love remains unsatisfied and turns into overweening and misdirected greed.

3. This split, enforced by starvation and fear of death through starvation on the one hand, and by love and the fear of associated murderous envy and hate on the other, produces a mental state in which the patient greedily pursues every form of material comfort; he is at once insatiable and implacable in his pursuit of satiation. Since this state originates in a need to be rid of the emotional complications of awareness of life, and a relationship with live objects, the patient appears to be incapable of gratitude or concern either for himself or others. This state involves destruction of his concern for truth. Since these mechanisms fail to rid the patient of his pains, which he feels to be due to lack of something, his pursuit of a cure takes the form of a search for a lost object and ends in increased dependence on material comfort; quantity must be the governing consideration, not quality. He feels surrounded by bizarre objects,[1] so that even the material comforts are bad and unable to satisfy his needs. But he lacks the apparatus, alpha-function, by which he might understand his predicament. The patient greedily and fearfully takes one beta-element after another apparently unable to conceive of any activity other than introjection of more beta-elements. To observe this taking place in analysis is to feel that the patient will never abandon his pursuit of a course of action which one would think he could not possibly fail to know was futile. He thinks the interpretations are without exception bad, yet he must have more and more of them. The patient however does not feel he is having interpretations for that would involve an ability to establish with the analyst the counterpart of an infant's

relationship with a breast that provides material wisdom and love. But he feels able only to establish the counterpart of a relationship in which such sustenance can be had as inanimate objects can provide; he can have analytic interpretations that he feels to be either flatus or contributions remarkable for what they are not rather than for what they are. The fact that the patient uses an equipment suited for contact with the inanimate to establish contact with himself helps to explain the confusion produced by the patient's awareness that he is in fact alive.[2] Although he feels there are no redeeming features in his environment, including in his environment the analyst's interpretations and his own lack of equipment to learn anything from his experience, the patient does ultimately grasp some of the meaning of what is said to him.

CHAPTER SIX

1. The patient's reactions to material comfort are shown by his reactions to the material comforts, the couch or other amenities, of the consulting room. Why must he have more and more of such "comforts"? Part of the answer lies in the splitting that was intended, by effecting a separation of material from psychical comforts, as an escape from fear of envy, either his own or another's.

2. The attempt to evade the experience of contact with live objects by destroying alpha-function leaves the personality unable to have a relationship with any aspect of itself that does not resemble an automaton. Only beta-elements are available for whatever activity takes the place of thinking and beta-elements are suitable for evacuation only—perhaps through the agency of projective identification. These beta-elements are dealt with by an evacuatory procedure similar to the movements of musculature, changes of mien, etc. which Freud described as intended to disencumber the personality of accretions of stimuli and not to effect changes in the environment; a muscular movement, for example, a smile, must have a different interpretation from the smile of the non-psychotic personality. The phenomena present in analysis are not identical with Freud's description of the personality acting, during the phase of dominance of the pleasure principle, to disencumber itself of accretions of stimuli. That personality is, within limits, normal; the personality I am describing is highly abnormal. Activity taking place, under the dominance of the pleasure principle, to disencumber the personality of accretions of stimuli becomes replaced, in the phase of dominance by the reality principle, by ejection of unwanted beta-elements. A smile or a verbal statement must be

interpreted as an evacuatory muscular movement and not as a communication of feeling.

The scientist whose investigations include the stuff of life itself finds himself in a situation that has a parallel in that of the patients I am describing. The breakdown in the patient's equipment for thinking leads to dominance by a mental life in which his universe is populated by inanimate objects. The inability of even the most advanced human beings to make use of their thoughts, because the capacity to think is rudimentary in all of us, means that the field for investigation, all investigation being ultimately scientific, is limited, by human inadequacy, to those phenomena that have the characteristics of the inanimate. We assume that the psychotic limitation is due to an illness: but that that of the scientist is not. Investigation of the assumption illuminates disease on the one hand and scientific method on the other. It appears that our rudimentary equipment for "thinking" thoughts is adequate when the problems are associated with the inanimate, but not when the object for investigation is the phenomenon of life itself. Confronted with the complexities of the human mind the analyst must be circumspect in following even accepted scientific method; its weakness may be closer to the weakness of psychotic thinking than superficial scrutiny would admit.

CHAPTER SEVEN

1. IF A MAN has an emotional experience when asleep or awake and is able to convert it into alpha-elements he can either remain unconscious of that emotional experience or become conscious of it. The sleeping man has an emotional experience, converts it into alpha-elements and so becomes capable of dream thoughts. Thus he is free to become conscious (that is wake up) and describe the emotional experience by a narrative usually known as a dream.

2. A man talking to a friend converts the sense impressions of this emotional experience into alpha-elements, thus becoming capable of dream thoughts and therefore of undisturbed consciousness of the facts whether the facts are the events in which he participates or his feelings about those events or both. He is able to remain "asleep" or unconscious of certain elements that cannot penetrate the barrier presented by his "dream". Thanks to the "dream" he can continue uninterruptedly to be awake, that is, awake to the fact that he is talking to his friend, but asleep to elements which, if they could penetrate the barrier of his "dreams", would lead to domination of his mind by what are ordinarily unconscious ideas and emotions.

The dream makes a barrier against mental phenomena which might overwhelm the patient's awareness that he is talking to a friend, and, at the same time, makes it impossible for awareness that he is talking to a friend to overwhelm his phantasies. The psychotic's attempt to discriminate one from the other leads to rational thought characterized by a peculiar lack of "resonance". What he says clearly and in articulated speech is one dimensional. It has no overtones or undertones of meaning. It makes the listener inclined to say "so what?" It has no capacity to evoke a train of thought.

3. The "dream" has many of the functions of censorship and resistance. These functions are not the product of the unconscious but instruments by which the "dream" creates and differentiates consciousness from unconsciousness.

To sum up: the "dream", together with the alpha-function, which makes dream possible, is central to the operation of consciousness and unconsciousness, on which ordered thought depends. Alpha-function theory of the "dream" has the elements of the view represented by classical psycho-analytic dream theory, that is to say, censorship and resistance are represented in it. But in alpha-function theory the powers of censorship and resistance are essential to differentiation of conscious and unconscious and help to maintain the discrimination between the two. This discrimination derives from the operation of the "dream", which is a combination in narrative form of dream thoughts, which thoughts in turn derive from combinations of alpha-elements. In this theory the ability to "dream" preserves the personality from what is virtually a psychotic state. It therefore helps to explain the tenacity with which the dream, as represented in classical theory, defends itself against the attempt to make the unconscious conscious. Such an attempt must appear indistinguishable from destruction of the capacity to dream in so far as that capacity is related to differentiating conscious from unconscious[1] and maintaining the difference so established.

CHAPTER EIGHT

1. I SHALL NOW TRANSFER all that I have said about the establishment of conscious and unconscious and a barrier between them to a supposed entity, that I designate a "contact-barrier"; Freud used this term to describe the neuro-physiological entity subsequently known as a synapse. In conformity with this my statement that the man has to "dream" a current emotional experience whether it occurs in sleep or in waking life is re-formulated thus: The man's alpha-function whether in sleeping or waking transforms the sense-impressions related to an emotional experience, into alpha-elements, which cohere as they proliferate to form the contact-barrier. This contact-barrier, thus continuously in process of formation, marks the point of contact and separation between conscious and unconscious elements and originates the distinction between them. The nature of the contact-barrier will depend on the nature of the supply of alpha-elements and on the manner of their relationship to each other. They may cohere. They may be agglomerated. They may be ordered sequentially to give the appearance of narrative (at least in the form in which the contact-barrier may reveal itself in a dream). They may be ordered logically. They may be ordered geometrically.

2. The term "contact-barrier" emphasizes the establishment of contact between conscious and unconscious and the selective passage of elements from one to the other. On the nature of the contact-barrier will depend the change of elements from conscious to unconscious and vice versa. In so far as dreams give us direct access to its study they retain the central position in psycho-analysis that Freud assigned to them.

The nature of the transition from conscious to unconscious and vice versa, and therefore the nature of the contact-barrier and its component alpha-elements affect memory and the characteristics of any given memory.

3. In practice the theory of functions and the theory of an alpha-function make possible interpretations showing precisely how the patient feels that he has feelings, but cannot learn from them; sensations, some of which are extremely faint, but cannot learn from them either. A determination not to experience anything can be shown to co-exist with an inability to reject or ignore any stimulus. Sense-impressions can be seen to have some meaning but the patient feels incapable of knowing what the meaning is.

4. Interpretations derived from these theories appear to effect changes in the patient's capacity for thinking and therefore of understanding. Such a response is itself sufficiently peculiar, in view of the phenomenon being investigated, to require explanation. In the first place the nature of the difficulties, if indeed they are being accurately described, would seem to rule out the possibility that the patient could grasp the description. Such a difficulty may be surmounted by an elucidation of different degrees of disability. From the point of view of technique it would be agreeable if the response to interpretations based on a use of a theory of functions, alpha-function and contact-barrier carried some element of confirmation that a realization approximated to these theoretical concepts. Scientifically, validation of the theory would then be supported by a correlation between evidence that capacity for thinking had been increased by analysis and evidence of the existence of a realization that corresponded to the abstract theoretical construct. There is in fact an "echo" effect when an interpretation is given that lends support to the idea that the theoretical concept of contact-barrier has a corresponding realization. Discussion of this is outside the scope of this subject and I leave it for another occasion.

In Chapters 3–8 I have used the concept of alpha-function to fill gaps in my knowledge of a state of mind which is met with in analytic practice and that I want to describe. I have thus been able to proceed with the communication without having to wait for discovery of the missing facts and without making statements that might appear to suggest that the facts were already known.

I must now show how the theory of functions is used as a tool in the analytic work. I give examples of the background of emotional experiences (realizations) from which the theory was abstracted and pass on to give examples of realizations, unknown when the theory was abstracted, that were subsequently found to approximate to the theory. The material unfortunately does not lend itself to such logical exposition without producing misleading distortion of the facts. In the next chapter emphasis is on the background of emotional experience from which the theory is abstracted. The description is of elements from which the abstraction was made but these are mixed with so many others that it is impossible to claim for it qualities that are ordinarily regarded as essential to a scientific production.

CHAPTER NINE

1. A SMALL NUMBER of patients with whom I have had to deal have presented prominently symptoms of disordered capacity for thought. In the course of their treatment opportunities for orthodox transference interpretations occurred and were taken, but the patient often learned nothing from them. The stream of disjointed associations continued. Interpretations based on theories of anal erotism in its various forms, theories of the patient's need to improvise a personality out of elements he felt were worthless and which he could therefore afford to lose, theories of splitting, projective identification, defence against assault and so on had only slight effect. There were signs of confusion that I had learned to associate with projective identification. I therefore assumed that I was the repository of a part of his personality such as his sanity, or the non-psychotic part of his personality. Before long I decided that further interpretations based on these theories were not likely to achieve any useful purpose. I tested the supposition that I contained the non-psychotic part of his personality, and then began to be aware that I was supposed to be conscious of what was going on while he was not. I was (contained) his "conscious". Sometimes I could visualize the situation, unfolding in the analysis, as one in which the patient was a fœtus to whom the mother's emotions were communicated but to whom the stimulus for the emotions, and their source, was unknown (see "model making", p. 66 below). At other times he seemed to have a rudimentary idea of what was going on, but no idea how he felt. I shall not here describe the variations on this theme, as they were not substantially different from those described by M. Klein, H. Rosenfeld and others. The problem which awaited

solution, and which I am now discussing, was to determine what this part was. The theory of functions offered a prospect of solving this problem by assuming that I contained unknown functions of his personality and from this to scrutinize the sessional experience for clues of what these might be. I assumed that I was "consciousness." Freud's theory that consciousness is the sense-organ of psychic quality, allowed an assumption that a separation was being effected between consciousness and psychic quality. This assumption proved fruitful, but only for a session or two and then I found myself in the same situation as before, or nearly so. I was still thinking of the problem as one that could be solved in terms of transference theory and projective identification, that is to say, that I could assume that patients felt under scrutiny by me and the parts of their personality I was supposed to contain. In the light of theories of transference and projective identifications the material poured out could be seen as the link between patient and analyst and I could interpret in the way described in Attacks on Linking. Interpretations had some success, but I did not feel that changes necessarily related to illumination received from interpretations. It then occurred to me that he was doing what I earlier described as "dreaming" the immediate events in the analysis—that is to say, translating sense impressions into alpha-elements. This idea seemed to illuminate sometimes but became dynamic only when I related it to *defective* alpha-function, that is to say, when it occurred to me that I was witnessing an inability to dream through lack of alpha-elements and therefore an inability to sleep or wake, to be either conscious or unconscious.

2. This could explain why I was a conscious that was incapable of the functions of consciousness and he an "unconscious" incapable of the functions of *unconsciousness*. (For the sake of simplicity I am supposing that this division of functions remained stationary, but in fact it was not so; roles were interchangeable.)

3. Now this situation does not correspond to the theoretical framework I have suggested, the theory, namely, of a contact-barrier owing its existence to the proliferation of

alpha-elements by alpha-function and serving the function of a membrane which by the nature of its composition and permeability separates mental phenomena into two groups one of which performs the functions of consciousness and the other the functions of unconsciousness.

4. In the new situation there is a division of sorts, suspended between analyst and patient as it were, but offering no resistance to the passage of elements from the one zone to the other. It is unsuited to the establishment of conscious and unconscious, and therefore conducive to defective or anomalous developments of a capacity for memory and repression. The difference in the two states derives from the differences between a contact-barrier composed of alpha-elements and one composed, if that is the right word, of beta-elements. These last, it will be remembered, appear to lack a capacity for linkage with each other. Clinically this screen of beta-elements presents itself to casual observation as indistinguishable from a confused state and in particular from any one of that class of confused states which resemble dreams, namely: 1. An outpouring of disjointed phrases and images which, if the patient were asleep, we would certainly believe to be evidence that the patient was dreaming. 2. A similar outpouring but expressed in a manner that suggests that the patient is feigning dream. 3. A confused outpouring that seems to be evidence of hallucination. 4. Similar to (3) but suggestive of an hallucination of a dream; I have not had occasion to suppose that the patient was having a dream that he was hallucinated. All four states are related to a fear lest the depressive position should precipitate a murderous superego and therefore to the need to have the emotional experience in which this might occur in the presence of the analyst. Clinically the screen of beta-elements to which I am referring bears a strong superficial resemblance to any one of these four classes and might be supposed to be identical with them.

5. Comparison of the beta-element screen with the confused states resembling dream shows the beta-element screen to be coherent and purposive. An interpretation that the patient was pouring out a stream of material intended to

destroy the analyst's psycho-analytic potency would not seem out of place. Equally apt would be an interpretation that the patient was concerned to withhold rather than to impart information. One peculiarity of the situation is the plethora of interpretations that would occur to anyone with any common sense. Yet they do not occur to the patient. These common-sense interpretations have a common characteristic in that all are accusatory, or, alternatively, laudatory as if far-fetched with intent to reassure the patient of his goodness in the teeth of the evidence. This is not fortuitous; it would be difficult in face of the evidence to maintain that it was. One is forced to a conclusion that is unexpected and surprising, namely, that the beta-element screen—I shall call it beta-screen for short in future—has a quality enabling it to evoke the kind of response the patient desires, or, alternatively, a response from the analyst which is heavily charged with counter-transference. Both possibilities require examination for their implications.

CHAPTER TEN

1. THANKS TO THE BETA-SCREEN the psychotic patient has a capacity for evoking emotions in the analyst; his associations are the elements of the beta-screen intended to evoke interpretations or other responses which are less related to his need for psycho-analytic interpretation than to his need to produce an emotional involvement.[1] The theory of counter transferences offers only partly satisfactory explanation because it is concerned with the manifestation as a symptom of the analyst's unconscious motives and therefore leaves the patient's contribution unexplained. First the patient for which these theories are intended is not employing articulate speech; he is demonstrating with evident sincerity an inability to understand his own state of mind even when it is pointed out to him. His use of words is much closer to action intended to "unburden the psyche of accretions of stimuli" than to speech. Second, he does not set to work to manipulate the analyst in the same way as the neurotic. There is a consistency in the characteristics of beta-elements. The language I must use to describe a dynamic situation produces a distortion because it is the language of a scientific method designed for the study of the inanimate. This distortion affects my claim that certain characteristics of the beta-screen are consistent. It would be more true to say that a dynamic situation evolves and that its evolution is betrayed by the emergence of a particular characteristic as one that pervades a growing number of elements and gives them consistency. The replacement of a contact-barrier by a beta-screen is a living process. The observations of the analyst, for reasons connected with the nature of the change from paranoid-schizoid to depressive position and vice versa,

contributes to the analytic situation an element which makes its development appear to be a transition from a series of discrete particles or elements to a synthesis of these same elements. One replaces the other in a manner analogous to the replacement of one judgment by another when we examine a figure illustrating reversible perspective.

2. The analysand contributes changes which are associated with the replacement of alpha-function by what may be described as a reversal of direction of the function.[1] Instead of sense impressions being changed into alpha-elements for use in dream thoughts and unconscious waking thinking, the development of the contact-barrier is replaced by its destruction. This is effected by the reversal of alpha-function so that the contact-barrier and the dream thoughts and unconscious waking thinking which are the texture of the contact-barrier are turned into alpha-elements, divested[2] of all characteristics that separate them from beta-elements and are then projected thus forming the beta-screen.

3. Reversal of alpha-function means the dispersal of the contact-barrier and is quite compatible with the establishment of objects with the characteristics I once ascribed to bizarre objects. The compatability would be much increased if, despite my warning that contact-barrier (a function) and ego (a structure) should not be regarded as interchangeable terms referring to the same thing, we could consider that the reversal of alpha-function did in fact affect the ego and therefore did not produce a simple return to beta-elements, but objects which differ in important respects from the original beta-elements which had no tincture of the personality adhering to them. The beta-element differs from the bizarre object in that the bizarre object is beta-element plus ego and superego traces. The reversal of alpha-function does violence to the structure associated with alpha-function.

4. To review the terms I have used so far: (1) the ego is a structure that, as Freud describes it, is a specialized development from the id having the function of establishing contact between psychic and external reality. (2) Alpha-function is the name given to an abstraction used by the analyst to

describe a function, of which he does not know the nature, until such time he feels in position to replace it by factors for which he feels he has obtained evidence in the course of the investigation in which he is employing alpha-function. It corresponds to that function of a number of factors, including the function of the ego, that transforms sense data into alpha-elements. Alpha-elements comprise visual images, auditory patterns, olfactory patterns, and are suitable for employment in dream thoughts, unconscious waking thinking, dreams, contact-barrier, memory. Clinically the bizarre object which is suffused with superego characteristics comes nearest to providing a realization to correspond with the concept of beta-elements. But the concept of beta-element includes only sense-impressions, the sense-impression as if it were a part of the personality experiencing the sense impression, and the sense-impression as if it were the thing-in-itself to which the sense-impression corresponds.

It is to be noted that the alpha-function may be regarded as a structure, a piece of mental apparatus producing the contact-barrier. In turn the contact-barrier may be regarded, as the name I have given it suggests, as having the characteristics of a structure. This is a repetition of the problem implicit in the differentiation from each other of ego, consciousness and alpha-function, and it is worth considering the implications of this peculiarity of psycho-analytic investigation, namely the use of concepts relating to objects which we need sometimes to consider as if they were related to machines, that is to say as if they were inanimate, and sometimes as if they were functions, which, since we are dealing with human beings and not machines, are certain to be suffused with the characteristics of life. In the case of alpha-function used as an unknown to correspond with a realization which is changing from unknown to known the name given these objects should make it clear whether we are to observe the object in its character as a function or as a structure or as an abstraction.

The contact-barrier may be expected to manifest itself clinically—if indeed it is manifest at all—as something that resembles dreams. As we have seen the contact-barrier permits a relationship and preservation of belief in it as an event in actuality, subject to the laws of nature, without having that view submerged by emotions and phantasies originating endo-psychically. Reciprocally it preserves emotions with endo-psychic origin from being overwhelmed by the realistic view. The contact-barrier is therefore responsible for the preservation of the distinction between conscious and unconscious and for its inception. The unconscious is thus preserved. It is being recruited by alpha-function with alpha-elements that need to be stored, but inhibited from intrusion into consciousness on occasions when their impingement on the man's grasp of the situation of external reality would be felt as an irrelevance or a dislocation of ordered thought.

CHAPTER ELEVEN

1. THE THEORY OF FUNCTIONS and the theory of alpha-function in particular makes possible further contributions to an understanding of thought processes. I shall consider the nature and function of thinking in any situation that seems to mirror an early age in the life of man, or his current primitive depths, where it would be possible to detect the qualities we associate with thought. In his paper on Two Principles of Mental Functioning Freud says "Restraint of motor discharge (of action) had now become necessary and was provided by means of the process of *thought*, which was developed from ideation. Thought was endowed with qualities which made it possible for the mental apparatus to support increased tension during a delay in the process of discharge. It is essentially an experimental way of acting, accompanied by displacement of smaller quantities of cathexis together with less expenditure (discharge) of them." He continues "For this purpose conversion of free cathexis into 'bound' cathexis was imperative, and this was brought about by means of raising the level of the whole cathectic process." He continues "It is probable that thinking was originally unconscious, in so far as it rose above mere ideation and turned to the relations between the object-impressions, and that it became endowed with further qualities which were perceptible to consciousness only through its connection with the memory traces of words." Implicit in Freud's statement is the part played by intolerance of frustration in producing tension, and then its relief, by the employment of thought to fill the interval between the need to unburden the psyche of accretions of stimuli and the actual unburdening. The

link between intolerance of frustration and the development of thought is central to an understanding of thought and its disturbances. Freud's statement suggests that the reality principle is sequent to the pleasure principle; it needs modification to make both principles co-exist. Though I shall not immediately discuss it I make a reservation that intolerance of frustration may be excessive, a quantitative change which almost becomes one of kind. Let us now suppose intolerance of frustration allied to hunger: suppose further that satisfaction of hunger is made impossible by other factors in the personality such as fear, greed, or envy that cannot allow the breast or its equivalent any success in satisfying the envious person. In such a situation greed would be intensified and so would the intolerance of frustration; the effect would be much the same as if the personality were endowed with an excessive intolerance of frustration. Does it matter if intolerance of frustration, or any other dynamic characteristic is primary or secondary? The distinction indicates the limitation of any treatment effecting changes in the personality to secondary factors for primary factors will not be altered.

It is likely from clinical evidence of the infant's need for material and psychological support that no distinction between material and psychological can be made by the infant. In analysis, however, it is possible to deduce whether the deficiency was one of physical or psychical quality. No matter how early such a deficiency might be, nor what it might be due to, it would be felt to be real and would demand a real solution, that is, one that appeared to remove the disease. The choice that matters to the psycho-analyst is one that lies between *procedures designed to evade frustration and those designed to modify it. That is the critical decision.*

There are other ways in which the procedure adopted may be classified, as, for example, those that are ultimately destined to reveal themselves as belonging to the class of muscular action (physical movement generally) and those that are destined to develop so that they are ultimately classified as pertaining to the realms of thought. The fact that the decision is related to such an ultimate classification is significant but for the present I wish to focus attention on phenomena genetically related to the co-existence in the personality of feelings of frustration, intolerance of feelings of frustration, related emotions and the decision that emerges from such a concatenation of elements.

CHAPTER TWELVE

1. The activity we know as "thinking" was in origin a procedure for unburdening the psyche of accretions of stimuli and the mechanism is that which has been described by Melanie Klein as projective identification. The broad outline of this theory is that there exists an omnipotent phantasy that it is possible to split off temporarily undesired, though sometimes valued, parts of the personality and put them into an object. In practice it is possible, and desirable in the interests of beneficial therapy, to observe and interpret the evidence that supports this theory and which this theory explains in a way that no other theory does.

2. It is also possible, and in fact essential, to observe evidence which shows that a patient in whom the operation of this omnipotent phantasy can be deduced is capable of behaviour which is related to a counterpart in reality of this phantasy. The patient, even at the outset of life, has contact with reality sufficient to enable him to act in a way that engenders in the mother feelings that he does not want, or which he wants the mother to have. To make theory correspond to these clinical findings I have suggested an emended version of Freud's pleasure principle theory so that the reality principle should be considered to operate co-existentially with the pleasure principle. An instance of an attempt to make the omnipotent phantasy a reality can be seen in the patient who has the impulse to force others to feel that he is capable of murdering the sexual parents so that he may feel capable of a loving sexual relationship free from the fear that he would murder his partner and himself if, as he would be bound to do, he observed himself and his partner displaying evidence of mutual sexual passion. I have suggested

that in an extreme form this may even lead to murder as a method of giving effect, in the world of reality, to the omnipotent phantasy of projective identification which, without such action, would remain only an omnipotent phantasy.

3. There are instances far less dramatic and therefore demanding some perspicacity in the analyst to discern them. It is of importance that the analyst should observe them. That is to say, he should observe and interpret the operation of the phantasy as a mental phenomenon deducible from the evidence and also observe signs that the patient is sufficiently adjusted to reality to be able to manipulate his environment so that the phantasy of projective identification appears to have substance in reality.

4. The more this realistic component is in evidence, and can be made evident to the patient, the more it is possible to judge the extent to which a gravely ill and indeed certifiable patient has contact with reality albeit a reality not always familiar to better developed individuals.

5. The patient's ability to gear his omnipotent phantasy of projective identification to reality is directly related to his capacity for tolerance of frustration. If he cannot tolerate frustration the omnipotent phantasy of projective identification has proportionately less factual counterpart in external reality. This contributes to the state Melanie Klein describes as *excessive* projective identification. The excess however must be scrutinized carefully. It may appear to be excessive because the analyst is forced to be aware of it by the realistic steps which the patient takes to make the analyst in fact experience emotions of a kind the patient does not want to have (M. Klein). *This* excess must be sharply distinguished from the excessive projective identification which represents a resort to omnipotent phantasy as a flight from reality, and in particular from feelings which are not wanted. But projective identification cannot exist without its reciprocal, namely an introjective activity intended to lead to an accumulation of good internal objects.

6. Let us now suppose that in reality the breast supplies the infant with milk and sensations of security, warmth,

well-being, love. Let us suppose further that the infant needs —I deliberately avoid saying "wishes"—to possess itself of the milk itself and the related sensations. We may make a distinction between milk and love by appropriate classification or we may emphasize, if it suits us, the respects in which they appear similar. Thus we may say that milk is a material substance and is related to alimentation and is presumably dealt with by the digestive tract. Love on the other hand we may regard as immaterial though comparable with milk for the mental welfare[1] of the child. We may place it in one or more of a number of different categories that philosophy, religion and other disciplines place at our disposal. The only reason for limiting our classificatory apparatus to one discipline is the desire to achieve simplicity. Whether we employ philosophical concepts, religious concepts, endocrinological concepts or concepts employed by the neuro-physiologist they will be open to the same objection, namely that they describe states of mind with which we are familiar and shall require them to describe phenomena, or the realities we assume to be the counterpart of those phenomena, with which we are not familar but believe we have correctly observed and correctly imputed to the infant. Two adults may mean widely different things by the same word "love", yet this word is one I must use to describe part of what I believe to be an infant's experience (I include lack of love). It is clear therefore that there are two major sources of error that immediately present themselves, one being the semantic gap which has to be bridged between adults discussing the problem and the other the scientific propriety of attributing to infant experience a modified yet recognizably similar experience.

7. The milk, we may assume with a degree of conviction we cannot feel about love, is received and dealt with by the alimentary canal; what receives and deals with the love? The question may be a formulation based on inadequate thinking, and therefore liable to lead to error, unless we consider what the situation is with the mother. As the infant receives the milk and deals with it by the alimentary system, so the mother provides it by the glandular system, yet milk has been known to fail and the failure has been attributed to emotional upsets.

The infant likewise has been supposed to suffer digestive disturbances originating in an emotional upset. It may be useful to suppose that there exists in reality a psycho-somatic breast and an infantile psycho-somatic alimentary canal corresponding to the breast.[1] This breast is an object the infant needs to supply it with milk and good internal objects. I do not attribute to the infant an awareness of this need; but I do attribute to the infant an awareness of a need not satisfied. We can say the infant feels frustrated if we assume the existence of some apparatus with which frustration can be experienced. Freud's concept of consciousness as that of "a sense-organ for the perception of psychical qualities", provides such an apparatus.

8. As the analyst treating an adult patient I can be conscious of something of which the patient is not conscious. Similarly the mother can discern a state of mind in her infant before the infant can be conscious of it, as, for example, when the baby shows signs of needing food before it is properly aware of it. In this imaginary situation the need for the breast is a feeling and that feeling itself is a bad breast; the infant does not feel it wants a good breast but it does feel it wants to evacuate a bad one.

9. Suppose the infant is fed; the taking in of milk, warmth, love, may be felt as taking in a good breast. Under dominance of the, at first unopposed, bad breast, "taking in" food may be felt as indistinguishable from evacuating a bad breast. Both good and bad breasts are felt as possessing the same degree of concreteness and reality as milk. Sooner or later the "wanted" breast is felt as an "idea of a breast missing" and not as a bad breast present. We can see that the bad, that is to say wanted but absent, breast is much more likely to become recognized as an idea than the good breast which is associated with what a philosopher would call a thing-in-itself or a thing-in-actuality, in that the sense of a good breast depends on the existence of milk the infant has in fact taken. The good breast and the bad breast, the one being associated with the actual milk that satisfies hunger and the other with the non-existence of that milk, must have a difference in psychical quality. "Thoughts are

a nuisance" said one of my patients, "I don't want them." Is a "thought" the same as an absence of a thing? If there is no "thing", is "no thing" a thought and is it by virtue of the fact that there is "no thing" that one recognizes that "it" must be thought? Before considering further how this difference in quality might be established I shall assume another situation. Let us suppose the infant to have fed but to be feeling unloved. Again it is aware of a need for the good breast and again this "need for a good breast" is a "bad breast" that needs to be evacuated. A number of different situations of this kind would pose problems requiring different solutions; in my first example the infant could be supposed to feel that the "need for the breast" bad breast was being evacuated if it passed a motion while taking milk; in that case it would associate a physical act with a result that we would call a change in its state of mind from dissatisfaction to satisfaction. If it is correct to suppose that the central question rests on discrimination of psychical quality and if consciousness is legitimately regarded as the sense-organ of psychical quality it is difficult to see how consciousness comes into existence. It clearly will not do to say that the infant is conscious of psychical quality and transforms this emotional experience into alpha-elements for I have already said the existence of consciousness and unconsciousness depends on the prior production of alpha-elements by alpha-function. We must assume that the good breast and the bad breast are emotional experiences. The physical component, milk, discomfort of satiation or the opposite, can be immediately apparent to the sense and we can therefore accord a chronological priority to beta-elements over alpha-elements. Intolerance of frustration could be so pronounced that alpha-function would be forestalled by immediate evacuation of the beta-elements. The mental component, love, security, anxiety, as distinct from the somatic requires a process analogous to digestion. What this might be is concealed by use of the concept of alpha-function but a value may be found for this by psycho-analytic investigations. For example, when the mother loves the infant what does she do it with? Leaving aside the physical channels of communication my impression is that her love is expressed by reverie.

10. Though the difficulties of penetrating the adult mind in analysis are great they are less so than attempting to penetrate the infant's by speculative hypothesis; investigation of reverie in the adult may afford us an entry into this problem. We may deduce from reverie, as the psychological source of supply of the infant's needs for love and understanding, what kind of psychological receptor organ is required if the infant is to be able to profit from reverie as it is able, thanks to the digestive capacities of the alimentary canal, to profit from the breast and the milk it supplies. Put in another way, assuming alpha-function as that which makes available to the infant what would otherwise remain unavailable for any purpose other than evacuation as beta-elements, what are the *factors* of this function that relate directly to the mother's capacity for reverie?

11. The mother's capacity for reverie is here considered as inseparable from the content for clearly one depends on the other. If the feeding mother cannot allow reverie or if the reverie is allowed but is not associated with love for the child or its father this fact will be communicated to the infant even though incomprehensible to the infant. Psychical quality will be imparted to the channels of communication, the links with the child. What happens will depend on the nature of these maternal psychical qualities and their impact on the psychical qualities of the infant, for the impact of the one upon the other is an emotional experience subject, from the point of view of the development of the couple and the individuals composing it, to transformation by alpha-function. The term reverie may be applied to almost any content. I wish to reserve it only for such content as is suffused with love or hate. Using it in this restricted sense reverie is that state of mind which is open to the reception of any "objects" from the loved object and is therefore capable of reception of the infant's projective identifications whether they are felt by the infant to be good or bad. In short, reverie is a factor of the mother's alpha-function.

12. Returning now to the infant containing[1] a "need for

the breast" which I have said is a feeling that is equated with a "bad breast".[2] This bad breast has to be exchanged for a good breast. An infant capable of tolerating frustration can permit itself to have a sense of reality, to be dominated by the reality principle. If its intolerance of frustration reaches beyond a certain degree omnipotent mechanisms come into operation, notably projective identification. This might still be regarded as realistic, in that it suggests awareness of the value of a capacity for thought as a means of softening frustration when the reality principle is dominant. But it depends for its efficacy on the existence of the mother's capacity for reverie. If the mother fails then a further burden is thrown on the infant's capacity for toleration of frustration for now its capacity for toleration of frustration of thought itself is tested. I am here supposing that projective identification is an early form of that which later is called a capacity for thinking. An infant endowed with marked capacity for toleration of frustration might survive the ordeal of a mother incapable of reverie and therefore incapable of supplying its mental needs. At the other extreme an infant markedly incapable of tolerating frustration cannot survive without breakdown even the experience of projective identification with a mother capable of reverie; nothing less than unceasing breast feeding would serve and that is not possible through lack of appetite if for no other reason. We have thus approached a mental life unmapped by the theories elaborated for the understanding of neurosis. I do not propose to pursue this investigation now, except in so far as it bears on alpha-function.

CHAPTER THIRTEEN

1. For effective use it is necessary to be able to regard alpha-function as constant by virtue of its status as an unknown. In so far as it is flexible its flexibility derives from the use of variables as factors that can be replaced, as I explained earlier, by theories and concepts of fixed value. The values given to the variables (the factors) must be genuinely constant so that once their value has been fixed the meaning of alpha-function is fixed. In practice even an approximation to precision is only possible in the sense that the factor must be clearly described or, in the instance of a theory, correctly quoted.[1]

2. As an example of an attempt at precise formulation I take alpha-function and two factors, excessive projective identification and excess of bad objects. Suppose that in the course of the analysis these two factors are obtrusive to the exclusion of other factors that the analyst has observed. If psycho-analytic theory were rationally organized it should be possible to refer to both these factors by symbols which were part of a system of reference that was applied uniformly and universally. The Kleinian theory of projective identification would be referred to by initials and a page and paragraph reference. Similarly, Freud's view of attention would be replaced by a reference. This can in fact be done, though clumsily, by reference to page and line of a standard edition even now. Such a statement could lend itself to mere manipulation, more or less ingenious, of symbols according to apparently arbitrary rules. Provided that the analyst preserves a sense of the factual background to which such a formulation refers, there are advantages in the exercise in precision and rigour of thought that is exacted by an attempt to

concentrate actual clinical experience so that it may be expressed in such abstract notation. Further the analyst can see from an inspection of his formalizations which theories he is using and which he neglects. From evidence of neglect he could deduce either that his psycho-analytic armoury was becoming impoverished or that certain psycho-analytic theories were not in his experience standing up well to the test of clinical usefulness. In either case this would be a valuable insight. The formula provides a shorthand summary of sessions over a period. It should be possible to see what links one summary has with another thence to predict by reference to the theoretical deductive systems in which these factors appear as hypotheses or premises analytical situations that may develop. Alpha-function may be a major pre-occupation of the analyst in a particular analysis, but it does not follow that it will continue to be so, or that, being so, it will have the same value in subsequent weeks. In the next group of sessions it may become clear that a belief that a bad object exists is being expressed as an expression of envious disparagement of a good object. In that case the formulation will reflect the change of factors. By the next week alpha-function may no longer be of central importance and other factors and some other function may have taken its place. The principle of applying the Theory of Functions remains the same whatever the function and whatever the factors of which it is the function.

3. As a method of making something clear to himself the analyst needs his own book of psycho-analytic theories that he personally frequently uses together with page and paragraph numbers that make their identification certain.

4. The capacity to remember what the patient has said needs to be allied to a capacity for forgetting so that the fact that any session is a new session and therefore an unknown situation that must be psycho-analytically investigated is not obscured by an already over-plentiful fund of pre-and misconception. Yet the analyst needs all the knowledge of the patient and the discoveries and work of his predecessor in the field that he can muster. This reinforces the need for a firm

structure, a theoretical framework of psycho-analysis which is yet capable of flexibility in action. If the rigidity of the theoretical structure is weakened by departure from theory such departures become easier to detect. For example, if reference to transference is made by specific quotation it can be seen that the writer is claiming to use the term with meanings already established. If conscious anxiety about the analyst is said to be a factor in the transference it would be apparent that the writer had in mind some phenomenon not the same as that described by Freud in the passage to which reference is made. Flexibility is conferred by working with functions that are variables whose value only becomes constant when for the variables of which it is the function there are substituted factors which are constants. At present the nearest to a constant in psycho-analysis is the use of a page and line reference to the theory that is being employed as a factor.

5. With the deterioration in the analyst's theoretical and analytical equipment I need not concern myself here; it is sufficient that a method of formulation would help to make it manifest, and enable the analyst to take such steps as he thought necessary. Diminished use of a psycho-analytic theory might show that it was not surviving the test of analytical practice.

6. A record of sessions that showed succinctly the progress of the analysis by representing the theories employed would thus serve a purpose that was more than an aid to the analyst's memory. Its value as a record of work done, and indirectly of the analyst's method of working, would be great, but the central problem concerns the need for a system of notation that is valuable both for recording analytic problems and working on them.

7. The system of notation must make it possible for the analyst to provide a record that he himself can understand, after a lapse of time, and that can be communicated to others without serious loss of meaning. Difficult as it may be to fulfil this ambition its achievement would not be enough. For development of psycho-analysis a notation must be found that records psycho-analytic work, as mathematical notation

records facts, but just as mathematical notation records facts and provides a means for calculation as well, so the ideal psycho-analytic notation must provide a means for working on the problem that the notation has enabled the analyst to record.

CHAPTER FOURTEEN

1. A CENTRAL PART is played by alpha-function in transforming an emotional experience into alpha-elements because a sense of reality matters to the individual in the way that food, drink, air and excretion of waste products matter. Failure to eat, drink or breathe properly has disastrous consequences for life itself. Failure to use the emotional experience produces a comparable disaster in the development of the personality; I include amongst these disasters degrees of psychotic deterioration that could be described as death of the personality. As always, the use of a model, as I am using the model of the digestive system here, is open to the dangers I discuss on p. 80. To moderate these dangers and make discussion scientific a notation to represent emotional experience is required. If the individual analyst built up for himself an anthology of working psycho-analytic theory on a foundation of a few good basic theories well understood and capable, individually and in combination, of covering a great many of the situations he might expect to meet, it might help the creation of a notation. What follows is a sketch to indicate the lines along which progress could be made and which I have found helpful.

2. The feelings we know by the names "love" and "hate" would seem to be obvious choices if the criterion is basic emotion. Envy and Gratitude, Depression, Guilt, Anxiety, all occupy a dominant place in psycho-analytic theory and would seem with Sex to be choices to place with love and hate. In fact I prefer three factors I regard as intrinsic to the link between objects considered to be in relationship with each other. An emotional experience cannot be conceived of in isolation from a relationship. The basic relationships

that I postulate are (1) X loves Y; (2) X hates Y; and (3) X knows Y. These links will be expressed by the signs L, H and K. What realization may exist to which these abstract links, L, H and K, correspond? Suppose an imaginary situation of a type with which an analyst is familiar; the patient Smith is talking freely and is co-operative and friendly; in the course of his associations he mentions that he knows a certain psycho-therapist, Jones, who is a very stupid man and knows virtually nothing about psycho-analysis. The patient knows him well and has good reason, he says, to dislike him. He once treated a friend of his, Mr. May, with shocking results. His friend's marriage, which had always been harmonious until his friend took up treatment . . . . etc. Obviously this is a complex communication. There is a link between the patient and the analyst; there are various links between the patient and the psycho-therapist, between patient and his friend, between the patient and his friend's analyst. For the link between the patient and analyst there is direct evidence. With regard to the patient's report of the other links the evidence is mostly indirect although the direct evidence which the session affords could be used, if thought desirable, to supplement the patient's own statements. The patient says he knows Jones. Is this to be recorded as Smith K Jones? He says he dislikes Jones. Should it be Smith H Jones? The patient says "his friend" Mr. May. Should this then be Smith L May? Or is there some previous material in the analysis, or some manner or intonation that suggests a link, Smith L Mrs. May? But perhaps there is some material that suggests there is a homosexual relationship between Smith and Mr. May? There need be no end to the questions stimulated by an imaginary episode or limit to the number of answers for each question. But it is hardly less true to say just that about a real session. Yet on the answers to the questions, which the analyst begins to entertain, will depend his interpretation of the direct evidence of the nature of the transference. It may seem, since the analytic situation is complex, that there can be no merit in recording it by one of three simple signs. Admitting that the sign is to express only one part of the emotional experience, the link, does not the imaginary episode show that either the signs, L, H and K, conceal a complex link which may have endless varieties under a sign of misleading simplicity, or, that they define a link with a degree of rigidity which makes their applications to a real analytical situation a hopeless falsification?

3. There is no reason for either of these alternatives to be true; the signs can be related to fact in a way that saves them from becoming meaningless symbols and can at the same time be sufficiently abstract to ensure that they are generally and not merely accidentally applicable to real emotional situations.

4. The analyst must allow himself to appreciate the complexity of the emotional experience he is required to illuminate and yet restrict his choice to these three links. He decides what the linked objects are and which of these three represents with most accuracy the actual link between them.

If the patient is friendly the link can be represented by L. It is not an adequate representation because it is necessary to record the state of the transference. I save the trouble of saying what I mean by that by recording transference in accordance with the system I suggested earlier (p. 40, para. 6).

It will be seen that the use of HKL, to force the analyst to establish the "key" of the session is not the same as using it to record an emotional experience; that is to say it is a usage that provides a less than full account of what is known to have happened. But it introduces an element that must be an essential part of any recording system before that system can be regarded as satisfactory, namely the working tool. To sum up an emotional episode as K is to produce an imperfect record but a good starting point for the analyst's speculative meditation. In this respect the system I have sketched out, despite its crudity and naivety, possesses the rudiments of the essentials of a system of notation—record of fact and working tool.

CHAPTER FIFTEEN

1. THE AIM IN MAKING the choice L, H or K is to make one statement that is to the best of the analyst's belief true. It need not be a statement that accurately represents a realization of which it is the counterpart; the statement must seem to the analyst to be a true reflection of his feelings and one on which he can rely for a particularly important purpose, namely to act as a standard to which he can refer all the other statements that he proposes to make. If L is chosen then L expresses a quality with which he compares other qualities. L also expresses quantity and by this quantity the analyst will measure all the other quantities he expresses. That is to say, if he means by L that the two objects are linked by strong feelings of love he will not then use K for a casual tie such as might be expressed by an impatient "Yes, I know". The choice of L or H or K is not determined by a need to represent fact but by the need to provide a key to the value of the other elements that are combined in the formalized statement. In psycho-analysis where a statement depends on other statements for its value the need for the recognition of such a key statement is pressing. It must be made clear that the analyst is basing the values of all the elements in his statement on the one statement. Theoretically I see no reason why he should not choose any element he likes for this purpose, but in practice much is to be said for choosing an element that has importance derived from other aspects of its position in the total statement. Obviously an element which has already such importance is more likely to support the burden that it must carry than one that has not. The L, H or K link is just such an element. When the analyst chooses his sign it must feel right and, it stands to reason,

he must keep it constant. If by reference to it other elements seem to make the statement incompatible with itself the other elements and relationships must be brought into harmony and the L, H or K left unaltered unless it becomes clear that it has been wrongly chosen or that the analysand has changed; in that case the whole statement will have to be abandoned and a fresh start made. It will be seen that I attach great importance to the choice of L, H or K; that I have a preference for choosing the sign representing the link as the element best suited to carry the load I wish it to bear, but have no difficulty in conceiving that there might be good reasons why an analyst should prefer to make his "true" statement one based on some different element; I do not think the choice presents any unreasonable degree of difficulty to a trained and practising analyst.

2. L, H or K have to be decided in such a way that the analyst *feels* he has established a point of reference. By doing so the danger of producing a system of abstractions, devoid of background and subject only to ingenious and arbitrary manipulation, is made less.

CHAPTER SIXTEEN

THE K LINK

1. I SHALL IGNORE L and H and discuss K as it is important for the analyst and is the link that is germane to learning by experience. In the course of discussing it I hope also to take up further points which are relevant to linking but with which I have not so far been able to deal. My first point is that L or H may be relevant to K but that neither is by itself conducive to K. x K y, the analyst K the analysand, I K Smith, these are statements that represent an emotional experience. Like L and H, K represents an active link and has about it a suggestion that if x K y then x does something to y. It represents a psycho-analytic relationship. As I propose to use it it does not convey a sense of finality, that is to say, a meaning that x is in possession of a piece of knowledge called y but rather that x is in the state of getting to know y and y is in a state of getting to be known by x. The statement x K y, in so far as it means that x has a piece of knowledge called y, falls in the category of a relationship between the person making the statement and the person to whom it is made *and* a relationship with x and y about whom it is made.

2. In so far as it is a statement meaning x is concerning himself to know the truth about y it corresponds to statements of relationship that are said to be informed by a scientific outlook. The techniques employed by those who have a scientific outlook have achieved most success when y is an inanimate object. The conviction that a scientific outlook prevails in the relationship x K y is more easily maintained if y is inanimate and if x can be made to seem to approximate to the inanimate, for example x uses a machine. Truth value

is felt to inhere in the record presented by a smoked drum or the record of the human voice in a way that is not felt to be the case in the report of human judgment. The simplicity of this view is exposed on occasions when it is believed that a photographic record cannot yield the evidence available to direct observation.

3. Doubts about human capacity to know anything underlie the inquiries of the philosopher of science; these doubts today spring from an inescapable awareness that the situation represented by these abstract terms x K y is identical with x L y or x H y in that an animate element exists intrinsically. That is to say that in proportion as inanimate machinery is introduced to displace the living element, L, H or K have ceased to exist. The problem with which philosophers of science have become associated has been given added significance by psycho-analysis and this for two main sets of reasons: x has the strength and is shown in detail to have the weakness of which he has always been suspected when he embarks on an investigation of y that is related to y's capacity for contact with reality. I do not propose to spend time on the philosophical problems involved as they can be found dealt with in Kant, Hume and their successors. I wish to emphasize that all that has been said about the problems of knowledge applies with particular force to psycho-analysis and that psycho-analysis applies with particular force to those problems.

4. The question "How can x know anything?" expresses a feeling; it appears to be painful and to inhere in the emotional experience that I represent by x K y. An emotional experience that is felt to be painful may initiate an attempt either to evade or to modify the pain according to the capacity of the personality to tolerate frustration. Evasion or modification in accordance with the view expressed by Freud in his paper on Two Principles of Mental Functioning are intended to remove the pain. Modification is attempted by using the relationship x K y so that it will lead to a relationship in which x is possessed of a piece of knowledge called y—the meaning for x K y repudiated by me on p. 47. Evasion on the other hand is attempted by substitution of the meaning

"x is possessed of a piece of knowledge called y" so that x K y no longer represents the painful emotional experience but the supposedly painless one.

5. Such a manœuvre is intended not to affirm but to deny reality, not to represent an emotional experience but to misrepresent it to make it appear to be a fulfilment rather than a striving for fulfilment. The difference between the aim of the lie and the aim of truth can thus be expressed as a change of sense in x K y and to relate to intolerance of the pain associated with feelings of frustration. The problem of translating private "knowledge" into public is the same for misrepresenting an emotional experience as it is for representing it. In the psycho-analysis of certain patients we have to concern ourselves with their failure to misrepresent emotional experiences even to themselves; it is possible to increase understanding of the insane by considering his failure to substitute a misrepresentation of the facts for the representation that corresponds to, and therefore illuminates, reality. The motive is likely to be explained in Freud's statement that "hallucination was abandoned only in consequence of the absence of the expected gratification". It will be necessary to approach the problem as if with two distinct aims, one concerned with knowing a person or thing, K in fact, and the other concerned with evasion of K and the emotional experience it represents. The procedure I am proposing, as part of K for the purpose of knowing "x K y" and what it represents therefore involves identification with a person that comes for analysis. It also involves abstraction from the realization to produce a formulation that represents the realization and might therefore correspond with and so represent realizations at present unknown.

CHAPTER SEVENTEEN

1. In the K activity on which I am engaged, namely in knowing, I have to be conscious of my emotional experience and able to abstract from it a statement that will represent this experience adequately. This abstraction engenders confidence if it then represents other experiences unknown when the abstraction is made. The sense of confidence is similar to that produced if a belief seems supported by common sense. Confidence is a concomitant of knowing that there is correlation between the senses (p. 51) or that more than one person in a group entertains what appears to be the same statement of the same representation of an emotional experience. Confidence in a representation is associated with (1) a belief that the representation is supported by common sense and (2) that it not only represents the emotional experience from which it is abstracted, but represents other realizations, unknown when the abstraction was accomplished. Thus an abstract formalization, employing the signs LH and K used for the evaluation of one emotional experience may itself be evalued if it can be seen to serve as an abstract representation of a different emotional experience.

2. Abstraction, then, can be seen as a step in publication which facilitates correlation by comparison of the representation that has been abstracted with a number of different realizations none of which is the realization from which the representation was originally abstracted. The concretization, by contrast, can be seen as a form of publication which facilitates correlation by common sense; that is, by stating something so that it is recognized as an object of one sense that can yet be tested as an object of another sense. The criterion for the statement must be its value in facilitating testing by

more than one sense or by the senses of more than one person. (In astronomy correlations are achieved although only the sense of sight and its data are available because the individual discoverer has been able to make his private experience public for testing by other observers contemporary or posthumous. The weakness incidental to an inability to employ the evidence of more than one sense has been compensated for by the ability to abstract a statement of an original emotional experience in terms of such rigour that realizations of the representation could be sought for, found, or accidentally recognized many years afterwards. The intuition of heliocentricity of Aristarchus could be confirmed hundreds of years later by Kepler.) Mathematical formulation is not yet available to the psycho-analyst though there are suggestive possibilities.

3. The reasons for making an abstract statement are these; (1) the analyst is impelled to formulate his basic hypothesis; (2) the analyst is able to detect from the record that such abstraction makes available any tendency for the theoretical armoury on which he relies to become jejeune; (3) the analyst is preserved from losing sight of the provenance of his theoretical equipment in the history of his scientific discipline; (4) the analytic practitioners will be able more readily to see that certain theories hitherto regarded as established have in fact become redundant or discredited by the test of experience itself, and (5) correlation of the abstract statement with realizations from which it was *not* derived becomes possible; (6) it helps to establish a standard to which all other statements can be referred. Examples will be seen in the later pages.

The process of abstraction to which I have made conscious resort is essential to the x K y emotional experience. It is not an incidental procedure which can be discarded at will.

4. Once we have given priority to the link and agreed to limit its representation to the three signs L, H and K, it is possible to approach the problem of representation by considering what steps would be needed to establish a successful method of *mis*representation. Since the process of abstraction is not incidental and one to be discarded at will

positive steps have to be taken for an individual to achieve the state of mind, seen in some psychotics, in which the capacity for abstraction is destroyed. The value, for example, of the word dog which does not refer to a specific animal but to a class, as a method of achieving abstraction and generalization, is destroyed so that it can no longer be used as the name of a thing but is the thing in itself, "words are things". In a formalized system, designed to represent the K link it is necessary to introduce elements that will represent mis-representation. This can be done quite simply by borrowing from algebraic geometry the procedure by which a change of sign, say for a line AB represents a change in sense of the line. K represents the link I have adumbrated: — K represents the link constituted by NOT understanding i.e. *mis*-understanding. The implications of this can best be grasped by noting that — L is not the same as H, nor — H the same as L.

5. For the present factors must be represented by a page and line reference to that part of the literature that gives the best definition of the factor to which reference is being made. The search for signs to represent factors thus following the procedure I have adopted with L, H and K, is premature because substitution of a sign for an ordinarily accepted term produces a formalized system so divorced from its background that it becomes meaningless whereas by keeping to a system of page and line reference the background of realization from which the theories are derived is never wholly lost to sight. Formalization and abstraction on the other hand have the effect, by removing the concrete and particular, of eliminating aspects that obscure the importance of the relationship of one element with another. The employment of specific terms notable for their concreteness though retaining the background from which they are derived obscures the fact that concrete terms are variables dependent for their value on the context in which they are placed. This means that the essential thing is to find a set of signs that will adequately represent a realization and also make it possible to display the relationship of one sign with another—its context.

CHAPTER EIGHTEEN

1. In the work done here (K activity) I have resorted to abstraction, in contrast to that reverse process of concretization by which words cease to be abstract signs but become things themselves. To demonstrate relationship adequately abstraction and formalization are essential.

2. The problem is not merely the use of words already invested with a penumbra of associations to describe an unprecedented situation; it is that this penumbra of associations has been acquired in pursuit of the establishment of a mental relationship with concrete objects. This pursuit, in the development of the individual, is far less exacting than the attempt to establish a mental relationship with a personality either the individual's own or that of another person. The senses present the personality with material on which work has to be done to produce what Freud calls the "conscious awareness attached to them", that is to the sense data. But it is hard to believe that sense data, as ordinarily understood, could bring much material of value when the object of the senses is an emotional experience of a personality (to whomever it may belong). The senses may be able in a state of fear or rage to contribute data concerning the heart-beat, and similar events peripheral, as we see it, to an emotional state. But there are no sense-data directly related to psychic quality, as there are sense-data directly related to concrete objects. Hypochondriacal symptoms may therefore be signs of an attempt to establish contact with psychic quality by substituting physical sensation for the missing sense data of psychical quality. It seems possible that it was in response to his awareness of this difficulty that Freud felt disposed to postulate consciousness as the sense-organ of

psychic quality. I have no doubt whatever of the need for something in the personality to make contact with psychic quality.

3. For personalities that seem to be incapable of true dreaming, the border-line psychotic and psychotic parts of the personality, the theory of consciousness as the sense-organ of psychic quality is not satisfactory; by the standards of clinical practice contradictions become apparent which are resolved if the problems are approached with a different theory. The weakness of this theory of consciousness is manifest in the situation for which I have proposed the theory that alpha-function, by proliferating alpha-elements, is producing the contact-barrier, an entity that separates elements so that those on one side are, and form, the conscious and on the other side are, and form, the unconscious. The theory of consciousness is weak, not false, because by amending it to state that the conscious and the unconscious thus constantly produced together do function as if they were binocular therefore capable of correlation and self-regard. Because of the manner of its genesis, impartial register of psychic quality of the self is precluded: the "view" of one part by the other is, as it were, "monocular". For these reasons, and others arising from clinical experience of psycho-analysis of that class of patient in whom the psychotic part of the personality is obtrusive, I find the theory of primary and secondary processes unsatisfactory. This theory is weak in the need to postulate two systems at the point where, in my theory of an alpha-function, an emotional experience is transformed into alpha-elements,[1] to make dream thought, unconscious waking thinking and storage in the mind (memory) possible. I attribute the appearance of beta-elements, the closely associated bizarre objects and the serious disturbances ordinarily associated with excessive obtrusion of the psychotic elements of the personality, to the failure of alpha-function.

CHAPTER NINETEEN

1. ATTRIBUTION OF A VALUE to the term alpha-function is a task of psycho-analysis and can be achieved in no other way. Its status, as I discuss it here, is that of an unknown variable to be used to satisfy the need for a system of abstraction adequate to the requirements of psycho-analysis. This and related problems are objects of the enquiry; they are also instruments by which the enquiry is conducted.[1] A distinction must be made between the concept of alpha-function and the realization which is felt to approximate sufficiently closely to the theory in which this concept is employed to warrant appropriation of the term alpha-function as a name, however temporary, for the realization.

2. The genesis of all abstraction is to be supposed, for purposes of analytic investigation, to be a factor in alpha-function. Such an hypothesis is compatible with the association of breakdown in alpha-function with predominance of beta-elements which are remarkable for their concreteness to a point where some patients regard words not as the names of things but as things-in-themselves. The hypothesis must be matched against emotional experiences that are a part of the clinical problem of establishing a value for alpha-function itself. First we need to know what is the counterpart of a sense impression in the relationship of a person with an emotional experience. The sense-organs, the awareness belonging to them and their realizations derive from the sensuous experience of concrete objects. What deals with the counterparts of a sense impression of an emotional experience? How are these counterparts of a sense impression then transformed into alpha-elements? It is helpful to postulate[1] sense impressions of an emotional experience

analogous to sense impressions of concrete objects. If there are such impressions we shall have to consider whether the alpha-elements into which alpha-function transforms the sense impressions of an emotional experience differ from the alpha-elements into which alpha-function transforms the sense-data of a concrete object and if so in what the difference consists. Freud suggested that the model for primary and secondary processes was the reflex apparatus; the application of the theory of functions requires that the model is formed first, and then inspected to see if it can be represented by the theoretical abstraction I have called a link and if it can represent, and if so how, the realization that has stimulated the production of the model. Alpha-function represents something that exists when certain factors operate in consort. It is assumed that there are factors which operate in such consort or alternatively that if for some reason they do not, that is to say that if the available factors have no alpha-function, then the personality is incapable of producing alpha-elements and therefore incapable of dream thoughts, consciousness or unconsciousness, repression, or learning from experience. This failure is serious because in addition to the obvious penalties that follow from an inability to learn from experience there is a need for awareness of an emotional experience, similar to the need for an awareness of concrete objects that is achieved through the sense impressions, because lack of such awareness implies a deprivation of truth and truth seems to be essential for psychic health. The effect on the personality of such deprivation is analogous to the effect of physical starvation on the physique.

3. By resorting to abstraction and its products, alpha-function and its factors, I have been able to discuss psychoanalytic unknowns. I continue by concretization, that is, by using terms approximating to those used on a level of empirically verifiable data, to speculate on what part of the early psychic apparatus it is that is deflected to the provision of the apparatus needed for thought. Freud, describing thought as providing a method of restraint for motor discharge which had become necessary, simply says it developed from ideation. In his discussion of dream interpretation

Freud was impressed by the value of reflex apparatus as a model for the psychic apparatus involved in dreaming and evolved his theory of primary and secondary systems in the light of this model.[1] I suggest that thinking is something forced on an apparatus, not suited for the purpose, by the demands of reality, and is contemporary with, as Freud said, the dominance of the reality principle. A modern analogy is provided by the fact that the demands of reality not only forced the discovery of psycho-analysis, but have led to the deflection of verbal thought from its original function of providing restraint for motor discharge to the tasks of self knowledge for which it is ill-suited and for the purpose of which it has to undergo drastic changes.

4. It will be seen that I ignore the nature of alpha-function and leave it as an abstraction for use as an unknown that is given a value only in the course of an analytic investigation.[1] I am therefore tackling a different problem from that which Freud investigated with his theories of ideation and his model of the reflex arc. I am assuming that an apparatus existed and had to undergo, still has to undergo, adaptation to the new tasks involved in meeting the demands of reality by developing a capacity for thought. The apparatus that has to undergo this adaptation is that which dealt originally with sense impressions relating to the alimentary canal.

In this system, as far as I can make out and as far as I am able to render what I have deduced in words, what takes place is this; the infant is aware of a very bad breast inside it, a breast that is "not there" and by not being there gives it painful feelings. This object is felt to be "evacuated" by the respiratory system or by the process of "swallowing" a satisfying breast. This breast that is swallowed is indistinguishable from a "thought" but the "thought" is dependent on the existence of an object that is actually put into the mouth. In certain conditions, dependent on factors of the personality, the sucking process and its attendant sensations are equated with evacuation of the bad breast. The breast, the thing in itself, is indistinguishable from an idea in the mind. The idea of a breast in the mind is, reciprocally, indistinguishable from the thing itself in the mouth. Keeping for the present to two situations only, one of which is an actual breast, indistinguishable from an emotional experience which in turn is thing-in-itself and thought, but in an undifferentiated state, and the other the bad "need-of-a-breast" bad breast which is equally an object compounded of emotional experience and thing-in-itself the two being as yet undifferentiated, it is clear that we have arrived at an object very closely resembling a beta-element. The realization and the representation of it in the mind have not been differentiated. The characteristics of this condition may be made clearer if I educe some manifestations of it. Thus an infant containing a "need-of-a-breast" bad breast may evacuate it by sucking at the breast. This obviously requires a topographically close relationship with an actual breast. It may evacuate it by the respiratory system; there need be no tactile sensation for this. It may evacuate it by seeing the actual breast; for this an actual breast needs to be in sight, that is to say it is in a position in which being in sight is the same as being in the mind's eye and both are the same as being in the mouth. When all these events are evacuations of the "need-of-a-breast" bad breast it is clear that if no breast is then in fact available the "no breast" will be felt to be not only bad in itself but made worse because it, as it were, is concrete evidence that this bad breast has been successfully evacuated. This situation corresponds to one in which a "bizarre object" rather than a "beta-element" would be the correct descriptive term for the object felt by the infant to exist.

CHAPTER TWENTY

1. WHEN EVACUATION of a bad breast is felt to lead to its presence externally, if the evacuation is achieved, apparently by sucking at a real breast, the aftermath of the evacuation is not painful as in the respiratory and other methods. This stimulates interaction between the reality and pleasure-pain principles. We may follow-up (1) the process of differentiation of the representation from the corresponding realization, the process by which the thing in itself is distinguishable from the idea, (Bradley, I.148) or (2) the effects of the correspondence between alimentation and thinking. The first course leads directly to a discussion of the importance of abstraction, which may, in this context, be regarded as an aspect of the transformation, by alpha-function, of an emotional experience into alpha-elements.

2. The Kleinian theory that the infant feels it has evacuated its bad object into the breast combined with the theory that satisfaction of a need can be felt as evacuation of a need, the need itself being a bad breast (to employ concrete terms) or what I have called a beta-element (to employ an abstraction) represents an infant's feeling that the breast in actuality is an evacuated object and therefore indistinguishable from a beta-element. Something must happen now if the child is to continue feeding. It is implied in the process I have described that the situation cannot be recognized as objective. If there is a good breast, a sweet object, it is because it has been evacuated, produced; and the same with the bad breast, the needed breast, the bitter breast, etc. It cannot be seen as objective and it cannot be seen as subjective. From these sweet, bitter, sour objects, sweetness, bitterness, sourness, are abstracted. Once abstracted they can be reapplied;

the abstraction made can be used in situations where a realization, not the original realization from which it was abstracted, approximates to it. For example an emotional experience is associated with the breast, in which the infant feels that there is an object existing independently of itself on which it can depend for satisfaction of its feelings of hunger; assuming a capacity for abstraction, the infant can feel that from the total experience he can detach an element which is a belief that an object exists that can satisfy his needs. The concrete statement might be: a breast exists that can be depended on to satisfy his hunger for food; abstraction from this might be: there is a something that can and does give him what he wants when he wants it.

3. Almost any number of statements can be made to represent what the infant feels when, in the view of a reputedly impartial observer, it has been fed at the breast. From that emotional experience and the statement that represents it, and all the other statements that could equally reasonably be felt to represent it, there can be abstracted a series of further statements. Since an enormous number can be made, the significance of this for scientific procedure, with particular reference to this preceding passage, will be discussed later. Presumably the infant also "can make a number of statements" and that it is with the nature of these "statements" that the analyst has ultimately to concern himself. The first level of statements are particular, derived from an actual episode, and concrete; the abstractions become further and further removed from the concrete and specific until their origin is lost to sight. The abstractions that are thus produced may then be reapplied to a realization when a realization is found that appears to approximate to the abstraction.

4. Situations met with in analysis are: (1) a patient, incapable of abstraction, strives to exist with a mental apparatus engaged in introjection and projection of beta-elements; (2) a patient capable of abstraction produces theoretical systems far removed from the background of realizations from which they have been abstracted, but proliferates these systems according to rules that make the abstractions in any system consistent with each other; (3) a

patient capable of producing abstractions proliferates systems that seem to obey no ascertainable system of rules. Though the original realization is unknown (in this respect resembling (2) above) and likewise the system of rules under which the abstractions have been manipulated, he may yet find realizations that approximate to his abstract statements; (4) a patient capable of abstraction and formation of systems in accordance with rules that ensure that the system is not incompatible with itself and yet unable to find a realization to which the abstract systems apply; (5) a patient capable of abstraction and of combining these abstractions into systems according to rules (whose nature can be demonstrated) that ensure that the systems are not incompatible with themselves. It may be possible to deduce what the original realization was from which the abstraction was derived. Further realizations can be seen to approximate to the deductive systems although the latter realizations may not have been known to exist when the abstraction that can be seen to represent them was first adumbrated.

5. I shall ignore (1) as it is a statement whose derived abstract systems form representations of realizations that are usually felt to be of a different kind from the realizations corresponding with (2), (4), (5). (3) represents a realization which we shall have to consider further. It is peculiar in that realizations approximating to this representation bear a superficial resemblance to the realizations approximating to (1) and other realizations approximating to the representations derived from (1).

6. Throughout discussion of (1), (2), (3), (4) and (5), abstraction may be usefully investigated as a factor in alpha-function. There are two tasks on which it is now necessary to embark. The first is the elucidation of original realizations of the abstraction. The second task is to elucidate the relationship of the model (as Freud uses the term in the passage in which he refers to the reflex apparatus as being the model for the apparatus involved in dreaming) to the realization from which the abstraction and the theoretical deductive systems have been derived; to what extent and in what circumstances can this original realization be seen to be, or

used as, a model for the abstraction derived from it? It can easily be used as such a model unwittingly. For example, I have spoken of certain locutions as being evidence not for memory but for "undigested facts" (p. 7). Implicit in this statement is the use of the alimentary system as a model for the processes of thought. There is reason to believe that the emotional experiences associated with alimentation are those from which individuals have abstracted and then integrated elements to form theoretical deductive systems that are used as representations of realizations of thought. There is reason for using alimentary system as a model for demonstrating and comprehending the processes involved in thought. No objection, except on grounds of inefficacy, can be raised against the procedure as one by which the original realization and the emotional experience to which it gave rise is transformed to provide representations for realizations that seem to approximate to them. Moreover the concrete image of the original realization can be used as a model for a subsequent realization. The distinction between the representation, formed from alpha-elements combined to produce an abstract theoretical deductive system, and a model formed from concrete images combined according to what were conceived to be the relationships between the components of the original realization, is important and must be preserved to avoid confusion. But what is to be said for using our knowledge of the alimentary system to form a model, not for the processes involved in thought but for the processes involved in thought about thought?

7. Problems associated with disturbance of thought compel us to think about thought and this raises a question of technique—*how* are we to think about thought—what is the correct method? It is clear that we can use our knowledge of the alimentary canal unwittingly when we are concerned to elucidate disorders of thought and therefore phenomena that are related to the patient's attitude to, and his capacity for, thinking about thought. The importance of this question lies in the fact that certain patients are influenced by the belief that they digest thoughts and that the consequences of doing so are similar to the digestion of food. That is to

say that if they attempt what might ordinarily be regarded as meditating on an idea, they believe that the thoughts so treated suffer a change analogous to that undergone by food that is turned into faeces: some ideas, or their verbal representations, survive and if expressed emerge not as evidence of the possession of an idea, but as evidence, embedded in a matrix of gibberish, that their thoughts have been destroyed and denuded of meaning in the way that faeces and its undigested particles can be regarded as food that has been destroyed and denuded of its value as food.[1] Interpretations addressed to such a patient need to be couched in terms that avoid words in which the model of the alimentary system is implicit. In practice if the difficulty is recognized by the analyst steps can be taken to prevent making the confusion worse confounded. But the problem stimulates the thought that unconscious employment of this model may be creating difficulties not only for the psychotic but also for the philosopher of science who is engaged on problems of methods of clear thinking. The term "clear thinking" that I have just employed is itself evidence of the extent to which the vocabulary of philosophy and of psycho-analysis, which may be regarded as having a relationship to philosophy analogous to the relationship of mathematics to applied mathematics, is saturated with models derived from sense impressions of material objects. We may thus resort unaware to the same methods of understanding, and that includes representing realizations in the realms of thought by the models employed in the original realization. It is true that the model with which present knowledge of the alimentary canal provides us will be very different from the model with which the infant's knowledge of the alimentary system provides him. A similar difference applies to the systems built on the alpha-elements that are derived as part of the process of abstraction; the infant's abstractions are not those of the adult.

CHAPTER TWENTY-ONE

1. THE USE OF A MODEL has a value in restoring a sense of the concrete to an investigation which may have lost contact with its background through abstraction and the theoretical deductive systems associated with it. Its merit in this respect is matched by its merit as a primitive approach to abstraction in that a whole experience, say feeding, is being used as a model for a later problem. The defect of the model as an instrument adds force to the need to produce abstractions.

2. A model has also qualities which enable it to fulfil some of the functions of an abstraction. It enables the investigator to use an emotional experience by applying it as a totality, to a subsequent experience, or to some aspect of it. These merits carry in themselves the elements that finally make the model outdated. No experience exactly matches a past experience; scientific deductive system and its abstractions, or the model and its associated images, can only be an approximation to the realization and vice versa.

3. I distinguish between the model and the abstraction by reserving the term model for a construction in which concrete images are combined with each other; the link between concrete images often gives the effect of a narrative implying that some elements in the narrative are the causes of others. It is constructed with elements from the individual's past, whereas the abstraction is, as it were, impregnated with preconceptions of the individual's future.[1] Its similarity with the model lies in its origin in an emotional experience and its application to a fresh emotional experience; its dissimilarity lies in the gain in flexibility and applicability which is obtained by loss of particular concrete images; the elements in the abstraction are not combined by narrative

but by a method intended to reveal the relationship rather than the objects related. The deductive system abstracts from an emotional experience those qualities that display the relationship between the elements in that emotional experience. The actual elements related are of lesser consequence. The model stresses the actual elements, the visual images, but the manner in which they are strung together is of subordinate significance.

4. The fact that any realization only approximates to the representation, be it abstraction or model, is the stimulus for further abstraction and further model making.

If the learner is intolerant of the essential frustration of learning he indulges phantasies of omniscience and a belief in a state where things are known. Knowing something consists in "having" some "piece of" knowledge and *not* in what I have called K.

The description of model making and abstraction in Chapters 20 and 21 is itself an example of model making and abstraction employed in K (or "knowing" in the sense of "getting to know" something). If the model making and abstraction imply a capacity for alpha-function they are compatible with all the states of mind mentioned on p. 60 except (1). If there is evidence of (1) the incompatibility of (1) with the others means that (1) and (2), (3), (4), etc. co-exist but are split off from each other.

CHAPTER TWENTY-TWO

1. THE WRITING OF THIS BOOK is a realization of K. The difficulties of the patient suffering from a "disorder of thought" are similar to those that beset scientists, and others concerned with the establishment of facts, in that they arise through failure to ascertain facts and so involve investigation of the nature of the failure. The failure of patients suffering from disorders of thought is patently within the personality. Psycho-analysis of that failure is impossible without understanding the problem of the philosopher of science and conversely his problem is incompletely stated without the aid of psycho-analytic experience of disorders of thought.[1] Investigation of abstraction as a part of the psycho-analytic armoury will be by this two-fold approach. I shall first discuss abstraction as a factor of alpha-function in a K-link.

2. Let us suppose the infant repeats an emotional experience in which the following elements are constantly conjoined; the sight of a man, a sense of being loved by the man, a sense of wanting the man, an awareness of the repetition of a phrase, by the mother, of "That's Daddy." "Da, da, da" says the child. "That's right; Daddy" says the mother. From the emotional experience the infant abstracts certain elements, what they are depending partly on the infant; these abstracted elements are given a name "Daddy" in other situations in which the same elements appear to be conjoined; thus a vocabulary is established. This is not a description of fact; I give it the status of a model from which I abstract a theory and expect to find that it is a representation to which some realization corresponds. The theory I abstract is: "Daddy" is the name of an hypothesis.[1] The

hypothesis called "Daddy" is a statement that certain elements are constantly conjoined.

3. The infant now meets another who also says Da-da-da, but in circumstances that do not appear to correspond with the circumstances with which Da-da-da is associated. There is a man, but it is the wrong one. Yet elements in this new situation correspond with elements in situations that the infant regards as realizations corresponding to the hypothesis of which the name is "Daddy". The hypothesis must be revised to represent the realizations. It may be abandoned for another or it may become a system of hypothesis, a scientific deductive system. The experiences continue and the scientific deductive system named "Daddy" becomes progressively more complex. Using the model to abstract a theory, the individual must be capable of abstracting from an emotional experience elements that appear to be constantly conjoined including one element which is at one and the same time the name of the theory or hypothesis or scientific deductive system; it is also the name of the realization that is believed to approximate to the theory. Thus, "chair" is: (1) the name given to a thing in itself, as it is supposed to exist in actuality; this, following Kant, cannot be known to us.[1] (2) the name given to the selected fact. (3) the name given to a selection of feelings, impressions, etc., that are felt, by virtue of the selected fact, to be related and coherent. (4) the name of the definitory hypothesis that states that these elements are constantly conjoined. (3) and (4) correspond to Kant's secondary and primary qualities. These distinctions of the nature of the content of the term "chair" are of practical importance to psycho-analysts who face the necessity for, and difficulty of, communication within the group. So far I have used only two words, Daddy and chair, as examples of names of hypotheses i.e. of elements abstracted from an emotional situation and given coherence by the name.

4. The use of the term hypothesis as a name for the object that would more often be described as a concept is an expression of the problem presented by (3) as it emerges when investigated psycho-analytically. The problem

presented by the psycho-analytic experience is the lack of any adequate terminology to describe it and in this respect it resembles the problem that Aristotle solved by supposing that mathematics dealt with mathematical objects. It is convenient to suppose that psycho-analysis deals with psycho-analytic objects and that it is with the detection and observation of these objects that the psycho-analyst must concern himself in the conduct of an analysis. (3) describes an aspect of these objects. I employ the term hypothesis provisionally because the meaning associated with the scientific use of this term has aspects that are shared by the psycho-analytic object. The identification of such an object depends on (*a*) the possibility of finding a means by which the nature of the object can be communicated. This involves the employment of the very methods that are the object of this investigation, and (*b*) the mental equipment that the observer can bring to bear. Both (*a*) and (*b*) are therefore adumbrations of problems on which these investigations must converge.

5. From all the elements in a realization only some have their corresponding sense data linked with each other as being constantly conjoined. These elements, and their corresponding sense data may therefore be regarded as abstracted from the totality of elements in the realization. A further abstraction takes place when the elements are given a name that is perceived to be different from the realization it represents. The abstraction must be capable of fulfilling the function of a pre-conception. The generalization must therefore be capable of particularization; the abstraction must be capable of concretization. Implicit in the term concretization is the model from which it is derived. The model supplies a background of meaning that can preserve my statement from being so far divorced from reality as to become unsuited for mating with its realization. But the implication that is its strength becomes a weakness when it is employed by a participant in a relationship in which the link is minus K. (Henceforward I shall write this "— K"; it is discussed in detail in Chapter 28). This weakness and its exploitation in — K becomes apparent in analysis of the patient who appears to be unable to abstract, the patient to whom words

are things—*the* things which the word is supposed to represent, but which are for him indistinguishable from their name and vice versa.

6. The problems associated with abstraction may be illuminated if regarded in reverse as problems of movement from the general to the particular, the abstract to the concrete. When I speak of concretization I employ, and hope to be understood to employ, a metaphor. This class of patient would not understand that. For him the word would be a lump of concrete.[1] This would equally be true if he tried as I am trying, to make my meaning clear by employing the term concretization. I can be aware of failing to make my meaning clear but I do not think my difficulty lies in passing lumps of concrete when what I want is to talk.

7. The theory that the concept is a statement that certain elements are constantly conjoined and that the word is the name of that statement, can be used as a model to formulate a more abstract and widely embracing theory. The realization of every emotional situation is an approximation to a theoretical deductive system that represents it, even though that scientific deductive system or representation has not been discovered.

8. It is now possible to formulate the nature of a psychoanalytical object more easily. Suppose ψ represents a constant, (ξ) an unsaturated element that determines the value of the constant once it has been identified. We may use the unknown constant ψ to represent an inborn pre-conception. Employing a model to give temporary meaning to the term "inborn pre-conception" I shall suppose that an infant has an inborn pre-conception that a breast that satisfies its own incomplete nature exists. The realization of the breast provides an emotional experience. This experience corresponds to Kant's secondary and primary qualities of a phenomenon. The secondary qualities determine the value of the unsaturated element (ξ) and therefore the value of ψ (ξ). This sign now represents a conception. The previously unsaturated element (ξ) together with the unknown constant ψ share a component, that is the inborn character of the personality. Let that be represented by $(\mathcal{M})$. The

psycho-analytic object may then be represented by ψ (ξ) ($\mathcal{M}$). The value of ($\mathcal{M}$), as of (ξ), is determined by the emotional experience stimulated by the realization, that is, in the model I have put forward, by the contact with the breast. The value of the psycho-analytic object ψ (ξ) ($\mathcal{M}$) is then determined by the identification of (ξ) ($\mathcal{M}$) that is precipitated by a realization.

9. This is not all. The extension of the concept of a psycho-analytic object, like the extensions of all biological concepts, includes phenomena related to growth. Growth may be regarded as positive or negative. I shall represent it by ($\pm$ Y). The plus and minus signs are employed to give sense or direction to the element they precede in a manner analogous to their mode of employment in co-ordinate geometry. To indicate this aspect of its extension I shall represent the psycho-analytic object by $\{(\pm \text{Y})\psi(\mathcal{M})(\xi)\}$. Whether (Y) is preceded by plus or minus sign will be determined only by contact with a realization. Abstraction from the psycho-analytic object will be related to the resolution of the conflicting claims of narcissism and social-ism. If the trend is social (+ Y) abstraction will be related to the isolation of primary qualities. If the trend is narcissistic (— Y) abstraction will be replaced by activity appropriate to — K, which I have not yet discussed.

10. K, to which the analyst is restricted, involves abstraction from the psycho-analytic object represented by $\{(\text{Y})\psi(\xi)(\mathcal{M})\}$. The abstraction must be capable of serving as the constant so that it can fulfil the function of an unknown and yet, by virtue of the analytic object from which it derives, have the attributes of a preconception that has, unlike the inborn pre-conception, a penumbra of meaning. It remains an unknown, but the range of values which can be conferred upon it by the identification of (ξ) is restricted. The term "*a priori*" knowledge can only apply to psycho-analytic objects where ψ is an unknown whose value can be determined by identification of (ξ) without restriction.

It is necessary and should be possible to find hypotheses that may be used in scientific deductive systems as either premises or as derived hypotheses. These scientific deductive systems, abstracted from emotional experiences, may then be found to represent other emotional experiences from which they have not been derived, but which can be seen to approximate to the representative scientific deductive system in question. The scientific deductive system may then be further abstracted to yield the equivalent of an algebraic calculus which would represent it.

CHAPTER TWENTY-THREE

1. H. Poincaré describes the process of creation of a mathematical formulation thus:

"If a new result is to have any value, it must unite elements long since known, but till then scattered and seemingly foreign to each other, and suddenly introduce order where the appearance of disorder reigned. Then it enables us to see at a glance each of these elements in the place it occupies in the whole. Not only is the new fact valuable on its own account, but it alone gives a value to the old facts it unites. Our mind is frail as our senses are; it would lose itself in the complexity of the world if that complexity were not harmonious; like the short-sighted, it would only see the details, and would be obliged to forget each of these details before examining the next, because it would be incapable of taking in the whole. The only facts worthy of our attention are those which introduce order into this complexity and so make it accessible to us."[1]

2. This description closely resembles the psycho-analytical theory of paranoid-schizoid and depressive positions adumbrated by Mrs. Klein. I have used the term "selected fact" to describe that which the psycho-analyst must experience in the process of synthesis. The name of one element is used to particularize the selected fact, that is to say the name of that element in the realization that appears to link together elements not hitherto seen to be connected. The representations of the selected facts may then be seen to have a similar coherence if the appropriate representation for a number of selected facts can be found. The selected facts, together with the selected fact that appears to give coherence to a number of selected facts, emerge from a psycho-analytic object or

series of such objects, but cannot be formulated in accordance with the principles governing a scientific deductive system. Before such a system can be created the selected facts have to be worked upon by conscious rational processes. Only then can the representation be formulated that will bring together the elements of coherent selected facts in a scientific deductive system. In the scientific deductive system the hypotheses of the system should be held together by rules but these do not correspond with that which, in the realization, appears to link together the elements whose relationship appears to be revealed by the selected fact. Now the rules that hold together the hypotheses in the system of hypotheses, namely the scientific deductive system, are the rules of logic. The relationship amongst the hypotheses of a scientific deductive system, namely the logical connection between them that has been brought into prominence by the deductive system, is characteristic of conscious rational thought but not of the relationship between the elements in a realization of which the phenomena appear to cohere as a result of the discovery of a selected fact. The selected fact is the name of an emotional experience, the emotional experience of a sense of discovery of coherence; its significance is therefore epistemological and the relationship of selected facts must not be assumed to be logical. The elements thought to be related have a counterpart in actuality of things-in-themselves. Are we to assume that the selected fact represents a thing-in-itself and similarly that the relationship, namely the logical relationship, between the elements in the deductive system has also a counterpart in actuality, a thing-in-itself that approximates to deductive logic? In fact the mathematical formulation has some of the characteristics of an attempt to formulate a system of relationships between mathematical objects to which some realization of relationships might approximate. In other words there is no reason why the rules governing the logical manipulation of the elements in a scientific deductive system should have any corresponding realization. It follows that the elements in an analytic object may be related to each other in a manner entirely different from the manner in which their representations are linked in a scientific deductive system. Progress in elucidation of the field of relatedness will probably depend on illumination by K of — K and the psycho-analytic objects peculiar to that.

3. The network of relationships discernible in the scientific deductive system or its corresponding calculus may not have any realization and for the following reasons. Successful investigations have been associated with inanimate objects which the animate object shares with the inanimate. In such cases the logical structure of the scientific deductive system and the algebraic calculus representing it appears to have a corresponding realization probably because it is abstracted from a similar realization. That is to say there is a realization that seems to correspond approximately to the actual network of relationships that is internal to the scientific deductive system itself. Investigation of elements that are essentially animate does not yield such a correspondence. The form of association between elements bound together by narrative is distinct from the form of association discerned through transition from paranoid-schizoid to depressive position.

4. The narrative form is associated with the theory of causation and the other with the depressive positions and the selected fact. There may be no realization that corresponds with these two theories.

5. Any experience may be used as a "model" for some future experience. This aspect of learning by experience is related to, and may be identical with, the function Freud attributes to attention when he says it had "periodically to search the outer world in order that its data might be already familiar if an urgent inner need should arise". The value of a model is that its familiar data are available to meet urgent inner or outer need. The selected fact precipitates the model. The coherence of the elements in the model that is identified with the realization is then felt to pertain to the elements of the realization.

6. Before an emotional experience can be used for a model its sense data have to be transformed into alpha-elements to be stored and made available for abstraction.

(In — K the meaning is abstracted leaving a denuded representation.) Model making during the experience relates to the model needed for that experience; alpha-function during the experience provides the elements needed for model making in a subsequent experience; the model is precipitated during the experience for which the model is needed. Elements are removed from mental storage to provide a model that is an approximation to the event it is to illuminate. The personality abstracts from experience the elements expected to recur and forms from these elements the model that will preserve something of the original experience but with enough flexibility to permit adaptation to new but supposedly similar experiences. He abstracts elements to construct either a model or an abstraction or both. I shall use the term model where the construct is forged to meet an "urgent need" for concreteness. (Construct, forged, concreteness. All three words carry implications of the models from which the words have been abstracted. I have left the passage as an example of the latent, though in this case noticeable, influence of the model.) If the need is for a model those elements will be abstracted from the store of alpha-elements that have, like visual images, a reminiscence of the emotional experience during which the alpha-element was formed. The more such elements are employed the more rigid the model becomes and the more restricted its application; the restriction is modified if the model formed from a combination of these elements is then submitted to further abstraction. The abstractions need then to be combined in accordance with the rules of logic. This system of abstractions is the scientific deductive system.

CHAPTER TWENTY-FOUR

1. SUPPOSE THAT THE PATIENT has produced a number of associations and other material. The analyst has available:

(1) Observations of the patient's material;
(2) Various emotional experiences of his own;
(3) A knowledge of one or more versions of the myth of Oedipus[1];
(4) One or more versions of psycho-analytical theory of the Oedipus complex;
(5) Other fundamental psycho-analytic theories.

Some aspects of the session will appear familiar; they will remind him of past experiences analytical and otherwise. Others will seem to bear a resemblance to the oedipal situation. From these sources the analyst can form a model; the problem is to decide whether the analyst is confronted by a realization of Freud's theory of the oedipus complex. The Oedipus theory, does not correspond closely to what a physicist would call a scientific deductive system but can be formulated to qualify for inclusion in such a category. Its weakness as a member of this class is likely to be its lack of abstraction and the peculiar structure by which its elements are related to each other. In part this is due to the fact that the more concrete the elements the less they lend themselves to variation of combination.

2. In addition two factors (1) the actual nature of the network of relationships in which the elements are held, and (2) the derivation of the elements from a myth contrast with the elements in a scientific deductive system as used by a physicist. The latter purports to derive from one realization

and to be able to represent another, whereas the psycho-analytic formulation is derived from and expressed by the emotional experience of a folk narrative and is said to represent a realization encountered in psycho-analysis. Freud derived his theory from the emotional experience of psycho-analytic inquiry, but his description could not be comparable with the formulations usually supposed to represent scientific discovery. I wish to discuss only two methodological weaknesses in the Oedipus theory and these are:

(1) The theory as it stands is so concrete that it cannot be matched with its realization; that is to say no realization can be found to approximate to a theory whose elements, concrete in themselves, are combined in a narrative network of relationships that is intrinsic and essential. Without the narrative the elements lose their value.

Conversely:

(2) If the elements are generalized the theory becomes an ingenious manipulation of elements according to arbitrary rules—the commonest formulation of this suspicion of the theory is the criticism that analyst and analysand indulge a taste for jargon.

3. A theoretical formulation that appears to be too concrete and yet too abstract requires to be generalized in such a way that its realizations are more easily detected, without the attendant weakness, most often seen in mathematics, of appearing to be an arbitrary manipulation of symbols. Can it retain its concrete elements without losing flexibility so essential in psycho-analytic application? It can be made more abstract though we may not find an algebraic calculus to represent the scientific deductive system. I shall say more about this possibility later.

4. I am convinced of the strength of the scientific position of psycho-analytic practice. I believe that the practice of psycho-analysts in making psycho-analysis an essential training experience deals with the fundamental difficulties for the time being because it makes conscious and unconscious available for correlation; but I do not consider the need less

pressing to investigate the weaknesses that spring from faulty theory construction, lack of notation and failure of methodical care amd maintenance of psycho-analytic equipment. ("Care", "maintenance", "equipment",—again the implicit model.)

CHAPTER TWENTY-FIVE

1. The model may be regarded as an abstraction from an emotional experience or as a concretization of an abstraction. The latter has affinities with the transformation of an hypothesis into terms of empirically verifiable data. In the group the myth has some claim to be regarded as filling the same role in the society as the model has in scientific work of the individual.

2. As an example of a model I take the imaginary story of the infant learning the word Daddy. This story does not purport to be a fact. It is derived from experience of patients in analysis, observation of children, desultory reading, some of it philosophical, and other sources; in short it is derived from experience—*my* experience. It is an artefact composed of elements that have been selected by me from my store of experience. But it has been formed for a specific purpose; the selection and combination of elements is not fortuitous but is made to "explain" or illuminate the problem of abstraction. It has, therefore, no value as evidence; its value lies in the ease with which it can be communicated and compared with facts. By contrast the account of the patient who feels that words are things is not a model but an example; what I describe purports to be a realization. The model was made to illuminate the experience I had with a particular patient and is used for comparison with the realization. Potentially, every realization approximates to an abstraction or scientific deductive system even if one to which it corresponds has not yet been discovered (p. 61). When I compare model and realization it may result in my receiving the illumination I desire; it may prove so unrewarding that I assume the model is worthless and discard

it. Models are ephemeral and differ from theories in this respect; I have no compunction in discarding a model as soon as it has served or failed to serve my purpose. If a model proves useful on a number of different occasions the time has come to consider its transformation into a theory.

3. A psycho-analyst may make as many models as he chooses out of any material available to him. It is important not to confound these ephemeral structures with realizations on the one hand or theories on the other. The model has a valuable function provided always that it is recognized for what it is. If the analyst believes he is describing an actual event he should make this clear and should not allow the distinction between an event, for the authenticity of which there is supporting evidence, and a model to become blurred. The same applies to the distinction between a model and a theory. I shall deal with the peculiar difficulties that beset the psycho-analyst in avoiding confusion in making the distinction between theory and model and between a model and the particular form of theory known as a psycho-analytical interpretation.

4. The process of abstraction from a realization may proceed directly from realization to scientific deductive system through the intervening phase of model making. Elements are selected from the model and used as elements in the scientific deductive system. The need for this procedure becomes apparent when a model is used to illuminate a realization that is thought to approximate to the model and the model is then found to be insufficiently similar to clarify the problem for which a solution is sought. I ignore the contingency that arises when the realization is mistakenly matched with the model; that failure is dealt with by the creation of a new model. An important failure is that which arises when the model is seen to be the nearest possible approximation to the realization, but nevertheless fails to mirror developments in the realization by the movement in its own internal structure. This failure can occur whenever model making is used; but there must be heightened risk of its occurrence when, as in psycho-analysis, we are concerned with growth and speak of "mental mechanisms". To

talk of "mechanism" suggests that, whatever the phenomenon is that is thus described, it is likely that the implied model is more suitable to the inanimate machine than to a living organism. It is likely to emphasize those aspects of the living organism which it shares with the inanimate. This defect is serious because we require models when the problem is most complex, that is when the characteristics of growth are central; and that is most of the time. The term mechanism implies the model of a machine which is precisely what the realization is not. The dangers of too great abstraction do not admit of an easy solution by discarding the use of models. Psychoanalysts are therefore certain to become familiar with the situation in which the model used to avoid the dangers of theorising, in which I include interpretation, suffers from the complementary defect of being so close to the realization from which it is derived that it is correspondingly intractable when required to represent a realization from which it is separated by its very concreteness. This defect resembles the defect of the beta-element as an element in thinking. The transformation which the model has to undergo to permit of its employment as a generalization is analogous to the process by which sense data are transformed into alpha-elements. The alternative to finding or making a new model is to resort to further abstraction. The model is then replaced by the Scientific Deductive System. As an example of the issues involved I shall take the scientific approach to the problems of the K relationships.

CHAPTER TWENTY-SIX

1. The terms Love, Hate and Knowing had precedent models. Link can imply a model or an abstraction. The failure of the patient to solve his problems may in some cases depend on the fact that he employs models wrongly. In making his own model the analyst needs in such cases to be aware of and to lay bare the model used by the patient. The analyst's model must be such that it enables him to arrive at an interpretation of the facts that present themselves for scrutiny. If the analyst supposes that the patient's thinking is at fault and is at the source of his troubles he will need a model and a theory of thinking of his own; he will need a model for the patient's mode of thinking and he will need to deduce from that what the patient's model for thinking is. He may then compare his model and abstraction with the patient's. The patient who thinks words are things-in-themselves does not feel he is doing the same thing as we think he is doing when we say he is thinking. To compare the ordinary view of thinking with such a patient's it is necessary to find a suitable model and theory. One model has, as we have seen, a wide-spread distribution, the model derived from the emotional experience of the digestive system. There is ordinarily no need to discard this model though its failings are obvious—it can still help to be able to speak of "undigested facts". But for a psycho-analytic investigation of thinking it is inadequate and some different model is needed. This need has become obvious in the psycho-analytic investigation of disorders of thought. Investigation of mental development shows that some individuals behave as if their model of thinking was not that of a healthy digestive system or perhaps of a digestive system at all. It is therefore necessary to discover what their model is.

2. Freud said thought provided a means for the restraint of motor discharge (Two Principles); it was no longer concerned with unburdening the mental apparatus of accretions of stimuli but was now employed in the appropriate alteration of reality. According to this, thought is a substitute for motor discharge although he does not say that motor discharge ceases to function as a method of disburdening the psyche of accretions of stimuli. But through projective identification thought itself takes on the function previously entrusted to motor discharge—namely ridding the psyche of accretions of stimuli; like "action" it may be directed to altering the environment, depending on whether the personality is directed to evasion of frustration or modification of it. "Thinking" can be regarded as the name given to a model or abstraction derived from a realization; with an actual patient the problem is to determine what he represents by the term thinking. An individual may mean that thoughts are being used and a thought is a not good breast, a "need for a breast" breast. The problem then would be to see how he uses this "object", particularly if the patient felt unable to evacuate it—to disburden himself of these accretions of internal stimuli.

3. The problem is simplified if "thoughts" are regarded as epistomologically prior to thinking and that thinking has to be developed as a method or apparatus for dealing with "thoughts". If this is the case then much will depend on whether the "thoughts" are to be evaded or modified or used as part of an attempt to evade or modify something else. If they are felt to be accretions of stimuli then they may be similar to or identical with beta-elements and as such would lend themselves to treatment by motor discharge and the operation of the musculature to effect the discharge. Talking therefore must be considered as potentially two different activities, one as a mode of communicating thoughts and the other as an employment of the *musculature* to disencumber the personality of thoughts.

4. An apparatus has to be produced to make it possible to think the already existing thought. As a "model" of thought I take a sensation of hunger that is associated with

a visual image of a breast that does not satisfy but is of a kind that is needed. This needed object is a bad object. All objects that are needed are bad objects because they tantalize. They are needed because they are not possessed in fact; if they were possessed there would be no lack. As they don't exist they are peculiar objects different from objects that exist. Thoughts then, or these primitive elements that are proto-thoughts, are bad, needed objects and to be got rid of because they are bad. They can be got rid of either by evasion or modification. The problem is solved by evacuation if the personality is dominated by the impulse to evade frustration and by thinking the objects if the personality is dominated by the impulse to modify the frustration. In analytic practice confusion and complication is produced for the analyst because both types of personality employ the same name for objects that are essentially dissimilar. The dissimilarity can be emphasized by comparison. If evasion dominates, the name denotes a beta-element, that is a thing-in-itself and not the name that represents it. The thing in itself is non-existent and therefore tantalizing. It is dealt with by divestment (evacuation). If modification dominates, the name denotes an alpha-element, that is the name is the name of the representation of a thing in itself. The name is of a thing in itself that exists and is therefore potentially available for use in achieving fulfilment. Further complication is produced because a patient is unlikely to be consistent and does not make clear what objects are being denoted by the names he is using.

5. If the patient cannot "think" with his thoughts, that is to say that he has thoughts but lacks the apparatus of "thinking" which enables him to use his thoughts, to think them as it were, the first result is an intensification of frustration because thought that should make it "possible for the mental apparatus to support increased tension during a delay in the process of discharge" is lacking. The steps taken by the patient to rid himself of the objects, the proto-thoughts or thoughts which to him are inseparable from frustration, have then led him to precisely the pass that he wished to avoid, namely to tension and frustration unalleviated by the capacity

for thought. The lack of a capacity for thought therefore implies a twofold failure. It is due to absence of alpha-elements and lack of apparatus to use alpha-elements if they exist. The double failure becomes significant in the psycho-analysis of the psychotic when the patient re-establishes alpha-function, and therefore his capacity for dreaming, and yet remains unable to think. He therefore resorts to projective identification as a mechanism for dealing with "thoughts". But if alpha-function has been developed there is a corresponding increase in dominance of reality principle and a corresponding change in projective identification which loses some of its quality of omnipotent phantasy and gains through the patient's ability to give it substance.

6. Clinically this shows itself in an increase in the patient of a sense of loss when he is speaking. The sense of loss appears to originate in an awareness that the thoughts being lost are good or valuable thoughts differing in this respect from beta-elements. The analyst likewise becomes aware of a change in the impact on himself of the patient's manipulations.

7. "Thinking", in the sense of engaging in that activity which is concerned with the use of thoughts, is embryonic even in the adult and has yet to be developed fully by the race. Quite conscious attempts are directed to this end. The problem is more accurately apprehended and investigated if it is seen to depend on (1) "thoughts" and (2) "thinking" which developed in response to the challenge presented by the existence of "thoughts". In the psycho-analysis of "disorders of thought", psycho-analytic investigation must be directed towards the development and nature of the "thoughts", alpha- and beta-elements, and then to the nature of the apparatus used for dealing with "thoughts". Only then can the investigation be devoted to what content or other factor contributed to the breakdown. The division into two classes and the attribution of priority to "thoughts" is subject to the limitations peculiar to the relationship existing in all scientific work between the realization and the representative theory to which it is believed to approximate. The division and priority are epistemologically and

logically necessary, that is to say the theory that thought is prior to thinking is itself prior, in the hierarchy of hypotheses in the scientific deductive system, to the hypothesis of thinking. A corresponding priority is epistemologically necessary in the realization corresponding to the theory of thinking I have adumbrated here.

8. The scientific deductive system is called for because the model made during the emotional experience which it is intended to illuminate is not sufficiently abstract. Its elements are derived from previous emotional experiences through the operation, concurrently with the emotional experience, of alpha-function. The model is formed by the exercise of a capacity similar to that which is in evidence when the two eyes operate in binocular vision to correlate two views of the same object. The use in psycho-analysis of conscious and unconscious in viewing a psycho-analytic object is analogous to the use of the two eyes in ocular observation of an object sensible to sight. Freud attributed this function, the sense organ of psychical quality, to consciousness alone. The scientific deductive system is elaborated away from the emotional experience and is a conscious act of construction in the course of which signs are chosen and rules for their manipulation formulated. Can such a procedure be profitably adapted to the psycho-analytic investigation of the development of thoughts and the apparatus that employs them? I shall answer the question by making the attempt in my last chapter and incidentally summarizing this book.

9. The first requisite for the use of a theory is proper conditions for observation. The most important of these is psycho-analysis of the observer to ensure that he has reduced to a minimum his own inner tensions and resistances which otherwise obstruct his view of facts by making correlation by conscious and unconscious impossible. The next step is for the analyst to bring his attention to bear. Darwin pointed out that judgment obstructs observation. The psycho-analyst however must intervene with interpretations and this involves the exercise of judgment. A state of reverie conducive to alpha-function, obtrusion of the selected fact,

and model-making together with an armoury limited to a few essential theories ensure that a harsh break in observation of the kind Darwin had in mind becomes less likely; interpretations can occur to the analyst with the minimum disturbance of observation.

10. The "selected fact", that is to say the element that gives coherence to the objects of the paranoid-schizoid position and so initiates the depressive position, does so by virtue of its membership of a number of different deductive systems at their point of intersection. Obtrusion of the selected fact is accompanied by an emotion such as is experienced in regarding the object in reversible perspective. The total process depends on relaxed attention; this is the matrix for abstraction and identification of the selected fact. From the model thus made and its matching with the realization a special theory, the psycho-analytic interpretation, must be abstracted. This abstraction involves the difference between a theory associated with a scientific deductive system and a psycho-analytic interpretation. The analyst has to concern himself with two models, one that he is called upon to make and the other implicit in the material produced by the patient.

11. I shall first consider the model that has to be made by the analyst. The model is produced by the analyst as a part of theory construction and is *not* itself an interpretation, except in the conversational sense of the term, of what is taking place. The relevant theory may be the Oedipus theory. The analyst must determine from the patient's material why he is producing it and what the correct interpretation should be. The model plays its part in the determination by enabling the analyst to match what the patient is actually saying, with the theory or theories known to psycho-analysis as the Oedipus complex. The model throws into relief two sets of ideas, those that relate to the patient's material and those that relate to the body of psycho-analytic theory.

12. Model making makes it possible to retain the structure of psycho-analytic theory without loss of the flexibility necessary to meet the moment to moment needs of

psychoanalytic practice. On the one hand the theory may become too set because of its concreteness and on the other open to endless proliferation because analysts, finding themselves in an impasse, may prefer to produce a new theory *ad hoc* rather than undergo the ardours of using existing theory properly. The advantage of the theory of functions and of the development of model making as an essential part of it, is that the analyst has plenty of scope for really satisfying himself, and therefore his patient, that it is the patient as a real man or woman whose affairs are under scrutiny and not just the supposed mental mechanisms of a dummy. At the same time the particularization necessary for this does not involve proliferating theories. The model makes it possible to find the correspondence between the patient's thinking and the main body of psycho-analytic theory by interpretations that are related closely both to theory and the statements and conduct of the patient. Model making thus increases the number of contingencies that can be met and decreases the number of psycho-analytic theories that the psycho-analyst needs as his working equipment. If every analyst set himself the task of producing a handbook of psycho-analytic theories to provide a foundation of the minimum number of premises from which a wide range of subsidiary theories could be deduced, I believe it would be possible with less than six major theories. Psycho-analytic virtue lies not in the number of theories the analyst can command but the minimum number with which he can meet any contingency he is likely to meet. The range of such theoretical equipment depends on the method of application and that on the procedure of model making. There will be less disposition to put forward new theories when none is called for if the distinction between model and theory is kept clear. The danger lies in being cramped by a theoretical system that is frustrating not because it is inadequate but because it is not being properly used.

CHAPTER TWENTY-SEVEN

THIS CHAPTER will be taken up with the construction of some theories that I have found serviceable. It is intended also to serve as an example of the use of the theory of functions and other ideas I have put forward and thus to take the place of a summary of the main items in the book.

THE K LINK

1. The theory of functions and alpha-function are not a part of psycho-analytic theory. They are working tools for the practising psycho-analyst to ease problems of thinking about something that is unknown.

2. The term "function", used in the sense of a function of the personality, has not the meaning it possesses for the mathematician or the mathematical logician though it has features partaking of the meaning of both. I propose it as a term for use in the practice of psycho-analysis; its full designation, if there is any doubt, is "psycho-analytic function of the personality" but otherwise it should be designated simply "function" and given the sign ψ. Alpha-function is a factor of ψ.

3. The term "factor" is the name of an element of any function. It may be represented by the unsaturated element (ξ) in ψ (ξ) and there must be a realization approximating to it. What the realization is that satisfies it, in the mathematical sense of satisfying the terms of an equation, is a matter to be determined by the psycho-analytical investigation itself.

4. The theory of functions, and alpha-function in particular, does not diminish or increase existing psycho-analytical theories. In this it differs from the arguments that follow.

5. Melanie Klein has described an aspect of projective identification concerned with the modification of infantile fears; the infant projects a part of its psyche, namely its bad feelings, into a good breast. Thence in due course they are removed and re-introjected. During their sojourn in the good breast they are felt to have been modified in such a way that the object that is re-introjected has become tolerable to the infant's psyche.

6. From the above theory I shall abstract for use as a model the idea of a container into which an object is projected and the object that can be projected into the container: the latter I shall designate by the term contained. The unsatisfactory nature of both terms points the need for further abstraction.

7. Container and contained are susceptible of conjunction and permeation by emotion. Thus conjoined or permeated or both they change in a manner usually described as growth. When disjoined or denuded of emotion they diminish in vitality, that is, approximate to inanimate objects. Both container and contained are models of abstract representations of psycho-analytic realizations.

8. The next step in abstraction is dictated by the need for designation. I shall use the sign ♀ for the abstraction representing the container and ♂ for the contained.

9. These signs both denote and represent. They are variables or unknown in that they are replaceable. They are constants in that they are only replaceable by constants. For syntactical purposes they are functors.

10. Reconsidering K in the light of previous discussion although K is essentially a function of two objects it can be considered as a function of one.

The earliest and most primitive manifestation of K occurs in the relationship between mother and infant. As a part object relationship it may be stated as a relationship between mouth and breast. In abstract terms it is between ♂ and ♀ (as I have proposed the use of these signs).

In K, L and H being factors and therefore subordinate, ♂ is projected into ♀ and abstraction, of a type that I shall use the term commensal to describe, follows. By commensal I mean ♂ and ♀ are dependent on each other for mutual benefit and without harm to either. In terms of a model the mother derives benefit and achieves mental growth from the experience: the infant likewise abstracts benefit and achieves growth.

11. The activity that I have here described as shared by two individuals becomes introjected by the infant so that the ♂ ♀ apparatus becomes installed in the infant as part of the apparatus of alpha-function. A model is provided by the idea of the infant who explores an object by putting it into his mouth. What talking was originally done by the mother, possibly a rudimentary designatory function, is replaced by the infant's own baby talk.

12. Using 11 above as a model from which to abstract a theory to represent the realization of the development of thoughts, I propose the following terms: (*a*) Pre-conception. This term represents a state of expectation. The term is the counterpart of a variable in mathematical logic or an unknown in mathematics. It has the quality that Kant ascribes to an empty thought in that it can be thought but cannot be known.

(*b*) Conception. Conception is that which results when a pre-conception mates with the appropriate sense impressions. I have used a phrase in which the implied model is obvious. The abstraction from the relationship of pre-conception to sense impressions is ♀ to ♂ (NOT ♂ to ♀).

13. To summarize. The relationship between mother and infant described by Melanie Klein as projective identification is internalized to form an apparatus for regulation of a pre-conception with the sense data of the appropriate realization. This apparatus is represented by a model: the mating of pre-conception with sense-impressions to produce a conception. The model is in turn represented by ♂ ♀.

14. The repetition of mating of pre-conception and sense data, that results in commensal abstraction, promotes growth in ♂ and ♀. That is to say the capacity for taking in sense impressions develops together with the capacity for awareness of sense data. Growth of ♂ and ♀ can be represented pictorially by models described in 16 and 17 below.

15. For the model for the growth of ♀ I shall borrow Elliott Jaques concept of the reticulum. (In doing so I do not propose alterations in his concept or claim that my use is justified by the intrinsic qualities of the concept. The relationship of his concept to my use of it as a model must be determined in the course of the development of psycho-analysis.) The model I propose is as follows:

♀ develops by accretion to produce a series of sleeves that are conjoined. The result is a reticulum in which the gaps are the sleeves and the threads forming the meshes of the reticulum are emotions. Borrowing from Tarski (*Introduction to Logic:* Oxford 1956 page 5) his simile of the questionnaire with blanks that have to be filled in, the sleeves can be likened to the blanks in the questionnaire. The structure of the questionnaire has as its counterpart the connecting threads of the reticulum.

16. The model for the growth of ♂ is a medium in which lie suspended the "contents". The "contents" must be conceived of as protruding from a base which is unknown. A two-dimensional image is provided by the parabola. The medium in a commensal relationship of ♂ and ♀ is tolerated doubt. That is to say that the developing ♂ can be visualized as being similar to the elements of the paranoid-schizoid position but without the sense of persecution. It is the state described by Poincaré, and quoted by me, as one in which elements are not seen to cohere.

17. Stating 15 & 16 above abstractly we have on the one hand (♀ ≠ ♀ + ♀. . .) and on the other (♂ . ♂ . ♂ . . .) where the + signs represent variables replaceable by signs representing emotions and . signs represent a constant representing doubt.

18. Growing ♂ ♀ provides the basis of an apparatus for learning by experience. Reconsideration of paras 5 to 17 shows that from thoughts and the development of thoughts there arises the apparatus for thinking the thoughts. I shall now consider the nature and operation of that apparatus. It cannot have the rigid clear-cut structure this attempt at exposition implies partly because the attempt is a clarification and partly because I have to use for something animate

terms such as apparatus and structure. I shall denote the growing ♂ ♀ by using the signs $♂^n$ and $♀^n$. The signs have no logical significance but are intended merely to save time.

19. Learning depends on the capacity for $♀^n$ to remain integrated and yet lose rigidity.[1] This is the foundation of the state of mind of the individual who can retain his knowledge and experience and yet be prepared to reconstrue past experiences in a manner that enables him to be receptive of a new idea. Using this last statement as a model from which to abstract, the elements (♀) of $♀^n$ must be held by a constant + that is capable of replacement, in other words it must function as a variable. Only then can it represent an apparatus capable of changing emotion. On the replacement of one emotion, represented by +, by another emotion, also represented by +, does the capacity for re-formation, and therefore receptivity, of $♀^n$ depend. Similarly the penetrability of ♂ elements in $♂^n$ depends on the value of ".". The value of "+" and "." is determined by the same factor, namely emotion and the emotion is a function of the personality.

20. Hitherto I have been describing a type of abstraction I have named commensal in which the link between objects is commensal. K has depended on that type of link between objects through all the phases of mental activity and growth. Since "+" and "." represent emotions it is evident that we need to know what emotions are compatible with a commensal relationship and therefore with K. The problem will receive some illumination in my next chapter in which I discuss — K.

21. The pattern ♂ ♀ represents an emotional realization associated with learning that becomes progressively more complex as it constantly recurs throughout mental development. This growing and recurring event, represented by $♀^n$ $♂^n$, I shall attempt to clarify by depicting one of its aspects, in its more developed and sophisticated stages, by a more sophisticated description.

$♀^n$ represents a late stage in a series of stages that commences with a few relatively simple undifferentiated preconceptions probably related to feeding, breathing and excretion.

22. The abstractions from the commensal mating of ♀

with ♂ include the formation of words that are names for various hypotheses stating that certain sense data are constantly conjoined. From such relatively simple beginnings the $♀^n$ $♂^n$ abstracts successively more complex hypotheses and finally whole systems of hypotheses which are known as scientific deductive systems. These extremely complex systems though hardly recognizable in their origins nevertheless retain the receptive qualities denoted by ♀. The phenomena related to realizations multiply as the realizations, though limited to the progress in experience of one man, are yet multiplied enough to reveal an expanding universe to which presumably an expanding realization corresponds. $♂^n$ must therefore have a phenomenological counterpart represented by the concept of infinity.

The elements of the many scientific deductive systems must be capable of recombination—the use of an hypothesis from one deductive system as premiss in a different deductive system is a familiar example. On the theory put forward here the freedom necessary for these recombinations depends on emotions suffusing the psyche because these emotions are the connective in which the scientific deductive systems and the elements of $♂^n$ are embedded. Tolerance of doubt and tolerance of a sense of infinity are the essential connective in $♂^n$ if K is to be possible.

CHAPTER TWENTY-EIGHT

— K

1. SOME PATIENTS who are concerned to prove their superiority to the analyst by defeating his attempts at interpretation can be shown that they are mis-understanding the interpretations to demonstrate that an ability to mis-understand is superior to an ability to understand. Interpretations based on this insight can lead to further development of the analysis. If the patient suffers from a disorder of thought, interpretations of mis-understanding lead to some illumination, but do not appear to carry matters much further. For this problem a more inclusive concept is necessary.

2. Using the procedures adumbrated here I first resort to the abstraction represented by the sign K and then reverse the sign to — K. Assuming that the signs of all factors in K are also reversed, I use the theories that represent factors in K as preconceptions to aid in my search for factors in — K. Those factors, now employed as pre-conceptions are employed, can be represented in their new employment by ♀. It may make my meaning clearer if I say that I am in a state of receptive observation as opposed to a state in which I pass judgment on what I observe. I can further describe it approximately by saying I become absorbed in my task of observation or that I am absorbed in the facts. In short there are many ways in which I can attempt to describe my mental activity; all of them may contribute to an understanding of what I am engaged on, but none of them does so with the precision that I think necessary for communicating psycho-analytic procedure. The advantage of employing a sign ♀ to designate the new role of factors in K is that it at least indicates

that the reader's comprehension of my meaning should contain an element that will remain unsatisfied until he meets the appropriate realization, an element that can be represented by the sign ψ (ξ), (ξ) being itself the sign for an unsaturated element.

3. The sections that follow are an attempt to describe the results of observation in which preconceptions are harnessed to the task of discovery and not treated as predilections to be eliminated if possible—for that is in any case not possible.

4. Inevitably one wonders at various points in the investigation why such a phenomenon as that represented by $-$ K should exist. The answer to that question must be sought in psycho-analytic work with individual patients. I shall consider one factor only—Envy. By this term I mean the phenomenon described by Melanie Klein in *Envy and Gratitude.*

5. I have described the role of projective identification in K as a commensal relationship between ♀ and ♂. In $-$ K, as exemplified in a patient represented by the sign ψ (ξ) in whom preliminary investigation reveals Envy as likely to be one of the factors needed to satisfy (ξ), the relationship of ♀ to ♂ is represented by ♀ + ♂ where + can be replaced by Envy. Using this formulation to represent infant and breast (to resort to less abstract signs) and using as a model an emotional situation in which the infant feels fear that it is dying, the model I construct is as follows: the infant splits off and projects its feelings of fear into the breast together with envy and hate of the undisturbed breast. Envy precludes a commensal relationship. The breast in K would moderate the fear component in the fear of dying that had been projected into it and the infant in due course would re-introject a now tolerable and consequently growth-stimulating part of its personality. In $-$ K the breast is felt enviously to remove the good or valuable element in the fear of dying and force the worthless residue back into the infant. The infant who started with a fear he was dying ends up by containing a nameless dread.

6. The violence of emotion that is associated with Envy, and can be one of the factors in the personality in which $-$ K

is in evidence, affects the projective processes so that far more than the fear of dying is projected. Indeed it is as if virtually the whole personality was evacuated by the infant. The process of denudation described in 5 is therefore more serious, because more extensive, than is implied in the simple example of the projection of a fear of dying. The seriousness is best conveyed by saying that the will to live, that is necessary before there can be a fear of dying, is a part of the goodness that the envious breast has removed.

7. Since the projection by the infant is also impelled by envy the projection is felt as an envious denudation of the psyche from which, in K, only the fear of dying would have been removed. There is therefore hardly any infant to re-introject or into whom the denuded fear of dying can be forced. In K, ♀ ♂ can find a habitat because the infant can re-introject the related pair. But — ♀ and — ♂ are returned to an object that covers them with little more than the semblance of a psyche.

8. The object that I described as being re-introjected as ♀ ♂ in K was one in which the relationship of the elements ♀ and ♂ was commensal. In — K it is envious and therefore it is necessary to consider — ♀ and — ♂ and — (♀ ♂) in more detail. There are a number of peculiar features that are difficult to reconcile in a coherent theory. I shall accordingly describe them first without any attempt at explanation.

9. In the first place its predominant characteristic I can only describe as "without-ness". It is an internal object without an exterior. It is an alimentary canal without a body. It is a super-ego that has hardly any of the characteristics of the super-ego as understood in psycho-analysis: it is "super" ego. It is an envious assertion of moral superiority without any morals. In short it is the resultant of an envious stripping or denudation of all good and is itself destined to continue the process of stripping described in 5, as existing, in its origin, between two personalities. The process of denudation continues till — ♂ — ♀ represent hardly more than an empty superiority-inferiority that in turn degenerates to nullity.

10. In so far as its resemblance to the super-ego is concerned — (♀ ♂) shows itself as a superior object asserting its superiority by finding fault with everything. The most important characteristic is its hatred of any new development in the personality as if the new development were a rival to be destroyed. The emergence therefore of any tendency to search for the truth, to establish contact with reality and in short to be scientific in no matter how rudimentary a fashion is met by destructive attacks on the tendency and the reassertion of the "moral" superiority. This implies an assertion of what in sophisticated terms would be called a moral law and a moral system as superior to scientific law and a scientific system.

11. Restating 10 in other terms, it can be seen as implying an attempt to retain a power to arouse guilt as an essential capacity. The power to arouse guilt is essential and appropriate to the operation of projective identification in a relationship between infant and breast. This guilt is peculiar in that its association with primitive projective identification implies that the guilt is meaningless. The — (♀ ♂) contrasts therefore with conscience in that it does not lend itself to constructive activity.

12. In contrast with the learning (K) function of ♀ ♂, — (♀ ♂) is engaged in the collection of meaningful ♂ elements for subjection to — ♀ so that these elements are stripped of their meaning and only the worthless residue is retained. The analyst's interpretations are a part of the ♂ elements that are so treated, with the result that they are denuded of meaning. This envious extraction is to be contrasted with the process of abstraction peculiar to ♀ ♂ in K. The ego-like function of — ♀ ♂ is unlike ego function in destroying rather than promoting knowledge. This destructive activity is tinged with "moral" qualities derived from the "super"-ego quality of — (♀ ♂). In other words — ♀ ♂ asserts the moral superiority and superiority in potency of *UN*-learning.

13. Successful operation of — (♀ ♂) has as its achievement growth in development and power of — ♀ and an ever-increasing accretion of ♂ elements for conversion to — ♂ elements. In other words alpha-elements, however obtained,

are acquired for conversion to beta-elements. In practice it means that the patient feels surrounded not so much by real objects, things-in-themselves, but, by bizarre objects that are real only in that they are the residue of thoughts and conceptions that have been stripped of their meaning and ejected.

14. The relationship of K to – K can be epitomized by saying that in K particularization and concretization of the abstract and general is possible, but in – K it is not because the abstract and general, in so far as they exist, are felt to become things-in-themselves. Conversely in K the particular can be generalized and made abstract, but in – K the particular becomes denuded of any quality it has; denudation not abstraction is the end product.

15. Finally, though I shall not follow it up here, the theories in which I have used the signs K and – K can be seen to represent realization in groups. In K the group increases by the introduction of new ideas or people. In – K the new idea (or person) is stripped of its value, and the group in turn feels devalued by the new idea. In K the climate is conducive to mental health. In – K neither group nor idea can survive partly because of the destruction incident to the stripping and partly because of the product of the stripping process.

NOTES

1.5.1. The term "realization" is used in the sense that it has if it is said that Euclidean geometry of three dimensions has the structure of ordinary space as one of its realizations. The expression is used in an easily comprehensible way in *Algebraic Projective Geometry*, Semple and Kneebone (O.U.P., 1956), Chapter 1, where the concept of geometry is discussed.

1.5.2. The term "deductive system", or "scientific deductive system", is used to cover any approximation to, or projected approximation to, the logical systems described in *Scientific Explanation*, Braithwaite (C.U.P., 1955), Chapter II and onwards.

1.7.1. Compare: *The Logic of Scientific Discovery*, K. R. Popper (Hutchinson, 1959), p. 35, note 2, where the difficulty is admirably illustrated.

2.1.1. *Two Principles of Mental Functioning* S. Freud. (C.P., 1911, Vol. IV), The quotations and references in this chapter, being intended to indicate the limits of the area in which I wish to use the concept of alpha-function are not selected with the rigour that I consider necessary if the selection is made for use in a scientific theory or as a factor for use with the theory of functions.

2.2.1. S. Freud (1954), *Interpretation of Dreams*, p. 615.

2.3.1. S. Freud, *Two Principles of Mental Functioning* (C.P.), Chapter IV, p. 15.

2.5.1. Notes on Some Schizoid Mechanisms, M. Klein, *Developments in Psycho-analysis*, p. 300.

2.5.2. M. Klein, *Ibid.*, p. 293.

2.5.3. Importance of Symbol Formation in the Development of the Ego. M. Klein, *Contributions to Psycho-analysis*, p. 236.

2.5.4. Differentiation of Psychotic from the non-psychotic Personalities. W. R. Bion.

3.2.1 and 2. I use the term "phenomena" to cover what Kant called secondary and primary qualities. The term "things-in-themselves" I hold with Kant to refer to objects that are unknowable to mankind.

5.1.1. The term 'envy' is here used to describe generally the phenomena described in detail by Melanie Klein in *Envy and Gratitude*.

5.2.1. *See* 4.4.

5.3.1. W. R. Bion, "The Differentiation of Psychotic from non-psychotic Personalities." *Int. J. of Psycho-analysis*.

5.3.2. *See* 6.2.

7.3.1. "Differentiating conscious from unconscious." This use of terms is typical of the difficulty of using ambiguous terms when no more precise terms are available. I do not mean "the" conscious or "the" unconscious because that would imply that an observer would be required to differentiate two objects. Yet I do not wish to exclude that shade of meaning because when elements have been differentiated, some becoming conscious and some unconscious, it is reasonable to say there is an unconscious if such a concept is valuable.

10.1.1. This suggests a capacity for intuition that seems incompatible with ordinary ideas of insanity. In so far as it is purposive conduct the purpose must be controlled and dictated by the non-psychotic part of the personality.

The evocation peculiar to the beta-screen, if successful,

means that the patient is starved of genuine therapeutic material, namely truth, and therefore those of his impulses that are directed to survival are overworked attempting to extract cure from therapeutically poor material.

10.2.1. The reversal of direction is compatible with the treatment of thoughts by evacuation; that is to say that if the personality lacks the apparatus that would enable it to "think" thoughts but is capable of attempting to rid the psyche of thoughts in much the same way as it rids itself of accretions of stimuli, then reversal of alpha-function may be the method employed.

10.2.2. The stripping of alpha-elements of the characteristics that differentiate them from beta-elements is important. A model is provided by the theory of the word as the name of a scientific deductive system, e.g. "Dada". The scientific deductive system consists of a series of hypotheses. The system is a statement that certain elements are constantly conjoined. The conjunction and the elements conjoined depend upon the pre-conception (*a priori* knowledge of the individual) and the realizations that have been found by the individual successively to approximate to the preconception and transform it into a conception. The conception in turn becomes an abstraction, or model, to which still more realizations are believed or found to approximate. It is these associations, now stated by the scientific deductive system to be conjoined constantly, (and by the fact of that statement *are* constantly conjoined in the mind of the individual) that are stripped from the word that is the name of the scientific deductive system so that finally only the name "Dada" remains. I am not considering the social value of the name "Dada" nor yet the social version of the scientific deductive system called by that name. The aspect I am discussing is that which exists before publication and is therefore private to the individual. It is that aspect of a phenomenon that would, in Kant's terms, be called secondary quality unless there was evidence, through publication, of the universality that Kant attributes to the primary qualities.

12.6.1. It would be impossible to proceed if I drew the reader's attention to the many instances where I myself am using phrases in which a model is implied rather than explicitly employed. Yet it may help in the elucidation of the problem with which I am concerned if I introduce such an interpretation occasionally as I do here. The term "welfare" itself suggests that mental development like physical development depends on the efficient working of a mental alimentary system. Similarly development may suggest an externalization opposed to envelopment that suggests internalization. One reader may be unconsciously affected by the term welfare, because of the effect of concretization inherent in the implied model, though the theory was not one with which he sympathized. On the other hand he might not be effected at all by the model implicit in "development". Readers of Fowler "The King's English" will be familiar with the problem as it presents itself to one concerned with writing good English (*see* his comments on metaphor in Chapter III). No one would accuse Fowler of treating the writing of good English lightly: yet he discusses this problem under the heading of "Airs and Graces". For the practising psycho-analyst it lies very near the root (or source, or matrix) of the problems of capacity to think and to communicate thought which in turn relate to the possibility or otherwise of achieving any real knowledge.

12.7.1. The term "breast" is used for the concept employed by Melanie Klein.

12.8.1. This idea may be compatible with Freud's statement (Interpretation of Dreams, p. 602) of the primary process.

12.12.1. "Containing." I accept the implied model of a container in this and other passages in which it is necessary to use terms such as "internal" or "external" objects. The model is one I employ with reluctance as I think it is more appropriate to immature than mature scientific thinking. Yet the nature of this work and the lack of a language adequate for a scientific approach to it compels the employment of models sometimes known and more often suspected to be inappropriate, but unavoidable because there is none better.

12.12.2. "bad breast." One of the problems of methodology with which I am attempting to deal is illustrated here, and instances of the same kind are plentiful in these pages: I shall not however mark them, leaving the reader to use his indulgence to remedy the faults in exposition.

If I am asked what I mean by "bad breast" I can only say I mean what the baby means. If I am asked what that is I can say that in the course of the empirical experience of analysis a patient shows certain feelings that I believe he has successfully communicated to me. I must, for reasons connected with the practice of analysis, say what those feelings are. To do so I can fall back on certain material, the source of which I describe later, to make a model. I compare this model with what is taking place in the room and I make my interpretation that amongst things the patient feels that he contains is a "bad breast". I can present the view, as I see it, of infant and analyst thus: A. I think the baby is having an unpleasant emotional experience. B. I think the baby thinks it contains a bad breast. A. I think the painful emotional experience is associated with the coming together of a pre-conception and a beta-element. B. Depending on the personality of the baby I think the baby can: (1) eject the beta-element and lay the foundation for incapacity to think (2) accept the beta-element with juxtaposition with the pre-conception, tolerate the intrinsic frustration, and thus be in process of alpha-function and the production of alpha-elements. I deal with the problem of pre-conceptions in my chapter on definitory hypotheses. In the practice of analysis of patients with disorders of thought the analyst requires, if possible, to establish a methodological framework for himself but, and this is the crux of the matter, he must also try to form some idea of what the infant thinks a feeling is. For in disorders of thought it is obvious that some problem of this kind has arisen in the infant's life and has not been solved. Yet it is but a short step from this point to the absurdity of attributing to the infant ideas, thoughts, concepts about what the grown up calls a "feeling" that would do credit to a Kant. Perhaps the answer is that only a Kant has such problems and can solve them. Those who are not Kant either (*a*) do not have these problems or (*b*) have these problems and develop disorders of thought.

13.1.1. What this means in practice is dealt with in the discussion of the anthology of theories. Some idea of the magnitude of the problem can be gained by a study of J. O. Wisdom's paper "A Methodological Approach to the Problem of Hysteria" (given to the Dutch Society for Psycho-Analysis, Amsterdam, 16th December 1957).

18.3.1. It is important to distinguish between the natures of the two theories. The theory of alpha-function is introduced to make it possible for the analyst to work without proposing a new theory prematurely: Freud's theory of consciousness as a sense organ for psychic quality is a part of recognized psychoanalytic theory. *See* Chapter 18.

19.1.1. The process that the analyst is activating is, in the cases in which he is investigating disorders of thought, designed to investigate the same process in the patient. What psycho-analysts call phantasies are, in some cases at least, the present day survivals of what were once models that the patient formed to match his emotional experiences. In this respect the Oedipus myth is the survival of a model designed to match an infant emotional experience. If the case exhibits a disorder of thought it will be found that this model was never properly formed. As a result the oedipal situation will appear to be imperfectly developed or non-existent. Analysis of such a patient will reveal attempts, if the analysis is progressing, to formulate such a model.

See also Frege *Grundgesetze*, Vol. 1, p. 3. Geach-Black translations, p. 154, in which he discusses the concept that is, as it were, unsaturated.

19.2.1. To postulate such objects is open to the objection expressed by Frege against postulating Logical Objects, pp. 55, 56, *Grundlagen der Arithmetik*. The psycho-analyst must rely on the emotional experience of the analysis to reveal elements that he regards as factors of alpha-function. If he thinks that some of these factors merit description as analogues of sense impressions of concrete objects, it will be time to formulate the appropriate definitory hypotheses or to assign to them already exisiting terms that appear to be the names of such definitory hypotheses.

The analyst is therefore in the position of one, who, thanks to the power of "binocular" perception and consequent correlation that possession of a capacity for conscious and unconscious thought confers, is able to form models and abstractions that serve in elucidating the patient's inability to do the same.

More detailed description of this belongs to a description of clinical psycho-analysis into which I cannot enter here except in so far as it is incidental to illustrating my theme, namely the analyst's problem of method in learning by experience.

19.3.1. S. Freud, *Interpretation of Dreams*, Chapter VII B.

19.4.1. A process similar to that whereby pre-conception and experience of a realization are matched to stimulate the genesis of a conception.

20.7.1. The significance of this phenomenon alters with the emotion accompanying the experience. The patient may believe his activity is an evacuation but the nature of the belief depends on whether he is feeling aggressive, depressed or persecuted. If his activity is what the analyst regards as a normal verbal communication the patient does not know "what he is feeling". Superficially the patient's behaviour closely resembles a dream state such as I have described in 9.4. It is in fact a β-screen and cannot effect separation of thoughts into conscious and unconscious. If it were true dream the clinical situation would afford evidence of separation of conscious from unconscious such as exists when the patient is identified with unconscious and the analyst with conscious or vice versa.

21.3.1. *See* 22.8.

22.1.1. *See* R. E. Money-Kyrle, *Man's Picture of his World*, Chapter IV. The problem discussed in his book is essentially the same as that discussed here in the restricted field of psycho-analytic method. Money-Kyrle shows that it confronts every-man in the tasks he faces throughout his life.

22.2.1. *See* H. Rosenfeld On Drug Addiction, *Int. J. of Psycho-Anal.*, Vol. XLI, p. 472, for an illuminating instance of the problem I have illustrated by the model of the infant use of "Dada". Although it is reported as occurring in a dream it is typical of an attitude of mind not restricted to sleep.

22.3.1. Kant, *Critique of Pure Reason.* Translated by N. Kemp Smith, B XXVII–XXVIII, Preface to Second Edition.

22.6.1. H. Segal, Notes on Symbol Formation, *Int. J. of Psycho-Anal.* 1957. With regard to concretization and abstraction see her comments on equation.

23.1.1. H. Poincaré. *Science and Method.* (Dover Publications).

24.1.1. *See* J. O. Wisdom, A Methodological Approach to Problem of Hysteria, *Int. J. of Psycho-Anal.*, Vol. XLII. Also An Examination of the Psycho-Analytical Theories of Melancholia.

27.19.1 Elliott Jaques, Disturbances in the Capacity to Work, *Inst. J. of Psycho-Anal.*, Vol. XLI, 1960. It seems to me that the process of lysis and scanning, as Elliott Jaques describes it, depends on the existence of a system of preconceptions that can be brought to bear on the incoherent elements of the paranoid-schizoid position. Highly developed scientific investigation appears to me to employ theories, or scientific deductive systems, as the tool through which the counterpart of scanning is effected.

INDEX

ELEMENTS OF PSYCHO-ANALYSIS

La response est le malheur de la question.

—Maurice Blanchot

(Or, as I understand it, the answer is the disease that kills curiosity.)

ACKNOWLEDGMENTS

It is a pleasure to acknowledge the help I have received from Dr. Elliot Jaques and other members of the Melanie Klein trust notably Dr. R. Money-Kyrle, who made a number of helpful criticisms when he read my manuscript, and Dr. Segal and Miss Betty Joseph. The book was completed before I heard Dr. J. J. Sandler's paper on *The Ego Ideal and the Ideal Self*, or I should have explored the significance of his approach for the matters discussed here.

A debt of a different kind I owe to my wife for her constant help and encouragement.

W. R. B.

CHAPTER ONE

Because psycho-analytic theories are a compound of observed material and abstraction from it, they have been criticized as unscientific. They are at once too theoretical, that is to say too much a representation of an observation, to be acceptable as an observation and too concrete to have the flexibility that allows an abstraction to be matched with a realization. Consequently a theory, which could be seen to be widely applicable if it were stated abstractly enough, is liable to be condemned because its very concreteness makes it difficult to recognize a realization that it might represent. Conversely, if such a realization is available, the application of the theory to it may seem to involve a distortion of the meaning of the theory.[1] The defect therefore is twofold: on the one hand description of empirical data is unsatisfactory as it is manifestly what is described in conversational English as a "theory" about what took place rather than a factual account of it[2] and on the other the theory of what took place cannot satisfy the criteria applied to a theory as that term is employed to describe the systems used in rigorous scientific investigation.[3] The first requirement then is to formulate an abstraction,[4] to represent the realization

[1] An instance of this can be seen in J. O. Wisdom's paper on "An examination of the Psycho-analytical Theories of Melancholia", p. 18, where he clearly states the need for an extension of theory, but sees that it involves making a supposition about what M. Klein's view could have been.

[2] In grid terms, too much G3 instead of D or E3.

[3] Too much C3 instead of G4.

[4] The concept of abstraction will be discussed at length; its use in the early stages is provisional. Such a formulation would be in G.3.

that existing theories purport to describe. I propose to seek a mode of abstraction that ensures that the theoretical statement retains the minimum of particularization. The loss of comprehensibility that this entails can be made up for by the use of models to supplement the theoretical systems. The defect of the existing psycho-analytic theory is not unlike that of the ideogram as compared with a word formed alphabetically; the ideogram represents one word only but relatively few letters are required for the formation of many thousands of words. Similarly the elements I seek are to be such that relatively few are required to express, by changes in combination, nearly all the theories essential to the working psycho-analyst.[1]

Most analysts have had the experience of feeling that the description given of characteristics of one particular clinical entity might very well fit with the description of some quite different clinical entity. Yet that same description is rarely an adequate representation even of those realizations to which it seems fairly obviously to be intended to correspond. The combination in which certain elements are held[2] is essential to the meaning[3] to be conveyed by those elements. A mechanism supposed to be typical of melancholia can only be typical of melancholia because it is held in a particular combination. The task is to abstract[4] such elements by releasing them from the combination in which they are held and from the particularity that adheres to them from the realization which they were originally designed to represent.

For the purpose for which I want them the elements

[1] Compared with the tendency to produce *ad hoc* theories to meet a situation when an existing theory, stated with sufficient generality, would have done. Compare Proclus, quoted by Sir T. L. Heath, on Euclid's Elements (Heath, T. L.: *The Thirteen Books of Euclid's Elements*, Chap. 9, C.U.P. 1956).

[2] A consequence of Ps$\leftrightarrow$D. See Chap. 18.

[3] A consequence of ♀♂. See Chap. 18.

[4] See footnote 4 on p. 1.

of psycho-analysis must have the following characteristics: 1. They must be capable of representing a realization that they were originally used to describe. 2. They must be capable of articulation with other similar elements. 3. When so articulated they should form a scientific deductive system capable of representing a realization suppose one existed: other criteria for a psycho-analytic element may be educed later.

I shall represent the first element by ♀ ♂; as I have discussed it at length in *Learning from Experience*[1] my account here will be brief. It represents an element that may be called, though with a loss of accuracy, the essential feature of Melanie Klein's conception of projective identification. It represents an element such that, if it were less it could no longer be related to projective identification at all; if it were more it would carry too great a penumbra of associations for my purpose. It is a representation of an element that could be called a dynamic relationship between container and contained.

The second element I represent PS ↔ D. It may be considered as representing approximately (*a*) the reaction between what Melanie Klein described as the paranoid-schizoid and depressive positions, and (*b*) the reaction precipitated by what Poincaré[2] described as the discovery of the selected fact.

I have already discussed the signs L, H and K, in *Learning from Experience*. They represent links between psycho-analytic objects. Any objects so linked are to be assumed to be affected by each other. The realizations from which they have been abstracted are usually represented by the terms "love," "hate," and "know."

[1] Bion, W. R.: *Learning from Experience*. Heinemann.
[2] Poincaré, H.: *Scientific Method*. Dover Press.

Using the notation R derived from the word "reason" and the realizations it is thought to represent, and *I* derived from the word "idea" and all realizations it represents including those represented by "thought"; *I* is to represent psycho-analytical objects composed of α-elements, the products of α-function. I have described what I mean by this term elsewhere (*Learning from Experience*). By α-function I mean that function by which sense impressions are transformed into elements capable of storage for use in dream and other thoughts. R is to represent a function that is intended to serve the passions, whatever they may be, by leading to their dominance in the world of reality. By passions I mean all that is comprised in L, H, K. R is as associated with *I* in so far as *I* is used to bridge the gap between an impulse and its fulfilment.[1] R[2] insures that it is bridged to some purpose other than the modification of frustration during the temporal pause.

[1] Freud, S.: *Two Principles of Mental Functioning.*

[2] I have not carried through the discussion of R because I do not yet feel in a position to see its implications. I include it because my clinical experience persuades me of the value of such an element and others may be able to use it incompletely worked out though it is. See Hume: *A Treatise of Human Nature*, Book II, Part III, Section 3. Clarendon Press 1896.

CHAPTER TWO

Psycho-analytic theories suffer from the defect that, in so far as they are clearly stated and comprehensible, their comprehensibility depends on the fact that the elements of which they are composed become invested with fixed value, as constants, through their association with the other elements in the theory. This phenomenon is analogous to the phenomenon of alphabetic script where meaningless letters can be combined to form a meaningful word. The elements in Freud's theory of the Oedipus situation, for example, are combined, by their association to form the narrative of the Oedipus myth, and so achieve a contextual meaning that gives them a constant value. As elements in a description of a realization that has been already discovered this is essential to their usefulness: as components of a theory that is to be used in the illumination of realizations yet to be discovered it is a defect because the constant value impairs the flexibility needed.

The abstractions intended to be elements of psycho-analysis should be capable of combination to represent all psycho-analytical situations and all psycho-analytical theories. For this to be true the chosen elements must be essential in the sense described on p. 7. I propose to devote discussion to this topic before pursuing the problem of abstraction[1] of which the solution is so important if the elements chosen, as the elements of psycho-analysis, are to be capable of use in the

[1] See Chap. 18.

construction of theoretical systems. The first step is to consider what phenomena of those present in analytical practice appertain to the elements of psychoanalysis. We may proceed by following three courses:

1. We may search for the elements as their secondary[1] qualities occur and may be recognized in psychoanalytical experience.

2. We may search for the elements as their representations occur and can be isolated in psychoanalytic theory.

3. We may investigate procedures 1 and 2, and combine them as a source from which to abstract elements.

I shall consider first the observability of the chosen elements, although it might be thought, since the elements enter into the composition of all psychoanalytic theories and are essential, that the first need would be to see if these elements can be detected in the theories.

If a patient says he cannot take something in, or the analyst feels he cannot take something in, he implies a container and something to put in it. The statement that something cannot be taken in must not therefore be dismissed as a mere way of speaking. It implies, furthermore, a sense of at least two objects. It might be stated ♀♂ ≥ 2. In certain circumstances, also observable in analysis, the sense of "two-or-moreness," may become obtrusive. For the present I shall ignore the implication of number although the element I wish to isolate cannot be correctly described unless it is understood that ♀♂ ≥ 2.

It is obvious that the number of occasions on which it is verbally stated that something is "in" something also might be innumerable and correspondingly insignificant. The patient is "in" analysis, or "in" a

[1] Secondary in the sense in which Kant uses the term.

family or "in" the consulting room; or he may say he has a pain "in" his leg.[1] Judgement of the importance or significance of the emotional event during which such verbalizations appear to be apposite to the emotional experience depends on the recognition that container and contained, ♀♂, is one of the elements of psycho-analysis. We may then judge whether the element ♀♂ is central or merely present as a component of a system of elements that impart meaning to each other by their conjunction.

Considering now whether it is necessary to abstract the idea of container and contained as an element of psycho-analysis I am met with a doubt. Container and contained implies a static condition and this implication is one that must be foreign to our elements; there must be more of the character imparted by the words "to contain or to be contained." "Container and contained" has a meaning suggesting the latent influence of another element in a system of elements. As the same objection can be levelled against "to contain or to be contained" I shall assume that both statements are contaminated by the presence of elements of an undeclared system of elements (e.g. the latent effect of the model discussed by me in *Learning from Experience*). I shall therefore close the discussion by assuming there is a central abstraction unknown because unknowable yet revealed in an impure form in statements such as "container or contained" and that it is to the central abstraction alone that the term "psycho-analytical element" can be properly applied or the sign ♀♂ allocated. From this definition it is clear that the supposed psycho-analytical element cannot be observed. In this respect it is not unlike Kant's concept of a thing-in-itself—it is not knowable though

[1] Cf. Ryle Gilbert: *Conception of Mind*, p. 22, not a category mistake but an expression of unconscious awareness of ♀♂ as the set to which all belong.

primary and secondary qualities are. Yet it is different in this respect. The phenomena of container and contained are knowable as secondary qualities. The central abstraction is only a phenomenon in that I as an individual am aware that it is convenient for me to postulate the existence of something that has no existence, as if in fact it were a thing-in-itself. If I postulate the existence of a table as a thing-in-itself, I do so because I believe it exists and that its existence is the explanation of the phenomena that I group together in a set with the name "table."

This explanation is necessary because I am anxious to establish the elements of psycho-analysis on a foundation of experience. The element I hope will be an abstraction of the type given by my example of ♀♂, container and contained. It will be a "central abstraction unknown because unknowable" but adumbrated, in an impure form, by its verbal representation. It will have the same status and quality as the object that we aspire to *represent* by the word "line" or a line drawn upon paper, has to the word "line" or a line drawn upon paper.

CHAPTER THREE

THE elements are functions of the personality.[1] Of them all it may be said that each is a function of something else and each has a function. In so far as each *is* a function the term "function" has a meaning similar to that with which it is associated in mathematics. It is a variable in relation to other variables in terms of which it may be expressed and on the value of which its own value depends. In so far as each function *has* a function the term "function" is used as the name for a set of actions, physical or mental, governed by or directed to a purpose. Whenever I use the term "function" I use it to denote something which is and has a function. In so far as it is a function it has factors: in so far as it has a function it has aims.[2]

For the present I propose that the elements of psycho-analysis are all without exception functions using the term in the sense I have just adumbrated. The sign representing an abstraction must therefore represent a function that is unknowable although its primary and secondary qualities (in the Kantian sense) are. As I propose to consider the elements as observable phenomena it must be assumed that I am talking about primary and secondary qualities of elements and not the abstractions or signs by which I represent them. What, of all that can be seen in the course of any analysis, are we to choose as the functions

[1] For further discussion of "function" see Bion, W. R.: *Learning from Experience.*

[2] This point will be clearer when reference can be made to the grid. See Chap. 6 *et seq.*

of personality that are also elements of psycho-analysis? The choice is already limited by the criteria I have proposed (Chapter 1, p. 6). We must now limit it further because the element must be a function in the sense that I have proposed for this term and, furthermore, must be "seen" in the course of analytic work. But how are the qualities of elements to be pronounced "seeable" in view of the notorious fact that some analysts purport to be able to see things the very existence of which is denied by others, a disagreement that is common enough between patient and analysand even though they share the "seen" experience?

As a criterion for what constitutes a sensible experience I propose common sense in the meaning that I have given it elsewhere, namely some "sense" that is common to more than one sense. I shall consider an object to be sensible to psycho-analytic scrutiny if, and only if, it fulfils conditions analogous to the conditions that are fulfilled when a physical object's presence is confirmed by the evidence of two or more senses. It is evident that it can only be analogous, for, in our present state of knowledge even anxiety, at least in others, is a deduction. The problem is to determine just how far we can go in accepting deductions from sensa as having, in the field of psycho-analysis, the same validity as sensa have in physics or philosophy. I have no doubt that my impression that a man is anxious has the same validity as my impression that a stone, say, is hard. But for my impression to be valid I consider it necessary to feel the stone to satisfy myself of its hardness and at least to look at it to satisfy myself that what I touch is a stone. The correlation thus established entitlés one to claim the term "common sense" to characterize one's view that the given object is a stone: and that the view that it is a stone is common to one's senses and therefore a common sense view, the term "common sense" being used with more than conversational precision. The problem is to establish some similar usage or convention to define the nature of the sense by which we apprehend a psycho-analytical element and, the counterpart of this, to define the nature of the dimensions of a psycho-analytical element. Implementation of this plan seems, as is so often the case in psycho-analytical investigation, to pre-suppose what we wish to discover. In writing this I have to start somewhere and this produces difficulties because the start of a discussion tends to impose an appearance of reality on the idea that the matter discussed has a start. Psycho-analytic investigation formulates premises that are as distinct from those of ordinary science as are the premises of philosophy or theology. Psycho-analytic elements and the objects derived from them have the following dimensions.[1]

1. Extension in the domain of sense.
2. Extension in the domain of myth.
3. Extension in the domain of passion.

An interpretation cannot be regarded as satisfactory unless it illuminates a psycho-analytic object and that object must at the time of interpretation possess these dimensions. In view of the importance I attach to these dimensions I shall discuss each of them in detail.

Extension in the domain of sense need not detain us long. It means that what is interpreted must amongst other qualities be an object of sense. It must, for example, be visible or audible, certainly to the analyst and presumably to the analysand. If the latter presumption turns out not to be the fact the grounds for the presumption must be such that the failure in correspondence must be regarded as significant in itself. Put in another way when the analyst gives an

[1] Discussion of the grid in Chap. 18 and later will explain more fully what I mean by these dimensions.

interpretation it must be possible for analyst and analysand to see that what he is talking about is something that is either audible, visible, palpable or odoriferous at the time.

It is more difficult to give a satisfactory explanation of what I mean by extension in the domain of myth.[1] I cannot conceive the possibility without it of model making as part of the equipment available to the psycho-analyst. Suppose that a patient is angry. More meaning is given to a statement to that effect if it is added that his anger is like that of a "child that wanted to hit his nanny because he has been told he is naughty." The statement in quotation marks is not an expression of a theory in a genetic exposition. It must not be supposed to express a theory that small boys hit their nannies if they are called naughty. It is a statement akin to the type of statement that philosophers contemptuously dismiss as mythologies when they use the term pejoratively to describe bad theories. I require, as part of analytical scientific procedure and equipment, statements of this kind. They are not statements of observed fact, or formulations of a theory intended to represent a realization: they are statements of a personal myth. Unless the experience of the psycho-analytical object is accompanied by a formulation by the psycho-analyst of a statement that has this type of component it lacks a necessary dimension. I shall refer to this dimension as the myth or "as if" component.

I have deliberately chosen the term "passion" rather than what might appear to be more usual terms for the last dimension, partly because the more usual terms have a meaning that should be left undisturbed. By "passion" or the lack of it I mean the component derived from L, H and K. I mean the term to

[1] The problem relates to the discussion of row C of the grid.

represent an emotion experienced with intensity and warmth though without any suggestion of violence: the sense of violence is not to be conveyed by the term "passion" unless it is associated with the term "greed."

It may seem that by introducing passion I am repeating what I have said already by including the L, H and K, as elements. This is not so; by passion I mean one of the dimensions which L, H or K must possess if it is to be recognized as an element that is present.[1] Furthermore the evidence that passion is present that may be afforded by the senses is not to be taken as the dimension of passion. That is to say, if the angry tone of the patient is judged to be evidence of hate it must not be assumed that passion has been discerned as a dimension of a psycho-analytic object, H in fact. Evidence may be afforded by the senses, in such an episode, that can be correlated with the evidence, sensuous perhaps but not sensible, of passion. Awareness of passion is not dependent on sense. For senses to be active only one mind is necessary: passion is evidence that two minds are linked and that there cannot possibly be fewer than two minds if passion is present. Passion must be clearly distinguished from counter-transference, the latter being evidence of repression. Further consideration of passion is not relevant to the immediate issue of passion as one of the dimensions of a psycho-analytic object and therefore of a psycho-analytic element.

[1] Cf. Chap. 19 on "feelings."

CHAPTER FOUR

In the first chapter I said that the development of psycho-analytical practice was hindered through lack of work on the elements of psycho-analysis and gave examples of what might be objects of a search for such elements. In the second chapter I discussed criteria by which objects proposed as elements might be judged, stressing observability in practice as one essential. In the last chapter I laid down that all elements must be functions of the personality and that they should be conceived of as having dimensions which, in the mind of the analyst, would be sense-impressions, myth and passion.

In this chapter I propose to approach the problem afresh by seeking an answer to the following question: considering any psycho-analytical session as an emotional experience, what elements in it must be selected to make it clear that the experience had been a psycho-analysis and could have been nothing else?

Many features of a psycho-analysis may be regarded as typical but they are not exclusively so. Departures from the common rule of meetings between two people may seem insignificant, but the number of such apparently insignificant departures taken together ultimately amounts to a difference that decides the need for a special term. A catalogue of such difference is likely to establish what constitutes an *imitation* of psycho-analysis rather than what is genuine, unless the difference can be stated in elements.

It would seem to avoid the disadvantages of cataloguing differences in detail by trying to focus on the emotional peculiarities of the experience but difficulty arises because it is common for patients to feel that analysis is coldly unemotional and yet provokes effects appropriate to an intense series of emotions. The surest guide is experience and to this I shall resort in the hope that it can be described in terms that enable others to compare their experience with it.

The dictum that an analysis must be conducted in an atmosphere of deprivation is usually understood to mean that the analyst must resist any impulse in himself to gratify the desires of his analysands or to crave gratification for his own. To narrow the expression of this statement without contracting the area covered by it; at no time must either analyst or analysand lose the sense of isolation within the intimate relationship of analysis.[1]

No matter how good or bad the co-operation may turn out to be the analyst should not lose, or deprive his patient of, the sense of isolation that belongs to the knowledge that the circumstances that have led to analysis and the consequences that may in future arise from it are a responsibility that can be shared with nobody. Discussions of technical or other matters with colleagues or relatives must never obscure this essential isolation.

Opposed to the establishment of a relationship yielding experiences of a sense of responsibility is the drive to be mean and greedy.[2]

The sense of loneliness seems to relate to a feeling, in the object of scrutiny, that it is being abandoned

[1] The point is discussed again under premonition.

[2] Terms such as "greed" are used because I am discussing the elements of psycho-analytic practice. Once such elements are clearly discerned as a part of the emotional experience the analyst can consider in what way they are illuminated by psycho-analytic theories of, for example, anal erotism.

and, in the scrutinizing subject, that it is cutting itself off from the source or base on which it depends for its existence.

To summarize: Detachment can only be achieved at the cost of painful feelings of loneliness and abandonment experienced (1) by the primitive animal mental inheritance from which detachment is effected and (2) by the aspects of the personality that succeed in detaching themselves from the object of scrutiny which is felt to be indistinguishable from the source of its viability. The apparently abandoned object of scrutiny is the primitive mind and the primitive social capacity of the individual as a political or group animal. The "detached" personality is in a sense new to its job and has to turn to tasks which differ from those to which its components are more usually adapted, namely scrutiny of the environment excluding the self; part of the price paid is in feelings of insecurity.

CHAPTER FIVE

The conclusions of the previous chapter suggest that decision requires further discussion; does it involve the translation of thought into action, or some analogous process, for example of thought into a fixed idea, a variable as it were into a constant? Since the analyst is constantly called upon to decide whether to intervene with an interpretation, decision, and its components of loneliness and introspection, should be regarded as an element of psycho-analysis at least from the point of view of the analyst and therefore probably from the point of view of both patient and analyst.

Introspection, that any practising analyst can carry out for himself, into what cliches he most commonly uses often suggests that the problem in analysis is to know which of possible interpretations is at a given time correct; it arises from awareness of the number of ideas expressed in papers on analysis and even more from the variety of human behaviour as it is experienced in ordinary life. In practice the impression is not so formidable: analytic interpretations can be seen to be theories held *by* the analyst about the models and theories the patient has *of* the analyst. It is believed and intended that the analyst's theories, if correct in content and expression, exert a therapeutic effect. Introspection will I believe show most analysts that the theories they employ are relatively few in number and may be seen to fall into the following categories:

1. Definition. Roughly such interpretations take the form that the patient is showing by his associations

that he is, say, depressed. In so far as it is a definitory hypothesis it is by way of saying "This, that you, the patient, are now experiencing is what I, and, in my opinion, most people, would call depression." In so far as it is to define for the patient what the analyst means by definition there can be no argument about it because the only valid criticism would be if the statement could be shown to be absurd because self-contradictory.

2. Statements representing the realization in such a way that the analyst's anxiety that the situation is unknown and correspondingly dangerous to him, is denied by an interpretation intended to prove to himself and the patient that this is not so. Any practising analyst appreciates that this state of affairs belongs to the domain of counter-transference and indicates analysis for the analyst. But as even analysts cannot have all the analysis they may consider desirable the theory used as a barrier against the unknown will remain in the armoury of analyst as well as patient.

3. Statements that are representations of present and past realizations. An example of such a statement would be a brief summary reminding the patient of something that the analyst believes took place on a previous occasion. This corresponds to the function Freud denotes by the term *notation*.[1]

4. Statements representing a scientific deductive system in so far as such a system can be expressed in ordinary conversational English. Such a statement has affinities with 3 above in that it may be regarded as representing a realization from which it has been derived. But essentially its function is similar to that of *attention* as described by Freud.[2] It is the statement one expects to follow an analyst's cliche. "I would like to

[1] *Two Principles* C.P. Vol. IV, p. 15.
[2] *Two Principles* C.P. Vol. XIV, p. 15.

draw your attention to . . ." It is similar to 5 below, but more passive and receptive, corresponding to reverie. It is a theoretical formulation, expressed with as much scientific rigour as the circumstances of analytical practice permit, whose function is to probe the environment. In this respect it has affinities with the pre-conception. It is essential to discrimination. One of its functions is receptiveness to the selected fact. (By selected fact I mean that by which coherence and meaning is given to facts already known but whose relatedness has not hitherto been seen.)

5. Similar to 1, 2, 3 and 4 as far as formulation is concerned—all are formulated by an identical representation, or, in other words, the interpretation can be verbally identical in each case—but it is a theory used to investigate the unknown. The most obvious example of this is the Oedipus myth as Freud has abstracted it to form the psycho-analytic theory. The function of the theoretical formulations in this category are interpretations being used with an intention to illuminate material, that would otherwise remain obscure, in order to help the patient to release still further material. The primary object is to obtain material for satisfaction of the impulses of inquiry in patient and analyst. Note that the probing quality of such interpretations may help to account for differences of reaction in the patient from those he would display to interpretations in category 1 or 4; this component can be distinguished from those derived from the content of the interpretation.

6. In this, the last category that I propose to distinguish, the statement, though still embodied in a representation identical with those employed in all the other statements, is used as an operator. The intention

[1] See Poincaré, H.: *Science and Method*, p. 30, and Hanson, N. R.: *Patterns of Discovery*, p. 121.

is primarily that the communication will enable the patient to effect solutions of his problems of development. (The patient of course can use it to effect solutions of his problems rather than solutions of his problems of development, that is, he can use the interpretation as advice not interpretation, but it is not here my intention to discuss these and other responses of the patient.) Functions of interpretations that fall in this category, and therefore the interpretations in this one of their aspects, are analogous to *actions* in other forms of human endeavour. For the analyst the transition that comes nearest to that of decision and translation of thought into action is the transition from thought to verbal formulations of category 6. From what I have said in Chapter 4 it is clear that activities of this category are those in which the sense of loneliness and isolation are most likely to be in evidence.

These categories are not exhaustive or exclusive. Experience it is to be hoped may lead to substitution by better categories. It is essential to resist an impulse to increase the number of categories unduly partly because that is very easy to do but also because what is needed for my present purpose is the least number of fundamental categories.

I must stress that though in practice interpretations will certainly be embodied in the most diverse formulations, theoretically the same interpretation formulated in the same terms may easily be used in all of these six, and yet more, ways in the same session. The categories I have drawn up to relate, not to the content of theory or the form in which it is represented, but to the work it is intended to do. I shall anticipate by saying that these categories apply to the use to which "thoughts" may be put, once they have been represented by patient as well as analyst. This chapter has been taken up with a particular aspect of what may broadly be called thoughts after the thoughts have been represented by words or combinations of words.

It is therefore a categorization of "*I*" (p. 4, Chap. 1) according to uses to which representations of *I* may be put. This treatment of *I* is a schematic exposition and excludes the component of time that is implicit in a genetic or developmental exposition. In view of the importance that *I* must now assume as a candidate for establishment as one of the elements of psycho-analysis I propose to devote the next few pages to a genetic, as opposed to schematic, exposition of *I* although it involves some repetition of ideas I have already put forward in my paper on Thinking.[1]

[1] "Symposium on Thinking." Int. Congress of Psycho-analysis. Edinburgh 1962.

CHAPTER SIX

The classification I have suggested for analytic interpretations can be applied to all statements whether made by patient or analyst. But I wish to introduce another mode of classification for the same material and for this I propose to draw on experience with patients suffering from disturbances of thought. In contrast with the scheme I have drawn up in the last chapter this will be framed genetically not systematically. Whether there is a realization approximating to it is a question I leave open for the present.

1. β-elements. This term represents the earliest matrix from which thoughts can be supposed to arise. It partakes of the quality of inanimate object and psychic object without any form of distinction between the two. Thoughts are things, things are thoughts; and they have personality.

2. α-elements. This term represents the outcome of work done by α-function on sense impressions. They are not objects in the world of external reality but are products of work done on the sensa believed to relate to such realities. They make possible the formation and use of dream thoughts.

3. I do not consider that there is or can be any evidence for the existence of a realization corresponding to β-elements, α-function, or α-elements, other than observed facts that cannot be explained without the aid of such hypothetical elements. For the remaining formulations the position is different. It can be supposed that there is evidence for the existence of

dream thoughts, preconceptions and the rest. To continue:

3. Dream thoughts. These depend on the prior existence of β- and α-elements: otherwise they require no elaboration beyond that which they have received in classical psycho-analytical theory. They are communicated by the manifest content of the dream but remain latent unless the manifest content is translated into more sophisticated terms.

With dreams one reaches a realm in which there is direct evidence of the phenomena with which one has to deal. At least there is direct evidence when a patient says he had a dream and proceeds to recount it. Unfortunately such assurance evaporates when the subject of investigation is thought itself. The statement that a patient has had a dream is ordinarily sufficient evidence to allow work to proceed, but not if we need to know what has occurred when the patient says he has dreamt. For example, if a patient complains that he had a pain in his leg are we to suppose, in the appropriate setting, that he *dreamt* that he had a pain in his leg or ought we to consider that sometimes the manifest content of a dream is a series of pains rather than a series of visual images that have been verbalized and linked by narrative?

4. The pre-conception.[1] This corresponds to a state of expectation. It is a state of mind adapted to receive a restricted range of phenomena. An early occurrence might be an infant's expectation of the breast. The mating of pre-conception and realization brings into being the conception.

5. The conception. The conception may be regarded as a variable that has been replaced by a constant. If we represent the pre-conception by $\psi(\xi)$

[1] This description of pre-conception is provisional. The concept is elaborated later, notably in Chap. 18 and subsequently.

with (ξ) as the unsaturated element, then from the realization with which the pre-conception mates there is derived that which replaces (ξ) by a constant. The conception can however then be employed as a pre-conception in that it can express an expectation. The mating of $\psi(\xi)$ with the realization satisfies the expectation but enlarges the capacity of $\psi(\xi)$ for further saturation.[1]

6. The concept is derived from the conception by a process designed to render it free of those elements that would unfit it to be a tool in the elucidation or expression of truth.

7. The scientific deductive system. In this context the term "scientific deductive system" means a combination of concepts in hypotheses and systems of hypotheses so that they are logically[2] related to each other. The logical relation of one concept with another and of one hypothesis with another enhances the meaning of each concept and hypothesis thus linked and expresses a meaning that the concepts and hypotheses and links do not individually possess. In this respect the meaning of the whole may be said to be greater than the meaning of the sum of its parts.

8. Calculi.[3] The scientific deductive system may be represented by an algebraic calculus. In the algebraic calculus a number of signs are brought together according to certain rules of combination. The signs have no properties other than those conferred on them by the rules of combination. $(a + b)^2 = a^2 + b^2 + 2\,ab$, is an affirmation of the rules of combination of a and b. a and b have no meaning[4] other than that

[1] Compare with what I say in Chap. 18 on the abstraction.

[2] Compare the state of logical relatedness with what I say in Chap. 18 on coherence.

[3] For a full description of the terms scientific deductive system and algebraic calculus as used in rigorous scientific method see Braithwaite, R. B.: *Scientific Explanation*, C.U.P. 1955.

[4] See discussion of coherence and meaning, Chap. 18.

they are replaceable by numbers and must be understood to be capable of manipulation in the manner defined by the statement $(a + b)^2 = a^2 + b^2 + 2\,ab$. In short to say that *a* and *b* have properties could only mean that they lend themselves to manipulation in accordance with rules and that the rules to which they conform can be deduced from the statement in that, like the conception, it retains a capacity for saturation.

This completes my genetic exposition. I propose now to combine it with the schematic exposition of Chapter 5. This, it will be remembered, adumbrated a provisional scheme by which the various *uses* to which "*I*" might be put could be categorized, thus contrasting with the scheme of the present chapter in which I suggest a scheme of various *stages* by which "*I*" might have developed. It is necessary to note that in the genetic scheme rows B–H inclusive may all be said to contain unsaturated elements that await a realization before they can be "satisfied" and become available for further employment as preconceptions. Row A differs from all others in that it has no unsaturated element and is therefore unsuited for use as preconception. Row B, the α-element, I propose for the present to leave undiscussed for a special reason. For the same reason I shall ignore important aspects of row C, the dream thoughts, and dreams themselves, until later. In the table on the end paper I set out the systematic and genetic expositions along different axes.

This formal table imparts an air of rigidity that may seem alien to a clinical approach. I hope that subsequent discussion involving its use will dispel any fears on that account—provided it is properly used. I shall indicate what that use is by taking up a few of the implications of the grid. The reference numbers are to the co-ordinates in the grid.

A1. This category may be defined as extremely primitive. It shows no clear differentiation of qualities such as we expect to find, say, in a dream as it is recounted by a patient. It shows no differentiation of animate qualities from inanimate, subject from object, moral from scientific. Since it is saturated it is unsuited for use as a preconception. The only sense in which it can be regarded as having a use as a definition is in the sense that to define something may be said to imprison it within certain limits: its meaning is not liberated by verbalization but denied an outlet. It is however suited to projective identification. To use the example I employed in my paper on Thinking—to save unnecessary burdening of the reader's memory by a multiplicity of examples I shall use very few and ask him to bear with the boredom of repetition—the infant experiencing a fear that it is dying, in so far as the terminology of adult sophistication can express the experience at all, imprisons it in a β-element (now placed in the grid category A1). This is projected into the container and its subsequent fate depends on a number of contingencies that I shall not anticipate here because I deal with them later.

A2. The indications I have given in A1 show that strictly speaking A2 must be a nul class, because A1 is incapable of development. Yet in some sense A1 can be used to fulfil some of the functions of A2 in that the imprisonment implicit in A1 denies any liberation of meaning. But comparison with G2 will show that there is a great difference between A2 and G2 (in so far as A2 can be said to exist by virtue of substitution of A1 and A2) and the implication of this difference must be correspondingly greater.

I shall not take up A3, A4 and A5 in detail for what I have said about A2 obtains with appropriate modifications. Essentially they are nul classes. But

A6 is worth brief comment in that the β-element, dealt with by projective identification, does lend itself to use as an operator. Its significance is more sharply defined by comparison with D6, E6, F6, G6 and H6, which I have not so far discussed.

In the situation where the β-element, say the fear that it is dying, is projected by the infant and received by the container in such a way that it is "detoxicated", that is, modified by the container so that the infant may take it back into its own personality in a tolerable form. The operation is analogous to that performed by α-function. The infant depends on the Mother to act as its α-function.

Stating this in other terms, the fear is modified and the β-element thereby made into an α-element. Restating this less abstractly still, the β-element has had removed from it the excess of emotion that has impelled the growth of the restrictive and explusive component; therefore a transformation has been effected that enables the infant to take back something, call it an α-element for convenience, that is now suitable for use as a definition or preconception. The change that is brought about by the mother who accepts the infant's fears, is one that is brought about later in personalities whose development is relatively successful, by α-function. By the same token α-function may be described as concerned with the change I have associated with the conception[1] and the concept (E and F in this chapter) as I have described these entities in my genetic exposition.

[1] See commencement of Chap. 6 for discussion in dynamics of growth and Chap. 18 *et seq.*

CHAPTER SEVEN

I SHALL represent the table set out in the last chapter by the sign *I*.[1] I do not propose to discuss what meaning if any is to be attached to classes represented by co-ordinates such as 5.1. We need not suppose that such elements exist. Nevertheless I do not wish to discard them for the present; I propose to reconsider the axes of the framework in the search for elements. When I use the sign *I*, I mean it to represent either the whole table or any one or more of the compartments I have distinguished by co-ordinates. As an example suppose that in the course of an analysis the material suggests the predominance of *I*. This impression should be gained as a result of relaxed or free-floating attention; this state of mind approximates to that represented by D4 (since I am already disposed by my personality and psycho-analytic training to entertain certain expectations). A state of attention, being receptive to the material the patient is producing, approximates to a pre-conception and therefore the change from attention to preconception is represented by a move from D4 on the grid to E4. If I seek confirmation from other material that the patient is presenting, E3 and E5 are swept into activity; if I begin to *verbalize* my impressions F5 is also involved. If it now appears that the time is ripe for an interpretation a further shift takes place, this time towards G6 with a view to a formulation intended to affect the patient.

[1] See Chap. 19 for discussion of feelings.

As aspects of the patient's behaviour relevant to his psycho-analysis fall in the class of phenomena represented by *I* they will be represented by certain of the tabulated categories. Suppose the patient has said, at the commencement of the session, "I know that you do not like me." From knowledge of the patient I may think he is referring to something in the previous session. It would then be a theory enshrining his view of a past event. In that case the realization may be regarded as approximating to G3. But if the G3 session leads me to think that the material is intended by the patient to support the supposition that I do not like him then I would consider that his remark belonged to the category represented by G1 that is to say that it approximated to a definitory hypothesis.

If the context of the statement leads me to suppose feelings of persecution are operating and that his preconceptions would interpret my behaviour as evidence, then his statement would lie in the category E4 and F4. If, however, I regarded it as intended to evoke a confirmation or refutation I would consider it to be classifiable under G6.

I have been supposing in this example that the significance of the patient's behaviour lay in the domain *I*. So far, however, I have in my example been considering the content of his thought in order to determine the category into which, in a given instance, it would fall. If the context of the analysis showed that the content related to an oedipal rivalry the categories of *I* to which it belonged would in most cases be of subsidiary importance, namely for determining the nature of the presenting oedipal material. But if *I* itself is in question the importance of content lies in its relevance to determination of the *I* category. All the categories in the table, with the possible exception of the row B sets, may be considered to play a part, sometimes more important, sometimes less, in any psycho-analytic material. The reader can see for himself that there are some categories in the table into which the analyst's thought processes ought not to fall. Except possibly in the writing of papers or in extra-analytic activities it is difficult to imagine how he could need calculi even if they were available: similarly but for different reasons, familiar to any analyst, he should not be employing any of the column 2 categories. The grid tabulation may help to make explicit features of the analytic situation that should always be watched for as possible disturbances of the analysis.

My immediate concern is with the use of the grid when the presenting problem is *I* itself. The table sets out to cover comprehensively all phenomena that might be described in ordinary conversation as "thoughts" though the right of some categories to be so described might be disputed. As I have said elsewhere[1] patients who suffer from disorders of thought seem to owe their disability partly to failures in development of thoughts themselves, exemplified in the table by the β-elements, and partly to failures in development of an apparatus for dealing with thoughts. It would be easy to say that the obvious thing to do with thoughts is to think them; it is more difficult to decide what such a statement means in fact.[2] In practice the statement becomes more meaningful when it is possible to contrast what a psychotic personality does with thoughts *instead* of thinking them, and how much discipline and difficulty a measure of coherent thinking involves for anyone. I shall ignore any of the uses to which organized thought is put partly because I have already included them as factors in *I*-function and partly because experience in disorders of thought show

[1] Bion, W. R.: *Learning from Experience.*

[2] See Chap. 18 below for mechanisms related to coherence and comprehension.

that their relevance to disorders of thought is chiefly to illuminate them by contrast.

I shall state the theory first in terms of a model, as follows: The infant suffering pangs of hunger and fear that it is dying, wracked by guilt and anxiety, and impelled by greed, messes itself and cries. The mother picks it up, feeds it and comforts it, and eventually the infant sleeps.

Reforming the model to represent the feelings of the infant we have the following version: the infant, filled with painful lumps of faeces, guilt, fears of impending death, chunks of greed, meanness and urine, evacuates these bad objects into the breast that is not there. As it does so the good object turns the no-breast (mouth) into a breast, the faeces and urine into milk, the fears of impending death and anxiety into vitality and confidence, the greed and meanness into feelings of love and generosity and the infant sucks its bad property, now translated into goodness, back again. As an abstraction to match this model I propose an apparatus, for dealing with these primitive categories of *I*, that consists of a container ♀ and the contained ♂. The mechanism is implicit in the theory of projective identification in which Melanie Klein formulated her discoveries of infant mentality.[1] I propose provisionally to represent the apparatus for thinking by the sign ♂♀.[2] The material, so to speak, out of which this apparatus is manufactured is *I*. The material with which this apparatus is designed to deal, is *I*. *I* develops a capacity for any one of its aspects to assume indifferently the function ♂ or ♀ to any other one of its aspects ♀ or ♂. We must now consider *I* in its ♂♀ operation, an operation usually spoken of in ordinary conversation as thinking. From the point of

[1] Klein, Melanie: *Notes on Some Schizoid Mechanisms* 1946.
[2] See Chap. 18 *et seq.* under coherence and comprehension.

view of meaning thinking depends on the successful introjection of the good breast that is originally responsible for the performance of α-function. On this introjection depends the ability of any part of *I* to be ♂ to the other part's ♀. The relevance of this to explanation and correlation I shall deal with elsewhere;[1] briefly, explanation may be seen as related to the attitude of one part of the mind to another, and correlation as a comparison of content expressed by one aspect of *I* to content expressed by another aspect of *I*.

[1] See Chap. 18 *et seq.* under coherence and comprehension.

CHAPTER EIGHT

CERTAIN contradictions and confusions must now be considered even though present knowledge may be inadequate for their resolution. First I propose to review the genetic axis in the light of the aspect of projective identification I have represented by ♀♂. Anticipating what I have to say in Chapter 17, I shall assume that the operation ♀♂ is benign and, as I have suggested, that it is responsible for the developments implied by the genetic ordering of the lettered axis, A to H. (To understand what I mean by the benign operation of ♀♂ see the model on page 35.) Inspection of A to H in the light of ♀♂ shows that the categories have a common relation to each other in that each category depends on changes, in the previous category, that fit it to operate as a preconception as well as a record. Thus E1 depends on mating D1 with a realization that enables the formation of a conception which is in turn capable of leading to F1. Putting this in other terms the element represented by D1 say, is increasing the scope of its function of notation in such a way that its function of attention (the terms "notation" and "attention" being employed in the sense used by Freud[1]) is also increased. Using the table to say this again in a different way, D1 develops through the stages represented by D3 and D4 to become E1.

The mechanics of change from one to another of the phases represented by A to H may thus be represented

[1] Freud, S.: *Two Principles of Mental Functioning.*

by ♀♂.[1] The link ♀♂ between the phases represented by categories A to H, is mechanical. What of the dynamic link? That is represented by L, H and K. The benignity of the operation ♀♂ will depend on the nature of the dynamic link.

The systematic axis of *I*, the uses to which a formulation may be put, consists of a series of categories that could be extended. Since the formulation is the same, only the use that can be made of it is varied; it is obvious that the link between the various categories of use is the formulation. In fact what has to be sought is the counterpart in the systematic axis of the mechanism that links the categories of the genetic exposition genetically. Such a search would involve investigation of mechanisms of evasion and modification of pleasure and pain into which I cannot enter here. It is probable that the mechanism by which transition from one use of the axis 1–6 is transformed into another, is that used in evasion or modification and the dynamic is pleasure and pain.

Melanie Klein's discoveries of the paranoid-schizoid and depressive positions required a theory that in certain situations apparently unrelated elements, associated with feelings of persecution, come together as an integrated whole associated with feelings of depression. I shall employ this theory together with the term "selected fact," borrowed from H. Poincaré.[2] Each "use" classified under the categories 1–6 of the schematic axis depends on the operation of this mechanism on the elements A–G. Thus the use that consists in the employment of an aspect of the categories A to H to inquire or research has come into being by virtue of this mechanism and itself effective by employment of this mechanism. This mechanism I represent

[1] Further consideration will show that this mechanism is related to growth.
[2] Poincaré, H.: *Science and Method*, p. 26. Dover Publications.

by the sign Ps $\leftrightarrow$ Dep. The dynamic link, as before, is L, H or K.

The process of change from one category represented in the grid to another may be described as disintegration and reintegration, Ps $\leftrightarrow$ D. The benignity or otherwise of change effected by the mechanism ♀♂ depends on the nature of the dynamic link L, H or K.

It will be observed that in the course of the discussion, commenced by making a distinction between thoughts and the apparatus for using them and then according them priority in time so that they could be studied separately from thinking, it has been necessary to reintroduce a primitive mechanics of thinking, or something very like it, to explain the development of the thoughts. In fact it is easier to believe that this spontaneous development in the discussion represents the facts with a greater approximation to the truth than is the case if the accord of priority to thoughts, convenient epistemologically, is to be taken as an accurate representation of the reality of thinking. Nevertheless there are grounds for supposing that a primitive "thinking," active in the development of thought, should be distinguished from the thinking that is required for the use of thoughts.[1] The thinking used in the development of thoughts differs from the thinking required to use the thoughts when developed. The latter is derived from the Ps $\leftrightarrow$ D mechanism that is considered in Chapter 9.[2] When thoughts have to be used under the exigencies of reality, be it psychic reality or external reality, the primitive mechanisms have to be endowed with capacities for precision demanded by the need for survival. We have therefore to consider the part played by the life and death instincts as well as reason, which in its embryonic form

[1] See growth and the interaction of ♀♂ and Ps $\leftrightarrow$ D in Chap. 18.
[2] And Chap. 18–20.

under the dominance of the pleasure principle is designed to serve as the slave of the passions, has forced it to assume a function resembling that of a master of the passions and the parent of logic. For the search, for satisfaction of incompatible desires, would lead to frustration. Successful surmounting of the problem of frustration involves being reasonable and a phrase such as the "dictates of reason" may enshrine the expression of primitive emotional reaction to a function intended to satisfy not frustrate. The axioms of logic therefore have their roots in the experience of a reason that fails in its primary function to satisfy the passions just as the existence of a powerful reason may reflect a capacity in that function to resist the assaults of its frustrated and outraged masters. These matters will have to be considered in so far as dominance of the reality principle stimulates the development of thought and thinking, reason, and awareness of psychic and environmental reality.

CHAPTER NINE

THE mechanism of projective identification enables the infant to deal with primitive emotion and so contributes to the development of thoughts. The interplay between the depressive and paranoid-schizoid positions is also related to the development of thoughts and thinking. It has been pointed out (by Melanie Klein and Segal) that symbol formation is related to the depressive position. It is compatible with a connection between a capacity for thinking and the interplay between the two positions. It would seem that there is a connection between Ps ↔ D and ♀♂ yet the dissimilarity makes it hard to see what form the connection, if there is one, could take.[1] The bringing together of elements that have apparently no connection in fact or in logic in such a way that their connection is displayed and an unsuspected coherence revealed, as in the example from Poincaré,[2] is characteristic of Ps ↔ D. The operation Ps ↔ D is responsible for revealing the relationship of "thoughts" already created by ♀♂. But in fact it seems as if Ps ↔ D is as much the begetter of thoughts as ♀♂. The development requires examination in some detail.

The earliest observation I have been able to make seemed to suggest that development of thinking through Ps ↔ D depended on the production of signs. That is to say the individual had to bring together elements to form signs and then bring signs together

[1] See below, Chap. 18, in discussion of growth.
[2] Poincaré, H.: *Science and Method*, p. 30. Dover Publications.

before he could think. In his case "writing" preceded not talking only but thinking. His actual speech was incomprehensible if I tried to unravel it by applying my knowledge of ordinary words and grammar. It became more meaningful if I thought of it as a doodling in sound, rather like tuneless and aimless whistling; it could not be described as speech, poetic speech, or music. Just as aimless whistling fails to be music because it does not obey any rule or discipline of musical composition, just as doodling fails to be drawing because it does not conform to the discipline of artistic creation, so his speech for lack of obedience to the usages of coherent speech did not qualify as verbal communication. The words employed fall into an undisciplined pattern of sound.[1] This pattern the patient believed he could see, because the words and phrases that he uttered were believed by him to be embodied in the objects in the room. Having uttered actual objects not phrases the pattern that they formed supposedly revealed their meaning, and this meaning he expected he could now take back. The resemblance this bears to projective identification will be noted.

The procedure I have just described qualifies as an attempt to establish thought, because although the verbalizations seemed to refer to the objects present, and to depend upon their being present, scrutiny showed that the objects were being used as signs to make thinking possible about objects that were *not* present. In this respect the objects in the room were being used as a mathematician might employ mathematical notation to solve a problem without having to rely on the physical presence of the objects on which the problem centred. Ordinarily if a man wished to know how many apples there were if four men had three each he would not need to have the men and the

[1] See below: coherence and meaning.

apples present because he could employ a mathematical notation and the rules for manipulation of its signs. The patient exhibiting the features I have described would, had he been able to employ the objects in the room successfully, have "thought about" objects *not* in the room. It is important to note that in this example the objects in the room are not symbols but signs. In so far as the patient has to wait the appearance of appropriate objects before he can think they are inadequate as signs: in so far as they are not the actual objects about which he is attempting to "think" they represent an attempt to invent and employ signs. To that extent *this* employment of actual objects represents a degree of liberation from the state of mind compelled to employ actual objects.

Amongst these object-signs, as I shall call them for convenience, there is felt to exist one that will harmonize them all: by virtue of its supposed functions it resembles Poincaré's "selected fact." It differs from the selected fact, as I use the term, in that it is not felt by the patient to be other than a thing in itself and this β-element, unlike the selected fact, depends on external fortuitous occurrence.

It is tempting to suppose that the transformation of β-element to α-element depends on ♀♂ and the operation of Ps $\leftrightarrow$ D depends on the prior operation of ♀♂. Unfortunately this relatively simple solution does not adequately explain events in the consulting room; before ♀♂ can operate, ♀ has to be found and the discovery of ♀ depends on the operation of Ps $\leftrightarrow$ D. It is obvious that to consider which of the two ♀♂ or Ps $\leftrightarrow$ D is prior distracts from the main problem. I shall suppose the existence of a mixed state in which the patient is persecuted by feelings of depression and depressed by feelings of persecution. These feelings are indistinguishable from bodily sensations and what might, in the light of later capacity for discrimination, be described as things-in-themselves. In short β-elements are objects compounded of things-in-themselves, feelings of depression-persecution and guilt and therefore aspects of personality linked by a sense of catastrophe:[1] fuller elaboration will have to wait on clinical discovery.

I do not claim the existence of a realization that corresponds to the description that follows; it must be taken as a representation of an hypothesis that is necessary to give coherence to diverse clinical observations.

The β-elements are dispersed; this dispersal should be terminated by Ps ↔ D and a selected fact unless the patient seeks a container, ♀, that compels cohesion of the β-elements to form the contained, ♂.

The dispersed β-elements, in so far as they seek the ♀, may be regarded as an abortive prototype of a container, a container loosely structured like the reticulum[1] of Dr. Jaques. They may equally be regarded as the abortive prototype of the contained, a loosely structured ♂ before compression to enter ♀.

This description can be restated in terms of Ps ↔ D: the cohesion of β-elements to form ♂ is analogous to the integration characteristic of the depressive position; the dispersal of β-elements is analogous to the splitting and fragmentation characteristic of the paranoid-schizoid position.

To restate the above description in more sophisticated terms: the dispersal of β-elements has analogies with the preconception that is to be mated with a realization to produce a conception; the expectation of a breast mating with the realization of the breast.

Although the compression of β-elements to form ♂

[1] There is a curious parallel in a description by R. B. Onians (*Origins of European Thought*, p. 369 C.U.P.) of the Greek ideas of the riddle and the sphinx.

and the dispersal to form a loosely-knit ♀ (a reticulum in search of ♂) is suggestive of Ps ↔ D in fact it cannot be regarded as equivalent because β-elements lack the valency necessary for true integration. The interplay between paranoid-schizoid and depressive positions belong to a stage when the elements can be integrated and the integration represented by verbal statements composed of articulated words. Such statements represent the realization by the nature of their formulation as well as their content. The concentration of β-elements is closer to agglomeration than to integration or coherence: the associated depression and persecution are correspondingly incoherent.

If the dispersed β-elements find no container (the model corresponding to ♀ is presumably the breast) the dispersed β-elements, functioning as we have seen as a loosely-knit reticulum (container in search of a container) become as it were far more actively depressed-persecuted and greedy. The expelling object, the centre of these β-elements, already impoverished by the dispersal, is then threatened with annihilation by its evacuated β-elements since the dispersed elements are searching for saturation. Developments that follow have been described by Melanie Klein and her co-workers and need not detain us now. My main object is to establish the theoretical relationship between the theory of projective identification and the theory of paranoid-schizoid and depressive position.

CHAPTER TEN

In the second paragraph of the last chapter I described behaviour designed to develop thought by the interaction of Ps ↔ D and objects in external reality that were regarded as β-elements. I likened the process to doodling or writing as a method of evacuating objects that could then be scrutinized or dealt with in some way that would cause them to yield a meaning. This process I have described as part of the development of a capacity for thought, the manipulation of β-elements by the mechanism PS ↔ D, may also be regarded as a stage in the development of self-consciousness; for β-elements are felt to contain a part of the personality in their composition. The significance of this will be seen to lie, when we reconsider what the elements of psycho-analysis are, in their supposed possession of characteristics such as greed, love, hate, envy, curiosity. The mechanisms involved in these primitive phenomena can be regarded, at their simplest, as PS ↔ D (or fragmentation ↔ integration) and ♀♂ (or expulsion ↔ ingestion). I shall describe these mechanisms now by reformulations in terms of models.

PS may be regarded as a cloud of particles capable of coming together, D and D as an object capable of becoming fragmented and dispersed, PS. PS, the particles, may be regarded as an uncertainty cloud. These elementary particles may be regarded as closing on to one elementary particle, object, or β-elements, a process that is a particular instance of the general movement represented by → D.

D may be regarded variously as an integrated object,

as an agglomeration produced by the convergence of elementary particles on to one particle or β-element, or as an especial instance of integrated object, namely, either ♀ or ♂. It may even be taken to represent the universe of dispersed fragmentations or elementary particles PS. That is to say, if the *field* of fragmentations is the significant feature then D may represent the whole field of elementary particles.

It will be observed that PS is capable of functioning as if it were a form of ♀. A realization corresponding to this abstraction may be seen in practice when a patient appears to pour out a series of incoherent, inarticulated and disjointed associations designed to evoke from the analyst a statement that is to fulfil the function of one of the following: (1) a selected fact that will give coherence to the whole (an interpretation), (2) meaningful comment from which the meaning will be extracted, (3) meaningful comment on to which the disjointed associations will fasten to destroy the meaning ("So What?" the patient may reply to the response he has evoked from the analyst), (4) a meaningful comment on which the disjointed associations will fasten in order to possess it. (The patient makes apparently no response whatever but subsequently produces the analyst's thought as his own.)

In sum, the two mechanisms can each operate in its characteristic manner or in a manner typical or reminiscent of the manner of operation of the other. The description I have given of PS operating as if it were a form of ♀ may be thought of as representing a situation in which the mechanism PS $\leftrightarrow$ D has become arrested at PS, but, in order to maintain its vital function, assumes the mechanical operative quality of ♀♂ and so retains its dynamic quality. Similarly ♀♂ can assume quality of operation characteristic of PS $\leftrightarrow$ D.[1]

[1] In particular ingestion of ♂ by ♀, and penetration of ♀ by ♂ replace some of the functions of the selected fact.

In the latter part of Chapter 7 and subsequently I have been concerned with the mechanics of thinking. I proposed that thoughts should be regarded as prior to the apparatus for using thoughts and in the course of the discussion modified this view by suggesting that "thinking" should be used as a term to describe the processes by which thoughts are produced and the processes by which they are subsequently dealt with. If "thinking" is to be used as a term covering the manufacture as well as the employment of thoughts it should be differentiated so that the activities of creation and employment can be considered separately. I then considered PS ↔ D and ♀♂ separately as mechanisms concerned with the elaboration and employment of thoughts. Lastly I have tried to show that PS ↔ D and ♀♂ are not to be regarded as representing a realization of two separate activities but as mechanisms each of which can at need assume the characteristics of the other. In all of this I have concerned myself with content only in so far as it helped to illustrate the mechanisms. Before I turn to content I must point out a difficulty in the use of the term "content." It is clearly appropriate to hypotheses of the kind I have represented by ♀♂. We have already encountered difficulties inherent in the use of terms such as "mechanism" because of the implied model and its unsuitability to convey a meaning when life is an essential element in the meaning that is to be conveyed. The difficulty involved in the use of the term "content" is similar. Although I shall speak of the Oedipal situation as if it were the content of thoughts it will be apparent that thoughts and thinking may be regarded as part of the content of the Oedipal situation. The term "Oedipal situation" may be applied to the (1) realization of relationships between Father, Mother and child, (2) emotional preconception, using the term "preconception" as I have used it here as that which mates with awareness of a realization to give rise to a conception, (3) a psychological reaction stimulated in an individual by (1) above. I trust the context will make it clear in which of these senses I employ the term.

Freud's use of the Oedipus myth illuminated more than the nature of the sexual facets of the human personality. Thanks to his discoveries it is possible by reviewing the myth to see that it contains elements that were not stressed in the early investigations because they were overshadowed by the sexual component in the drama. The developments of psycho-analysis make it possible to give more weight to other features. First, the myth by virtue of its narrative form binds the various components in the story in a manner analogous to the fixation of the elements of a scientific deductive system by their inclusion in the system: it is similar to the fixation of the elements in the corresponding algebraic calculus where that exists. No element, such as the sexual element, can be comprehended save in its relationship with other elements; for example with the determination with which Oedipus pursues his inquiry into the crime despite the warnings of Tiresias. It is consequently not possible to isolate the sexual component, or any other, without distortion. Sex, in the Oedipal situation, has a quality[1] that can only be described by the implications conferred on it by its inclusion in the story. If it is removed from the story it loses its quality unless its meaning is preserved by an express reservation that "sex" is a term used to represent sex as it is experienced in the context of the myth. The same is true of all other elements that lend themselves to abstraction

[1] This point becomes more clear when I discuss the use of ideational content of a statement as a method of expressing feeling. See Chap. 19 *et seq.*

from the myth.[1] In so far as I am concerned to elucidate the elements of psycho-analysis I shall regard the train of causation, as it is expressed in the myth, as an element as we may think it necessary to abstract, but otherwise to be subordinate to the function of linking all elements to confer upon them a particular psychic quality. In this respect the elements suffer modification analogous to that of letters of an alphabet held in combination to spell a particular word. Combination of the elements in the story is analogous to the combination of hypotheses in a scientific deductive system.

The chain of causation is necessary to express the moral system of which it is an integral part. The riddle traditionally attributed to the Sphinx is an expression of man's curiosity turned upon himself. Self-consciousness or curiosity in the personality about the personality is an essential feature of the story: psycho-analytic investigation thus has origins of respectable antiquity. Curiosity has the same status in the myths of the garden of Eden and the tower of Babel—it is a sin. Ignoring the narrative chain of the story except for its contribution to linking the components with each other I isolate the following elements:

1. The pronouncement of the Delphic Oracle.
2. The warning of Tiresias, blinded for his attack on the serpents whose coupling he had observed.
3. The riddle of the Sphinx.
4. The misconduct of Oedipus in arrogantly pursuing his inquiry and thus being guilty of hybris.

Added to these are a series of disasters:

5. The plague inflicted on the population of Thebes.
6. The suicides of the Sphinx and Jocasta.
7. The blinding and exile of Oedipus.

[1] Particularly curiosity—the K link.

8. The murder of the King.

It is noteworthy that:

9. The original question is posed by a monster, that is, by an object composed of a number of features inappropriate to each other.

This concludes my brief review of the Oedipus myth in the light of psycho-analytic theory. I shall consider in what respect it is meaningful to regard the Oedipus myth as an important component of the content of the human mind.

CHAPTER ELEVEN

DISCUSSION of the Oedipus myth as a part of the content of the mind meets with inherent difficulties at the outset. The first is typified by the employment in this context of a locution that implies the model of a container. The second is the peculiar feature of the myth in that the following elements seem to correspond to the numbered axis of the grid.

1. The pronouncement of the oracle defines the theme of the story and can be regarded as a definition, or definitory hypothesis. It resembles a preconception, or an algebraic calculus, in that it is an "unsaturated statement" that is "saturated" by the unfolding of the story; or an "unknown," in the mathematical sense, that is "satisfied" by the story. It is the statement of the theme of the story that is to unfold; the description of the criminal who is wanted.

2. Tiresias may be regarded as representing the hypothesis, known to be false, that is maintained to act as a barrier against the anxiety anticipated as a concomitant of any hypothesis or theory that might take its place.

3. The myth as a whole may be taken as the record of a realization and therefore to fulfil the function Freud attributed to notation.

4. The Sphinx stimulates curiosity and threatens death as the penalty for failure to satisfy it. It can represent the function Freud attributed to attention, but it implies a threat against the curiosity it stimulates.

5. Oedipus represents the triumph of determined curiosity over intimidation and may thus be used as a symbol for scientific integrity—the investigatory tool.

It may seem that I am forcing the myth to fall in with preconceptions of my own, but little ingenuity is required to see these facets of meaning. The classical psycho-analytical employment of the myth sheds light on the nature of L and H links; it is equally illuminating for the K link. Features that can serve as symbols for the mechanics of thinking contribute to my suspicion that it is inadequate to regard the Oedipus situation as a part of the *content* of the mind. I propose to leave discussion of the conception of the mind as having content in abeyance until I have dealt later on with the Oedipus myth in its function as a pre-conception.[1]

I turn now to a clinical experience in which analyst and analysand appear to be speaking the same language, to have many points of agreement and yet to remain without any tie other than that of the mechanical fact of continued attendance at analytic sessions. Progress of the analysis reveals a divergence which I shall sum up as follows:

The analyst is, and thinks he is, in a consulting-room conducting an analysis. The patient regards the same fact, his attendance in analysis, as an experience affording him the raw material to give substance to a day dream. The day dream, thus invested with reality, is that he the patient being extremely intuitive, is able without any analysis, to see just where his difficulties lie and to astonish and delight the analyst by his brilliance and friendliness. The patient reports, and the analyst believes, that he, the patient, has had a

[1] See below, Chap. 15, towards the end, and Chap. 19 on the function of the Oedipus myth as an inborn pre-conception intended to match the realization of the parental relationship.

dream. The patient reports, but does NOT believe, that he has had a dream. The dream, an experience of great emotional intensity, is felt by the patient to be a straightforward recital of the facts of a horrifying experience.[1] He expects that the analyst, by treating it as a dream requiring interpretation, will give substance to his day dream that it was only a dream. In short, the patient is mobilizing his resources, and these include the facts of the analysis, to keep at bay his conviction that the dream not only was but is the reality and the reality, as the analyst understands it, is something to be appreciated only for those elements that are suited to refutation of the "dream."

This account is not of a new theory of dreams, but is a description of a state, seen in an extremely disturbed patient, but probably of fairly common recurrence. The "dream," whether it is correctly described by inclusion in the category of dreams or not, is something that would emerge in the session as a hallucination if the patient's capacity for day dream weakened.

The description fails to bring out one marked peculiarity of such a situation and that is the extent to which analyst and patient agree about the facts. But the agreement on facts is similar to the agreement that two people might have about the disposition of lines, light, and shade in a drawing illustrating reversible perspective–one sees a vase while the other sees two faces: what then are the facts on which both are agreed?

In the example of reversible perspective it may be supposed that it is the actual visual impressions and that the divergence is in the domain of preconceptions. It is possible that this might fairly represent the situation with the patient, but it is a matter that has to be

[1] For the grid categorization of this phenomenon see the later discussion on the application of the grid to feelings: Chap. 19.

determined by clinical observation of each case in which such phenomena appear. I prefer not to lay down a general rule. The principle should be that clinical observation must determine where the intersection of the analyst's and patient's views is.

The significance of the agreement between analyst and patient lies in the fact that the agreement is obvious and obtrusive but the disagreement, which may be just as obtrusive, is by no means obvious. It lies in the use of the agreed facts by the patient to deny what he is convinced are the facts. The conflict between the view of the patient and analyst, and in the patient with himself, is not therefore a conflict, as we see it in the neuroses, between one set of ideas and another, or one set of impulses and another, but between K and minus K (−K) or, to express it pictorially between Tiresias and Oedipus, not Oedipus and Laius.

The common-sense view of mental development is that it consists in an increase of capacity to grasp reality and a decrease in the obstructive force of illusions. Psycho-analysts suppose that the exposure of archaic phantasies to modification by a sophisticated capacity for approximation to a series of theories, that are consistent and compatible with the reception and integration of further experience, is therapeutic in its effects. This supposition cannot stand up to rigorous examination, but has to be received with indulgence to yield meaning of value. Is it possible to find any description in which scientific rigour can make up for absence of indulgence? On the answer to this question depends the possibility of arresting the processes of mental and personality deterioration as those terms are understood medically. The first problem is to see what can be done to increase scientific rigour by establishing the nature of minus K (−K), minus L (−L) and minus H (−H). I shall start by considering the mechanics of thinking. I shall not consider further the ♀♂ mechanism as I do not wish to add anything to what I have said about the denudation of each component by the other. The PS ↔ D mechanism may be briefly dismissed: instead of an interaction involving dispersal of particles with feelings of persecution (Chapter 8) and integration with feelings of depression we have in −PS ↔ D disintegration, total loss and depressive stupor, *or*, intense impaction and degenerate stuporose violence. Although these descriptions of −♀♂ and −PS ↔ D are incomplete they may serve until further experience is forthcoming. I must now consider the nature of the mechanism that I have likened to reversible perspective.

Clinically the picture presented is curiously baffling. There is usually no doubt about the severity of the patient's disability, but it is difficult even for the patient to say why he seeks analysis. It may also be possible at first to underestimate the degree of severity of the disturbance. But before long the lack of contact between analyst and patient and the lack of signs of ordinary conflict begin to build up an unmistakable picture. There is evidence that the patient is a prey to extremely painful emotional experiences: the analyst usually has to rely on the patient's report as the only evidence of these. If they take place in the session the patient invariably has a facile "explanation" of what is taking place. The explanation is often couched in terms that successfully disguise the real nature of the experience. If the patient has been in analysis for some time they are manipulated in such a way that they invite interpretation in terms that the patient has learned to expect from the analyst—the "agreed" intersection is thus maintained. Between analyst and patient there is thus established what I have elsewhere[1] called a contact barrier. Is it possible to glean from the mechanisms involved in this behaviour any material that will throw light on minus phenomena (−L, −H and −K) and incidentally on the problem of establishing the elements of psycho-analysis?

[1] Bion, W. R.: *Learning from Experience*. Heinemann.

CHAPTER TWELVE

THE model of reversible perspective, when applied to the analysis, reveals a complex situation. The patient detects a note of satisfaction in the analyst's voice and responds in a tone conveying dejection. (What was said is irrelevant to our immediate concern.) The patient detects a moral supposition in an interpretation: his response is significant for its silent rejection of the moral supposition. That which makes one person see two faces and the other a vase remains insensible, but in the domain of sense impressions there is agreement. The interpretation is accepted, but the premises have been rejected and other silently substituted.

In any interpretation there is a significant assumption, one being that the analyst is the analyst: this assumption may be denied silently by the patient. Although he appears to accept the interpretation he denies its force by having substituted another assumption. Further associations may show what *his* assumption is.

The debate between analysand and analyst is therefore unspoken;[1] what the analyst says is shown to be agreed by both parties to the analysis, but—it is insignificant. The conflict is therefore kept out of discussion because it is confined to a domain which is not regarded as an issue between the analyst and analysand. The supposition that the analyst is the

[1] The analyst can detect this situation if he uses the grid to categorize interpretations and the responses they evoke and then compares the relationship of the grid categories to each other. See Chap. 20.

analyst and the analysand the analysand is but one of these domains of disagreement that is passed by silently.

Suppose it is brought into the analysis: the patient and the analyst are at once in agreement, for what proposition could be more obvious, or one more loyally accepted by the patient? But the mode of acceptance will indicate that the significance, in the patient's opinion, of the analyst's interpretation lay in the analyst's premises—his false premises. The nature of the falsity is not pressed: it lies in the implication that the premises are of the kind that lead one person to see two faces when he might with equal propriety have seen a vase.

A difference of opinion about the significance of known facts differs from the phenomenon I am describing; on such occasions the difference is overt and concerns the facts. In "reversed perspective" the disagreement between analyst and analysand is apparent only when the analysand appears to have been taken unawares; there is a pause while he carries out a readjustment.

The pause may seem indistinguishable from one that a neurotic patient will make in order to digest the interpretation he has heard. I doubt whether the true nature of the pause can be clinically observed; it may be that an ability to differentiate depends always on long experience of the patient's pauses and the discovery, later rather than sooner, that after many months of apparently successful analysis the patient has gained an extensive knowledge of the analyst's theories but no insight. The pause is not being employed to absorb fully the implications of the interpretation, but rather to establish a point of view, not expressed to the analyst, from which the analyst's interpretation, though verbally unchanged and unchallenged, has a meaning other than the one the analyst intended to convey.

Any growth of insight depends on the extent to which the patient has been forced to digest the interpretation in order to effect the change in his point of view. Such misinterpretation differs from the common run of resistances; the patient will often seize on an ambiguity in the analyst's phrasing or intonation to give his interpretation a slant that the analyst does not intend. The difference is difficult to observe because the patient who reverses perspective also employs the common modes of misinterpretation sufficiently frequently to obscure the more serious condition. He will welcome interpretations of these misunderstandings if they emphasize the deliberate aspects of his contribution; it is a relief to believe that his difficulty is under conscious control.

The following is an example from the analysis of an intelligent man who gave the impression, in session after session, of co-operation that was both friendly and informed—if his responses were not scrutinized too keenly. "My secretary," he said, "complains bitterly of his wife: he says that she does not understand him. He says she complains constantly of him: bitter criticisms and hostility about his lack of understanding, inability to love and so on . . ." In the context of this and similar communications of which his analysis consisted, it was evident that a wide range of transference phenomena might be discussed. In view of the patient's experience of analysis, his undoubted ability and sensitiveness, it would be reasonable to suppose that he would observe a transference relationship between his secretary and himself and that he would be able to understand what his communication of this material would imply about his feelings for me. On several occasions his manner of communicating associations made me suspect that the episodes described might have been invented by him to illustrate a theory of transference that he had picked up in the course of his analysis.

I gave interpretations to this and similar communications, all, as I hoped, being reasonably apposite and given sufficient cogency by the context. His responses were varied; they ranged from an almost stupefied silence to apathetic acquiescence followed by more material—more "free associations." Sometimes he would say that he had been "thinking" during the silence, "about what you said." Sometimes he would disagree with the interpretation, or some aspect of it, and then, as if striving to achieve a solution, would come round to agree that I was probably, no—certainly right. On other occasions, when I felt that my interpretation was one with which he must surely be familiar, he would blandly agree as if it were a cliché that hardly stirred a ripple in his thoughts. It was not till I was able to suggest that he made this class of communication because he felt that the episodes he mentioned were utterly incomprehensible that he made a response showing that this was indeed the case. Such a blank failure to understand would be remarkable at any time, but doubly so in a man who had had so much experience of being analysed. It could not be explained by lack of intelligence, lack of sensitiveness, lack of experience, or ineptitude of my analysis; for the instances he communicated were nearly all of the kind that might be chosen to illustrate psycho-analytic theories.

This last characteristic of these communications is, in this context, particularly baffling: if the patient has no psycho-analytic acumen how is the evidence of careful selection in accordance with psycho-analytic principles to be accounted for? If the evidence of selection is admitted how is one to explain the failure of comprehension?

I exclude the hypothesis of deliberate conscious or semi-conscious denial of the analyst's work. My reason, of which I shall say more later, is the evidence of pain. There was ample evidence, after interpretations had established the reality of the patient's inability to comprehend, of the severity of his pain.

In each instance, the perspective that enabled me, but not the patient, to grasp the meaning of the associations, was that afforded by the Oedipus theory. In every instance, that which appeared to cause the patient to reverse the perspective, was the Oedipus myth. I say myth, not theory, because the distinction is important: the Oedipus theory and its various formulations, belongs to the area of the grid, covered by F4, G4, F5, G5. The myth pertains to the area C.

The patient's capacity for learning but not using analytic theories is a failure to match pre-conceptions with the realizations that approximate to them. The unsaturated element remains unsaturated.

Melanie Klein described a situation in which the personality attacked its object with such violence that not only was the object deemed to become minutely fragmented, but the personality likewise. In the situation I describe there appears to be no dynamic splitting. It is as if the splitting was arrested in a static pose action being no more necessary than it is when hallucination is substituted for reality. The patient does not have to disagree with the analyst or experience Oedipal conflicts within himself: he reverses the perspective. It is important to consider more closely what this means.[1]

Reversing perspective is not the same as evacuation of β-elements. That is an active process and the patient's behaviour in the analysis affords evidence

[1] The "static" splitting and failure to match pre-conception with realization will be better understood when it is related to discussion in first half of Chap. 19.

that is, to put it no higher, quite compatible with a theory that he is taking action to "disburden his psyche of accretions of stimuli" as Freud described it.[1] As near as I could tell the patient regarded the analyst's interpretations as evidence that he, the patient, had evacuated β-elements, a state of mind more akin to hallucination than delusion. The search for elements involves further investigation of pain, reversible perspective and the Oedipus myth.

[1] Freud, S: *Two Principles of Mental Functioning.*

CHAPTER THIRTEEN

Reversible perspective is evidence of pain; the patient reverses perspective to make a dynamic situation static. The work of the analyst is to restore dynamic to a static situation and so make development possible. As I said in my last chapter, the patient manoeuvres so that the analyst's interpretations are agreed; they thus become the outward sign of a static situation. Since the analyst's interpretations are unlikely to permit this and the patient is unlikely always to command sufficient nimbleness of mind to match the interpretation with a shift that reverses the perspective in which the interpretation is viewed, the patient employs an armoury that is reinforced by delusion and hallucination. If he cannot reverse the perspective at once he can adjust his perception of the facts by mis-hearing and misunderstanding so that they give substance to the static view: a delusion is in being.

If this is not sufficient to keep the situation static the patient resorts to hallucination. For simplification, I can restate this as hallucination in order to preserve, temporarily, an ability to reverse perspective; and reversed perspective in order to preserve a static hallucination.

The prolonged resort to reversible perspective is thus accompanied by delusions and hallucinations that are difficult to detect because they are both static and evanescent. Moreover, since their aim is to preserve the analyst's statements (interpretations) as an overt expression of agreement and a defence against change, the true significance of the patient's behaviour as a sign of delusion or hallucination is not apparent unless the analyst is alert to this possibility. The analyst's expressed thoughts belong to the area F5, G5 and G6: the same formulation is accepted by the patient but as an expression of thought belonging to F1, G1, G2.

An analysis that is taking this course appears to be curiously unsatisfactory because the lack of real progress obtrudes only slowly and then appears to be stable, unspectacular and dull. In reality the situation is unstable and dangerous. The clue to it lies in the fact I mentioned at the start of this chapter—pain. The patient's manoeuvres appear to lack an aim because, though the ready acceptance of interpretations arouses suspicion, it is not apparent that they are directed against change, *any* change, and pain. It is the dynamic quality of the interpretation that evokes evasive reactions. That is to say, the objection to the interpretation is that, *whatever* the content may be, it has the qualities appropriate to columns 5 and 6 of the grid.

Reference to the grid would lead one to suspect that if the patient manoeuvres to shift all *I* to the area of columns 1 and 2, with the possible addition of 3, he must tend to do the same with his own *I* phenomena. That is in fact the case and it helps to explain some of the features of his dreams, pre-conceptions and theories.

The lesson to be drawn from this discussion is the need to deduce the presence of intense pain and the threat that it represents to mental integration. I shall therefore consider pain as one of the elements of psycho-analysis.

Pain cannot be absent from the personality. An analysis must be painful, not because there is necessarily any value in pain, but because an analysis in which pain is not observed and discussed cannot be regarded as dealing with one of the central reasons for the patient's presence. The importance of pain can be dismissed as a secondary quality, something that is to disappear when conflicts are resolved; indeed most patients would take this view. Furthermore it can be supported by the fact that successful analysis does lead to diminution of suffering; nevertheless it obscures the need, more obvious in some cases than in others, for the analytic experience to increase the patient's *capacity* for suffering even though patient and analyst may hope to decrease pain itself. The analogy with physical medicine is exact; to destroy a capacity for physical pain would be a disaster in any situation other than one in which an even greater disaster—namely death itself—is certain.

In reversible perspective acceptance by the analyst of the possibility of an impairment of a capacity for pain can help avoidance of errors that might lead to disaster. If the problem is not dealt with the patient's capacity to maintain the static situation may give way to an experience of pain so intense that a psychotic breakdown is the result.

The case for acceptance of pain as an element of psycho-analysis is reinforced by the position it occupies in Freud's theories of the pleasure-pain principle. It is evident that the dominance of the reality principle, and indeed its establishment, is imperilled if the patient swings over to the evasion of pain rather than to its modification; yet modification is jeopardized if the patient's capacity for pain is impaired. As I have discussed the relationship of the establishment of the reality principle to psychosis in *Learning from Experience* I shall say no more about it here.

Pain cannot be regarded as a reliable index of pathological processes partly because of its relationship with development (recognized in the commonly used phrase "growing pains") and partly because intensity of suffering is not always proportionate to the severity of the disturbance. Its degree and significance depend on its relationship with other elements.

Implicit in the discussion of reversible perspective as a means of preserving a defence against pain is the concept of growth. Growth is a phenomenon that appears to present peculiar difficulties to perception either by the growing object or the object that stimulates it, for its relationship with precedent phenomena is obscure and separated in time.[1] Difficulty in observing it contributes to the anxiety to establish "results," e.g. of analysis. It will be necessary to trace its relationship with PS ↔ D, ♀♂. Its dependence on a capacity to entertain the social and narcissistic components of the Oedipal situation involves further discussion of the Oedipus myth, the Babel myth (Genesis XI, 1–9) and the early version of the Eden myth (Genesis II, 8–3 passim). The primitive models for mental growth are the Tree of Knowledge, the Tower and city of Babel and the Sphinx. The myths (Row C of the grid) provide a succinct statement of psycho-analytic theories which are relevant in aiding the analyst both to perceive growth and to achieve interpretations that illuminate aspects of the patient's problems that belong to growth.

[1] One of the advantages of reference to the grid is that grid categorization of the patient's response to interpretation should reveal growth.

CHAPTER FOURTEEN

In Chapter 3 I described personal myth as an important tool in psycho-analytic work. In chapters 11 and 12 I attributed augmented though similar significance to the Oedipus myth because it has public and racial, as opposed to private, status. The advantages of transition from private to racial myth are analogous to the transition from private to public communication.[1]

The Oedipus myth will be differently read by different people, but the measure of agreement makes it a channel of public communication as Freud's use of it has shown. I shall use the myths of the garden of Eden and the Tower of Babel to reinforce the expression, already implied by the Sphinx in the Oedipus myth, of attitudes of a god inimical to the gaining of knowledge by human beings whose search is felt to imperil his supremacy.

In the garden of Eden, possessed by the Father, eating of the Tree of Knowledge of good and evil is forbidden. The serpent, or Satan disguised, incites the woman to defy the ordinance of the Almighty. The relevation of disobedience is associated with guilt and nakedness. The outcome is banishment as it is in the Oedipus myth. In the Babel myth the use of the tower is to effect an entry into realms regarded by Jahweh as his own—heaven. The outcome is exile, as in the garden of Eden and Oedipus myths, but an important precursor is the destruction of a common language and

[1] Compare *Scientific Explanation*—R. B. Braithwaite, p. 6, and his reference to Heinrich Her tz on p. 91.

the spreading of confusion so that co-operation became impossible.

The components of these myths that I wish to use are those which pictorialize, in the sense of internal pictures or symbols that we make for ourselves, features that might turn out to be the psycho-analytical elements that I seek.

1. There is a god or fate, omniscient and omnipotent though modelled anthromorphically. This god belongs to a moral system and appears to be hostile to mankind in his search for knowledge, even moral knowledge.

2. In all, penetration into, or ingestion into, or expulsion from, a blissful place or state is prominent. Sexual knowledge and pleasure is a prominent feature of the knowledge sought and forbidden.

3. In Eden and Oedipus myth there is a stimulation of forbidden desires—the serpent incites desire for the fruit: Oedipus instigates the search for the criminal: in the Babel myth there is a significant variation—the people come together and are dispersed, the language is one and is replaced by a number of languages. The Sphinx incites to curiosity by its riddle. Using these myths as a source for pictorial representation of the elements in the horizontal axis of Table 1 the definitory function of a formulation may be represented by the oracle and the statement of aims as expressed in the phrase "let us build us a city and a tower." The repressing force exerted by the formula used in col. 2, by Tiresias or the god of fate of whom he is the representative. The action column 6 is represented by the outcome, exile or dispersion.

It is not my object to establish an exact correspondence; I suggested in Chapter 11, that these myths serve as a primitive counterpart of the sophisticated formulations whose employment in scientific work I have placed on the horizontal axis of the grid. Since they are primitive and pictorial they are vital but lack precision—hence the need for sophisticated formulations as in science. Therefore to make the correspondence between the horizontal axis and the elements of the myth appear to be exact would be a falsification that obscured the nature of the myth. Equally failure to see that there is this correspondence obscures the value of the myth as a fact-finding tool. I wish to restore it to its place in our methods so that it can play the vitalizing part there that it has played in history (and in Freud's discovery of psycho-analysis) and it is for that reason that I have introduced it in Chapter 3. It is also an object for investigation in an analysis as part of the primitive apparatus of the individual's armoury of learning.

If the Oedipal myth in addition to the place it already occupies in analytic theory is recognized as an essential part of the apparatus of learning in primitive stages of development, a number of elements discernible in the debris of a disintegrated ego assume a new significance.

In certain highly disturbed patients the patient according to Melanie Klein attacks his object with such violence that not only is the object felt to disintegrate but the personality delivering the attack also. This disintegration is characteristic of the patient who cannot tolerate reality and has therefore destroyed the apparatus that enables him to be aware of it. The private myth, corresponding to the Oedipus myth, enables the patient to understand his relationship with the parents. This private myth, in its investigatory role, if impaired or maldeveloped or subjected to too great a stress, disintegrates; its components are dispersed and the patient is left without an apparatus which would enable him to comprehend the parental relationship and so to adjust to it. The Oedipus debris will in these circumstances contain elements that are components of the Oedipal myth that should have operated as a pre-conception. How are the scattered components of a disintegrated ego to be recognized? In this instance the analyst who seeks to illuminate the fragments of the patient's apparatus of learning may be led to recognize them by noting isolated[1] fragments of the Oedipal myth (and the myths I have associated with it).

The private myth has this important role in the individual's attempt to learn from experience analogous to that played by public myths as systems of notation and record in the development of groups. Conviction comes only from clinical experience in which material resembling Oedipal components appears, the components being dispersed and evocative in tendency. The myth must be expected to appear in a private version. The operation follows the pattern of the fragments in PS $\leftrightarrow$ D as I have described it at the commencement of Chapter 10. The verbalizations of the patient, and behaviour associated with them, seem to vary from something incoherent and meaningless to formulations that appear vaguely to be inviting comment, sometimes even suggesting the comment that they invite.

Search for the elements of psycho-analysis is restricted to that aspect of them that it is the business of the psycho-analyst to discern. They cannot be represented, either by abstract signs, such as I have suggested, or by mythological narratives evoking visual imagery, in such a way that anyone other than a trained and practising psycho-analyst could recognize the realization approximating to the representation. In this chapter I hope that by showing a correspondence

[1] Such fragments appear, particularly in psychotic material, widely dispersed in analytic time. One of the problems of interpretation is to show that these temporarily dispersed fragments are related.

between myth and the items of the horizontal axis of the grid analysts, who are used to observing patients in the light of the preconceptions with which psycho-analytic Oedipal theory endows them, will find it easier to make the transition from theoretical background to consulting-room phenomena. The gap remains and can only be bridged by training and experience and, to some extent, by interpolation, between the concept of "Oedipal components" and the events of the consulting room, of description of those events in terms that are vivid and exact. Such description would tax the powers of a writer and would then represent a degree of particularization unsuitable except for short and relatively infrequent passages of a total analysis.

Although I aim to isolate elements of the reality of psycho-analytic practice and not of theory I have to represent them by signs and myths that belong to the domain of representation of abstractions and the high-level hypotheses of a scientific deductive system. This must not obscure the fact that every sign is intended to represent phenomena that a psycho-analyst might experience in analytic sessions. The signs chosen to represent the elements are to aid in working on and thinking about the experience of the analysis.

CHAPTER FIFTEEN

In this chapter I reconsider transference. The elements of the transference are to be found in that aspect of the patient's behaviour that betrays his awareness of the presence of an object that is not himself. No aspect of his behaviour can be disregarded; its relevance to the central fact must be assessed. His greeting, or neglect of it, references to couch, or furniture, or weather, all must be seen in that aspect of them that relates to the presence of an object not himself; the evidence must be regarded afresh each session and nothing taken for granted for the order in which aspects of the patient's mind present themselves for observation are not decided by the length of time for which the analysis has endured. For example, the patient may regard the analyst as a person to be treated as if he were a thing; or as a thing towards which his attitude is animistic. If ψ (ξ) represents the analyst's state of mind *vis-à-vis* the analysand it is the unsaturated element (ξ) that is the important one in every session.

The peculiarity of a psycho-analytic session, that aspect of it which establishes that it is a psycho-analysis and could be nothing else, lies in the use by the analyst of all material to illuminate a K relationship. The transference interpretation is peculiar in that it refers to all material without discrimination, but is highly selective in appraising its significance. The patient communicates information that has significance by virtue of criteria of his own: the analyst is restricted to interpretations that are an expression of a K relationship with the patient. They must not be expressions of L or H.

Ordinarily an analyst would not expect to go through a series of conscious speculations on the nature of simple statements. But if he wishes to do some "homework," that is to say extra-analytic meditation, on a session, either to train and amplify his capacity for intuitive deduction, or because he has some doubts about the accuracy of the work he has been doing, he may refer the doubtful material to the grid. Suppose the patient had said "I know that you hate me": his speculations might take some form such as the following: On the face of it the sentence is grammatically and semantically straightforward, but there is need to examine it critically to determine which of the grid categories apply.

The context of the statement, taken together with the (ξ) element of ψ (ξ), representing the patient's state of mind, could make it probable that the significance lay in its being for the patient a disguised expulsion of flatus: in that case the analyst would assess the chance that it was a β-element pertaining to row A.

The session might indicate that the phrase related to a dream that the patient had had or was perhaps part of a phantasy. In that case it would belong to rows B or C.

In yet another context it might be more appropriate to suspect that it was a pre-conception and should lie in the class represented in row D.

Suppose however that the statement had followed a critical interpretation that could itself have been interpreted by the patient as an expression of hostility: it might then be appropriate to regard it as, from the patient's point of view, a mating of a pre-conception with a realization.

It cannot be supposed to lie in row H; it might, however, be correctly attributed to row G, but for this to be appropriate the analyst would need to be able to draw on a number of attendant circumstances that led him to suppose that the statement represented a hardening of belief into a more nearly permanent fixed idea.

Let us now consider the horizontal axis. The columns in this axis represent the functions that a statement is being made to perform. The statement may be an oracular pronouncement, an announcement of the theme of the session, a definition in the light of which the remainder of the session is to be understood. In short it may fall in the category represented by column 1.

If it seems rather to fall in the column 2 category it will mean that the statement is known to be false but provides the patient with a theory that will act as a defensive barrier against feelings and ideas that might take its place.

If it seems to fall in columns 3, 4 or 5, it is a probing statement and is quite compatible with co-operation in the analytic investigation.

If it belongs to column 6 it is a warning of acting out, in which I include the use of the analysis itself as a form of acting out. To illustrate the value of the grid as an instrument to aid the analyst in thinking about an analytic problem, that is to say, as an instrument of notation that provides a record of fact and a sign that can be manipulated in a manner analogous to a number in mathematics, I shall contrast A6 and F6 by considering the significance of each.

A.6 indicates that the statement "I know that you hate me" is to be regarded as a β-element employed as an act. If the analyst concludes that the statement falls in this category it can only mean that the session must be regarded as an acting out rather than as an ordinary analytic session. The muscular movements necessary to express the words, since they are intended to disburden the psyche of accumulations of stimuli, must be regarded as of primary significance. The words indicate that the patient has a feeling (which is apparently regarded by him in much the same light as a normal personality would regard a concrete object) that was part of his personality (also regarded as a concrete object) that he can by his muscular movements detach and expel. The end-product of this manoeuvre is that he has achieved a state of mind in which he is no longer burdened by the feeling that the analyst hates him. He is now, supposedly, free to feel that the analyst is his friend.

To turn now to F6. If this is the category to which the statement belongs it now means that the patient is convinced that the analyst is his enemy. It means furthermore, by virtue if its membership of column 6, that the patient is already acting, or is about to act, on this supposition. The analytic significance of the patient's statement is very different in the two instances; it is a matter of importance to distinguish between the two categories and to decide to which of the two the statement belongs.

Consider the statement "I know that you hate me" as it appears in another category; suppose that it belongs to the categories lying in row C, because the patient said that he had dreamt it. Or it might be part of a phantasy or day dream: in such a case the characteristics of visual imagery, or perhaps myth, would be prominent. The intensification of this element is bound to affect the elements expressed by the headings of the horizontal axis of the grid. Such interplay is implied by the grid. Consequently the columns 1–6 tend to become pictorialized and personified in the way I have suggested by equating each of them with a character from the Oedipus myth. For example, if the statement appears to be appropriate to C6 when a break in analysis is impending the break would be related to exile and the analyst should anticipate the appearance of other features of the Oedipal situation. I stress the importance of recognizing the category to which material belongs as a step towards anticipating and therefore recognizing related phenomena in the material. If the material fits category C5 one would expect an intensification of the determination with which curiosity was pursued: if in category C2 an intensification of resistance to the emergence of new material. I shall leave the significance of the emotion expressed—"I know that you *hate* me"—to the next chapter.[1]

The description I have given is not of a process of thought appropriate to actual contact with the patient. The analytic session is too precious an opportunity for observation to be jeopardized by pre-occupations of the kind my description implies; the theme of this book is a scheme to facilitate thinking about analytic work *outside* the sessions themselves. The object of such extra-sessional work is to substitute creative thinking for laborious and frequently meaningless note-taking; it provides practice, analogous to the musician's scales and exercises, to sharpen and develop intuition. It becomes increasingly possible to arrive at conclusions instantaneously which at first are the fruits of laborious intellectualization.

[1] And in the latter part of Chap. 19 where I discuss feelings.

CHAPTER SIXTEEN

PROBLEMS of instinct and emotion belong to the main body of psycho-analytic theory and must be considered for inclusion amongst the elements of psycho-analysis as they appear in psycho-analytic practice.

The emotion to which attention is drawn should be obvious to the analyst, but unobserved by the patient; an emotion that is obvious to the patient is usually *painfully* obvious and avoidance of unnecessary pain must be one aim in the exercise of analytic intuition. Since the analyst's capacity for intuition should enable him to demonstrate an emotion before it has become *painfully* obvious it would help if our search for the elements of emotions was directed to making intuitive deductions easier. The sexual instinct is an integral part of psycho-analytic theory, but the element of sex in the sense of something for which I need to look is not sex but that from which the presence of sex may be deduced. But for my purpose the term "element" cannot be properly used to denote something that would appear to be a property of some more fundamental thing whose presence it betrays. Therefore the element I choose is not a sign of sexuality but a precursor of sexuality. Amongst the elements that we seek there must be the precursor of emotion, not an emotion itself unless it is the precursor of some emotion other than itself. Thus, if the hate that a patient is experiencing is a precursor of love its virtue as an element resides in its quality as a precursor of love and not in its being hate. And so for all other emotions.

I am adumbrating, in the domain of emotion, something that is reminiscent of the relationship of preconception to conception.

If interpretations forestall the development of emotions by illuminating their precursors it follows that sexual and other feelings should not be regarded as elements. The counterpart of the preconception is the *premonition*. Directly observed emotional states are significant only as premonitions.

I have defined the pre-conception as an element private to the individual, possibly not conscious; the same is true of the pre-monition.

Lest it seems confusing to use the term preconception as something to be distinguished from a scientific deductive system and then speak of an analytic theory as an analyst's preconception I shall use the term pre-conception to distinguish it from a preconception. Pre-conception, as I have placed it in row D of the grid, is a term representing a stage in the development of thinking; preconception, in the sense of the analyst's theoretical preconceptions refers to the use of a theory and so belongs to columns 3 and 4 of the grid. As an example, the analyst may have a hunch that something of which he is not properly aware is going on in the session. This state might be represented by D3. As he feels greater conviction about the development, his state of mind changes until, say, he conceives that oedipal material is emerging; his state of mind is now represented by G4 or G5. In other words he thinks that Freud's oedipal theories will give point and direction to his probing curiosity. To return to the significance of emotional drives that are active in the course of the analytic experience and the manner of their elucidation; when a patient comes for a first consultation his premotions give information about him that cannot be obtained from other factors. From them it is possible to obtain some idea of the use that he is likely to make of an analysis.

The term "premonition," as I propose to use it represents emotional states rather than ideational content, thus leaving the term "pre-conception" to represent the latter. I do not dissociate "pre-monition" from its association with a sense of warning and anxiety The feeling of anxiety is of value in guiding the analyst to recognize the premotion in the material. The premonition can therefore be represented by (Anxiety (ξ)) where (ξ) is an unsaturated element.

Analysis must be conducted so that the conditions for observing pre-monitions exist, a conclusion compatible with Freud's definition of the analytic situation as one in which an atmosphere of deprivation[1] is dominant. If premonitions cannot be experienced correct interpretation becomes difficult for the analyst to give and difficult for the analysand to grasp; unnecessary pain, of which I have already spoken, becomes more likely.

The distinction between pre-conception and premonition facilitates the creation of a system for thinking about analytic practice; it is no more of a falsification than the separation, implied in the use of the term "sex" or "fear," of one emotion from another. Freud showed that in certain hysterical palsies and anaesthesiae the distributions corresponded to *ideas* of anatomical structure, rather than to the nerve distribution known to an anatomist. An anatomist can use the concept of a hand provided he does not allow his view of anatomical structures to be obscured by using it in investigations to which it is inappropriate. A patient says he feels fear but does not know of what he is afraid. We also suppose that man can feel fear but not sex. What is the model implicit in a statement

[1] See Chap. 4, p. 16 above.

that a man feels afraid, but does not know why? One possibility is that it is derived from the model of himself that the parents have presented him with. It would seem to suggest that "feeling afraid" and "knowing why," or "sex" and "fear" are different things. Correct treatment depends on the view we take of a patient who has lost all feeling "in his mind." By analogy it is important to know what the premises are on which we base a view that "sex" and "fear," or "feeling afraid" and "knowing why" differ. The supposition that pre-conception and premonition are to be distinguished in this universe of discourse and its implication that there is a similarity between the objects thus distinguished leads me to the point I wish to establish, namely that the categorization of ideational content that is facilitated by the grid is equally significant if it is applied to the emotional experience. For example we may regard the statement "I feel that you hate me" is significant for the idea it expresses. This idea can then be placed in one of the grid categories. Or we may regard the statement as significant for its expression of an emotion. The emotion (or pre-monition) can then be placed in one of the grid categories. The matter will be discussed more fully after we have considered the problem of "feelings" which is raised in Chapter 19.

CHAPTER SEVENTEEN

THE grid itself can obviously be categorized in accordance with its own categories. Thus the horizontal axis may be described as a series of definitions of various uses. In so far as it is employed to define the horizontal axis belongs to the categories of column 1. But as it is, its use could qualify it for inclusion in row F. But suppose it were desired to test out the value of some of the suggestions made in this book; in that case the horizontal axis might be regarded as a pre-conception to which one wished to find a matching realization. As the object of investigation it would fall in the category of a bound constant conjunction, a definitory hypothesis that stated that certain elements are constantly conjoined. As the object of further investigation it would then be treated in a manner intended to invest it with meaning or expose whatever meaning it might have.

As I have set it out in the grid the horizontal axis is represented by abstract signs, in a manner, as I said above, that can qualify it to belong to one of the categories of row F. But, following a suggestion implicit in the grid, I shall take the "uses" of the horizontal axis and substitute personifications, thus incidentally restating it in terms that would qualify it for categorization in row C.[1]

It might be convenient to substitute any sign or

[1] The preceding suggestions are examples of the use of the grid to choose a mode of employment for a concept. It contrasts with the use of the grid to find the category for a psycho-analytic object that has been employed already.

symbol that I chose, for example, the sign ψ for column 2. By proceeding in this way I can fill the line with signs and symbols that have meaning for me and thereby establish the basis for private communication, that is, for communication private to myself. Instead of the sign ψ I can use the sign "Smith" a man known to me who has a significance private to myself. Since however this discussion is intended to be public, I shall employ signs representing symbols that are public already and are consequently more likely to effect a public communication. This I can do by using elements in a myth familiar to the audience I hope to reach. It must be appropriate to the matter to be symbolized on the one hand and to culture of the group to which I want to address myself on the other. As this is addressed primarily to psycho-analysts I shall use the Oedipus myth, in the way indicated at the end of Chapter 15, the Jehovistic account (the second in Genesis) of the Creation and the account in Genesis XI of the building of the Tower and City of Babel. Both accounts are Jehovistic and anthropomorphic, the latter characteristic contributing to their value for this discussion.

Since I am using a myth as the course of my symbols the substitution is itself an artificial[1] use of row C elements rather than those of, say, G or H. I can choose characters to correspond to the separate columns 1, 2, 3, etc., or I can place the entire myth in each of the compartments C1, C2, C3, etc., or any single character, symbolizing 1–6 can be placed in *all* the columns 1–6 in row C. Thus Tiresias, symbolizing col. 2, may now appear in cols. 1, 3, 4, 5, 6. If it is used in column 2 it would represent a symbol representing an idea entertained for the purpose of denying the emergence of a more accurate but more frightening idea. In this

[1] See previous note.

instance it would represent the adherence to a myth of a repressing force, for use as a repressing force.

Since Tiresias is a symbol for the use represented by col. 2 it may seem that it would be shorter and simpler to say that any use represented in cols. 1–6 may be placed in any other column—and its own. But in fact this is not so: a use cannot act as a use; C2 cannot be meaningful placed in C2.[1] But a symbol representing a mode of thought, as "Tiresias" represents dream or myth or model, can, by being placed in column 2, represent a dream or mythological thought used to inhibit another mode of thought even though this other mode of thought is being used to inhibit. Thus a deductive system used to inhibit the emergence or other thoughts may itself be inhibited by a dream of mythological thought used for that purpose. Tiresias, or a corresponding private symbol, may be used to inhibit the use of a scientific theory to inhibit further thoughts. Stating this abstractly, in terms of the grid, C2 can be used to inhibit G2.

The reformulation of the uses to which thought can be put by the substitution of symbols drawn from myth has expressed the uses in terms that bring them into the category designated by row C. The new formulation should therefore make it possible to subject the reformulated statement to the treatment or process, whatever it is, that governs the transition of the elements in the vertical axis from one to the next below—a process I have described as one of growth, positive or negative. The uses, formulated in terms of myth, row C, may now be successively diminished in quality till they become analytical objects represented by the

[1] "C2" represents an abstract statement. But the category C2 is intended to contain dream thought not sophisticated statements. C2 in C2 would therefore mean either that C2 or what it represents was wrongly categorized, or, what comes to the same thing, C2 only appears to be a scientific concept but is a myth.

β-elements of row A, or be stimulated to grow so that they can be represented by signs appropriate to the elements of rows D, E, F, G and H.

The categorization from which we started, namely that expressed by the signs used to represent the uses to which a statement may be put (the numbers representing the columns) can itself be seen to belong to row G. The numbers are used purely as a means of notation. They can be seen therefore to be classifiable under column 3.

To substitute personifications as symbols for the "uses" could be described as effecting a transition in the vertical axis from below upwards—from row G to row C—a matter of manipulation of signs and topographical distribution in the grid.

If the total myth is placed in each of the compartments of row C, the compartments represent a primitive scientific instrument[1] for scanning the analytic material. It may itself be represented by F or G5 an instrument for a macroscopical view of the analytic material. If only one component of the myth is used, instead of the whole myth, the grid reading represents an instrument affording a more restricted view of the material—a view analogous to microscopic scrutiny. The movement → A diminishes sophistication of the component represented, but the movement → H increases it, the latter being approximate to a prelude to interpretation.

The grid as the representation of an instrument used by the analyst in scrutinizing the patient is equally a representation of the material produced by the patient as an instrument for scrutinizing the analyst. But if the analyst scrutinizes the material (the realization) to see in what grid category the representation

[1] Cf. Chap. 19. The use of the Oedipal myth as a pre-conception intended to mate with the parental realization to produce understanding of the parental relationship.

lies to which the realization approximates the grid is an instrument and not merely its representation.[1] The realization to which his attention (Col. 4) is directed is the reality of pre-conception and premonition.

So far I have been concerned with manipulations of signs in the grid. Is it possible to say that these manipulations correspond with the dynamics of the realizations represented by the readings in the grid? There is no difficulty in supposing that growth takes place but are the processes of growth, as deduced from observations in the consulting room, approximate to the rules of manipulation of the signs in the grid? The movements can be said to represent the results of growth or diminution—I am not discussing acquisition and denudation related to greed and envy—but for the present the actual manipulation of symbols must not be taken to represent growth or diminution itself. This matter can be reconsidered after discussing the vertical axis.

In the Jehovistic version of the creation a feature of the myth of the expulsion is the apparent conflict between the thirst for knowledge and the will of the deity. In the story of Babel, the god is also opposed to the will of the people; it appears to impinge on his right to occupy heaven undisturbed. The god in both is anthropomorphic in the manner typical of J sources. The Eden shows him opposed to eating that confers a knowledge of good and evil: the Babel myth shows him opposed to language because the common language confers on the people capacity to co-operate in building both a city and a tower, the latter facilitating entry into the god's heaven. The punishment in Eden is expulsion from the garden: in the Babel story the integrity of the language is destroyed, each fragment becoming a new language, confusion supervenes

[1] See Hanson, N. R.: *Patterns of Discovery*, p. 100, §5 (*d*).

and the differing language groups are scattered. The exile theme common to both stories is discernible in the exile of Oedipus. In all three sex is implied. Knowledge is related to eating in Eden and to morality in so far as it makes discrimination between good and evil possible. In Babel knowledge seems to be referable to scientific rather than to moral standards though the god's possession of heaven is a "moral" issue.

The elements in each of these three myths bear a resemblance to the elements of the other two; from them symbolic representations of oral sexuality and scattering, repressive super-ego, linkage through language, learning and self-knowledge, genital sexuality (e.g. tower and city) may be readily obtained. The difference in the apparent content is due to the form of narrative by which the elements are linked in each story. The relative importance of the elements will depend on the nature of the exploration for which they are used and the fact selected to bring coherence to the elements when they are re-integrated in the process of analysis. Re-integration is not something occurring once for all; throughout an analysis elements of the analytic material are seen by the analyst to be inappropriately assembled and a fresh integration and cohesion is made possible by the elucidation his interpretations afford. The selected fact that gives coherence, can be an idea or it may be an emotion. What emotions give rise to the patient's integrations and disintegrations must be deduced from inspection of the premonitions.

CHAPTER EIGHTEEN

THE vertical axis (A–H), related to a genetic rather than a systematic exposition, involves a premiss of growth dependent on (*a*) psycho-mechanics, (*b*) an alternation of particularization and generalization, (concretisation and abstraction), (*c*) successive saturations, and (*d*) emotional drives.

(*a*) The relationship between the mechanisms of projective identification and the alternation of paranoid-schizoid and depressive positions in K presents difficulties that seem due to an incompatibility. A solution may be approached through investigation clinically of the destructive splitting attacks that transform ♂ into fragments which nevertheless retain in their fragmented form an association with each other sufficient to permit *penetration* of a problem. Similar fragmentation of ♀ leaves an association of fragments that still perform the function of ingesting or introjecting. The objection to attributing priority to splitting lies in the fact that it does not allow primary quality to the alternation between paranoid-schizoid and depressive positions: yet both projective identification (♀♂) and paranoid-schizoid ↔ depressive positions must be regarded as potentially primary.

(*b*) The "alternation between particularization and abstraction" as a method of describing a theory is open to the objection that "abstraction" is a term that implies removal of a quality from something. The theory is more likely to match realizations if the *formulation* of an abstraction or generalization is seen to be the significant feature of the transaction and not extraction of qualities from a known representation or its corresponding realization. Generalization (or abstraction) must be recognized as a process by which the saturation of an unsaturated element is bound in order to consolidate the gain. The abstraction, or formulation, of a generalization consists in the naming[1] of a new entity. What has been regarded as a dynamic state in which elements of a realization are abstracted selectively to form an abstraction, generalization or, more abstractly still, an algebraic calculus, should be regarded as the mating of a pre-conception with a realization to form a conception and *thus* a reformulation: the reformulation is a *naming* of the total constellation of pre-conception and conception to prevent the loss of the experience by dispersion or disintegration of its components. The process known as abstraction is related to notation (as described by Freud) and an enlargement of memory. It is relevant here to consider in more detail the idea of growth positive and negative (Chap. 17, p. 5).

I introduce the idea of negative growth as a method of approaching an aspect of learning from experience; I do *not* mean denudation which I associate with hostile and destructive impulses such as envy. Denudation implies impoverishment of the personality. What I mean is exemplified by the restatement of the horizontal axis of the grid in mythological symbolism rather than in the terms appropriate to a deductive system (row C rather than row F or G). A capacity for negative growth is needed partly to revivify a formulation that has lost meaning, partly to establish a link in making

[1] Compare Condillac's theory that ideas become fixed by being associated with a sign or word: (Etienne Bonnet de Condillac. Essay on the origin of Human Knowledge): Hume on constant conjunction, and Freud on thinking "became endowed with further qualities which were perceptible to consciousness only through its connection with the memory traces of words." (Freud, S.: *Two Principles of Mental Functioning.* 1911.)

private knowledge public, but perhaps most important of all to achieve naivety of outlook when a problem is so overlaid by experience that its outlines have become blurred and its possible solutions obscure. One of the advantages of the grid is that its use in thinking about material that emerges in psycho-analytic practice stimulates reconsideration of familiar phenomena such as dreams or Oedipal material and their corresponding psycho-analytical theoretical formulations. The ability of an analyst to retain the substance of his training and experience and yet achieve a naïf view of his work allows him to discover for himself and in his own way the knowledge gained from his predecessors.

(*c*) The theory implicit in the representation of a pre-conception by a constant ψ together with an unsaturated element (ξ) has its convenience provided it is remembered that the sign ψ (ξ) is a representation of a complex realization. We do not know the nature of the process of saturation or how the extent of the suffusion of the psyche by the stimulus of a new experience is to be determined. I find it a useful representation till it can be discarded for a better.

(*d*) To what I have already said about emotional drives I add a reminder that the analyst's concern is with the premonitory aspects of these drives and that the political nature of the human being should be borne in mind in assessing the force and direction of these premonitions. The determining factors in even intimate manifestations of sex or aggression may lie outside the personality and within the group.[1]

A vertical axis related to a genetic exposition depends on a concept of growth; in the formulation of this axis I have been governed by the idea of pre-conception as central. Hitherto it has served to suppose that abstractions and generalizations are extracted or

[1] Freud, S.: *Instincts and their Vicissitudes.*

abstracted from an already existing concept.[1] With patients in whom disorders of thought are prominent this view of abstractions and generalization fails to explain the nature of his thoughts. The fault lies in the model implicit in the term "abstraction." The term I require must express in the domain of psycho-analysis what is expressed in mathematics when it is said that a formula, already discovered, has been, and may at some future date be, approximated to by a realization. This meaning is inherent in the term "pre-conception" as I wish to use it. It is the meaning I wish to express in terms such as "generalization" and "abstraction." The scientific deductive system (G) and the algebraic calculus (H) may also share the quality of a pre-conception; different terms in the vertical axis express differences in degrees of sophistication rather than differences in function. Stating the same thing in another way terms in the vertical axis vary but all have the same use whereas in the horizontal axis all terms are the same but the "uses" vary. The significance of the formulation I am putting forward lies in its use to establish the theory that any term such as "dog," "unconscious," "dream," "table," comes into existence when a set of phenomena are recognized as having a coherence of which the meaning is *unknown*.

An object is not perceived and given the name of "dog" because from the object perceived a quality of "dogginess" is abstracted. The term "dog" ("unconscious," "dream," "table," etc.) is used when and because a set of phenomena is recognized as being related yet *un*known. It is used to prevent the scattering of the phenomena. Having found the name, and thereby bound the phenomena, the remainder of history, if so wished, can be devoted to determining what it means —what a dog *is*; the name is an invention to make it

[1] See Chap. 1.

possible to think and talk about something before it is known what that something is. To postulate an α-element or α-function as I have done, is, according to this theory, merely a conscious sophisticated extension of normal spontaneous procedure that has always existed and is inherent in the development of language. The term "dog" or the term α-function comes into existence, the one spontaneously and unconsciously, the other by premeditation and contrivance, because phenomena are meaningless and need to be bound together so that they can be thought about. Once a name has been given and the scattering thereby prevented, meaning can begin to accumulate. How readily and spontaneously this can occur is illustrated by the observation[1] that attempts to contrive a term devoid of a distorting penumbra of associations is often defeated by the speed with which such a meaningless term collects a meaning. To sum up: the pre-conception awaits its realization to produce a conception: the term "dog" waits for a real dog to provide it with meaning. The algebraic calculus awaits a realization to approximate to it. In this way mathematicians who say mathematics have no meaning are justified. The mathematical formulae are analogous to pre-conceptions, as I use the term, and await a realization that approximates to them before they can be said to have meaning. The grid, as I have adumbrated it here, itself shares the qualities I attribute to the pre-conception.

It will be observed that this theory of the name as that which prevents scattering of phenomena so that they can function as a pre-conception, is at variance with the theory, that I have already used, that Euclidean geometry, for example, is abstracted from the realization of space and finds therefore its realiza-

[1] Popper, K. R.: *The Logic of Scientific Discovery*, Chap. II, 9 and 10.

tion in space. The theory of pre-conception I am putting forward requires a readjustment in our views about concretization, particularization and β-elements The term "pre-conception" is ambiguous because it denotes a tool, the function for which it exists and the use to which it may be put; the two last may of course be the same.

The genetic view of an abstraction differs from the conception of an abstraction as a representation of something that has been removed from something. A readjustment of our idea of the concrete is required. The term "dog" and all others terms apparently possessing a definite meaning must be seen to have no meaning until they acquire one through accretions of experience. A theory that such terms must be regarded as binding phenomena helps to dissipate contradictions inhering in the theory that an abstraction is something that has been removed from something else. Hume's postulation of constant conjunction is quite compatible with a theory that the term "dog" comes into existence in order to be a sign that certain discrete and previously incoherent phenomena are constantly conjoined. There is no difficulty if this fact is kept clearly separated from any idea that the term implies that the constantly conjoined elements have any meaning other than that the elements are constantly conjoined. The genesis of the term "dog" is thus adequately accounted for as a product of the PS $\leftrightarrow$ Dep mechanism. But only after the term "dog" has served to signalize and perpetuate the conjunction does the question of meaning arise. It might be stated thus: "These phenomena are constantly conjoined. I record this fact and bind the phenomena to each other so that they shall remain constantly conjoined by the sign 'dog.' Now that I have bound the phenomena I can try to find out what their constant conjunction means. Thus we shall arrive at the *meaning* of the term 'dog'."

The mechanism ♀♂ comes into play and the product of its operation is meaning.

The nature of the relationship between PS ↔ Dep and ♀♂ thus receives some clarification. On the PS ↔ Dep operation depends the delineation of the whole object: on the successful operation of ♀♂ depends the meaning of the whole object.

CHAPTER NINETEEN

The choice of axes may appear arbitrary without further reasons; it stems from the analytic situation itself.

The patient's activity most in evidence in an analysis is thinking. The analyst can see the use he makes of the analytic situation. He may appeal for help, exploit the possibilities of cruelty to the analyst, seek an outlet for love and generosity and so on. This he does by thinking silently, talking to the analyst, thinking aloud and occasionally by action. He makes statements classifiable under the headings of the vertical axis A–H. The information available for communication is selected, withheld, or expressed according to the use to which he wishes to put it. Since this is so the significance of the content of the communication can be assessed from the use, only *one* of the features of the patient's contribution, but it is a feature that is most continuously significant and is therefore worthy of attention, isolation and elevation as the 1–6 axis of the grid.

Since self-knowledge is an aim of psycho-analytic procedure the equipment for attaining knowledge, the function and apparatus of pre-conception, must be correspondingly important. Growth and a capacity for growth are equally fundamental. The vertical axis (A–H) represents both the stages of growth and the function of pre-conception.

Representation of a process, such as growth continuing, by the headings A–H gives a misleading impression of discrete, clear-cut entities; transition from one to another must be assumed, for lack of evidence, probably to be gradual.

Choice of the Oedipus myth as a reservoir on which to draw for symbols to replace the horizontal axis (1–6) enables me to illustrate a feature of the myth as a pre-conception. The Oedipus myth may be regarded as an instrument that served Freud in his discovery of psycho-analysis and psycho-analysis as an instrument that enabled Freud to discover the Oedipus complex. I turn now to the part played by the myth, or its counterparts in α- and β-elements, in the growth of the psyche.

The myth may be regarded as a primitive form of pre-conception and a stage in publication, that is, in communication of the individual's private knowledge to his group. Any scientific theory must ultimately be represented by a medium that facilitates publication. The processes by which private knowledge is communicated within the individual is obscure and elucidation waits on advances that psycho-analysts have yet to make. The dream has fresh significance if it is regarded as a private myth. Oedipal material in a dream requires the accepted classical theory that it displays the Oedipus situation as yielded up by the unconscious under the impact of the analytical investigation, but in certain cases this material must also be regarded as evidence of a primitive mechanism of pre-conception, a private version of what later becomes publicly communicable through its correspondence with the Oedipal myth. When the issue is capacity for thought the same is true of the Eden and Babel myths. Analysts need accordingly to consider that the Oedipal material may possibly be evidence for primitive apparatus of pre-conception and therefore possessing a significance additional to its significance in classical theory. I am postulating a precursor of the Oedipal situation not in the sense that such a term might have in Melanie Klein's discussion of *Early Phases of the Oedipus Complex*, but as something that belongs to the ego as part of its apparatus for contact with reality. In short I postulate an α-element version of a private Oedipus myth which is the means, the pre-conception, by virtue of which the infant is able to establish contact with the parents as they exist in the world of reality. The mating of this α-element Oedipal pre-conception with the realization of the actual parents gives rise to the conception of parents.

If, through envy, greed, sadism or other cause, the infant cannot tolerate the parental relationship and attacks it destructively, according to Melanie Klein the attacking personality is itself fragmented through the violence of the splitting attacks. Restating this theory in terms of the Oedipal pre-conception: the emotional load carried by the private α-element Oedipal pre-conception is such that the Oedipal pre-conception is itself destroyed. As a result the infant loses the apparatus essential for gaining a conception of the parental relationship and consequently for resolution of Oedipal problems: it does not fail to solve those problems—it never reaches them.

The significance of this for practice is that scraps of what appear to be Oedipal material must be treated with reserve. If the evidence is related to a disaster to the ego, the destruction of the pre-conception and consequently of the ability to pre-conceive, interpretations based on the supposition that fragmental Oedipal material is evidence of a destroyed object will be only partly successful. The investigation must be directed to distinguishing amongst the elements of Oedipal material those that are fragments of Oedipal pre-conception from those that are fragments of the fragmented Oedipal situation. Since the experience of learning from which the patient is thus debarred is that of the parental relationship, the importance for the patient's development and for a successful outcome of analysis, depending on resolution of the Oedipus complex, are gravely prejudiced.

I must leave the development of this theme for future treatment when I hope to show in greater detail the manner of using the grid for penetrating to a clearer perception and understanding of clinical material. The nature of the elements is determined by their position relative to the two axes (1–6) and (A–H).

What might be called the psycho-mechanics of thinking, represented by the interplay between ♀ and ♂ and between paranoid-schizoid and depressive positions (PS ↔ Dep and the selected fact) provides the link between row and row.

At the beginning of this chapter brief reasons were given for the choice of "uses" for the axis 1–6. In the genetic axis the psycho-mechanisms represented by PS ↔ D and ♀♂ were accorded an importance that requires further discussion. At the end of Chapter 18 I said that when hitherto unrelated elements were discovered, by the operation of PS ↔ D, to be coherent their relatedness was fixed by nomination. The name had a function, analogous to that of the mathematical formulation, in fixing the constant conjunction that it represented. In this respect the fixing of the cohering elements is identical with the mating of preconception with realization to produce a conception. We must now consider the process by which the name accumulates meaning through the operation of ♀♂.

I have discussed the part played in the understanding of thinking by the model of the alimentary canal. Detailed discussion of the mechanisms and dynamics involved in the growth of meaning is helped by introducing a shift of emphasis in our scrutiny of the phenomena represented by the vertical (A–H) axis of the grid. I shall represent this shift of emphasis by using the term "feeling" instead of the term "thinking". This substitution is based on the common usage, in analytic practice, of phrases such as "I feel I had a dream last night," or, "I feel you hate me," or "I feel that I am going to have a breakdown." Such locutions imply an emotional experience and are therefore more appropriate to my purpose than the more austere implication of "I think . . ." Communications introduced by terms such as "I feel . . . ." are often methods of expressing emotions or premonitions. It is in their function as expressions of emotion that I wish to consider these phenomena. I propose to leave the grid unaltered; the categories represented by the co-ordinates of the grid apply equally to classes of "I think . . ." and "thoughts" as to classes of "I feel . . ." and "feelings." In order to indicate emphasis of the emotional content I shall speak of "feeling" rather than "thinking," but the grid remains unchanged for the categorization of "thoughts" or "feelings."

Regarding the statements whose development is represented by the vertical (A–H) axis as expressions of feeling, the mechanism ♀♂ by which change from one row of the grid to another is effected, may be represented by models other than that provided by the digestive tract. Of these the most suggestive are (1) the respiratory system, with which is linked the olfactory system; (2) the auditory system with which is linked transformations such as music ↔ noise, and (3) the visual system. Each of the three provide models for the mechanism ♀♂ representing projective identification as employed for purposes of K. The sense of touch is usually employed as an antidote to the confusion that can be incidental to the employment of ♀♂. Its use to establish the reassurance obtained from feeling there is a barrier between two objects, a limiting boundary that is absent in the container ↔ contained relationship characteristic of models (1), (2) and (3), produces the paradoxical effect that the topographically closer relationship implied by tactile contact is *less* intimate, i.e. confused, than the more distant relationship implied by the models (1), (2) and (3).[1] It is worth noting that clinical manifestations of asthma become psycho-analytically more meaningful if their relationship to the respiratory model for thinking-feeling is recognized.

Views of thinking and feeling, stated in terms appropriate to row G, can be restated, by use of these models of digestive tract, respiratory system, auditory system and visual system in terms appropriate to row C and vice versa.

The mechanism PS ↔ D allied with the mechanism ♀♂ is thus responsible for growth of pre-conception either in the direction of naivety or of sophistication.

Since we can use the grid categories to represent feelings much will depend on the analytic context in which statements are made. The analyst must decide whether the idea that is expressed is intended to be an instrument whereby feelings are communicated or whether the feelings are secondary to the idea. Many subtle expressions of feeling can be missed if the ideas by which they are expressed are regarded, wrongly, to be the main burden of the communication. The facility with which subtle shades of feeling can be expressed makes the communication of what appear to be ideas an ideal vehicle for the communication of premonitions; the "ideas" should be scrutinized accordingly.

[1] A psychotic patient can have genital intercourse without confusion but will become seriously confused by (1), (2) and (3).

If the grid categories are as appropriate to "feelings" as "ideas" there should be an emotional counterpart of β-elements. In the limited field to which I have restricted them hitherto I have suggested that the term "β-elements" should be used to cover the area of phenomena such as the "thoughts" that some psychotic patients regard as indistinguishable from "things." In the domain of feelings and those aspects of thought in which feelings are dominant the term "β-elements" should be extended to cover the analogous phenomena. I am not sure what these analogous phenomena, if any, are. But the same patients who regard "thoughts" as "things" show every sign of regarding what I am used psycho-analytically to believe are phantasies as "facts." I therefore suggest provisionally that the β-element categories of the grid should not be dismissed off-hand as non-existent, but should be thought of, in the domain of expressions of feeling, as related to phantasies that are felt to be indistinguishable from facts. These phantasies that are indistinguishable from facts must be considered as the emotional counterpart of β-element "thoughts" that are indistinguishable from "things." In other words the β-element categories of the grid should be regarded as representations to which some realization, discovered psycho-analytically, may be found to approximate.

CHAPTER TWENTY

Before I summarize the main themes of this book I must make it clear that the grid, though genetically related to a number of analytic theories, differs from the object which the term "theory" is usually taken to represent. Its nature is better indicated by describing it as a convention for construing psycho-analytical phenomena.[1] But if an analyst uses this convention he entertains a pre-conception of which the grid, as printed or written, is a representation. Thus the analyst's state of mind, which is approximating to the representation, the grid as printed or written, can be classified under one of the grid categories according to the use to which it is being put and the position it occupies in the genetic development of the analyst's scientific equipment. Since the grid and the associated theories may be used for whatever motives the analyst chooses it can be used to keep knowledge at bay (column 2) as well as to further it (cols. 1, 3, 4, 5, etc.). Equally, since use of the grid means that the analyst entertains a preconception, it is possible that his use of it can be categorized more precisely if we employ the vertical axis for this purpose and see the appropriate grid category in row D. If, therefore, the reader does not wish his state of mind to be disturbed he will either not use the grid or employ it as a means of expressing feelings and thoughts that can be represented by D2. If on the contrary he is disposed to employ the grid for further investigation he will be employing it as a means

[1] But note the discussion at beginning of Chap. 17.

of expressing feelings and thoughts that can be represented by D (or, according to the degree of sophistication he brings to bear, F (or G)4.

I am aware that the grid not only can be but requires to be improved. I have felt that col. 2 might be replaced by a negative sense to the horizontal axis. It is plausible and would conform to a pleasing similarity with the system of cartesian co-ordinates as used in the development of algebraic geometry. Furthermore, it would simplify some difficulties if, instead of the present arrangement, the horizontal axis read

$$-(n), -(n-1) \ldots -5, -4, -3, -2, -1, \\ 1, 2, 3, 4, 5, \ldots (n-1)\ (n)$$

with the 2 column standing for what is, in the present grid, column 3. Then one might say that all the "uses" $1 \leftrightarrow n$ can be used negatively, as a barrier against the unknown or known but disliked. But I am primarily concerned to sketch out the uses to which the phenomena represented by the vertical axis are put and not to embark on the complexities of the "uses" to which "uses" may be put, regarding the latter as an extension best left to clinical investigation.

I turn now to uses of the grid. The summary is not intended to be exhaustive.

A. Meditative Review. 1. Suppose that at the end of the day's work the analyst wishes to review some aspect of his work about which he is doubtful. Assume further that the preoccupation centres on some phrase of the patient's. Recalling the session, the context of the statement, the patient's intonation, the analyst can place the statement in a category which, in the light of after knowledge, he thinks is correct. Such meditation is related to notation and memory. It is akin to recording what took place and is an example of using the grid and the theories it represents for the purposes of notation. Even if he does not commit his work to paper the analyst is doing something that will stamp the episode in his memory.

2. The analyst may place it speculatively in any grid category he chooses. He can then give direction to his speculations by considering what the implications would be if in fact the statement belonged to the category in which he had provisionally and speculatively placed it. This means that he has "bound" a number of elements and can proceed to discover the meaning of their supposed conjunction. The grid assists in giving direction to his speculations.

3. In the course of 1 and 2 he will be considering the possibility of other categories in which the statement might with propriety have been placed. Such activity is a stimulant to the analyst's capacity for attention.

4. The analyst can scrutinize his interpretations by subjecting them to the same procedure as that to which he has submitted the patient's associations in 1, 3, and 4.

5. The analyst can place the association and its actual, or proposed interpretation, in the appropriate categories and thus examine the *couple*, association and interpretation. Thus he can compare and examine the relationship not of the association to the interpretation but of the category of the association to the category of the interpretation. Thus a basis can be provided for investigation of the developmental value of interpretation and association according to the nature of the relationship of their categories.

6. The analyst can take conflicting statements in the patient's associations, place them according to their respective grid categories, and then scrutinize the nature of the conflict by a comparison of the *categories* of the conflicting statements. It should then be

possible to see what is contributed to conflict by the nature of the categories of the conflicting statements.

B. The psycho-analytic game. In A I have proposed uses for the grid closely associated with actual analytic experiences. The grid may, however, be profitably used in a kind of analytic make-believe in which the experiential element is far less dominant. Such an imaginative exercise is closer to the activity of the musician who practises scales and exercises, not directly related to any piece of music but to the *elements* of which any piece of music is composed. This brings me back to the elements of psycho-analysis and their elucidation. I define the elements of psycho-analysis as being those phenomena whose various aspects can be seen to fall within the grid categories even though some categories must for the time being remain empty. Such phenomena are—

(*a*) Ideas as described in Chapters 1–18.

(*b*) Feelings as described in Chapter 19, including pain.

(*c*) Association and Interpretation.

(*d*) The couple (association and interpretation).

(*e*) Conflicting pairs (I use the term "pair" so as to leave the term "couple" free for the phenomena of (*d*) above).

(*f*) The two axes of the grid (as special cases).

In Chapter 3 I suggested that the psycho-analytic object had three "dimensions," sensa, mythology and analytic theory. Translating this into terms of grid categories any analytic object before qualifying as such must display features categorized in rows B, C and G. An analytic object is not the same as an element but may be regarded as having a relationship with an element analogous to that of a molecule to an atom. The analytic object is not necessarily an interpretation though an interpretation is an analytic object. An interpretation must be based on evidence of analytic objects and is itself an analytic object composed of analytic objects. The analytic object emerges as a result of the operation in the observer of PS ↔ D and ♀♂. To the analytic observer the material must appear as a number of discrete particles unrelated and incoherent (PS ↔ D). The patient may be describing a dream, followed by a memory of an incident that occurred on the previous day, followed by an account of some difficulty in his parents' family. The recital may take three or four minutes or longer. The coherence that these facts have in the patient's mind is not relevant to the analyst's problem. His problem—I describe it in stages—is to ignore that coherence so that he is confronted by the incoherence and experiences incomprehension of what is presented to him. His own analysis should have made it possible for him to tolerate this emotional experience though it involves feelings of doubt and perhaps even persecution. This state must endure, possibly for a short period but probably longer, until a new coherence emerges; at this point he has reached → D, the stage analogous to nomination or "binding" as I have described it. From this point his own processes can be represented by ♀♂—the development of meaning. It has been necessary to give this somewhat schematic description of the analyst's mental working to introduce a discussion of certain apparent anomalies to which I now turn. I shall take the statement I made (Chap. 17) that the whole Oedipus myth could be placed in a single category, or, alternatively, that parts of the myth could occupy a single compartment in the grid. It may seem that this is not compatible with the distinction I have made between a psycho-analytic object and an element of psycho-analysis. The anomaly disappears however if it is appreciated that, in the context in which the myth is mentioned, it is the shortest and most compact representation that can be devised to express, say, a sense of foreboding of a particular quality. In this instance the importance of the myth lies in the fact that it represents a feeling and as such its place in a grid category denotes a psycho-analytic element. Taken with other similar psycho-analytic elements it and the other elements together form the field of incoherent elements in which it is hoped that the selected fact, that gives coherence and relatedness to the hitherto incoherent and unrelated, will emerge. Thus "nominated," "bound," the psycho-analytic object has emerged. It remains to discern its meaning. This verbally same myth may then be a psycho-analytic object which is instrumental in giving meaning to the totality of elements, one of which was the feeling represented by the myth in its grid category. Correct interpretation therefore will depend on the analyst's being able, by virtue of the grid, to observe that two statements verbally identical are psycho-analytically different. To reiterate, a verbal statement observed to have aspects falling in rows B, C and G represents a psycho-analytic object. A verbally identical statement seen to fall in, say, D2 is a psycho-analytic element. In the example I have taken the myth in category D2 represents a *feeling* of foreboding and is a premonition of a particular kind employed to exclude something else. (Incidentally the whole of the preceding discussion can be taken as an example of the use of the grid for an exercise designed to develop intuition and the capacity for clinical discrimination.) To conclude: the *elements* of psycho-analysis are ideas and feelings as represented by their setting in a *single* grid-category; psycho-analytic objects are associations and interpretations with extensions in the domain of sense, myth and passion (*see* Chap. 3), requiring three grid categories for their representation. It follows that the classes a-f above are only elements if they fall in one grid-category only. The practical significance of this is that if they are elements, despite any appearance to the contrary, it is necessary to know of what psycho-analytic object they are a part.

INDEX

TRANSFORMATIONS

Ay, in the catalogue ye go for men,
As hounds and greyhounds, mongrels, spaniels, curs,
Shoughs, water-rugs, and demi-wolves are clipt
All by the name of dogs.

—Shakespeare, *Macbeth*

ACKNOWLEDGMENTS

AGAIN it is a pleasure to me to acknowledge help and criticism of this book from a number of colleagues and friends who have read it in proof.

Professor Elliott Jaques, Miss Betty Joseph, Mr. Money-Kyrle and Dr. H. Segal have all helped with advice and criticism. I am also indebted to Dr. J. O. Wisdom for many helpful criticisms of my previous work, and in particular of *Learning from Experience*, which have made me more aware of the pitfalls in this one. But whether I have avoided them is another matter. I would thank them all, but would not have them debited with my faults.

As always there remains my debt to my wife which I can acknowledge but cannot repay.

W. R. B.

INTRODUCTION

I had hoped to write this book so that it could be read independently of *Learning from Experience* and *Elements of Psycho-Analysis*, but I soon found this impossible without an intolerable degree of repetition.

The other two books are therefore still necessary for the understanding of this one. I regret this; there are some things I said before which I would now say differently. But any reader who thinks the subject is as important as I do will find it rewarding if he can think the thought through despite defects of presentation.

W. R. B.

CHAPTER ONE

SUPPOSE a painter sees a path through a field sown with poppies and paints it: at one end of the chain of events is the field of poppies, at the other a canvas with pigment disposed on its surface. We can recognize that the latter represents the former, so I shall suppose that despite the differences between a field of poppies and a piece of canvas, despite the transformation that the artist has effected in what he saw to make it take the form of a picture, *something* has remained unaltered and on this *something* recognition depends. The elements that go to make up the unaltered aspect of the transformation I shall call invariants.

The artist is not the only person involved in looking at a picture; recognition of what the picture represents could not occur if the observer were to rely exclusively on his sense of smell. The wider his experience of art the more likely he would be to interpret the painting correctly.

In many pictures the effectiveness of the representation would depend on perspective. A peculiar feature of this domain is that a completely circular pond, for example, might be represented by an ellipse, or a path with borders running parallel to each other might be represented by two lines that meet. Indeed the representation of pond or path would be less adequate if it were a circle or parallel lines. Accordingly we assume that in ellipse and intersecting lines, circular pond and parallel borders, is some quality that is invariant under artistic creation.

Suppose now that we view a stretch of railway line that is straight as far as the eye can see. The two lines of the track will be seen to converge. We know that if we were to test the convergence by walking up the line this convergence would not be confirmed; but, if we were to walk far enough and to look back the way we had come, the convergence would appear to lie behind us and to be confirmed by our sense of sight; the two parallel lines meet in a point. Where then is this point?

One theory would explain the apparent meeting as an optical illusion. I propose not to accept this explanation, for in a domain in which the sense of sight only is employed correlations based on common sense[1] are not available; furthermore, the explanation, though valid in its sphere, does not promote development in the domain of this investigation.

In Euclidean geometry definitions of terms such as "point", "straight line" and "circle" are so closely wedded to marks on paper and similar realizations that these definitions, which are really suggestive descriptions, serve well enough. But points and straight lines as defined in Euclidean geometry are not things-in-themselves. The mathematician has found that the extensions which his subject demands are not served by these definitions. The point and straight line have to be described by the totality of *relationships* which these objects have to other objects.[2] I shall leave on one side the problem of the extent to which the totality of relationships can be either explored or ignored.[3] The mathematician can investigate invariants common to circular object and ellipse, that represents it, by algebraic projective geometry. In his investigations statements about length, angles or congruence cannot find a place in the theorems of projective geometry, though they are a part of Euclidean geometry; therefore psycho-analysts need not be dismayed if it can be shown that there is no place in their theories for measurement and other entities that are a commonplace of disciplines accepted as scientific. Just as there are geometrical properties invariant under projection, and others that are not, so there are properties that are invariant under psycho-analysis and others that are not. The task is to find what are the invariants under psycho-analysis and what the nature of their relationship to one another.

What is the relationship of the point at which parallel

[1] See Bion, W. R.: *Learning from Experience*, in which I discuss the use of the term "common sense".

[2] The definitions of such commonplace physical substances as zinc are summaries of relationships, described as "properties".

[3] Heisenberg, W.: *Physics and Philosophy*, p. 82.

lines meet to the points at which lines that are not parallel meet? The railway lines of my example can be seen to meet; the surveyor would not confirm the finding and nor would the neurologist. Though this problem is not of consequence to the psycho-analyst it may resemble problems which are. To them I shall now turn.

In his paper, "Fragment of an Analysis of a Case of Hysteria" (1905),[1] Freud gives a description of a patient Dora. The paper may be regarded as analogous to, but differing from, a painting, in that it is a verbal representation of an analysis; we can gain an impression of the experience as we can gain an impression of a field of poppies though the original field of poppies or the original analysis are unknown to us. There must then be something in the verbal description of the analysis that is invariant. Before the invariants in the printed description can be effective certain precedent conditions must exist; the layman must be literate: the invariants in Freud's description I shall accordingly describe as "invariant under literacy."

Not all laymen would understand the same thing from the printed description; "invariance under literacy" therefore is not an adequate limitation. We must therefore consider briefly some of the problems that are involved in establishing the limitations of the field. We are introduced to some of these problems in Freud's Prefatory Remarks to this paper; he points out that it can be read as a *roman à clef* designed for private delectation. The understanding of such a reader will depend on invariants under prurience and is not what Freud intends to bestow on his reader. He indicates this by his reference to the *Studies in Hysteria* and subsequent developments of psycho-analytic technique; invariants under pornographic literature[2] are not invariants under psycho-analysis. To use the visual arts to provide an analogy, invariants in photography are not the same as invariants in impressionist painting.

For my purpose it is convenient to regard psycho-analysis

[1] Freud, S.: "Fragment of an Analysis of a Case of Hysteria" (1905), Standard Edition, Vol. VII.

[2] See Freud, S.: Prefatory Remarks to "Fragment of an Analysis. . . ."

as belonging to the group of transformations. The original experience, the realization, in the instance of the painter the subject that he paints, and in the instance of the psycho-analyst the experience of analysing his patient, are *transformed* by painting in the one and analysis in the other into a painting and a psycho-analytic description respectively. The psycho-analytic interpretation given in the course of an analysis can be seen to belong to this same group of transformations. An interpretation is a transformation; to display the invariants, an experience, felt and described in one way, is described in another.

Freud's reference to developments that had taken place in psycho-analytic technique indicates one direction in which this inquiry must be pursued. Since psycho-analysis will continue to develop we cannot speak of invariants under psycho-analysis as if psycho-analysis were a static condition. In practice it is undesirable to discard established theories because they seem to be inadequate to particular contingencies; such a procedure would exacerbate a tendency to the facile elaboration of *ad hoc* theories at times when it were better to adhere to established discipline. It is therefore advisable to preserve a conservative attitude to widely-accepted theories even when it has become clear that some adjustment needs to be made. For my present purpose it is helpful to regard psycho-analytical theories as belonging to the category of groups of transformations, a technique analogous to that of a painter, by which the facts of an analytic experience (the realization) are transformed into an interpretation (the representation). Any interpretation belongs to the class of statements embodying invariants under one particular psycho-analytic theory; thus an interpretation could be comprehensible because of its embodiment of "invariants under the theory of the Oedipus situation."

The advantage of classifying psycho-analytic theories as members of groups of transformations will be discussed later,[1] but I shall anticipate some of the main considerations here. The painter by virtue of his artistic capacity is able to

[1] See Chapter 2.

transform a landscape (the realization) into a painting (the representation). He does so by virtue of invariants that make his representation comprehensible. The invariants depend on the technique he employs: thus the invariants in an impressionist painting are not the invariants of a painting by a member of, say, a realist school of painting. Similarly, the invariants in a description of a family situation by a layman will not be the same as they are in a description of the same family situation by a psycho-analyst using oedipal theory. The various psycho-analytic theories enable the psycho-analyst to effect similar transformations. Analytic theories, or groups of theories, can be combined to transform the realization into a representation or series of related representations (interpretations). The analytic theories thus associated may then be classified by their association with the type of transformation (and its associated invariants). The type of transformation will depend on the analyst and his assessment of the demands of the clinical situation. Thus an analyst may employ theories of splitting and the oedipal theory to effect a transformation such that the invariants ensure understanding in his patient. His theories, transformation (or group of theories) and interpretation (or group of interpretations) will be analogous to the artist's techniques, transformation and end-product. Just as impressionism can be regarded as a method of transforming landscape into a painting, so the grouped analytic techniques are part of transformation of analytic experiences into interpretation. As the painter's transformations vary according to the understanding his painting is to convey, so the analyst's transformation will vary according to the understanding he wishes to convey. Kleinian transformation, associated with certain Kleinian theories, would have different invariants from the invariants in a classical Freudian[1] transformation. Since the invariants would be different so the meaning conveyed would be different even if the material transformed (the analytic experience or realization) could be conceived

[1] In practice I should deplore the use of terms such as "Kleinian transformation", or "Freudian transformation". They are used here only to simplify exposition.

of as being the same in both instances. Similarly the painting of the same scene by a realist and an impressionist would convey different meanings. Further particularization is achieved, for one Kleinian analyst's transformation and therefore interpretation would differ from another's. Nor would the interpretations by two impressionist painters be alike though both painters could be recognized as belonging to the same school (of transformation). For the problems of diagnosis the approach I am making may have value in that clinical entities might be defined and classified according to the transformation[1] (I refer now to the method and its component theories) and invariants employed.

Throughout this book I suggest a method of critical approach to psycho-analytic practice and not new psycho-analytical theories. By analogy with the artist and the mathematician I propose that the work of the psycho-analyst should be regarded as transformation of a realization (the actual psycho-analytic experience) into an interpretation or series of interpretations. Two concepts have been introduced, transformation and invariance. The book will be devoted to these concepts and their application to the problems of psycho-analytical practice. I use borrowed philosophical and other terms for psycho-analytical purposes because the meaning with which they are already invested comes near to the meaning I seek to convey. When I write "transformation" or "invariance" I leave it to be understood that I am discussing psycho-analysis. What I mean by these terms will, I hope, become clearer as I use them.

Psychotic mechanisms appear in the course of a psycho-analytically controlled breakdown, but the analyst may be called upon to deal with them after such a breakdown has occurred, or, because something has happened, despite the work of the analyst, to precipitate such a breakdown during analysis. I discuss the latter contingency because the material illuminates transformation and invariance as a function of patient and analyst. The clinical description is designed for reasons of discretion to be impossible to apply

[1] Transformation is discussed in detail later. See Chapter 2.

to any one of whom I have heard, but the reader will not be misled if he treats it as true.

The man[1] could be regarded, in view of the predominance of psychotic mechanisms and bizarre behaviour, as a borderline psychotic. Analysis seems to proceed slowly and there may be little evidence open to observers or members of the family that his behaviour is different from what it has been.

Then a change: friends or relations who have been denying that there is anything the matter cannot ignore his illness. He has been strange: he spends hours seated morosely in a chair; he appears to be hearing voices and seeing things. On this latter point there is some doubt; in the consulting room it is difficult to say if the patient is describing a delusion or indulging his fancy. In analysis he is hostile and confused. There is sudden deterioration. The alarm of relatives is evident in letters and other communications from them or the family doctor. There appears to be reason for the analyst to be alarmed, or, if he is not, to lay himself open to grave miscalculation and consequent blame.

In such a situation the common view is so pervasive that it is difficult to suppose that the analyst's anxieties and those of the relatives could be regarded profitably as anything other than rational and appropriate to the facts. Preservation of an analytic view, of what is taking place, is made difficult because it can fit so easily into a pattern of denial, by the analyst, of the seriousness of his predicament. In such a situation the analyst will take such steps as his experience in the management of analytic cases dictates. He will try to assess the contribution that his own psychopathology may be making. I mention these points without discussion save for their bearing on transformation and invariance. In the material I wish to include the analyst's anxieties and, in so far as he has access to them, those of the patient's relatives and friends. The analyst's main concern must be with the material of which he has direct evidence, namely, the emotional experience of the analytic sessions themselves. It is in his approach to this that the concepts of transformation and invariance can play an illuminating role.

Change from an analytical experience, confined to the

[1] Later referred to as A.

consulting room, to a crisis that involves more people than the pair is remarkable for a number of features. It is catastrophic in the restricted sense of an event producing a subversion of the order or system of things; it is catastrophic in the sense that it is accompanied by feelings of disaster in the participants; it is catastrophic in the sense that it is sudden and violent in an almost physical way. This last will depend on the degree to which analytical procedure has produced a *controlled* breakdown. Since, for the purposes of this description, it is easier to deal with phenomena whose characteristics are exaggerated I shall rely on the description of events pertaining to the less analytically controlled episode. It must be borne in mind, however, that the analytically controlled event is more difficult to deal with in that the reactions being more restrained the elements in the situation are correspondingly unobtrusive and difficult to detect. Furthermore, in the analytically controlled event the catastrophic elements bear the same relationships to other elements as katabolic features bear to anabolic features in metabolism. I shall therefore ignore complications which I do not for the present wish to introduce.

To return to my illustration: there are three features to which I wish to draw attention: subversion of the system, invariance, and violence. Analysis in the pre-catastrophic stage is to be distinguished from the post-catastrophic stage by the following superficial characteristics: it is unemotional, theoretical, and devoid of any marked outward change. Hypochondriachal symptoms are prominent. The material lends itself to interpretations based on Kleinian theories of projective identification and internal and external objects. Violence is confined to phenomena experienced by psychoanalytical insight: it is, as it were, *theoretical* violence. The patient talks as if his behaviour, outwardly amenable, was causing great destruction because of its violence. The analyst gives interpretations, when they appear to be appropriate to the material, drawing attention to the features that are supposed by the patient to be violent.

In the post-catastrophic stage, by contrast, the violence is patent, but the ideational counterpart, previously evident, appears to be lacking. Emotion is obvious and is aroused in the analyst. Hypochondriachal elements are less obtrusive. The emotional experience does not have to be conjectured because it is apparent.

In this situation the analyst must search the material for invariants to the pre- and post-catastrophic stages. These will be found in the domain represented by the theories of projective identification, internal and external objects. Restating this in terms of clinical material, he must see, and demonstrate, that certain apparently external emotionally-charged events are in fact the same events as those which appeared in the pre-catastrophic stage under the names, bestowed by the patient, of pains in the knee, legs, abdomen, ears, etc., and, by the analyst, of internal objects. In brief, what present themselves to the outward sense of analyst and patient as anxious relatives, impending law-suits, mental hospitals, certification, and other contingencies apparently appropriate to the change in circumstances, are really hypochondriachal pains and other evidences of internal objects in a guise appropriate to their new status as external objects. These then are the invariants or the objects in which invariance is to be detected. I shall turn now to the relationship of violence to the change that has taken place from pre- to post-catastrophic.

The change is violent change and the new phase is one in which violent feelings are violently expressed. By analogy with an explosion, the patient's state of violent emotion sets up reactions in the analyst and others related to the patient in such a way that they also tend to be dominated by their over-stimulated internal objects thus producing a wide externalization of internal objects.[1] In practice in the pre-catastrophic stage, the violence of the emotions has to be deduced and this is true even of the post-catastrophic stage if the breakdown is analytically controlled. Though adequate as a theory there is advantage in using an explosion and its expanding pressure-waves as a model. I shall do so.

The catastrophic event may be described in terms of the

[1] Contrast with this state—shock, the seeping away of sanity into his own "mental tissues."

theory of transformations: this involves regarding the transformation, implied by employing the theory of transformations, as itself belonging to the group of transformations. That is to say that I transform the *facts* I describe by regarding them in a particular way. My description is therefore a transformation, analogous to the artist's painting that is a product of the particular artist's approach. For convenience I shall call my approach here transformation 'A.' Within this usage I have used the term "transformation" in three ways that need to be distinguished from each other: the term "transformation" related to (i) the total operation which includes the act of transforming and the end product: for this I shall use the sign T; (ii) the process of transformation: sign $T\alpha$; and (iii) the end product: sign $T\beta$.

Further distinctions are needed to minimize ambiguity. In my illustration it is possible that we shall need to discuss the lay point of view, such as that involved in concluding that the patient is not simply a normal person being difficult, but that he is mentally disturbed. Evidently the final opinion ($T\beta$) will not be the same when the facts are viewed in the light of a belief that the patient is normal as it is when the belief is that the patient is mentally disturbed. If discussion of the lay point of view is necessary we shall need to distinguish T still further; for example, by a sign T (lay) or a sign T (lay: normal) or T (lay: mental). To illustrate this notation: if we wish to categorize the description given by relatives who think that the patient has gone mad, it is first necessary to categorize the transformation (T). In this instance it would be: T (lay: mental). This however by itself could mean all of three things: (i) the relatives' point of view, (ii) the particular processes of thought leading to the description, and (iii) the description itself. Since we are concerned only to employ a sign for the last of these, the full sign would be: T (lay) β.

In general it may be said that the cultural background against which analytic work must be done is hardly a matter with which the individual analyst can concern himself; yet the culture may concern him. In the exceptional case, notably Freud himself, psycho-analytic work has profoundly affected the social outlook. Therefore it is a matter of importance to analysts that the public image of our work is not distorted to produce a climate of opinion in which difficulties, already great, are enhanced. That image will be influenced by patients, their analysts, and the societies and groups that analysts form. In the event of catastrophic change such as I postulate in my illustration there is a further transformation T (public), and therefore, since we are concerned with the end product, the opinion the public has formed: T (public) β. In some instances it may be of consequence to determine the content or meaning of the realization represented by the signs T (public), T (public) α, and T (public) β.

In the catastrophic event the concern of the analyst must be with transformation manifested in the patient. In this notation the representative signs are T (patient) standing for change in his point of view and including T (patient) α, the processes by which he effects the change from the realization to T (patient) β; the end product or transformed material is what is presented to the analyst.

Finally, we come to the analyst. In general terms the analyst's point of view differs from those we have considered because it is psycho-analytic. He will observe the pre-catastrophic state and make his own description, usually embodied in interpretations. In so far as the catastrophe may affect the armoury of theories on which he relies there will be a need to represent two transformations, one pre-catastrophic and the other post-catastrophic. This change must be reflected in the sign employed for the transformation. If he makes no change the signs will be T (analyst) and this will include T (analyst) α and T (analyst) β. If there is a change we can replace "analyst" by a sign representing the cycle of transformation, pre- and post-catastrophic.

If the reader considers the first chapter in the light of his experience he will realize that any apparent strangeness lies in the method of approach and not in the experience described. It will help understanding if he will satisfy himself before he reads further that phenomena described are already familiar to him.

CHAPTER TWO

THE term "transformation" may mislead unless the limitations of the implication of "form" are recognized. In painting, in geometry, it is safe to think in terms of form, but I am concerned with a function of personality in the process of being represented and it may introduce errors to suppose that a function of personality has a form. In severely disturbed persons a transformation T (patient) may be a deformation. Such a patient, abandoning one transformation for another, may produce T_2 (patient) β which has no obvious resemblance to T_1 (patient) β. Suppose that T_2 (patient) β is a shapeless lump, the term "deformation" is not likely to mislead. But if T_2 (patient) α is the patient's experience of being greeted by the analyst and T_2 (patient) β is the patient's representation of the event as a hostile attack made on him by the doctor, it may seriously obstruct understanding of what has taken place in the mind of the patient to suppose that either T_2 or $T_2\beta$ have, or are, forms.

The grid in *Elements of Psycho-Analysis*[1] affords a method of escape from the implications of "form" through resort to signs for abstract categories (the various grid compartments) to represent the content of $T_2\alpha$ and $T_2\beta$. A sign to represent the realization would denote, to take the example in Chapter 1, the landscape as a thing-in-itself, and therefore distinguish it from both $T_2\alpha$ and $T_2\beta$. The sign would denote something that is not a mental phenomenon and therefore, like Kant's thing-in-itself, can never be known. I introduce the idea of the thing-in-itself to make clear the status of $T_2\alpha$ and $T_2\beta$ as signs for mental phenomena.

The use of these signs may be clarified by an illustration: The patient enters and, following a convention established in the analysis, shakes hands. This is an external fact, what I have called a "realization". In so far as it is useful to regard it as a thing-in-itself and unknowable (in Kant's

[1] Bion, W. R.: *Elements of Psycho-Analysis.*

sense) it is denoted by the sign O. The phenomenon, corresponding to the external fact, as it exists in the mind of the patient, is represented by the sign T (patient) α. This sign I mean to replace by a grid category. The grid category is determined by picking on that category to which my clinical observation of the patient's behaviour seems most closely to approximate. Suppose the handshake is intended as a denial of hostility that the patient experienced in a dream about me. His action would then fall in a category in column 2 and row C. The sign then would be C2.

The associations following this start to the session would have yielded the evidence for choosing the sign C2. In addition I expect to find evidence on which to determine the category in which I shall place the representation that has resulted from his transformation, T, of the episode, O, (thing-in-itself), to T (patient) α and thence to T (patient) β —this last being the representation, his representation, of the episode. This sign T (patient) β I shall now replace, as I have already done with T (patient) α, by a grid category. Once more the grid category must be determined by assessment of the associations. Suppose the evidence suggests that the patient's experience is that my handshake was a sexual assault on him. The context shows me that this approximates to a definitory hypothesis; I expect accordingly to find the category in column 1. If, from my knowledge of him, I am convinced that the patient is not experiencing this as a thought or idea or even as a dream, but as an actual fact, I assess the category to lie in row A—the β-elements. The category with which I replace T (patient) β is A1.

Using the facts (of my illustration) to achieve a formulation in terms of a theory of transformations, I arrive at the following: the total analytical experience is being interpreted as belonging to the group of transformations, denoted by the sign T. The experience (thing-in-itself) I denote by sign O. The patient's impression, T (patient) α, is replaced by grid category C2. The patient's representation, a resultant of the transformation he has effected, T (patient) β, is replaced by grid category A1. Since we have not yet come to a decision about the nature of the process of transformation it is convenient to employ a sign showing that the abstraction represented by T is unsaturated.

The emotional experience of my illustration, as I have described it verbally, can be represented in the form of an equation as follows: $T = C2 \rightarrow A1$.

This formulation can be regarded as analogous to a model: a man observing that certain elements are constantly conjoined, binds the conjunction by using a sign, say the term "dog". Once the elements observed to be constantly conjoined are bound by the term "dog", the person thus binding them can set about discovering what meaning is to be attributed to the term "dog".[1] By analogy, we, having bound the constantly conjoined elements of the analytic experience by the formulation $T(\xi) = C2 \rightarrow A1$, may now resort to further analytical experience for evidence which will provide us with meaning: in other terms, to saturate the unsaturated element (ξ); or, again, to put it in another way, we hope to find evidence from analysis for a more precise understanding of this particular patient's transformation. The investigation of this and other analytical experiences should in time enable us to see different types of transformation and perhaps to arrive at some classification of the different sets of transformation which together make up the group of transformations.

In practice this means that if a patient is encountered with whom the analyst has experiences of which my illustration is typical, the analyst should be able to distinguish phenomena of the type $C2 \rightarrow A1$. This would enable him to formulate characteristics of T implying the existence of sets of T. It may help to clarify my meaning if I anticipate the findings of our investigation by provisional formulation of what such sets of transformation might be. Further it will serve the purpose of setting bounds to the area in which we search for clinically based theories of transformations. I therefore propose provisional hypotheses as an apparatus for

[1] An analogical counterpart can be seen in the group: if I succeed in binding a constant conjunction by writing this book the group can take over the task of discovering what it means.

further inquiry.[1] They are to be replaced by formulations to which the realization of psycho-analytic practice more closely approximates.

I assume that mental disorders fall into one of two categories, neuroses and psychoses, and ignoring existing criteria used to distinguish one category from the other I shall attempt to distinguish them on the basis of the theory of transformations. I shall therefore assume that the material provided by the analytic session is significant for its being the patient's view (representation) of certain facts which are the origin (O) of his reaction.

In practice this means that I shall regard only those aspects of the patient's behaviour which are significant as representing his view of O; I shall understand what he says or does as if it were an artist's painting. In the session the facts of his behaviour are like the facts of a painting and from them I must find the nature of his representation (or, in terms of my notation, the nature of that which I denote by the sign T (patient) β). From the analytic treatment as a whole I hope to discover from the invariants in this material what O is, what he *does* to transform O (that is to say, the nature of T (patient) α) and, consequently, the nature of T (patient). This last point is the *set* of transformations, in the group of transformations, to which his particular transformation (T (patient)) is to be assigned. As I am concerned with the *nature* (or, in other words, meaning) of these phenomena, my problem is to determine the relationship between three unknowns: T (patient), T (patient) α, and T (patient) β. Only in the last of these have I any *facts* on which to work.

I shall call on clinical experience to illustrate the next stage in this investigation. The patient[2], a man of 40, married, with one son, whose childhood was spent in a well-to-do professional family of father and mother with three older brothers, had complained of insomnia. The occasion was the last session before a weekend, and he commenced it by saying he had dreamt that a tiger and a bear

[1] In fact another instance of binding—this time by provisional hypotheses.

[2] Referred to earlier as A (see pp. 7 and 10).

were fighting. He felt dreadfully frightened lest the animals in their ferocious maulings would stumble across him and kill him. He woke in dread with a shout ringing in his ears. It was his own shout. The dream reminded him of a story by a famous big game shot; he could not remember the name of the man. The tiger who was very well known to be the fiercest of animals was driven off its kill by a bear. But the bear had its nose bitten off. It made him shudder to think of it. (Here he screwed up his face and shuddered.) He could not think of any more. He went on after a pause: The girl he was once engaged to for a year had broken off the engagement because she wanted to be free to flirt with other men. It still made his blood boil. Pepper was the man she married. He was very fond of pepper himself. Pepper was hot stuff with the girls. So unlike himself who was always afraid of them. With his wife it was different, but she was dull. At this point he became confused and I omit the rest of the session.

I have chosen this illustration because it lends itself easily to interpretation. The reader can see that the stimulus of the week-end break might be the trigger for the dream and its associations. There is no lack of analytic theories that might be appropriate and with the knowledge of the patient I had—he had been in analysis with me for two years—I was able to narrow choice of interpretations to two or three. But even two or three interpretations can be an embarrassment when one only is wanted and that one correct in the context in which it is given. I am therefore ignoring here, and throughout this book, any discussion of psycho-analytic theories. I am however concerned with theories of psycho-analytic observation, and the theory of transformations, the application of which I am here illustrating, is one of them. Can this theory be applied to bridge the gap between psycho-analytic preconceptions,[1] and the facts as they emerge in the session?

First I shall apply the theory to my own account of the

[1] The grid category of "psycho-analytic pre-conceptions" as I use the term here is F4, not D4 or 5, because I use the term "pre-conception" to denote "use" not "genesis".

session: something occurred during the session—the absolute facts of the session. What the absolute facts are cannot ever be known, and these I denote by the sign O. My description is of the facts as they appear *now* to have been at the time they took place: it is a description of phenomena and the description can be represented, in conformity with the theory of transformations, by the sign T (analyst) β. My mental processes, by which the phenomena were transformed to become the description I have given (T (analyst) β) are represented by the sign T (analyst) α. Since I may want to talk about them even if I do not know what they are, it is convenient to be able to refer to them by the sign T (analyst) α.

I shall not discuss T (analyst) α or T (analyst) β except to point out that the session is the stimulus for discussion and can therefore be represented by O and my description of it by T (analyst) β. As the patient is to be discussed we shall be concerned with a different O, call it O (patient), and T (patient) α and T (patient) β. To discuss O (patient) I shall represent the phenomena, to which he reacted by T (patient) α and T (patient) β, as T (patient).

The first question is, What is O (patient), or, to express it in more conversational terms, what was the patient talking *about*? One answer is that he was talking about the week-end break. Let us examine this.

Such a solution cannot be arrived at by any ordinary view of his statements. To re-state question and answer in terms of transformation theory: O (analyst), the patient's statements, have been transformed by me, my mental processes being represented by T (analyst) α, to form a view, T (analyst) β, from which I deduce that T (patient) = the week-end break. Or rather that I have assumed that a week-end break, O, exists, and that the phenomena associated with O by the patient is something I denote by T (patient). In some circumstances it may be adequate to say that the patient was talking about the week-end break. It may be adequate to say this in an analysis. But, as analysts know, such a statement will not provide an answer that is adequate to all breaks in analysis. The question itself lacks precision and is yet overloaded with meaning. In discarding the conversational expression for something more precise but less encumbered with meaning, for example, T (patient), and then falling back on the analytical experience and procedure to invest it with meaning, lies the justification for "naming". Analytically trained intuition makes it possible to say the patient is talking about the primal scene and from the development of associations to add shades of meaning to fill out understanding of what is taking place. I have chosen this session because, although the reader has not the emotional experience itself, he will be able to make deductions from the material that will serve for understanding this that I am saying without my own deductions. I shall proceed on the assumption that the reader will draw his own conclusions and from them see in what way his view of the session might be enhanced by a theory of transformations.

I shall now consider the state of mind in the patient which makes him see the week-end break as he does, that is, the *process* of transformation T (patient) α. By what mental processes does the patient come to experience the week-end break as an object of fear? What, when he contemplates the week-end break, does he see? In other words, what meaning are we to ascribe to T (patient) β? The material should show both what he sees and how he comes to see it as he does, the process of transformation and the product of that process.

I shall propound my views in general terms known to every analyst. As far as the process is concerned I assume that transference plays a predominant role and that the end-product, T (patient) β, is what an analyst would call a transference neurosis. The aspect of transference important in transformation is that which Freud[1] described as a tendency "to repeat as a current experience what is repressed" instead of recollecting it as a fragment of the past. He goes on to say, "This reproduction appearing with unwelcome fidelity always contains a fragment of the infantile

[1] Freud, S.: *Beyond the Pleasure Principle* (1920). Standard Edition, Vol. 18, p. 18.

sex life, therefore of the Oedipus complex and its off-shoots, and is played regularly in the sphere of transference, i.e. the relationship to the physician." It is this "unwelcome fidelity" that helps to make the term "transference" so appropriate. At its worst the fidelity of the reproduction tends to betray the analyst into interpretations that have a repetitive quality seeming to suggest that what the patient says about someone else applies almost unchanged to what he thinks and feels about the analyst. Though such interpretations are a parody of what transference interpretations should be they contain a germ of truth. The feelings and ideas appropriate to infantile sexuality and the Oedipus complex and its off-shoots are *transferred*, with a wholeness and coherence that is characteristic, to the relationship with the analyst. This transformation involves little deformation: the term "transference", as Freud used it, implies a model of movement of feelings and ideas from one sphere of applicability to another. I propose therefore to describe this set of transformations as "rigid motions". The invariance of rigid motion must be contrasted with invariance peculiar to projective transformations.

In the clinical illustration I said the patient became confused; I shall use an instance of the type of confusion he displayed for an illustration of a session for this chapter, but it will be from a different patient[1] and will be more intense. Here it is: The patient came in, but, though he had been attending for years, seemed uncertain what to do. "Good morning, good morning, good morning. It must mean afternoon really. I don't expect anything can be expected today: this morning, I mean. This afternoon. It must be a joke of some kind. This girl left about her knickers. Well, what do you say to that? It's probably quite wrong, of course, but, well, I mean, what do *you* think?" He walked to the couch and lay down, bumping his shoulders down hard on the couch. "I'm slightly anxious . . . I think. The pain has come back in my knee. You'll probably say it was the girl. After all. This picture is probably not very good as I told him but I should not have

[1] Referred to later as B.

said anything about it. Mrs X. . . . thought I ought to go to Durham to see about, but then" and so on. I cannot do justice to the episode because I remember only the general impression and the general impression depending on changes of tone expressing depression, fear, anxiety, confidentiality, and others, was itself intended to give a general impression.[1] The short report is verbally nearly correct; yet as I read it again I see it is a misleading record of the experience. I shall therefore make another attempt to describe this fragment of session but without attempting verbal exactitude. After his pause of uncertainty he whispered his good mornings as if he were pre-occupied with an object he had lost but expected to find close at hand. He corrected himself in a tone that might imply a mental aberration that had led him to think it "good morning". The speaker of the words "good morning", I gathered, was not really the patient, but someone whose manner he caricatured. Then came the comment that nothing could be expected. That was clear enough, but who was making the comment, or of whom nothing could be expected, was obscure. It might have been myself; I did not think it was he. Then he spoke of the joke. The way this term was used implied that the joke had no tincture of humour about it. To me it could mean a cruel joke, but such an interpretation depended on an assumption that the words retained the meaning that they would have in sane conversation and that the emotion expressed, by and with them, had the value that it would have in ordinary speech. When he spoke of "this" girl it was evident that I was supposed to know her; in fact I did not nor did I know whether she had left her knickers lying about or given notice on account of some episode connected with her knickers. "What do you say to that?" meant that in either case I would know as well as he did what her behaviour signified, though, as his next sentence showed, the significance (unmentioned) attached to her behaviour by both of us was probably mistaken, girls being what they are.

When he lay on the couch he did so as if trying to express surreptitiously his wish to damage my property. I thought

[1] See Chapter 1.

his next comment compatible with this surmise in that it might mean that, being confused with me and yet detached from both of us, he hazarded a guess that I was anxious at his violence, that I supposed him to be anxious and not aggressive, that he thought the feelings he experienced were what I would call anxiety. His reference to the pain in his knee was typical of certain very rare statements in that it meant "The pain in my knee, which I now experience, is what you as analyst think is really the girl inside me." Such a statement meant that despite evidence to the contrary he had knowledge of my analytic theories and that he was now having an experience which I would explain by that particular theory. It might mean that he wished me to know what experiences he was having and that the correct interpretation could be arrived at through the theory of internal objects. Such interpretations were rare but previous experience had convinced me that they occurred and had the significance I have attributed to this one. But the flatness of tone, the tortuosity of the communication and the ambiguity made it probable that I would either fail to grasp the latent meaning, or, in searching for some such meaning, would fail to notice the almost obvious sense.

His "after all" is typical; it is meaningless, but can act as a stimulus to speculation. Subsequent remarks meant that what had been taking place in the session was a pictorial representation, an externalization of a visual image, not likely to be regarded by me as good and therefore evacuated by me with such force that this fragment of his personality would be projected as far away from me as Durham is from London.

It will be observed that this, my second account of the episode, contains a very high proportion of speculation. The speculations depend on my theoretical pre-conceptions. In addition to classical analytical theory I have had in mind Kleinian theories of splitting and projective identification. I expected to find that some part of the confusion would be illuminated by applying the theory of projective identification to the patient's inability to distinguish between himself and myself. I also assumed that experience of hallucinations, as I have described them in my paper, "On Hallucinations", would stand me in good stead. But beyond preserving an awareness of such a background of theory I allowed myself to be as open to clinical impressions as possible. I have already indicated what some of these impressions were. The experience, as usual, was one of stimulation and frustration. The sense of being at a loss, which will be apparent to the reader, is not quite so profound in the consulting room as the written account makes it appear, because the clinical experience affords a mass of detail that cannot be communicated in print; even though it is grasped imperfectly it is sure to make an impact. Yet an account that contains so much speculation to so little fact must be unsatisfactory to a scientist. To what extent is the patient's communication the most direct and informative instrument he can employ, obscure though it may appear? Is its obscurity due to the difficulty of the matter of the problem for which he seeks help or is it due to his need to conceal? The analyst's task is to distinguish one from the other. In terms of T, it is necessary to determine whether T (patient) β is characterized primarily by the need to conceal O or by the need to give as direct a representation of O as possible in view of its obscurity to him; in the illustration I have given the characteristic of T (patient) β is revelatory rather than obscuring.

It may seem perverse to judge it as revealing, especially since in fact the patient could, though extremely rarely and then only for short periods, speak coherently. My reason lies in the experience of many sessions of which the cumulative effect was to give an impression of O. The impression was often difficult to express in words. Sometimes it was strong, but hard for me to formulate without feeling my interpretation, even to myself, was fanciful. At other times I was satisfied that my formulation was a correct translation into words and that it was a valuable communication; such occasions made interpretations to the patient likely to be analytically sound. The decision that the communication is revelatory must depend on the strength of the impression received by the analyst and this weighed against the fact that the patient appears to choose an obscure method of communication. Later I shall consider the possibility of classifying the types of communication[1] T (patient) β, as well as the process of communication T (patient) α. In my next chapter I shall discuss the illustration in terms of the theory of transformation.

[1] See Chapter 5.

CHAPTER THREE

THE clinical illustration of Chapter 2 made a distinction between the patient's experience O and the analyst's experience O. When the stimulating experience is the analytic session itself, O is the same for patient and analyst and the distinction has to be made between the processes by which the patient transforms his experience to achieve his representation of it and the processes by which the analyst does so; similarly between the patient's representation and the analyst's between T (patient) α and T (analyst) α, between T (patient) β and T (analyst) β. I shall abbreviate these signs further to Tp α and Ta α, Tp β and Ta β.

The experiences illustrated in Chapter 2 differ, but the illustrations may not display these differences adequately. The inadequacy lies in notation for the presentation of psycho-analytic phenomena with the precision required.

B has an emotional background which I believe to be typical, though this will need confirmation. From the first, it was evident that the resources of psycho-analysis might prove inadequate to the demands of such a patient. In terms of time and money alone treatment would be costly. Patience and a capacity for taking risks were also soon seen to be necessary. It was only necessary for the patient to feel that one demand was satisfied for him to make it the prelude for further exactions; this attitude pervaded all aspects of relationship with me and apparently with life at large. Typical of the development of awareness of a situation to a point at which I could venture on a verbal impression of it, was the fact that awareness grew gradually so that it was difficult to say, when an aspect had been clarified, what material, in the immediate circumstances, was sufficient to sustain the burden of interpretation I wished to lay on it. An interpretation therefore appeared to lack the scientific quality that is conferred by supporting evidence. I have drawn attention to the high degree of speculation in my second description of B. A series of such doubts sprang naturally from the fact, obvious at the outset, and therefore of slight significance in the immediate analytic setting, that any collaboration, and particularly an analytic one, with such a patient would be unrewarding and even dangerous. Such premonitions have two mainsprings: the first from the analysis itself, which is so transformed that the intention that the analytic association should be healing and rewarding is frustrated by actions intended to wound; the second from perceptions of the patient's material as it coheres to form his representation of O. This first transformation is analogous to that of the landscape gardener who works to transform the landscape itself; the second transformation is analogous to that of the painter who transforms the landscape into a painting. It is doubtful whether the transformation of the analysis into something wounding[1] should be included amongst transformations in the sense in which I have used the term so far. The state of mind in which such behaviour is dominant may be described as the patient studying the interpretations he receives (Ta β). The object of his study is to arrive at action by which he may destroy psycho-analysis. It is a necessary part of the process to arrive by Tp α at Tp β as a prelude to destructive activities, but the transformation does not require special categorization because of the end it is to serve. The danger that the colloquial sense of a "transformation of the analysis" will infect the meaning I wish to reserve for the theory of transformation is one against which I wish to guard by using the sign T. The "transformation of the analysis" refers to a change of "uses" as set out on the horizontal axis of the grid.[2] The subject is one to which I shall return after investigating illustration B.

I shall make three assumptions: (i) that the patient is talking about something (O); (ii) that something, O, has impressed him and that he has transformed the impression by the process represented by Tp α, and (iii) that his representation Tp β is comprehensible.

[1] The transformation into action approximates to grid category A6.

[2] See End-paper, and Bion, W. R.: *Elements of Psycho-Analysis* where the grid system is more fully discussed.

According to the theory of transformations the emotional experience gives the analyst the opportunity of deciding whether he is faced by evidence for Tp (that is the impression of O gained by the patient), Tp α, or Tp β. Ideally the analyst should be in the state of mind presented by C3, C4, C5 and D3, D4, D5, with the exception of moments when he intends to give an interpretation. In fact, this is unlikely because the patient's attacks on his state of mind can be incessant and, in my experience, not infrequently successful.[1] Attacks may be generalized and depend for their force on the patient's capacity for being a liability in any situation in which he finds himself. Or they may be given particularity by the evocative use of sundry words such as "police . . . what are you doing?" "My uncle . . . I am saying 'madness' for some reason," and so on, depending on material that has been presented at various times during the analysis. I ignore distraction produced by counter-transference as I have nothing to add to what is already known about it or the methods of dealing with it.

The problem of classifying the material is complicated because it contains elements of all three: Tp, Tp α and Tp β. It is a matter of consequence because the decision depends on what is most convenient for the analyst.[2] If it seems the best approach to interpretation to narrow scrutiny (say C4 and D4) to those aspects of the material that are expressions of Tp β the analyst should adjust accordingly. The problem is to reformulate Tp β in conversational, but precise, English. This aim is to produce statements that could be appropriately categorized by the grid category F, or G1. That is to express a definitory hypothesis. In my second version of B, sundry speculative statements cannot be classified as F1 or G1, for that implies too great a degree of scientific sophistication. I suggest the category C1.

Suppose the approach to be fruitful: this would mean that I was gaining an impression of the patient's picture of some event—O. What, then, is Op?

[1] See Chapter 5. p. 54

[2] And the decision the analyst makes is to identify with a particular vertex: see Chapter, 6.

At this point defects in this approach obtrude because the nature of the speculations indicates that the differences of B from A are such that the signs Ta and p, Ta and pα, Ta and pβ are insufficient. Their inadequacy derives from the fact that the combined operation by patient and analyst receives an accession of emotion from the confusion, in the patient's mind, between himself and the analyst. I shall anticipate by marking the difference between the transformation of A with that in B by calling the former a Rigid and the latter a Projective Transformation.

A patient[1] was speaking of problems in his office. But for certain peculiarities which I shall come to in a moment, his account seemed to be realistic, coherent and rational. The peculiarities lay in his response to interpretations. When I referred to something he had just said, a row with his secretary, for example, he would reply blankly "What row?" as if the topic were strange to him. On these occasions there seemed to be nothing that I could say that did not have the effect of leading him away from the theme of his communication and destroying the coherence of the material. About a half of the session was employed in this way and the mood was not replaced by another till I had given a number of interpretations to the effect that his questions showed that the thread in his apparently coherent account was precariously maintained. Every sentence was a series of tenuously connected splits so that if I drew attention to something he mentioned at the beginning of a sentence he had forgotten it by the time he had reached the end; interpretation was made meaningless. My interpretation was based on the assumption that the episode approximated to the Kleinian theory that an attack was being delivered against analytic potency by means of splitting which had the incidental effect of splitting him. Judged by the change of mood and the associated developments, the interpretation appeared to be correct.

Assumption of hostility depended less on the matter of his communication than on the manner and particularly on the peculiarities stressed here. Once the assumption of hostility was made it became possible to see the analytic significance

[1] Referred to later as C.

of the matter he was communicating. The problem depends for its solution on observation of the patient's behaviour over a relatively short period and contrasts with the problem of hostility spread out over a long period and expressed in episodes of short duration. The individual episode is easier to deal with than the totality of episodes. In so far as they are dealt with they contribute to the solution of the whole, yet the problem of the whole comprises far more than the sum of the parts. I shall illustrate this by a situation that is built up over, and endures for, years. In the last chapter I pointed out that with some patients any association is unrewarding to both associates. This applies to the class of patient to which the one of whom I am writing belonged. Consequently such analysis brings about a progressive discrediting of patient, analyst and psycho-analysis in the eyes of all who know the case socially. Together with this, and essential to it, is arduous and devoted effort, directed towards both attendance and work in the session itself. The essential feature is stimulation and frustration of hope, and work that is fruitless except in discrediting analyst and patient. Destructive activity is balanced by enough success to deny the patient fulfilment of his destructiveness. A helpful summary of such a case is to describe it as "chronic" murder of patient and analyst, or, an instance of parasitism; the main features are dependence of the patient, the parasite, on analyst and the associated group, or family, or wider social group. The patient draws on the love, benevolence, indulgence of the host to extract the knowledge and power which enables him to poison the association and destroy the indulgence on which he depends for his existence.

I could give instances, such as example C, which are essential to the production of this result but which are none of them individually of obvious consequence; that aspect is apparent only when they are repeated and then only if seen to form part of a coherent whole. A total view is possible for the analyst; the problem, in face of constant splitting and projective identification is how to make it clear to the patient. The theory of transformations affords an approach to a solution in the following way.

First, the problem needs to be stated in terms of the theory. I have at my disposal the following signs: "Invariants", "O", "T", "Tp α", "Ta α", "Tp β", "Ta β". Preceding chapters have indicated the universe of discourse to which they are intended to apply and the domain of that discourse to which each term is assigned. To that extent each sign may be said to represent a meaning. The status of the meaning represented by each sign is indicated by grid category C4;[1] that is to say that the genetic stage of thought is that of dream or myth—the pejorative philosophical expression for a doubtful theory as a mythology—and column 4 that it is to be used to focus attention on appropriate facets[2] of material.

In practice the next development would be dictated by the experience of the session; according to the form taken by it one or more of the signs would become invested with meaning. Reliance on clinical observation for accretion of meanings is central to the use of the theory of transformations. But in this theoretical discussion we may substitute an inquiry into the meaning to be sought for any sign, for the stimulus which would in practice be supplied by the material; no significance is to be attached to the choice I make other than the convenience of exposition. I shall commence with Op and Oa.

The advantage of this is that the facts are limited to the experience shared by patient and analyst.

I shall reduce O to the simplest terms by considering first the facts known to the analyst, Oa. With modifications appropriate to the individual Oa may be said to consist of the following components: two people, patient and analyst, are met together in conditions of privacy. The furniture of the room, remaining unchanged, should be quite familiar to the analyst. The same should be true of features such as the usual sounds of the household and neighbourhood. The familiarity of the surroundings may blind the analyst to the possible significance of them for the patient and he must be on his guard against this. This completes, in general terms, the constant features.

[1] End-paper and Bion, W. R.: *Elements of Psycho-Analysis.*

[2] See vertices, Chapter 6.

Amongst changing features must be listed absence of patient or analyst, or, notably during breaks, of analyst and patient. To these must be added changes in time-table and others likely to be significant. *All* change is a component of O, but one is constant, namely that which flows from the passage of time.

The personality of the analyst is recognized as a feature of the analytic situation but he may not attach enough importance to the strength and weakness of aspects of his personality that are relatively unrelated to psychopathology and have to be learned from experiences other than those of his own analysis.

O, subjected to Ta α, eventuates in Ta β, the analyst's view of himself and extensions of his personality.

Turning to the patient, we find some features of Oa and Op intersect to give Oa and p. Patients vary in what they include in O. In the group of projective transformations, events far removed from any relationship to the analyst are actually regarded as aspects of the analyst's personality. Thus a patient reported angrily that the milkman had called. The patient was angry with me and went into a sulk. For about five minutes he would not talk, but then began to complain about the noise. I knew he was referring to a boy who was whistling cheerfully in the street. I was certain that the milkman had called and that the patient made no distinction between the milkman and myself; conversely, my presence in the consulting room was not distinguished from the milkman's call; this phenomenon differs from transference. A patient might use the milkman's visit to express emotions arising in his relationship with me and it could be interpreted accordingly. That transformation belongs to the set of rigid motions. In this illustration the interpretation might be couched in terms suitable for a transference interpretation and it would probably still be effective. But the difference between rigid motion and projective transformation on other occasions might be important. The importance lies in the fact that the patient believes that the "milkman" me did in fact visit his house and that this same "milkman" me has just appeared to him.

If I do not seem to know about the milkman's visit it makes the patient feel I cannot be aware of my behaviour and am therefore not responsible for my actions—that I am, in short, "mad". Contrasting this with a session where I have to deal with his reactions, say to my absence during a week-end, in the latter instance I know what he is talking about, what Op is, but on other occasions I am confronted with his reaction to Op without knowing what Op might have been—though I can always attempt to guess.

It does not meet the case to suppose that Op, as I am describing it here, is a manifestation of transference for the term "transference" should be reserved for the description of the response to a stimulus; whereas I am concerned to delineate the stimulus. Op, in projective transformations, must not be regarded as identical with Op in rigid motion transformations. The necessity for establishing the nature of the difference springs from the exigencies of psycho-analytic practice. When I assigned O to denote the reality, the impressions of which the individual submits to the process $T\alpha$, I had in mind what Kant describes as the unknowable thing-in-itself. Tp β or Ta β denotes the analyst's or patient's representation of what is a private communication understood only by the individual whose processes have effected the transformation. They are thus denoting a representation that is related to what Kant describes as a primary process. If patient and analyst agree on an interpretation the interpretation can be correctly denoted by the sign Tp and Ta β. Since this is shared by two people it is no longer a private communication but has become public. In this respect it is related to what Kant describes as a secondary quality and is by way of qualifying for recognition as common-sense, as I have defined that expression.[1] In rigid motion transformations the invariants establish the relationship with O. But in projective transformations the differences between Op and Oa do not permit of a process of arguing back from Tp and Ta β to Op and Oa as it can be done in rigid motion transformations. The crux lies in the nature of Op in projective transformation. Op is

[1] See Bion, W. R.: *Learning from Experience*.

apparently the stimulus; yet it has qualities which seem to be appropriate to Kant's primary quality. The difficulty becomes less formidable if Op in projective transformation is a psychic reality and has the same capacity for initiating a train of mental events as is possessed by an event of external reality such as a break in the routine of sessions. A feeling of dread might be such an internal psychic reality.

The artist stimulates a reaction in his public by his representation of the subject of his painting. Recognition that a painting depicts a field of poppies depends on invariants common to the original landscape and the representation, to O and T β. Such an invariant might be that which stimulated, in landscape and painting, the impression of redness. A transformation dependent on a "red-to-red" invariant would not be likely to produce the effect achieved by the "great" artist who produces a "great" painting. The problem is the transformation that issues in an end-product, T β, which communicates an *emotional* experience, such as the artist intends to produce, in the greatest number of the people in whom he intends to produce it. The components of T β in this class of transformation are: emotional experience, precision of communication, universality and durability.

The psycho-analyst tries to help the patient to transform that part of an emotional experience of which he is unconscious into an emotional experience of which he is conscious. If he does this he helps the patient to achieve private knowledge. But since scientific work demands communication of discovery to other workers the psycho-analyst must transform *his* private experience of psycho-analysis so that it becomes a public experience. The artist is used here as a model intended to indicate that the criteria for a psycho-analytic paper are that it should stimulate in the reader the emotional experience that the writer intends, that its power to stimulate should be durable, and that the emotional experience thus stimulated should be an accurate representation of the psycho-analytic experience (Oa) that stimulated the writer in the first place.

It will be observed that in model and psycho-analytic experience the following parallels exist: landscape and psycho-analytic experience, painting and scientific paper, emotions stimulated by landscape and analytic session, emotions represented by painting and scientific paper. We may regard the transformation as extending beyond the limits I have imposed if we consider the progression from O to T β as a link in the progression from O to the emotional state stimulated by T β in the observer of the painting, or the reader of the paper. If the emotion stimulated in the recipient of the communication is a *representation* of the emotion stimulated by O in the artist we may regard the artist's intervention in the chain of events as one that does not stop at the disposal of patterns of pigment on canvas, but extends to the emotional state evoked in the individual, or group, and to giving durability to the power to evoke emotion.[1] The sign T can be made to denote either canvas, or paper, or the emotional state of the recipient of the communication. Our model serves psycho-analytic needs better if T β denotes the emotional state stimulated in the recipient and T represents the emotional state, stimulated in the analyst by O, which Ta α is to transform. The same value must be given to each sign throughout any given universe of discourse; if the universe of discourse is transformation in the domain of emotion, T β, for example, must not at one moment denote canvas and pigment and at another the emotional state of the recipient of the communication.

To bring the discussion into closer approximation to the needs of psycho-analysis—no one can ever know what happens in the analytic session, the thing-in-itself, O; we can only speak of what the analyst or patient *feels* happens, his emotional experience, that which I denote by T. We know what the participants *say* happens, or the emotional state engendered by the verbalization of analyst or patient in the listener. By analogy with the model we must decide whether to use T β to denote (*a*) the verbalization (association or interpretation) or (*b*) the emotional state *produced* by

[1] The theme of "Vixere fortes ante Agammemnona multi. . . ." Horace Odes, Bk. IV, 9.

the association or interpretation.[1] Similarly we must decide whether the significance of the association or interpretation lies in its being an emotional response to O or in its intention to evoke or represent an emotional response. If it is the former, then it belongs to the category represented by T. If T, then it is necessary to know whether it is significant because it *is* the emotional response or merely represents it. The model of the artist retains its value, but it may become misleading and lead into paths that are irrelevant; the signs may lack specificity or tend to a proliferation that obscures rather than illuminates. I shall retain both model and signs until something better becomes possible.

To forestall misgivings and criticisms which may have an insidious appeal for the psycho-analyst: a book on psycho-analysis in which the first chapters contain no substantial reference to sexuality, conflict, anxiety, or Oedipus situation, may seem irrelevant, or of specialized interest and minor consequence. In fact, if the matters I am discussing are regarded as seriously as I think they should be, it becomes possible for the analyst to have a firm and durable grasp of the reality of the analytic experience and the theories to which it approximates. The theory of transformations and its development does not relate to the main body of psycho-analytic theory, but to the practice of psycho-analytic *observation*. Psycho-analytic theories, patient's or analyst's statements are representations of an emotional experience. If we can understand the process of representation it helps us to understand the representation and what is being represented. The theory of transformations is intended to illuminate a chain of phenomena in which the understanding of one link, or aspect of it, helps in the understanding of others. The emphasis of this inquiry is on the nature of the transformation in a psycho-analytic session.

T β may be expressed through the medium of speech. Psycho-analysts agree that correct analysis demands that

[1] Strictly speaking the interpretation *draws attention* to an *existing* emotional state; but it *produces* the emotional state of awareness of an emotional state. In fact the decision depends on whether we think the analyst or patient works in words or in emotions.

the analyst's interpretation should formulate what the patient's behaviour reveals; conversely, that the analyst's judgment should be embodied in an interpretation[1] and not in an emotional discharge (e.g. counter-transference or acting out). To this we may add provisionally that his contribution may be regarded as embodied in the change in the patient's emotional state.

I shall not discuss transformation in scientific communications except to illustrate transformation in analytic practice.

The analyst conducting a session must decide instinctively the nature of the communication that the patient is making. I suggested, in *Elements of Psycho-Analysis*, a method of classification to aid in developing capacity for such instinctive decisions and have embodied it in the grid.[2] If exigencies of the analysis demand emphasis on the growth of the patient's thought the analyst's attention will dwell mainly on the row that determines the category—the vertical axis. If emphasis is on the use that the patient is making of his communication the analyst's attention will be directed to the horizontal component. The content of the communication, so important in analysis, will be touched on only incidentally in the discussion of transformations; it will depend on O as deduced from the material in the light of the psycho-analyst's theoretical pre-conceptions. Thus, if the content is oedipal material I do not concern myself with this but with the transformation it has undergone, the stage of growth it reveals, and the use to which its communication is being put. This exclusion of content is artificial, to simplify exposition, and cannot be made in practice.

Since I shall refer to phenomena related to Melanie Klein's theories of projective identification, transition from paranoid-schizoid to depressive positions, and vice versa, it may seem that I am concerned primarily with psychotic personalities, but this is not so. These mechanisms are operative in neuroses and psychoses alike. But their investigation is a prime consideration in psychotic disorder, secondary in neuroses. This has been discussed further after elaboration of the theory of transformations[3] has shown the

[1] F1, 3, 4. [2] See End-papers. [3] See Chapter 2, p. 15.

possibility of making a fresh distinction between neurosis and psychosis.

To review briefly the points made in this chapter: we must be prepared to find the model of the painter misleading though still useful. The theory of transformations is to be developed, not as an addition to or alteration of psycho-analytic observation. I shall use the grid categories and in particular refer to column 6. This will involve some explanation of what I mean by the term, loosely employed, "action" in column 6. I shall start by taking the last point first.

In his paper on "Two Principles of Mental Functioning"[1] Freud distinguishes between a stage where muscular action is taken to alter the environment and a stage when a capacity for thought exists. I propose to include in the category represented by the term "action" phantasies that the mind, acting as if it were a muscle and a muscle acting as a muscle, can disburden the psyche of accretions of stimuli. I include the Kleinian concept of the phantasy known as projective identification in this category of "action". The growth of insight depends, at its inception, on undisturbed functioning of projective identification. If it is disturbed, mental development is hampered by the phantasy that insight depends on what is regarded, even by the sophisticated mind, as action. There are thus two attitudes distinguishable in patients of whom some behave as if action were precedent to action. The first I associate with projective transformations, the second with rigid transformations.

Since there is a breakdown in the early stages of development of insight many elements[2] involved in projective transformations will be represented by the first row of the grid. The existence of elements A2 and A3 is questionable, but I include them because their exclusion would be equally debatable.

Elements and objects in rigid transformations are likely to be found in all grid categories.

[1] Freud, S.: "Two Principles of Mental Functioning" (1911). Standard Edition, Vol. XII.

[2] See Bion, W. R.: *Elements of Psycho-Analysis.*

CHAPTER FOUR

THEORY leaves us free to give Ta β the value of the analyst's verbalization of his experience in the session, or the emotional state induced in his patient. That the analyst works on his patient's emotions as a painter might work on his canvas would be repugnant to psycho-analytic theory and practice. The painter who works on his public's emotions with an end in view is a propagandist with the outlook of the poster artist. He does not intend his public to be free in its choice of the use to which it puts the communication he makes. The analyst's position is akin to that of the painter who by his art adds to his public's experience. Since psycho-analysts do not aim to run the patient's life but to enable him to run it according to his lights and therefore to know what his lights are, Ta β either in the form of interpretation or scientific paper should represent the psycho-analyst's verbal representation of an emotional experience. An attempt to exclude by restriction to verbal expression any element from Ta that would make it pass from the domain of communication of knowledge to propaganda would be inadequate. Verbal expression must be limited so that it expresses truth without any implication other than the implication that it is true in the *analyst's opinion*. How this is to be attempted lies outside the scope of this discussion, but for certain implications which I shall now consider. The first concerns the route by which we have arrived at this conclusion. It is sometimes assumed that the motive for scientific work is an abstract love for truth. The argument I have followed implies that the grounds for limiting the values that may be substituted for Ta β to true statements lies in the nature of values *not* so limited and their relationship to other components in the T theory. If truth is not essential to all values of Ta β, Ta β must be regarded as expressed in and by manipulation of the emotions of patient or public and not in or by the interpretation; truth is essential for any value of Ta β in art or science. How is truth to be a criterion for a value proposed to Ta β? To what has it to be true and how shall we decide whether it is or not? Almost any answer appears to make truth contingent on some circumstance or idea that is itself contingent. Falling back on analytic experience for a clue, I am reminded that healthy mental growth seems to depend on truth as the living organism depends on food. If it is lacking or deficient the personality deteriorates. I cannot support this conviction by evidence regarded as scientific. It may be that the formulation belongs to the domain of Aesthetic. In practice the problem arises with schizoid personalities in whom the super-ego appears to be developmentally prior to the ego and to deny development and existence itself to the ego. The usurpation by the super-ego of the position that should be occupied by the ego involves imperfect development of the reality principle, exaltation of a "moral" outlook and lack of respect for the truth. The result is starvation of the psyche and stunted growth. I shall regard this statement as an axiom that resolves more difficulties than it creates.

The medium in which the psycho-analyst works is verbalized thoughts. Using the grid[1] to categorize the verbalized thoughts more precisely, they should be true and fall within the categories of rows E, F, and possibly D and G, and columns 1, 3, 4 and 5. Row G and H apply to phenomena endowed with a greater degree of sophistication and precision than any to which psycho-analysis attains at present. If the statements made in the course of interpretation are expressions of feeling they should fall in the same categories. The patient's contribution is not restricted and may fall in any grid category; the grid categories are intended to be adequate for all the elements and psycho-analytic objects met with in the practice of psycho-analysis. They should therefore be adequate for the requirements of a theory of transformations.

By considering psycho-analytic experience in the light of[2] a theory of transformations it is possible to see the problems

[1] See End-papers and Bion, W. R.: *Elements of Psycho-Analysis*.

[2] Or, with a vertex having the value T. See Chapter 6.

of thinking afresh. Freud associated thinking with the dominance of the reality principle and showed that it interposed a stage between awareness of an impulse and the action necessary for its fulfilment; he drew attention to its ameliorating effect on frustration. Its absence exacerbates frustration. Transformations have a number of functions, such as notation and record, private and public communication and the pursuit of knowledge; I shall consider an aspect of the latter, seeking an analogy with mathematics for the purpose.

A mathematical illustration is afforded by the use of numbers for enumeration and record. An increase in sophistication marks the manipulation of numbers to solve a problem *in the absence of the objects giving rise to the problem.* Applying this analogy to the elements of psycho-analysis, as I have categorized them in the grid, it is evident that an advance in sophistication separates the categories of columns 1 and 3 from the categories in all other columns. A distinction must be made between categories in column 2 and those of columns 4 to n-1, n, but in this case the distinction is one of kind, not sophistication.

Columns 1 and 3 represent uses of a relatively simple kind; if a word, hypothesis, theoretical system, myth, or transformation were limited to uses represented by those columns, it would not be suitable for working with. An analyst's notes on his cases are useless for the statement of problems and adumbration of solutions if their form prevents extension beyond definition and record. The theory of transformations must serve to illuminate and solve the problems that lie unsolved at the heart of certain forms of mental disturbance; and to do the same for problems inherent in the psycho-analysis of such disturbances.

A theory of transformations must be composed of elements and constitute a system capable of the greatest number of uses (represented by the horizontal axis of the grid) if it is to extend the analyst's capacity for working on a problem with or without the material components of the problem present.

This may seem to introduce a dangerous doctrine opening

the way for the analyst who theorizes unhampered by the facts of practice, but the theory of transformations is inapplicable to any situation in which observation is not an essential. Observation is to be made and recorded in a form suitable for working *with* but inimical to wayward and undisciplined fabrications. As grid categories show any scientific theory can be used in accordance with the categories of column 2 but it may be possible to prevent unpredictable changes from the uses of one grid column to the uses of another. In short, the theory is to aid observation and recording in terms suitable for scientific manipulation without the presence of the objects.

One problem in analysing the psychotic patient seems to be his difficulty in working without the actual presence of the objects for and about which work must be done.[1] If we could suppose that there was a failure to develop a system of notation and record which could also be used for manipulation in the absence of the object it might explain a number of features associated with the psychotic's behaviour. I have noticed that he sometimes behaves as if in order to "think" something he had to wait for that thing to appear in the world of external reality. Similarly he seems unable to think or imagine a situation but has to act it out. Stating this in terms of a theory of transformation the patient is not able to transform T (the phenomenal counterpart of O) into Tp β. Indeed he talks as if he felt unable to transform O into T. It is as if in one view man can never know the thing-in-itself, but only secondary and primary qualities; whereas in the other view he can never "know" anything *but* the thing-in-itself. This apparent attitude has similarities with another apparent attitude, namely, that postulated by the theory of projective identification. He behaves as if parts of his personality had physical properties and could be split off and projected into others as physical objects which the other object could modify or use.[2] Since a psychotic

[1] Hence the tendency to produce problem situations instead of solving problems.

[2] See Klein, M.: "Notes on Some Schizoid Mechanisms." In: *Developments in Psycho-Analysis*.

patient can express words and sentences it seems reasonable to suppose that he can think. But thinking, in the sense of manipulating words and thoughts to do work in the absence of the object, seems to be just what the patient cannot do. I have said[1] that such patients do not have memories but only undigested facts. The breakdown appears to occur in the necessity for an object into which the patient feels he is able to project parts of his personality for their development and manipulation. If he feels there is no such object, and no such possibility as "splitting off parts of his personality" disturbance is set up.

The use of transformation to produce T β such that T β can be worked with in the absence of O is one aspect of transformation theory. The theory must be extended to be adequate to cover transformation of this kind and the projective transformations of which I spoke earlier.

The similarity of phenomena associated with the theory of projective identification to those associated with lack of any differentiation of thing from its corresponding thought is probably due to their being different aspects of the same state of mind.

If the apparent inability to transform O to T corresponds to a real inability it would mean an end to the discussion—no theory of transformations could apply as no transformations take place. I have, however, deliberately described the patient as talking *as if* he could not transform O to T so as to leave the matter open to discussion; patients who show, or appear to show, this disability are in fact able to communicate with the analyst. The communication, though words are used, is more akin to musical or artistic than verbal communication. It contrasts with what I have said (on pages 24–26) about the nature of Ta β, the analyst's contribution.

Ordinary language is already more than a method of recording and enables work to be done, like mathematics, in the absence of the object worked on, but it is less effective in precision and universality. So long as our communications are reliable only in the presence of the objects we study,

[1] See Bion, W. R.: *Learning from Experience.*

we work under disabilities analogous to those of the psychotic and quality must suffer correspondingly. The theory of transformations is designed to decrease the disabilities of the psycho-analyst in his study of similar disabilities in the patient. I propose therefore to study alternately the transformations of the patient and the transformations of the analyst with a view to formulating a theory of transformations superior to those already used consciously and unconsciously.

The next task will be to examine afresh the group that I have provisionally called projective transformations. In this group Tp β appears to require two personalities, an object into which something is to be projected and an object responsible for the projection. Associated with this is the problem of deciding what the nature of Tp β is, if the object, into which the projection is made, is missing.

The mathematician in the absence of other than mathematical objects can work with his notation and formulations to solve a specific problem. To some extent the analyst can do the same with verbal communications; he can work with a patient, transform his experience into words, communicate his results to patient, or make them available to another analyst who can in turn use them and the work already done, in his task with a new patient and a new problem. Work has thus been done, in the absence of a patient, to carry forward the solution of a *general* problem and make it available for *specific* use in a specific instance. This can be likened to the process whereby growth[1] has been promoted, from the state represented by the earlier rows in the grid, to the state represented by row D. Such a transformation of the communication fits it for one of the uses in the horizontal axis, in this instance, column 4.

This description is of a characteristic common to several types of mental growth. Starting with the simplest example discussed, namely, from the name of an object, and

[1] "Growth" here refers to the growth of a mental formulation. It is interesting to consider the relationship that exists when the growth of a mental formulation appears to be matched by a realization of growth that approximates, or is "parallel" to, the mental formulations.

proceeding to quite complex combinations of objects, the growth process can be described as passing through a number of stages from β-element to algebraic calculus. Each stage is a record of a previous stage and a pre-conception of the subsequent stage. Each stage can be used in ways indicated in the headings of the horizontal axis. Each "use" represented in the horizontal axis can be seen to be representable by a term used to represent a stage on the genetic axis. "Pre-conception" can represent equally the use which is being made of a statement and the genetic stage of the statement. It is therefore appropriate to ask if the investigation would gain and the grid be improved by bringing stages and uses into clearer approximation to each other. Thus columns 4 and 5 might be amalgamated and be represented by the term "pre-conception". The term would then denote a use, but in the vertical axis it would continue to represent a stage in growth. But if each stage can be regarded as an element that is both record and pre-conception it may be objected that there is no need for terms such as "β-element", "dream", "concept", etc. In practice this is not so; it is useful for psycho-analysis to be able to signify degrees of growth and to represent these by stages with their proper sign.

Hitherto I have spoken of "growth" and "increased sophistication" when speaking of the progression from A to H; is it possible to give more precise meaning to these terms? I shall consider some possibilities.

Growth from elements of one row to the row next below cannot very well be measured by an increase in the "uses" (represented by the columns of the horizontal axis) to which the element can be put for I have already supposed that any element in its character as member of a row also can have a character derived from its membership of any column of the horizontal axis and in practice it is useful to retain this supposition. An approximation to universality of uses to which a row can be put is therefore unlikely to provide a criterion for growth. It may be that some rows are better suited to serve a multiplicity of uses than others. Similarly some uses may be served more effectively by some rows than by others. For example, I have said that β-elements lend themselves to projective identification when that mechanism is employed to evacuate a part of the personality, but are useless, or at best extremely unsuited, for use in thinking—which is to say for any use other than those of columns 2 and 6. A possible approach may therefore be provided by considering the nature of the match between the stage (or row) and the use matching row and column in terms of the appropriateness of one to the other, but this only shelves the problem by postponing it to a later stage in the discussion, for it necessitates criteria by which to judge appropriateness. Some of the pitfalls are less dangerous in the practice of analysis than they are in an abstract discussion of the problems. Thus in practice it is easier to feel that β-elements are not appropriate to thinking than to discuss in the abstract a criterion for the appropriate. Herein lies one advantage that the psycho-analyst possesses over the philosopher; his statements can be related to realizations and realizations to a psycho-analytic theory. What psycho-analytic thinking requires is a method of notation and rules for its employment that will enable work to be done in the *absence* of the object, to facilitate further work in the *presence* of the object. The barrier to this that is presented by unfettered play of an analyst's phantasies has long been recognized: pedantic statement on the one hand and verbalization loaded with unobserved implications on the other mean that the potential for misunderstanding and erroneous deduction is so high as to vitiate the value of the work done with such defective tools. I would retain the freedom to speak of "incorporating" a particular theory "in the main body of analytic theory", with the precision necessary for use[1] of Melanie Klein's theories of internal objects. This means that there must be psycho-analytic invariants, of which I have already written, psycho-analytic variables, and psycho-analytic parameters. These mathematical terms, used in this sentence as models, row C, need transformation to fit them for psycho-analytic use as row F, G and H elements.

[1] Columns 1, 3 and 4.

By writing "psycho-analytic" invariants, variables and parameters I have limited the universe of discourse; only within this universe of discourse can these terms be described as representing invariants or parameters. There is opportunity for ambiguity if this is not recognized; the term "variable" may describe something which, in a particular universe of discourse, is given a constant value and so qualifies for description as a parameter (as in a mathematical formulation, say $ax + by - c = 0$, the signs a, b, c, representing variables are given constant value).

According to Heisenberg, in atomic physics a situation has arisen in which the scientist cannot rely on the ordinarily accepted view that the researcher has access to facts, because the facts to be observed are distorted by the very act of observation. Furthermore, the field in which he has to observe the relationship of one phenomenon to another is unlimited in extent, and yet none of the phenomena "in" that field can be ignored because all interact. It follows that the fact that the universe of discourse is finite is not matched by a corresponding fact in the relationship to each other of the realizations supposedly approximating to the universe of discourse. The universe of discourse itself must always be defined (thus falling into the categories of grid column 1) if its terms are to have meaning. Yet, by virtue of this very fact it becomes of doubtful validity unless it is realized that to the finite universe of discourse no realization corresponds.

The point may not be of immediate importance, but it may be a source of error and it *is* a part of the psycho-analyst's methodological problem. The situation of the psycho-analyst dealing with psychotic transformations is similar to that attributed to nuclear physicists. He has to deal with relationships of a domain that has no finite limitations. The terms psycho-analytic invariant, variable and parameter are meaningful in a universe of discourse that has in one important respect no realization corresponding to it; his interpretations have characteristics of relatedness that are applicable to his universe of discourse, but not to the phenomena they represent, since those phenomena possess a relatedness, if there is one, appropriate to an infinite universe. If a patient says that he knows that his "char" is in league with the postman because his friend left white of egg in the bathroom the relatedness implied by his statement may differ from forms of relatedness to which I am accustomed because his statement represents phenomena related to each other in an infinite universe.

Freud made a statement, which is similar in principle, when he adumbrated the universe of discourse in which conscious behaviour is studied by postulating an unconscious, but the characteristics of *relatedness* remain unchanged in the new universe of discourse. The differentiating factor that I wish to introduce is not between conscious and unconscious, but between finite and infinite. Nevertheless I use, as my model for forms of relatedness in an infinite universe, forms of relatedness operative in a finite universe of discourse and its approximate realization. It follows therefore that the model is likely to be faulty.

When I used the concrete elements of a transformation (namely the subject stimulating the artist) at one end of the chain of events and the finished painting at the other, I did so to provide a model for a part of the whole—the part that takes place in the mind of the artist. The psycho-analyst's domain is that which lies between the point where a man receives sense impressions and the point where he gives expression to the transformation that has taken place. The principles of this investigation must be the same whether the medium is painting, music, mathematics, sculpture, or a relationship between two people, whether expressed verbally or by any other means. These principles must be determined so that they remain constant whether the transformation is effected in a mind which is sane or insane.

I take an illustration from an analysis in which the patient had considerable adjustment to reality. He entered the room, and, avoiding my glance, walked to the couch and lay down while I was going to my chair. On these facts, as it appeared in the session, there was agreement between us, but he showed great anxiety and told me that he felt, when walking to the couch, that I was attacking his genitalia from behind. He was able to tell me that this was as real to him as the agreed facts. He did not know why he was anxious. That, as near as I can make it so, is a correct account of what took place and is my transformation (Ta β) of what took place (O). Is it advantageous to regard this episode as a transformation and, if so, in what respect?

I propose to consider this episode in detail though in analysis this was not, and could not be, possible. I shall use the proposals I have made in *Learning from Experience*, *Elements of Psycho-Analysis*, and the preceding chapters of this book.

The discussion has a two-fold aim; to carry the investigation further and to give an example, in doing so, of my method of applying my methods. First I shall divest myself of pre-conceptions approximating to the state of naivety[1] which translate roughly into words: "*not* knowing to make room for a pre-conception that will illuminate a problem that excites my curiosity."

A lake in calm bright weather reflects trees upon the bank on the shore opposite the observer. The image presented by the trees is transformed in the reflection: a whole series of transformations is effected by atmospheric changes. Suppose the observer could see only the reflection; he would be able to deduce the nature of O from what he saw. Provided conditions were not too disturbed, the demands on the observer's deductive powers would be relatively simple if he were expected only to recognize that he observed the reflection of trees, more difficult if he were called upon to pronounce on the species of tree and impossible if he were to state the nature of microscopical features of leaf structure.

The change in atmosphere from light to darkness or from calm to turbulence would influence the transformation sometimes slightly, at others so deeply that the observer would have to exercise all his perceptiveness to deduce the nature of O. Just as the demands on him could be impossibly exacting so that atmospheric conditions could be impossibly distorting.

I shall use this as a model for the analytic observation of

[1] See *Elements of Psycho-Analysis*, p. 86.

transformations. It will be convenient to suppose that the L, H, K links influence the transformation in a manner analogous to the atmospheric changes in the model: convenient, but not necessarily true, as will be obvious by reference to analytic experience when the emotional tie is extremely complex; so are atmospheric conditions. I do not suggest that turbulence and distortion are invariably the outcome of emotion, but wish to leave myself free to consider the situation when emotions might provide a constant and the variations might be due to some other factor.

In the model, the trees at the lake-side are supposed to be the manifestation of O. What is the nature of the counterpart of O in analysis? Can we suppose that it is invariably a fact known to analyst and analysand, or at least knowable to both? In fact there is no choice in the matter, for if we postulate that O might be *any* circumstance in the patient's life whether known to the analyst or not we postulate a condition that makes analysis impossible. There *are* such facts, but analytic effectiveness depends on their being irrelevant to the analytic procedure or relevant only in so far as some aspect of such a fact *is* available to both analyst and analysand. I therefore postulate that O in any analytic situation is available for transformation by analyst and analysand equally.

I shall ignore disturbance produced by the analyst's personality or aspects of it. The existence of such disturbance is well known and its recognition is the basis for analytic acceptance of the need for analysts to be analysed and the many studies of counter-transference. While other scientific disciplines recognize the personal equation, or the factor of personal error, no science other than psycho-analysis has insisted on such a profound and prolonged investigation of its nature and ramifications. I ignore it therefore so as to keep an already over-complicated problem down to its simplest terms. I shall assume an ideal analyst and that Ta α and Ta β are not distorted by turbulence—though turbulence and its sources are part of O.

To summarize the preceding discussion:

1. In psycho-analysis any O not common to analyst and

analysand alike, and not available therefore for transformation by both, may be ignored as irrelevant to psycho-analysis. Any O not common to both is incapable of psycho-analytic investigation; any appearance to the contrary depends on a failure to understand the nature of psycho-analytic interpretation.

2. Transformation, i.e. Tp α or Ta α, is influenced by L, H and K. The analyst is assumed to allow for or exclude L or H from his link with the patient and Ta α and Ta β are assumed for purposes of this discourse to be free from distortion by L, H (i.e. by counter-transference). Tp α and Tp β, on the contrary, are assumed always to be subject to distortion and the nature of that distortion, in so far as it is an object of illumination through psycho-analytic interpretation, is the O of the transformation that the analyst effects in his progress from observation to interpretation. This brings me to consider whether or not it is possible to put a further limitation on what must be considered to lie in the domain of O in psycho-analysis; so far I have suggested O must be available to Ta α and Tp α and to this have added that the transformation of the patient must always be the O that is transformed when the analyst works to arrive at an interpretation. But the analyst must have a view of the psycho-analytic theory of the Oedipus situation. His understanding of that theory can be regarded as a transformation of that theory and in that case all his interpretations, verbalized or not, of what is going on in a session may be seen as transformations of an O that is bi-polar. One pole of O is trained intuitive capacity transformed to effect its juxtaposition with what is going on in the analysis and the other is in the facts of the analytic experience that must be transformed to show what approximation the realization has to the analyst's preconceptions—the preconception here being identical with Ta β as the end-product of Ta α operating on the analyst's psycho-analytic theories.

Freud stated as one of the criteria by which a psycho-analyst was to be judged was the degree of understanding allegiance he paid to the theory of the Oedipus complex. He thus showed the importance he attached to this theory and time has done nothing to suggest that he erred by over-estimation; evidence of the Oedipus complex is never absent though it can be unobserved.

Melanie Klein, in her paper on "Early Phases of the Oedipus Complex", made observations of Oedipal elements where their presence was previously undetected; methods of observation, notation and record, should make failure to detect relevant material less frequent. Part of the equipment of observation is pre-conception used for preconception—D4. It is in its D4 aspect that I wish to consider the Oedipal theory; that is, as part of the observational equipment of the analyst. The behaviour which this apparatus, "Oedipus complex D4", is to scrutinize bears qualities of rows A and B.

But now, difficulties. The first step seems simple enough: to set out the theoretical apparatus with which I shall investigate the material. The theories with which I propose to investigate the patient's material should, in accordance with the theories in the previous part of this book, be described as transformations of the experience of training and learning that I have had. They may be denoted by the sign Ta β of O1, O1 here being the stimulus provided by my accumulation of experience, and Ta β of O2, O2 being the experience of the session I am investigating. Ta β, the end product of my transformation of theories that were passed on to me in personal analysis and training, can now be categorized, according to the degree of sophistication with which it is expressed, as belonging to columns 1, 3, 4, 5, and rows D to F. But the state of free-floating attention, usually regarded as desirable in the analyst, is the more effective the more it approximates to being represented by a wide spectrum of grid categories. Therefore the analyst's state of mind should not be limited to categories E4 and F4, say, but rather to the area of categories C $\rightarrow$ F by 1, 3, 4, 5. In practice this means that the analyst should be cognizant of dreams in which patients appear, though his interpretation of the significance of their appearance will relate more to their characteristics as column 2 phenomena than to their significance as evidence of his own psychopathology.

The analyst's theoretical equipment may thus be narrowly described D4, E4, F4, but the state of mind in which the theories are available in the session should cover a wider spectrum of the grid. With this proviso in mind I propose to limit the following description of theories to statements that fall in the categories E1, E3, E4 and E5. I mean to employ the following theories:

(1) The theory of projective identification and splitting; mechanisms by which the breast provides what the patient later takes over as his own apparatus for α-function.

(2) The theory that some personalities cannot tolerate frustration.

(3) The theory that a personality with a powerful endowment of envy tends to denude its objects by both stripping and exhaustion.

(4) The theory that at an early stage (or on a primitive level of mind) the oedipal situation is represented by part objects.

(5) The Kleinian theory of envy and greed.

(6) The theory that primitive thought springs from experience of a non-existent object, or, in other terms, of the *place* where the object is expected to be, but is not.

(7) The theory of violence in primitive functions.

As I have already written of these theories in *Learning from Experience* and *Elements of Psycho-Analysis* I shall say no more of them here. These theories, as extensions of the oedipal situation, must be present in the analyst's mind in a form that enables them to be represented in a wide range of grid categories.

I shall now consider phenomena that the state of expectation represented by these theories might be expected to reveal. One difficulty, of those to which I referred on page 5, concerns the communication of material from an experience that is ineffable; the scientific approach, as ordinarily understood, is not available and an aesthetic approach requires an artist. Therefore the reader will need to be indulgent if he is to grasp the meaning I wish to convey; he will find the clinical experience, if it comes his way, simpler than my description makes it appear.

The external stimulus, O, is provided by an impending break of sufficient duration to excite more powerful reactions than those observed at weekends. I knew envy and intolerance of frustration to be powerful factors in the analytic situation and that violence was a prominent function in the patient's personality; he feared violence, his own and other people's; his emotions were violent, his ambitions violently pursued and obstructed, his course of action violently maintained. His thought processes were extremely disturbed, many of his utterances being incomprehensible even after prolonged analysis. When I thought I grasped his meaning it was often by virtue of an aesthetic rather than a scientific experience. There were short-lived lucid communications in which words and syntax were combined in a conventional manner. My own theoretical pre-dispositions I have already indicated. For reasons of discretion references to actual clinical material will be few, and drawn from more than one patient, but this I believe will not produce distortion in matter relevant to the discussion. I shall draw on a wide range of illustration, including historical matter, to fill gaps that I cannot leave without obscurity or fill without disclosure of private matter.

CHAPTER FIVE

THE patient's reaction to O is primitive with material belonging to the categories of rows A and B.

His presence shows that he knows that *I* am present. This fact is used, conformably with column 2 categories, to deny my *absence*. He reacts in the session as if I were absent. This behaviour, in accordance with column 2 categories, is intended to deny my *presence*. Though "absence" and "presence" are each characteristic of column 2 they are brought together at this stage in the analysis, in accordance with A4 and B4 categories.[1]

The state of mind I have described is represented for me by a model—that of an adult who *violently* maintains an exclusively primitive omnipotent ↔ helpless state. The model by which I represent *his* "vision" of *me* is that of an absent breast, the place or position, that I, the breast, *ought* to occupy but do not. The "ought" expresses *moral* violence and omnipotence. The visual image of me can be represented by what a geometer might call a point, a musician the staccato mark in a musical score. As this attitude is important I shall deal with it in detail, using ideas expressed earlier in the book.

The name given an object, often regarded as the sign for a quality abstracted from something,[2] or from which something has been abstracted,[2] is by me defined as genetically related to a selected fact. It is a sign intended to mark, and bind, a constant conjunction. It is therefore significant, but devoid of meaning.[3] It receives its accretion of meaning from experience. It is similar to a theory in that both imply that certain qualities are constantly conjoined; therefore, it cannot properly be described as true or false in its relationship to O; these terms express judgements on the health-giving effect of the theory to which they are applied, upon the

[1] Second cycle of transformation.

[2] See Paton, H. J.

[3] Compare Russell, B. *Principles of Mathematics*, Chap. XXVII.

personality entertaining the theory. The differentiation to be made to the name, or theory, is between "useful" and "not useful"; it can be categorized according to the terms of the 1 — n axis.

Implicit in the name as that which signifies constant conjunction, and inseparable from this significance, is the quality of negation. A constant conjunction, thus bound by a name, is *not* whatever the personality has observed as existing previously, but may be similar to it. This has been a cause of difficulty as far back as Aristotle.[1] In practice it presents difficulty to the patient who cannot tolerate frustration, and in whom envy, greed and cruelty are dominant.

In the illustration the problem centres on the fact that the absent breast, the "no-breast", differs from the breast. If this is accepted the "no-breast" can be represented by the visual image of the point. But if this is a column 2 phenomenon the point lacks the quality of a definitory statement and approximates to an object with column 3 characteristics. It therefore has the meaning that it is a breast that has been reduced to a mere position—the place where the breast was. This state appears to the patient to be a consequence either of greed that has exhausted the breast, or of splitting that has destroyed the breast leaving only the position.

The patient's relationship with himself is prejudiced if he *cannot* advance to recognition of a new experience and so falls back on existing meaning, or *does* progress and has to face frustration he cannot tolerate. He can decide, if such a term is permissible in this context, whether to make destructive attacks on his link with his object and so destroy his embryonic thought processes, or to tolerate it and allow his apparatus for thought to develop. A patient with the characteristics postulated will be likely to suffer disturbances of thought either way, for acceptance of the "no-breast" confronts him with the problem of what to do with the attendant "thoughts". The problem does not exist in one dimension only; tolerance of frustration involves awareness of the presence or absence of objects, and of what a developing personality later comes to know as "time" and (as I

[1] Aristotle: *Topics*, VI.6, 143 b 11 (p. 158).

have described the "position" where the breast used to be) "space".

The factors that reduce the breast to a point, reduce time to "now". Time is denuded of past and future. The "now" is subjected to attacks similar to those delivered against space, or more precisely, the point. It is both exhausted and split. This leads to expressions which can mislead for such a patient will say "at the moment" when he means "never" and "yesterday" or "tomorrow" when he means a split-off fragment of "now"; such beliefs contribute to the problems of a patient who cannot tolerate staccato markings in a musical score.

To turn now to the problems that await the personality that can accept "thoughts". As I have said, the definitory aspect of the name can be seen to have a negative foundation, that is, *not* a, b, c, etc.; or significance without meaning (thereby taking on the uses of column 4, the counterpart in "use" of what I have called, in the genetic axis of the grid, a pre-conception).

The "thoughts" can be combined with other "thoughts" in accordance with rules of syntax if they are verbally stated, rules of mathematical manipulation, if they are mathematically stated, or rules of musical composition if musically stated. But such rules are easier to conceive of in an advanced state of mental development than in the primitive domain with which I am dealing here and I shall leave the discussion of rules of combination on one side till later.[1]

According to Proclus, objection was raised against the term *στιγμη* by Plato on the grounds that it meant puncture and therefore suggested a background of reality that was not appropriate to geometric discussion. The objection resembles that of a patient to the visual image of the point because of its unwelcome penumbra of associations. He had evaded the difficulty by a neologism; my concern is not with the solution of the problem, but with its resemblance to the scientific difficulty of using terms with a long history to express novel situations.

The Pythagoreans regarded the point as having position,

[1] See Chapter 10, p. 133.

but Euclid did not include this in his definition, though he and Archimedes and later writers used the term *σημετον* instead of *στιγμή*; Aristotle in discussing the prevalent notion of the relatedness of the point to the line objected that, the point being indivisible, no accumulation of points can give anything divisible such as a line.[1] The significance of the discussion lies in the wish to establish the connection felt to exist between the point and the line. An analyst reading contributions to the establishment of scientific geometry would see that elements appear that invite psychoanalytic interpretation of the kind indicated. I shall have reason to quote illustrations that strengthen the impression of the sexual component in the mathematical investigation, but I do not propose to go into this aspect of geometric history.

Granted that a patient is capable of visual images, represented by the words "point" and "line", two apparently divergent courses appear to be open to him; he can *think* them, that is, use thoughts in accordance with rules which are acceptable to, and understandable by, others. This leads to the proliferation of a range of statements that fall into grid categories H1, H3, H4, etc. (I ignore H2, though that is possible also) and ultimately to the scientific structures of modern mathematics. *Or*, he *cannot* think them (if we exclude splitting, exhaustion and projection or evacuation as outside what is ordinarily meant by thought) and does not elaborate or employ rules of combination and manipulation that are widely acceptable. Such a patient, as in an instance quoted by Segal,[2] has no difficulty in seeing that a man playing a violin is masturbating in public: the fact that he is giving a public performance on the violin is significant, in the sense I have given the term, and it has a meaning, but the meaning it has for him is not the same as the meaning which it has for the ordinary person who regards the performer's activity as a part of music. The ordinary view of it as a musical activity is as alien to him as his view is to the ordinary person. Why then, to revert to the point and

[1] *Physics*, IV, 8, 215, big.
[2] Segal, H.: *Introduction to the work of Melanie Klein.*

line, do these visual images lead in one case to the efflorescence of mathematics and in the other to mental sterility? And is it certain that "mental sterility" is a correct assessment? The question implies the validity of a theory of causation which I consider misleading and liable to give rise to constructions that are basically false; if it is fallacious we may discard it for one as fallacious—which may be true of the formulation, by Heisenberg,[1] of the problem of multiple causation. Both views have proved of value in the development of science, but developments of physics by the Copenhagen school appear to have made the theory irrelevant. If so, the logical step would be to bother no longer with causation or its counterpart—results. In psycho-analysis it is difficult to avoid feeling that a gap is left by its disappearance and that the gap should be filled. Over a wide range of our problems no difficulty is caused by regarding the theory of causation as fallacious, but useful. When it comes to problems presented by disturbances in thought the difficulty cannot be met in this way. For though it is possible, as in the chain of reasoning I have reported,[2] to see that the patient has a theory of causation that requires assessment, such assessment cannot be made without contrasting it with some other theory—presumably the analyst's own.

Melanie Klein's theory of the part played by intolerance of depression illuminates the problem presented by the chain of causation I have reported.[2] The patient is persecuted by the meaning of certain facts that he feels to be significant. Further, he is persecuted by the feelings of persecution. This is explicable if we accept that the patient is intolerant of depression and that this hinders the $Ps \leftrightarrow D$ interchange. The proposed chain of causation can then be seen as a *rationalization* of the sense of persecution. Furthermore, if the patient is capable of seeing that his proposed chain of causation is nonsensical he may use it to deny the persecution and thus evade any explanation that would reveal the depression that he dreads.

[1] Heisenberg, W.: *Physics and Philosophy.*

[2] Chapter 4 above.

In putting forward such a suggestion I am postulating a chain of causation in the phenomena I witnessed. I shall risk being misled by an inadequate theory and suggest, as I did in the actual analysis, that the fear of depression depends on the dominance in the patient of a cruel super-ego.

I shall employ mythology to clarify the next stage in my discussion. In terms of the grid I use thought that belongs to the category C4, and in particular the myth (Eden) that an omniscient and harsh god, opposed to knowledge, is dominant. The Babel myth of the god that confounds language, or the myth of fate attending the Sphinx in the Oedipus myth would serve equally well.

The logical formulation of the problem points to a conflict between omniscience on the one hand and inquiry on the other. Further steps will show that the logical causal approach produces a circular argument. Is there any objection to this and, if so, is there an approach that is better? We have to consider not the patient's "theory of causation" only but that of the analyst also. As the problem is methodological psycho-analytic findings on all that touches learning cannot be separated from it.

The patient in the illustration was attempting to convince himself, or me, of the validity of a causal chain as something to which reason automatically owed allegiance. I was invited to collude with him in agreeing that this particular causal chain was valid. And "valid" in this context meant "not requiring scrutiny". This interpretation is my assessment of the emotional scene in which I was witness and participant. It is an experience that cannot be understood by any that have not experienced it and I cannot demonstrate that the account given represents the facts accurately but at some future date an experience, mine or another's, might approximate to this description.

The accounts that I have given, and the one that I am about to give, might be described as "theories" of what took place. In view of the associations that belong to the term "theory" I prefer the term "transformation". The accounts I give of this episode are transformations in the sense that I have given the term in Chapter 1 and subsequently. The reader may use the grid for evaluating the transformations printed in this book. My overt aim is to write something that could correctly be described as falling within the categories F1, 3, 4, 5; but the reader may assess them differently and attach different grid categories to the communication according to the facets that he sees.

To return to the episode: in the session the patient was passing rapidly from one visual image to another. In so far as the visual images were parts of his own personality he was identifying himself first with one and then with another. They could not be synthesized; that is to say, he could not allow himself the experience of the selected fact which gives coherence to elements not previously seen to be coherent. Nor could he dismiss the persecuting elements so long as he could not permit coherence. The chain of causation was designed with the express purpose of preventing coherence. But the feeling of persecution itself becomes a persecution, this persecution being "bound" by the idea of a cause. In this context the term "cause" and the associated theory of causation relates not to external reality but psychic reality. The source of anxiety in the patient is his fear of depression and an associated fear of the $Ps \leftrightarrow D$ interchange, the mechanisms of the selected fact. I categorize the idea of cause, in this context, as D2, that is, a relatively primitive pre-conception used to prevent the emergence of something else. The patient's communication in so far as it is to be described as logical, is a circular argument, supposedly based on a theory of causation, employed to destroy contact with reality, not to further it. In this respect it qualifies for one of Freud's criteria for psychosis—hatred of reality. But the reality that is hated is the reality of an aspect of the patient's personality.[1]

To avoid complexity and the risk of confusion, I shall assume that my interpretations were governed by the need to establish my own and the patient's contact with his psychic realities. If I employ a theory of causation and give

[1] The theory of causation is only valid in the domain of morality and only morality can *cause* anything. Meaning has no influence outside the psyche and causes nothing.

it expression in a circular argument[1] my transformation differs from that of the patient; his transformation falls in category C2 and mine in F3 and F4.

This account implies that the apparatus is secondary to the impulses that lie behind its employment—a conclusion which would not surprise a psycho-analyst. Nevertheless the apparatus matters. The impulses concerned determine (i) the way in which the apparatus is employed, and (ii) the fate of the apparatus itself. In severe disturbance it is possible to see apparatus employed in a manner calculated to destroy it. What, in a less disturbed patient, appears as a hostile attack on either the oedipal situation or a part-object oedipal situation, must, in the severely disturbed patient, be seen as an attack on the oedipal, or part-object oedipal, *pre-conception*—the apparatus that should make the relationship between the parents comprehensible and give it meaning. In disorders of thought interpretations must illuminate the condition of the apparatus of thinking, the nature of its deficiencies and the nature of the associated impulses. In practice I find I have constantly to give interpretations in the form that some impulse "leads to" a particular defect (or characteristic) of the mode of thought; or that some characteristic of the mode of thought "gives rise" to a particular impulse, as, for example, that frustration, engendered by failure to solve a problem, "leads to" a destructive attack on the analytic approach. I regard these statements as conversational formulations employing a theory I know to be false because it serves a useful purpose in the absence of the correct theory. This may, and often does, prove adequate in practice—it is usually adequate to speak in everyday life of sunrise. Nevertheless there are analytic situations, particularly when psychotic material is to the fore, when this is *not* adequate. The patient seems unable or unwilling to make for himself the adjustment of a conversational phrase which would make that phrase meaningful for him. The theory implicit in the interpretation must be exact. As I shall show later, this also applies to the emotional tone accompanying the interpretation: if

[1] For circular argument, see p. 111.

I am attempting to establish a K link, which is after all the case with any interpretation, there must be no emotion belonging to the H or L group. This may seem a commonplace of counter-transference theory, but it is not. A neurotic patient makes some allowance for human frailty; the psychotic patient either behaves as if the verbal communication had not been received, or, that it is a vehicle for transmission of some aspect of L or H—usually projection of it by the analyst into the patient.[1]

The patient's apparent demand for exactitude both with regard to the verbal communication itself and the emotional accompaniment seems to have some relationship to what I have said about the point "now". I spoke of this as associated with denudation of the elemental or primitive breast. In this context it is associated with inability to receive anything but a communication that is "pure".

Analysts are so accustomed to the fact that the link between analyst and patient is verbal that certain implications of this may escape scrutiny. These can be made to emerge more clearly by considering the verbal exchanges as transformations.

The analyst's transformations employ the vehicle of speech just as the musician's transformations are musical and the painter's pictorial. Though the analyst attempts to transform O, in accordance with the rules and discipline of verbal communication, this is not necessarily the case with the patient. He may, for example, transform O into what may *seem* to be a verbal communication but is to the analyst something akin to hallucination.[2] Such transformation (Tp β) belongs to the domain not of verbal communication but of hallucination, be it auditory, visual or tactile. It should therefore be helpful if, by analogy with painting, music or verbal communication, it were possible to understand the discipline and rules, so to speak, of hallucination.

[1] In successful analysis the patient brings to bear quite brilliant intuitive grasp of the possibilities that his analyst's deficiencies offer his super-ego for demolition of the analyst.

[2] What I say here is not exclusive of, but in addition to, what I have said about hallucination elsewhere.

The patient as receptor seems to receive everything as if it had the characteristics of the point, whether he is to understand time, or space, or meaning: as emitter he can only express transformations that are effected in a domain with the discipline of which we are unfamiliar. What "rules" govern the transformation of O into a visual hallucination rather than an auditory hallucination, or vice versa? or into hallucination rather than music or art or more ordinary forms of communication?

In discussion of transformation I drew attention to invariants; in painting there must be something that is invariant to the representation and that which is represented. It may be that the reaction stimulated is the element common to both object represented and representation. Yet one feels that something more is required than the reaction of the beholder—something present in object and its representation. If so, what is invariant in the word "cow" and the object it represents? If the word is onomatopoeic the sound can be regarded as invariant but such an element is relatively rare. It cannot satisfactorily be supposed that there is some simple factor like learning by heart that the name cow belongs to a particular animal. That memorization is present seems to be supported by incidents where an adult repeats to a child "Look, there is —— (whatever or whoever it is)!" when it reappears. If so, it may be part of being taught by communication of adult experience as opposed to learning from experience direct. It is easier to accept it as true that someone "cannot understand music" or "cannot understand painting" than to accept that a similar difficulty exists with regard to speech. Yet sometimes I think that this is so; the actual *medium* of speech is not understood.

The mother's inability to accept the projective identifications of the infant and the association of such failure with disturbances in understanding is matched by complications arising through the existence of an extremely understanding mother, particularly understanding by virtue of ability to *accept* projective identification. A reaction associated with this resembles character disorder, an unwillingness to face loss of an idyllic state for a new phase and suppression of the new phase because it involves pain. It is against this background of hallucinosis, projective identification, splitting and persecution, accepted as if it were the ideally happy state, that I want to consider the domain of verbal communication. The sense of well-being engendered by a belief in the existence of the perfectly understanding mother (or analyst) adds force to the fear and hatred of thoughts which are closely associated with, and may therefore be felt to be indistinguishable from, the "no-breast". A painful state of mind is clung to, including depression, because the alternative is felt to be worse, namely that thought and thinking mean that a near perfect breast has been destroyed.

The name, in its function of binding a constant conjunction, partakes of the nature of a definition; it commences by being significant, but meaningless, till experience gives it accumulations of meaning; it derives negative force both by virtue of its genesis as part of thought and by the necessary logic of its coming into existence precisely because the constant conjunction it binds is *not* any of the previous and already named constant conjunctions. Dislike of it is therefore derived from its genesis and from fear of the implications of its "use".[1] As naming and definition are inescapable this contributes to dislike of the unknown and the challenge it presents to the learner. The intensity of dislike depends on other factors. At what point the dislike of the unknown and its impact on the development of procedures which are a part of finding out must be regarded as pathological is an academic question; it is decided for the analyst whenever there is evidence of a desire to learn and an inability to do so. In such a situation primitive levels of thought are stimulated to discover the "cause" of the obstruction.[2] Evidence of the employment of a theory of causation is evidence of the operation of a theory that is not adequate. I shall consider the genesis of a theory of causation and its use with the aid of the grid and its two axes. Appearance

[1] Cf. Aristotle and definitions. *Topics*, VI, 4, 141b, 21.

[2] Cf. Hume, D.: *Enquiries Concerning Human Understanding*, Q 43–45. See also circular argument later, p. 111.

in a given situation—inquiry obstructed either by analyst or patient—must be assessed on the category in the grid to which it should be relegated. If it appears to belong to column 2 categories the presumption of a pathological origin will be strong. If it belongs to column 4 it is evidence, especially in a K link such as an analysis ought to be, for something compatible with healthy growth.

Ideally this inquiry should deal simultaneously with the process of transformation by which O is converted into thought, or whatever the alternatives to thought may be, and the processes of development (or transformation) which are associated with the *link* between thoughts and the *links* between the various alternatives to thought.

Invariant to β-elements and bizarre objects, in so far as they share the characteristics of β-elements, is the moral component of such objects. The moral component is inseparable from feelings of guilt and responsibility and from a sense that the *link* between one such object and another, and between these objects and the personality, is moral causation. The theory of causation, in a scientific sense in so far as it has one, is therefore an instance of carrying over from a moral domain an idea (for want of a better word) into a domain in which its original penumbra of moral association is inappropriate.[1]

The observation of constant conjunction of phenomena whose conjunction or coherence has not been previously observed, and therefore the whole process of $Ps \leftrightarrow D$ interaction, definition and search for meaning that is to be attached to the conjunction, can be destroyed by the strength of a sense of causation and its moral implications. Patients show[2] that the resolution of a problem appears to present less difficulty if it can be regarded as belonging to a moral domain; causation, responsibility and therefore a controlling force (as opposed to helplessness) provide a framework within which omnipotence reigns. In certain

[1] Usurpation of ego-function by super-ego. See Chapter 4.

[2] And not only patients. The group is dominated by morality—I include of course the negative sense that shows as rebellion against morality—and this contributed to the atmosphere of hostility to individual thought on which Freud remarked.

circumstances, to be considered later,[1] the scene is thus set for conflict (reflected in controversies such as those on Science and Religion). This situation is portrayed in the Eden and Babel myths. The significance for the individual lies in its part in obstructing the Ps $\leftrightarrow$ D interaction.

Hume's objection to a theory of causation supposes that since neither a hammer nor a nail can feel force it is not correct to speak of a nail being forced into position by the hammer, the term "force" being properly applicable only to the sense-experience of a human being who exerts force or on whom it is exerted. He supposes therefore that to speak of force as an external reality is a projection of human feeling. The fact that one merely follows the other is thus obscured. This argument does not satisfactorily dispose of an objective link between hammer and nail. To begin with, why is a selection made so that only the movement of the nail is considered and then only in relation to the hammer? There must be precedent "causes" that lead to the presence of nail and hammer. Furthermore it takes no account of the need of the human mind to apply a term, already with its penumbra of association and proper domain, in a different domain and because of its value as a model. For the analyst there is the added complication that, since he is dealing with beings like himself, there would appear to be justification for supposing that the relationship between two people was force if identification with one or other leads him to think that in such a situation he would feel force was being applied. The problem of conflict, which I shall name "Science versus Morals" as a prelude to finding meaning, will be found to be illuminated by the transformation of scientific thought into moral thought that is necessary for the former to be made suitable for action—column 6.

In spite of these objections I think Hume's argument has validity for psycho-analysis. In its extreme form it could mean that scientific validity was denied to a conjecture even though it was supported by common sense. (But the argument must not be supposed to be employed in an extreme form; if it is so employed it would be wise to consider why

[1] See below, p. 169.

the argument was employed in a manner that qualified it for column 2.) Hume's theory that an idea owes its genesis to a sense impression contrasts with the theory of force as the link between hammer and nail, for the latter is derived from an animistic outlook.

The earliest problems demanding solution are related to a link between two personalities. The breast, as analytic experience shows, can be regarded as an object with personality or as inanimate. Or it may be that no distinction between animate and inanimate is made. Sometimes a problem is "dealt with"[1] by regarding the object as a thing, sometimes by regarding it as if it were a person—an infant person. In either case O is being transformed; judgment of either operation must hinge on whether the solutions attempted are growth-producing or the reverse. If the solution is a pre-conception, and can be used in accordance with columns 3, 4, 5, it is growth-producing.

Patients can be observed to change their attitude to an object by changes in view-point[2] which may be perverse or analogous to changes of position that a surveyor, terrestrial or astronomical, uses to estimate the range of a distant object. The procedure involves splitting in time and space and, depending on the nature of the intention, may aid the solution of a problem by providing a substitute for "binocular vision" when "binocular vision" is not available, or hinder a solution by destroying "binocular vision"[3] when it is available.[4] The immediate relevance of this lies in the use of splitting as a method of achieving correlation. The mechanism involves bringing together the splits. The

[1] I use an ambiguous phrase deliberately.

[2] See discussion of vertices.

[3] See also circular argument, p. 111.

[4] Throughout this book I employ precisely the mechanism I attempt to describe as observable in analytic practice. To draw attention to these occasions at all frequently would burden the text with so many digressions that it would make a difficult subject appear more difficult. In this instance I am using a phrase taken from a domain of scientific statements appropriate to Optics and a high category of sophistication, row E or F, to provide a model which would be best classified as a member of row C. It is an example of the mechanism I am discussing as related to correlation. See also circular argument.

obstacle to correlation for a personality whose splitting is motivated by destructive impulses, is the need for two objects to be brought together creatively.

The instances examined in this chapter indicate that the mechanisms remain the same, but that the situation changes according to the emotional drives in operation—a banal enough conclusion, but its significance lies in what it may portend. I associated K with curiosity, but it is necessary to consider other impulses, emotions and instincts (I do not distinguish these terms because no distinction is precise enough) namely, the phenomena I have lumped together as L and H and the effect of the intrusion of one group on the other.

Hitherto I have considered the use of the grid almost entirely in terms of K and have not questioned its applicability to relationships with L and H dominant. To return to my "conclusion" that the character of a dynamic situation changes according to the emotional drives in operation even though the mechanisms are unaltered: I put the term "conclusion" in inverted commas because I am using it in a special way unrelated to any belief that some discussion has been "concluded". The statement made is a premise and is intended to fulfil the function of premises and postulates. That function I regard as marking a point of view[1] which is used as part of the mechanism of splitting and correlation to which I have referred.

This "view", which appears to ascribe a dominant position to emotion, is not a report, fact or discovery. In psycho-analysis there is difficulty in deciding when a statement is intended by its maker to represent a theory to be used if and when any realization appears to approximate to it (columns 4—n−1, n., of the grid), and when it is intended to be a statement of fact ("notation": grid 3). It is therefore often criticized in a way that would be appropriate to one belief but not to the other.

I shall combine the theory of dominance of emotion with the theory of transformation and use the grid to investigate both.[2]

[1] See vertices, Chapter 6.

[2] It would be more correct to say I shall correlate the three and see what eventuates from the correlation.

In Chapter 1, I used as a model of transformation the instance of the painting and its relationship to the object it purported to represent. I shall now use the image of reflection in water and the movement of air that disturbs it (Chapter 4). A representation, though distorted by emotion as a reflection in a lake might be distorted by a breeze, can be seen to have a relationship with the object. Equally, emotions that are active can be seen to have a relationship with the object even if disturbed by the representation. Again, the representation can be seen to be related to the emotions, and vice versa, even if disturbed by the object. To illustrate by clinical examples: a patient is dominated by hate of the analyst because of the transformation (Tp β) the analyst has undergone and the representation (Tp β) of the analyst that he now entertains. The patient entertains a representation (Tp β) of the analyst that is compatible with the hatred that has effected his transformation (Tp β). The patient entertains a transformation (Tp β) (it might be of a loved object) because of the hatred he feels for the person O of the analyst. It is inadequate to say there is a cause[1] for any of these situations. Yet I have said there is a relationship between the elements, and this means that one element effects and is effected by the others. Hume's argument that such a belief is a projection of an animistic outlook may not seem to apply to the view that one human being entertains of another. The fact that it is animistic may be obscured by the accident that the object observed is a human being. I shall suppose that the relationship is a "constant conjunction", that is to say, that the relationship is an element in the mind of the observer and may or may not have a counterpart in reality. I make no claim for objective reality, as far as I understand the meaning usually attributed to the term, but for me, a factual situation (conjectured) an emotional state (say hate, also conjectured) a representation (Tp β) are constantly conjoined and I record (grid E3) or bind (grid E1) it by the term "transformation".

It follows from the theory of transformations that whenever

[1] But see circular argument for the *value* of such a theory (p. 111).

I see one element of the equation O, Tp α, Tp β + L, or H or K, the others must be present. But I shall *not* assume that one causes the other, though for convenience I may (as I have already done when I used the phrase "because of the hatred", etc., p. 68) employ a theory of causation to express myself.[1] Indeed the object of binding what seems to be a constant conjunction of elements by a name "transformation" is in the hope of discovering the meaning of the constant conjunction.

The constant conjunction does not *have* to be marked by one word; it may be marked by two—e.g. "constant conjunction", or by a phrase, or an entire deductive system. Indeed such expansion may be an expression of the growth of meaning once the constant conjunction has been bound or recorded. (Columns 1 and 3.)

To return to the model of the reflection in water and its representation of transformation: in analysis all transformations, patient's or analyst's, are conventionally supposed to be expressed verbally. Such a supposition cannot legitimately be entertained with patients who transform in hallucinosis or some other unknown realm. The following problems may be discerned.

1. What is invariant to a name and the object named? For example, it appears that there is a flower rose (O) called "rose". What is it that leads a man who hears this word to relate it to a particular flower? What is invariant to the following marks on the paper—rose—and the flower visible in a garden?

2. Since I am proposing to classify statements, such as "rose", according to grid categories, and these statements are representations of transformations; since furthermore we know that a statement such as "I hate you" can be used in a manner compatible with column 1, or 6, or 2, and therefore represents a transformation whose elements are in a state of balance that differs according to whether it properly belongs to column 1 or 2 or 6, what difference does it make if the grid is being used to investigate an H link rather than K?

[1] I shall not draw attention to this, leaving the reader to note instances for himself, unless there is some especial reason for doing so, e.g. p. 68.

or L rather than H? The balance is different because the components are different and to suppose that a change in components makes no difference can only mean that in the domain of the psyche the observer is incapable of discrimination and therefore of recognition of the selected fact that gives coherence and meaning where none existed before. Can the grid be used for situations other than K? And if not, does this mean a defect in the grid or some basic difference between L, H or K?

In analytic practice it is generally agreed that love or hate between analyst and patient should not obtrude. Curiosity cannot be banned if patient and analyst are to learn anything. It is a part of common experience that strong feelings of love and hate affect ability to discriminate and learn. Therefore it is worth considering what grid categories the statements made by the two parties to an analysis, analyst and patient, are when L or H obtrude in what should be a K relationship. But the problem can also be regarded as concerned with the appropriateness of the grid as an instrument to be used for investigating L or H links. Considering the horizontal axis, there is no difficulty in retaining the headings found useful for K because an L relationship clearly cannot be regarded as excluding K either in logic or reality. Therefore a statement expressing love might perfectly well fall in column 1 as a definitory hypothesis. But the question, in practice, is not simply whether a statement *can* fall in a particular category. There are two questions involved. One is, whether I can formulate a theory that a transformation associated with L, or suffused with love, or perturbed by love, can be conceived of as falling in categories of column 1. The other is, is a particular statement illuminated by being thought of as belonging to one of the column 1 categories? The latter question is one that must be answered through the analytic process. The former must be answered with due consideration for methods of theory-formation and the construction of instruments (such as the grid) which are based on theoretical pre-conceptions. Is the grid soundly constructed for use not only in K but also for L and H links? If so, what is the difference between, say, D1 in K and D1 in L? There must be a difference because it is hard to imagine a transformation, and all statements are transformations in the view I am putting forward, that is, affected by L being correctly placed, that is, placed in a manner that increases meaning, if it is placed in the same category as a transformation affected by K.

Though I am speaking of "transformations affected by . . ." and so implying causation, I do not wish the reader to infer my belief in the implied theory, except as a convenience in verbal communication. At this juncture a theory of causation is a hindrance to understanding the theory I wish to advance, namely, that any element in a transformation can appear to the analyst to affect any other element and vice versa. It appears to affect other elements in the transformation (on the analogy of atmospheric change, affecting the reflection) but other elements can be regarded, indifferently, as affecting L. Using the model to show its inadequacy to represent my meaning: the atmospheric change disturbs the reflection, but (it would be necessary to say), the disturbed reflection affects (or "causes") the atmospheric change. Such a theory would not commend itself as a useful theory about reflections in lakes but it is the theory of transformation that I wish to put forward. The transformation represents a constant conjunction and the idea that it has a cause, or that one element causes another I regard as derived from forces within the observer and not necessarily having a part in the conjunction observed. In short, the idea that the constant conjunction has a meaning may be logically (meaning psycho-logically) necessary but is not necessary to the constant conjunction. The importance of this for this discussion lies in the fact that L, H and K must be regarded as an essential element amongst all the elements seen to be constantly conjoined. This is true of the analyst's constant conjunctions and of those that he thinks are an aspect of the analysand's personality. Any transformation may thus be regarded as (*a*) an instance of the analyst's seeing a number of elements as constantly conjoined and therefore worth binding by the name "transformation", and (*b*) an instance of the analysand's seeing a number of elements as constantly conjoined and therefore to be bound by whatever name he regards as adequate. The interpretation given should then afford an opportunity for analyst and analysand to contrast two sets of transformation, the analyst's and the analysand's, and the analysand's and the analysand's (when the latter is affecting two transformations of the same O—which is commonly the case in conflict).

A common instance of the factors I am discussing can be seen in pictorial art where the picture (transformation) can be classified as a portrait, or a caricature, or a cartoon, and so on. O may be the same in all representations, but a different name is given according to the components of the transformation. In the named examples the dominance of L or H or K will influence classification of the whole.

I shall now consider "meaning" and "constant conjunction" in more detail, leaving discussion of L, H and K till later.

CHAPTER SIX

A CONSTANT conjunction is a function of consciousness in the observer. The observer feels that it is a necessity *for him* that the conjunction should have a meaning *for him*. Meaning is a function of self-love, self-hate or self-knowledge. It is not logically, but psycho-logically necessary. The constant conjunction, once named, must then be found, as a matter of psychic necessity, to have a meaning. Once psycho-logically necessary meaning has been achieved reason, as the slave of the passions, transforms psycho-logically necessary meaning into logically necessary meaning. Inadequacy of hallucinatory gratification to promote mental growth impels activity designed to provide "true" meaning: it is felt that the meaning attributed to the constant conjunction must have a counterpart in the realization of the conjunction. Therefore the activity of the reason as the slave of the passions is inadequate. In terms of the theory of pleasure/pain principle there is a conflict between pleasure principle and reality principle to obtain control of the reason. The objection to a meaningless universe (however big or small it may be thought to be) derives from fear that the lack of meaning is a sign that meaning has been destroyed and the threat this holds for essential narcissism. If any given universe cannot yield a meaning *for the individual*, his narcissism demands the existence of a god, or some ultimate object, for which it has a meaning from which meaning he is supposed to benefit. In some instances meaninglessness is attacked by splitting and projected into an object. Meaning or its lack, in analysis, is a function of self-love, self-hate, self-knowledge.

If narcissistic love is unsatisfied the development of love is disturbed and cannot extend to love of objects.

Disturbed self-love is accompanied by intolerance of meaning or its lack. The one contributes to the other. If the theories put forward in this book are felt to have or to lack meaning, they and the reasons for rejection, or acceptance, must be regarded as functions of L, H and K links of the self with the self.

The significance of self-love, -hate and -knowledge in psycho-analytic practice may be contrasted with its philosophical, moral or religious significance as it appears, to take one example, in the saying of Jesus that "No man hath greater love than this, that he lay down his life for another." Psycho-analysis is concerned with love as an aspect of mental development and the analyst must consider the maturity of love and "greatness" in relation to maturity.

The value of the vertical axis of the grid as marking steps in maturation or L or H could be supported from experience with patients. The analyst may ask himself which of his clinical experiences of L might appear to approximate to the category D4; and so with other categories.

Superficially an analytic session may appear boring, or featureless, alarming, or devoid of interest, good or bad. The analyst, seeing beyond the superficial, is aware that he is in the presence of intense emotion; there should be no occasion on which this is not apparent to him.

The intense experience is ineffable but once known cannot be mistaken; this chapter must be understood to relate to and be in preparation for participation in it for if such a contact is maintained the analyst can devote himself to evaluating and interpreting the central experience and, if he sees fit, the superficialities in which it is embedded.

One such group of superficialities pertains to the circumstances in which analysis is conducted. These are usually physically comfortable and bear the stamp of unadventurous civilized existence. They therefore conspire against awareness that analysand and analyst are engaged on a venture which is as hazardous as activities in which the perils are more obvious and dramatic. In what the danger consists will depend on circumstances, but danger and awareness of danger are features of the situation with which the analyst should be in contact. The approach to it, to be effective, is "binocular"; the analyst must be aware, while attending to the patient's material, of the dangers of his association with that particular patient: he should also be able to see what the danger is that the patient is inviting him by his presence to share. I stress these points because what I have to say about the grid and transformations is incomprehensible without it.

An explorer's knowledge of instruments must be such that he can use them in situations of stress. The analyst must use instruments that are altered by the circumstances they are devised to study. The grid and the concept of transformations are altered by the situation they are devised to examine in proportion as they are brought to bear on it. They retain their character so long as they are employed *away* from the tense situation; after a session in which they have been employed, though so transformed by Ta α and by the tension of the session that the analyst may not be able to see that grid and transformation are in use, they resume the characteristics they possess extra-analytically. This is disquieting, but no one who tries to use the grid or transformation concepts in a session would doubt that it is true. Unless transformed so that the instrument (O = the grid) has become Ta β it loses power to illuminate during the session, but regains it afterwards. Untransformed, they would reduce the analyst to the state of a musician who, aware that the composition of which he was giving a concert performance was made up of scales and arpeggios, began to play it as if it were an exercise in scales and arpeggios.

No one can understand the grid or transformations without experience of their use as part of psycho-analytic practice.

Suppose that this essential contact is established and that the patient is making his contribution: the more it were possible to go into it the more complex would the contribution appear to be. If the analyst's attention is slanted to pick up the characteristics that determine grid classification it would be selective attention. Therefore construction of the grid is such that it picks up what is wanted for psycho-analysis.

Although home work is not done in an atmosphere of emotional tension, grid and transformation theory are applied to the recollection of such situations. The analyst's intuition, which it is the object of these reviews to exercise and develop, is operating in contact with the tense situation. It is important to distinguish between the grid (as it appears in my scheme) operating in tranquility on recollections, and the grid as part of the analyst's intuitive contact with the emotional situation itself.

The appearance in psycho-analysis of black-heads, spots, dots, staccato marks in musical scores, points, etc., can all be represented by the geometer's point; similarly the variety of supposedly phallic symbols can be represented by the geometer's line. I shall take advantage of this to demonstrate the difference of K and −K.

The point and the line, representing all Tp β's, are used by certain patients, who believe others do the same, as if they or their signs in painting, music, words, etc., were things. That is to say, such a patient hearing me say "point", or seeing a dot, behaves as if the point, however it is signified or represented, marks the place where the breast (or penis) was. Now this "place" seems to be invested by the patient with characteristics that less disturbed people might attribute to an object they would call a ghost. The point (·) and the term "point" are taken as sensible manifestations of the "no-breast". In so far as I can express it in ordinary terms, the patient seems to think that the fact that the word "point" is used, is a sign of the presence of a non-existent breast, "the place where the breast was" having many of the characteristics of a breast that is hostile because it no longer exists. In short, the word "breast" is not recognized as a word representing a breast, but is thought to be the outward manifestation of a "no-breast", one of the characteristic qualities, so to speak, of the "no-breast" itself. It is in this way that a certain class of patient "concludes" that a thought is a thing, albeit a "thing" in a sense that a rational being does not ordinarily understand. Such a view contrasts with that which enables a mathematician to use a point, however represented, to elaborate a geometric system.

Similarly, it contrasts with the ordinary view of the word "breast" or "point" that enables it to be used to elaborate anatomical or physiological or artistic or aesthetic (in the philosophical sense) systems.

I can differentiate the views by regarding the extra-ordinary view as backward-looking and relating to what has been lost, and the ordinary view as forward-looking and relating to what can be found. Such a differentiation is not convenient because it implies a penumbra of associations, and therefore has implications, that limit my freedom of discussion. I shall therefore denote the extra-ordinary view by the sign —K and the ordinary view by the sign K. I shall continue the process of differentiation of the ordinary from the extra-ordinary view by using as a model a system of co-ordinates, analogous to that employed by the algebraic geometer, in which two axes intersect at a point O. K will lie to the right of O, —K to the left. I shall further suppose that O can be replaced by the point or the line or a word such as "breast" or "penis" or any other sign representing any constant conjunction. For this discussion I shall suppose the point replaces O as the origin. For the point to become adequate for manipulation in geometric systems it is clear that it should not be invested with a penumbra of inappropriate associations. Now the associations of a statement include feelings: indeed many of the associations of a verbal statement represent feelings. The objection to Aristotle's term for point, on the ground that it "meant" puncture and therefore was too closely tied to reality, may be matched by Aristotle's objection that Plato called the point the beginning of a line (*Metaph.* 992. a. 20). It suggests that the importance of a definition is to mark a constant conjunction without the evocation of feelings; but something seems real only when there are feelings about it. The negative quality of a definition, then, relates to the need to exclude existing emotion as well as ideas. If "point" is to be available for use in K it must be defined to exclude the penumbra of associations with which it is invested; it has to be developed so that it reaches the stage represented by D category. The realization which will approximate to it will be an emotional experience. It must lend itself to saturation by an emotional experience and its sign should represent this.

As I do not attempt clinical description except by way of illustration I shall very briefly sketch the development in K of the geometrical elaboration. The sketch represents clinical experience and is accurate as far as only one experience can be.

The geometrical elaboration proceeds as follows: commencing with a point, line or any more complex figure such as those associated with the theorem of Pythagoras, the proposition is read off the figure, that is to say, it seems to be regarded as self-evident from the nature of the figure. Inspection of the figure may be followed by a formulation in terms other than pictorial. Plutarch gives a fanciful and oedipal description[1] of the 3, 4, 5 triangle. The mathematical development may have been achieved by transformation of the visual image into an arithmetical formulation. However that may be, my analytical experience is compatible with a development that proceeds from the *complete* visual image to elaboration in non-visual terms; that is from row C categories to row H, though I did not witness a row H transformation. I have no evidence for mathematical formulations that are not geometric in origin (other than material suggesting a relationship between having a third son and having three sons). What is not clear is the reason for a geometric rather than verbal development.

As I have no evidence in my experience, with one possible exception, of mathematical change in —K I shall confine myself to verbal transformations.

The point has appeared clinically as dot or dots, spot or spots ("spots" in or before the eyes is a fairly common phenomenon). I have described the point or line as an object indistinguishable from the place where the breast or penis was. Owing to the difficulty of being sure what the patient is experiencing I resort to a variety of descriptions, each of which is unsatisfactory. The spot, for example, seems to be part conscience, part breast, part faeces, destroyed, non-existent yet present, cruel and malignant. The inadequacy of description or categorization as thought at all has led me to the term β-element as a method of representing it. The spoken word seems significant only because it is invisible and intangible; the visual image is similarly

[1] Quoted by Heath: *The Thirteen Books of Euclid's Elements*, vol. 1, p. 417.

significant because it is inaudible. Every word represents what is not—a "no-thing", to be distinguished from "nothing".

The patient's attention passes from one β-element to the next, all linked by a chain of pseudo-causation to deny that their "cause" or genesis lay in the destruction and dispersal of their common origin. Such manifestations are compatible with Melanie Klein's theory of splitting and projective identification which she elaborated to describe aspects of the infant's relationship with the breast. The aspect that is most relevant to discussion of K and −K is the breast's association with provision of meaning. It will be remembered that a fear that it is dying is, in accordance with Melanie Klein's theory, projected into the mother's breast. It should be taken back purged of its painful quality and invested with more benign associations, but as I said in my paper on thinking[1] it may in some circumstances be denuded of such meaning as it has, so that the transaction terminates in the infant dominated by a re-introjected nameless dread.

I recall this to explain the behaviour of the patient who strives to link in a chain of pseudo-causation a number of visual images (or other elements) in the way described.[2] In K and −K the analyst and analysand are searching for meaning. The column 4 categories, which I have described as corresponding to Freud's term "attention" are searching for meaning. Any element categorized by the column 4 use is therefore being employed to discover meaning. (Contrasted with 3, notation, which is concerned with retaining meaning and 5, which may now be further differentiated from 4 as being concerned with the search for *moral* meaning.)

Pseudo-causation is the −K version of causation (which falls in the K domain). Both pseudo-causation and causation are "linear" in character. That is, the elements in a chain of causation may be represented geometrically by points in a line. The idea of causation is itself an assertion (in grid terms it falls in one of the categories of column 1) that certain elements are constantly conjoined and that the conjunction

[1] Bion, W. R.: *A Theory of Thinking*, 1961.

[2] See Chapter 4.

is one of cause and effect. It is therefore an assertion that the conjunction has a meaning.

Both representations may be compared with P $\leftrightarrow$ D and selected fact.

Suppose we regard the linear representation, as it occurs in K and —K, in the light of the theory of transformations: the line of points in —K may then be regarded as a version of the straight line of points in K. Furthermore, we may consider the line in —K as a disturbed version of the straight line in K, or vice versa. What then is the disturbance?

From the psycho-analytical point of view the most likely source of disturbance can be regarded as emotional. This source can be further regarded as lying in the individual's (*a*) narcissism and (*b*) social-ism. In so far as the geometrical representation can be regarded as a visual image it can be related to the model[1] of the reflection of objects in a disturbed surface such as a sheet of water. The reflecting surface and the source of the disturbance would both represent parts of the personality.

Narcissism and social-ism may be regarded as at opposite poles; I shall not consider what they are poles of but shall suppose that the intensity of narcissism falls off as the intensity of social-ism increases, and vice versa. Further, I shall suppose that the increase of intensity in narcissism is accompanied by a narrowing or concentration of emotion till it can be said to be one emotion such as love or hate or fear or sex or any other. Similarly the intensity of social-ism is accompanied by a widening of the spectrum of emotions. I shall further suppose that the total range from intense narcissism to intense social-ism is subject to splitting. In other words, that there can be a state in which intense narcissistic hate is split off from all other feelings and that this is true of all feelings in turn. The same description will apply to splitting of the social feelings.

Splitting need not be associated with L or H. It may be a function of K in which case it is what is scientifically known as analysis and is quite commonly used in psycho-analysis. If the range narcissism $\leftrightarrow$ social-ism is regarded as split, for

[1] See Chapter 4.

whatever reason, it may be represented geometrically by points on a line. As we shall have later to consider the geometrical representation of certain states by control (from a point) and parallel projection (from a series of points) and the transformations and invariants associated with them, splitting of the range narcissism ↔ social-ism is important.

The importance for the psycho-analyst of the range narcissism ↔ social-ism can be grasped by considering the close relationship of meaning and narcissism.[1]

The infant's experience of the breast as the source of emotional experiences (later represented by terms such as love, understanding, meaning) means that disturbances in relationship with the breast involve disturbance over a wide range of adult relationships. The function of the breast in supplying meaning is important for the development of a capacity to learn. In an extreme instance, namely the fear of the total destruction of the breast, not only does this involve fears that he has ceased to exist (since without the breast he is not viable) but fears that meaning itself, as if it were matter, had ceased to exist. In some contingencies the breast is not regarded as the source of meaning so much as meaning itself. This anxiety is often screened by the fact that the analyst gives interpretations and thus seems to provide evidence that meaning exists. If this is not observed the patient's intolerance of meaninglessness is not interpreted: he will pour out a flood of words so that he can evoke a response indicating that meaning exists either in his own behaviour or in that of the analyst. Since the first requisite for the discovery of the meaning of any conjunction depends on the ability to admit that the phenomena may have no meaning, an inability to admit that they have no meaning stifles the possibility of curiosity at the outset. The same is true of love and hate. The need to manipulate the session to evoke evidence of the existence of meaning extends to a need to evoke evidence of the existence of love and hate. Anyone with experience of the psychotic personality will be familiar with the probing, incessantly active, designed to tap sources of counter-transference. The patient's associations

[1] See Chapter 6.

are directed to obtaining evidence of meaning and emotion (here broadly divided into two all-embracing categories of love and hate). Since the patient's attention is directed to finding evidence of meaning, but not to finding what the meaning is, interpretations have little effect in producing change until the patient sees that he is tapping a source of reassurance to provide an *antidote* to his problem and not a *solution* of it.

The thought, represented by a word or other sign, may, when it is significant as a no-thing, be represented by a point (·). The point may then represent the position where the breast was, or may even *be* the no-breast. The same is true of the line, whether it is represented by the word line or a mark made on the ground or on paper. The circle, useful to some personalities as a visual image of "inside and outside", is to other personalities, notably the psychotic, evidence that no such dividing membrane exists.

Intolerance of a no-thing, taken together with the conviction that any object capable of a representative function is, by virtue of what the sane personality regards as its representative function, not a representation at all but a no-thing itself, precludes the possibility of words, circles, points and lines being used in the furtherance of learning from experience. They become a provocation to substitute the thing for the no-thing, and the thing itself as an instrument to take the place of representations when representations are a necessity as they are in the realm of thinking. Thus actual murder is to be sought instead of the thought represented by the word "murder", an actual breast or penis rather than the thought represented by those words, and so on until quite complex actions and real objects are elaborated as part of acting-out. Such procedures do not produce the results ordinarily achieved by thought, but contribute to states approximating to stupor, fear of stupor, hallucinosis, fear of hallucinosis, megalomania and fear of megalomania.[1]

I now explore some implications of the concurrence of elements of verbal with elements of geometrical formulation.

[1] See Chapter 12.

The association of the circle with "in and out" contributes to the difficulty of understanding the concepts of the line that cuts a circle in points that are conjugate complex. The difficulty arises from the supposition that the line that does so lies "outside" the circle; as opposed to the line that cuts it in two points, whose roots are real and distinct, and is supposed to lie "inside" the circle. The difficulty is diminished if there is no intolerance of the no-thing to contend with and therefore no opposition to a term of which the meaning is undetermined.

The simple example I have taken of the straight line that may cut a circle in two points that are (i) real and distinct, or, (ii) real and coincident (if the line is a tangent), or (iii) conjugate complex (if the line lies entirely "outside the circle") poses a problem that the mathematician has been able to solve by taking a mathematical point of view, but I use it to illustrate the nature of the psychological problem. I shall state this as follows: in the domain of thought where a straight line can be regarded as lying within, or touching, or wholly outside, a circle, a transformation has been effected whereby certain characteristics, lending themselves to mathematical manipulation, have been manipulated mathematically to adumbrate and then solve a mathematical problem. The residual characteristics however retain their problem, un-named (un-bound) and so uninvestigated. Hallucinosis is a domain, analogous to that of mathematics, in which their solution is sought. The mathematical problem resembles a psycho-analytic problem in that it is necessary that the solution should have a wide degree of applicability and acceptance and so avoid the need to apply different arguments to different cases when the different cases appear to have essentially the same configuration. Any analyst will recognize the confusion that is caused, or at best the sense of dissatisfaction that prevails, when a discussion by members makes it quite clear that the configuration of the case is apprehended by all, but the arguments formulated in its elucidation vary from member to member and from case to case. It is essential that such a state of affairs should be made unnecessary if progress is to take place. The search must be for formulations that represent the essential similarity of the configurations, recognized by all who deal with them, and thus to make unnecessary the *ad hoc* nature of so many psycho-analytic theories.

The individual error can always be recognized and allowed for if once the lack of a unifying theory, applicable to all similar configurations, has been recognized and eliminated. It will be noted that in writing of "similar configurations" I am pre-supposing the presence of invariants which are consciously or unconsciously recognized as such.

The geometric problem may appear more intractable than it need be by the apparatus of circles and straight lines drawn on paper. Included in this apparatus and of paramount importance, for the paper representations are not necessary, is the mental equipment of concepts such as inside and outside and the rules for their manipulation. Ignoring for the present any question of psycho-pathological inhibitions, it is evident that the inadequate apparatus must be replaced by a better. If we place ourselves in the position of the mathematician before Cartesian co-ordinates had been invented and before the geometric approach could be transformed into an algebraic approach (or in the position of the therapist before psycho-analysis was discovered or invented), it is easy to suppose that our dilemma would be the result of inadequate knowledge and experience, or simply lack of mental acuity. Such an explanation, however convincingly supported by the facts, is open to the objection that is levelled against the state of affairs where a number of different arguments are educed to apply to what appear to be different cases of the same configuration. For I have in this present argument proposed ignoring the presence of psychopathological inhibitions, and it is evident that such an exclusion makes any theory based on it exclude the similarity of the configuration in the two cases: in one, of the person unable to tolerate the no-thing, and in the other, the person who lacks the knowledge of Cartesian co-ordinates and algebraic manipulation. I propose therefore to suppose that the personality who cannot tolerate the point (breast, penis, and other verbal representations) and the pre-Cartesian mathematician (the prefix, pre- being used not in a social-temporal sense but as a term for a stage in individual development) to be in the same predicament. This I shall do by assuming that the mathematician is unconscious of the system of co-ordinates or algebraic manipulation.

By this means the two personalities can be differentiated by reference to the same frame. This disturbed patient can be said to be conscious of a "past" that no longer exists and the mathematician to be unconscious of a "future" that has not come to pass.

I now transform the theory adumbrated in the preceding paragraph to the domain of the mind; in doing so, the temporal component is first transformed into a scale at one end of which is the past and at the other the future. This description is inadequate as I wish to divest the concept of its associations of time and space. I shall do this by giving the term unconscious a sense, thus: $\overrightarrow{\text{unconscious}}$ and $\overleftarrow{\text{unconscious}}$; reciprocally, $\overrightarrow{\text{conscious}}$ and $\overleftarrow{\text{conscious}}$. The state of mind of the mathematician unaware of mathematical formal artifices can then be represented by $\overrightarrow{\text{unconscious}}$ and that of the disturbed patient by $\overleftarrow{\text{conscious}}$.

It will be seen that as it stands the last statement is ambiguous for it can be taken to represent a passive statement that the patient knows of his past as any ordinary personality might do. In fact it must represent an active hallucinatory state in which he is conscious of being in a past that replaces and excludes the present. Similarly $\overrightarrow{\text{conscious}}$ does not represent an awareness that events of some sort will take place in the future: it represents a replacement and exclusion of the present by a hallucinatory state of gratification either of foreboding or of pleasurable anticipation. An instance would be a patient who was conscious of unknown (because nothing has taken place) dread in a state of perpetual imminence or reciprocally of unknown pleasure equally imminent. The tone of $\overleftarrow{\text{conscious}}$

and $\overrightarrow{\text{conscious}}$ is determined by factors I am not at present discussing. $\overleftarrow{\text{Unconscious}}$ and $\overrightarrow{\text{unconscious}}$ will be marked by the presence of elements belonging to column 2 categories. Typical of this would be theories about the past or future that are known to be false. If it is correct to assume that column 2 categories are related to $\overleftarrow{\text{unconscious}}$ and $\overrightarrow{\text{unconscious}}$ we must consider what relationship exists between column 4 categories and $\overleftarrow{\text{conscious}}$ and $\overrightarrow{\text{conscious}}$ for it is natural to suppose there is a relationship between *attention* to a problem and *consciousness* of it. If it is to be assumed that this is true of a problem it is legitimate to assume it is also true of a state of pleasure or unpleasure. It can now be seen that conscious and unconscious, with a sign for sense, are signs for something that is a denial of "the present" and can accordingly represent the Kleinian theory of splitting and projective identification. The realization represented by these theories and signs, annihilated time, can be visualized as a point—"where the present used to be".

By definition the term conscious relates to states within the personality; consciousness of an external reality is secondary to consciousness of an internal psychic reality. Indeed consciousness of an external reality depends on the person's ability to tolerate being reminded of an internal reality.[1] If he cannot tolerate being reminded of an internal reality it may involve widespread employment of column 2 categories to keep awareness of aspects of real external objects at bay.

Before proceeding further, the reader may find it helpful to reconsider any difficulties he has in understanding formulations involving differences in point-pairs. If he has difficulty in understanding points that are conjugate complex, real and coincident, real and distinct, he can compare this experience of difficulty with the difficulty he may feel in understanding the following problem:

Two breasts have disappeared. Or perhaps it would be

[1] Relationship between the external and internal reality is thus similar to the relationship between pre-conception and the realization approximating to it. It is reminiscent of Plato's theory of Forms.

more accurate to say they have shrunk or faded away until only two points remain. The protagonist may feel reconciled to this fact or he may feel quite unable to tolerate these spots (or points or (·)) as to him they are either places where the breasts were, or, more poignantly, no-breasts. As he watches they appear to come together until they are coincident with each other and the boundary of his personality. They might just as well have travelled towards each other in a straight line and so coincided without touching him. But suppose they have travelled towards, or been drawn towards, him at the same time: then the line along which they travel to meet each other has been pulled into a curve that touches his personality at the point of coincidence. Then they disappear. Where have they gone? If he had an inside or an outside they might have gone inside him or gone out the other side. But suppose they are not inside or outside. Worse still, suppose there is no inside or outside, that he himself is only a place-where-he-used-to-be, a place-where-inside-and-outside-used-to-be?

The elements of the problem are: (i) the no-breast, or point, or (·), (ii) the no-penis, or straight line or (———), and (iii) the no-inside-or-outside, or circle or (○).

We can now allow our lack of understanding to impel curiosity along paths that are apparently different. Starting, say, at the no-inside-or-outside, we may proceed towards sophistication by one of two paths, which lead respectively to the concept of a circle in one instance (the geometer's view) and in the other to the concept of depersonalization.

Or, we may proceed by using both paths; before this I shall discuss some problems of the no-penis, straight line, (———).

It will be noticed that some configurations in which the no-breast and no-penis are involved suggest the possibility that it is unnecessary to have two concepts, of straight line and point, and that they could be replaced by a single concept.

The pre-Euclidean definition of a straight line, given by Plato, seems to depend on a visual impression of a straight line as it would appear to an eye placed at one end. The geometer's need to make the definition independent of an implied appeal to vision can be expressed in grid terms as a process of transformation from C1–H1. I shall use the sign to imply sense from ↑ for H to A, and for ↓ A to H.

I shall commence my investigation of the point and line as visual images. As I propose first to explore their characteristics as "no-things" the sense will be towards β-elements. Therefore the trend of the investigation of the point and line can be indicated by writing the category of the objects concerned as C1 ↑. When I wish to indicate that I am reversing the trend I shall write the category of the object with the appropriate sign.

Reversing the procedure of the geometer, who needs to divest the straight line C1 of its visual implications and does so by resort to algebraic calculi H1, we progress H1 ↑, C1 ↑ to A1.

The category A1 indicates that the straight line is a thought that is indistinguishable from a thing and is related to the β-elements as I have at various times described them. In view of the preceding discussion we may describe the straight line of category A1 as being, indifferently, a no-thing, a no-thought (in so far as it is a "thing"), a no-penis; in short, many descriptive expansions may be applied to it, but all will be characterized by the vice attributed to fundamental definitions of geometry, namely, that all are negative.

I have previously given my reasons for supporting the definition of a definition as something negative *in essence*; a definition should implicitly or explicitly be a statement that the statement itself is not any *past* statement (if not, where would be the need for the statement?) and has no meaning (if it had there would be no need for a definition) to bind the constantly conjoined elements; for they are to be bound so that their meaning can be determined. It is therefore quite appropriate that we should arrive by way of discussion of the no-thing at characteristics which are impregnated with a quality regarded by the scientist (proceeding in thought to H1 ↓) as undesirable.

To return to the straight line. Suppose we approach it as it is in category C1. As a visual image we can subject it to a number of manipulations that are excluded by the rules that govern its manipulation as an H1 object. Any mathematical terms I employ must be considered likewise to be freed from the rigour that governs the regulation of H1 elements when they are H1 elements themselves.

We may start with a mental image of a line in front of us. We can suppose that the two ends of the line are joined to our eye or that our eye projects the line outwards to a point where we want it. In both instances the eye is the vertex of a configuration of lines. We can rotate the line so that it is end-on to our "line of sight" and so appears as a point. Or we may consider that the point is projected outward while remaining attached to the eye. If projected outwards while remaining attached it becomes stretched out and can be considered therefore as a line. The line "seen" end-on and the point stretched out may be regarded as duals, or, the same object transformed under projection and possessing a different sense according to whether it is supposed to be proceeding from the eye or drawn in to it. I have already discussed other manipulations of these visual images and shall not therefore elaborate further; the reader can continue the exercise for himself. The immediate question is whether it is helpful to consider point or line as separate entities or whether it is better to consider them as different manifestations of one entity. But this raises the immediate question, better or useful to whom and for what? So long as I concern myself with visual images there seems to be freedom. If I want to use the point to enclose an object I can make it stretch out so that it catches up with its tail, the object to be enclosed lying inside the circle described. But is this a point with a tail, or a circle?

Suppose for the purposes of discussion it is convenient to replace point and line by a single object. This involves simplification in that we now have one object for all configurations but it involves restriction to objects of category C1 and resort to projection from a vertex.

Suppose the problem chosen (enclosure) proves recalcitrant[1]; we may vary the choice of vertex spatially, or from one sense to another, say visual to auditory. The no-thing owes its existence to the alimentary system as a model of the mind in its function of employing thought. Assuming the visual mental system, despite its freedom, is inadequate to provide a solution to problems of enclosure, is it possible to find some shift of vertex that will neutralize the obstacles encountered in employing the eye as a vertex of the mental visual system? There is nothing out of the way in making such an approach; as we saw, conversational English betrays the widespread use of alimentary metaphor when processes of thought are in dispute.[2] Equally common are locutions such as being "hot on the scent" of a problem, "smelling a rat", etc., but change to a vertex provided by the mental counterpart of a sense of smell, so poorly endowed verbally, simplifies the problem of enclosure, thanks to ideas of inspiration and expiration, but complicates all else further.

To shift from a vertex of one "sense" or "system" to another affords a way out of a difficulty that use of one vertex alone makes impossible. Apart from the problem of transformation of olfactory, or respiratory, representation into verbal representation the respiratory mental counterpart is no less effective than the visual in accepting point and line. The use of an aural mental counterpart to provide another vertex reveals some interesting comparisons with the alimentary, visual and respiratory vertices. Noise presents problems that sound, treated musically, can transcend. Musical methods of notation are in their adequacy reminiscent of algebraic methods of geometrical notation. But the important and striking feature revealed by a comparison of the mental counterparts of visual with other vertices is the superior power of the visual vertex to illuminate (I find I turn spontaneously to the use of verbal representations of visual elements to express my meaning) a problem over that of all other mental counterparts of the senses. Reversal of

[1] As it well may—even to the infant.

[2] See Bion, W. R.: *Learning from Experience.* Chapter 3.

direction in the system of which the vertex is a part is associated with what are ordinarily known as hallucinations. The supremacy of the visual vertex contributes to my belief that the solution of the problem of communicating psychoanalytically will have to be found through row C elements to geometrical formulation and thence to row H elements.

Before leaving the discussion of choice of vertices I shall consider the vertex provided by the mental counterpart of the reproductory system. First I deal with a matter that may have puzzled the reader, namely my use of the term "mental counterpart".

If the reader visualizes a point or a line, without representation of it on paper, he does something that has been variously described as "using his inward eye", "visualizing", "seeing in imagination", etc. I consider this activity to depend on a "mental counterpart of the sense of sight". Similarly the "bitterness" of a memory is dependent on a mental counterpart of the alimentary system; similarly with others including the reproductory system.

The "inner" reproductory system, as I may call the mental counterpart of the reproductory system by analogy with the "inward eye" of the mental counterpart of the visual system, must not be confused with awareness of reproductive activity any more than visual images that are related to the activity of the mental counterpart of sight are to be confused with objects of sight. The mental counterpart of the reproductory system is related to premonitions of pleasure and pain. The second source of confusion may lie in my use of the term vertex. I am unwilling to use a term such as "point-of-view" because I do not wish to be reduced to writing "from the point of view of digestion", or "from the point of view of a sense of smell" when the distinctions between metaphorical and literal usages are fine yet difficult to preserve. I can describe my use of the term "vertex" as an example of taking a mathematical term, (grid category H1) and using it as a model (grid category C1). With the reproductory mental counterpart as vertex, transformation of the point or line is into a surface or plane. In the last sentence I resort to verbal representation of geometrical visual images. This occurs so naturally as to suggest that the visual mental counterpart has supremacy over other mental counterparts; visual images lend themselves to transformation in different media. In using the term "vertex" I employ a geometrical concept of a high degree of sophistication, but as used by me its grid category is C1.

To sum up: The point/line may be transformed by central projection from any one of a number of vertices, or it may be transformed by parallel projection by a single point at infinity. What this may mean must be discussed below, together with the use of the point to mark a vertex of projection.

CHAPTER SEVEN

THE "point" and the "line" represent visual images which remain invariant under a wide range of conditions. The same is true of the visual images associated with the propositions of Euclid; hence the propositions themselves are communicated over long periods of time and between widely separated cultures and races. This may appear to be true of any visual representation, such as cave paintings, but although the column 3 component, record or notation, is strong, the artistic representation does not appear to be so rich in ideational content as the geometrical representation is. The geometer Bhāskara (b. A.D. 1114) drew four right-angled triangles inwards one on each side of the square of the hypotenuse and left it with the comment "See!"[1] There are two dissimilar observations that can be made. One is mathematical and can be stated: $C^2 = 4\frac{ab}{2} + (a - b)^2 = a^2 - b^2$; the other is mythical and can be stated: of the 3, 4, 5, triangle 3 is the first odd number and is perfect, 4 is the square on an even side 2, while 5 partly resembles the father and partly the mother, being the sum of 3 and 2, "and we must then liken the perpendicular to the male, the base to the female and the hypotenuse to the offspring of both".

The mathematical statement of the theme has been profitable and has led to development. The mythological statement, though widely spread, has not. Is it possible to release it from its fetters by reverting to point and line?

If we use the point alone to construct a square we can produce the following effects:

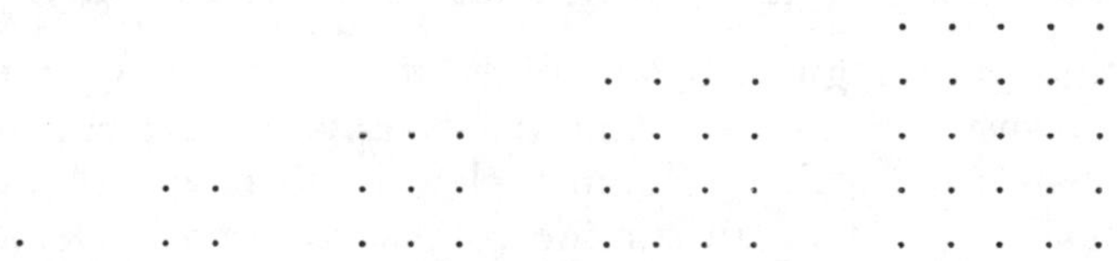

1 2 3 4 5

[1] Heath, T.: *The Thirteen Books of Euclid's Elements.*

In each case we have added a gnomon to the previous figure. It could represent accumulative if not creative activity. It adds to something or someone not specified. Whether we regard it as creative or not depends on whether ↑ ↓ represent its direction and a process of coherence or disintegration. If the direction is ↑ the trend is destruction of the capacity for thought. In verbal terms, if the process is from square to fragmentation of the square[1] it can be distinguished from the process of integrating fragments to make a square by calling the former creative, the latter destructive. If the horizontal axis represents uses there should be some relatedness between the elements of one column to the preceding and subsequent column, such as I have established between rows and put forward tentatively for the columns. It is easy to see that such a relationship might exist between 1, 3, 4, and 5 in that the order may be seen as one of increasing curiosity, at least in K, and possibly in L and H also. But 2 does not fit into such a progression. It might be better to replace it by a sign ← indicating that the element so distinguished was a use of that particular element to suppress another. $\overleftarrow{3}$ would then indicate the element was being employed to note or record something with the express purpose of exclusion of a true statement. But the antithesis I require is to a use in its fundamental nature. The $\overleftarrow{\text{square}}$ should mean the total denial of any initiative that $\overrightarrow{\text{square}}$ could effect. $\overrightarrow{3}$ would mean notation that is growth-producing: $\overleftarrow{3}$ would mean notation that was growth-inhibiting. But in fact I want to give the ← the quality of binding or definition as I have described it and that being so it must be understood to have no meaning that exists already.

What meaning can be attributed to $\overleftarrow{1 - n}$? It is *not* that 4 is transformed into 3, unless we suppose that curiosity, once aroused so that column 3 elements become column 4 elements, might again subside so that column 4 elements

[1] The points can be so disposed that their number represents a square but their visual impression does not: which "view" (vertex) are we to adopt?

left a residue of column 3 elements. This change is better represented by denoting the terminal categories thus: $3 \leftarrow 4$. If we assume that the progression of uses is not linear there is no difficulty in writing $n \rightarrow 2$ or $2 \leftarrow n$ without assuming any transition from column 5 to 4 to 3 to 2. Suppose $3 \rightarrow 4$ accompanied by suspicion. Suppose 4 leads to stimulation of impotent envy and hate. Destructive retreat takes place $4 \rightarrow 1$. The fragmentation of point and line cannot go beyond the point; though the line may be annihilated, having been transformed into a series of points, to a single point, to the place where the point was, this last is still a point. The point is thus indestructible. A patient's state of mind could be represented by such a model on occasions when he continues attack after attack on objects by which he is persecuted.

Such behaviour is determined more by the strength[1] of emotions than by their character. A desire to be loving and creative turns to hate and destructiveness if it is frustrated by disparity between equipment and ambition. This is true of every impulse to act, including impulses to change from one state of mind to another. Such an impulse is analogous to the impulse to translate thought into action.

It sometimes helps to illuminate an analytic problem by speaking of a characteristic as appearing to the patient a "ghost of the past". The infant experiences what may be called ghosts of the future. Such locutions are possible to adult investigations for maturity provides terms born of experience together with facility in their manipulation. But the facts of personality, its own and that of others, exist for the infant and present him with problems that he must solve. Is there some adult problem that will provide an analogy for what the infant appears to experience? What analogy is available to the infant by aid of which it can approach its problems of personality? What past problems provide us with analogies for our present problems? What in our present problems is analogous to problems we have encountered in the past?

The problem of the personality at the crossroads, the

[1] See Hyperbole.

problem of what impulses must dominate when thought is translated into action,[1] or from meditation into decision, or from one state of mind into another, may be regarded as one of power and the seizure of a commanding position. This struggle may be regarded indifferently as taking place within the psyche, outside it, or tangentially; the model may be that of Oedipus at the crossroads at Thebes or the circle whose circumference is intersected at two actual and separate points, two points that are actual and coincident or two that are conjugate and complex.

The advantage of using the Oedipus myth to represent the row C category version is economy and avoidance of a whole series of *ad hoc* models and theories for different problems that have the same configurations. The circle cut by the line offers a connection with point and line and a model for inside and outside. Later we shall have to consider the appropriateness or relevance of inside and outside to emotional states recognized to be "infectious" or "contagious".

Emergence of a group of impulses as dominant in the psyche involves conflict within the personality and crisis outside but this same crisis can be seen as the point at which $T\alpha$ gives rise to $T\beta$.

A proper use of the oedipal elements is obstructed by a tendency to allow the narrative form of the myth to impose a cause-and-effect outlook on the investigator. The theory of causation is implied in and inseparable from the narrative form of the myth, but the narrative form is a function of column 3 categories and is related directly to notation. The confusion of notation, particularly in its association with narrative and a theory of causation, with categories of columns 4 and 5, attention and investigation, obscures the importance in learning from experience of the mechanism of $Ps \leftrightarrow D$. The essential of the narrative form is that it permits of an easy memorization, as one might memorize a mathematical formula, of a constant conjunction. The narrative form, with its implication of causation, is relevant and significant to the myth's function to record a constant

[1] See Transformation: super-ego vertex and ego vertex.

conjunction, but the relationship in which the constantly conjoined elements are combined depends on the relationship of the conjunction to Transformation. I shall therefore reconsider Transformation.[1]

Transformation may be a transference of characteristics from one situation to another, from one medium to another, a rigid motion, or a projective transformation. A musician or artist may transfer or project an emotional experience through T α to the finished product, T β, which may be a musical composition or a painting. If the transformation is considered to extend to the state of mind of the artist's public the emotional experience O may be regarded as transformed into the same medium—another emotional experience.

If the transformation is in the same medium one man's state of mind serves to produce, not *any* state of mind in another man, but a *particular* state of mind in which the invariants are such that T β, in the second man, can be seen to relate to T, the first man's emotional response to O.

The transformation cannot occur without an emotional experience such that its proper model is the scene of violence at the crossroads at Thebes. Stating the model in other terms, the elements that must be formulated to establish their relation to each other are: the no-penis (one that is yet to be) with the no-penis (where the penis used to be).

Narrative and cause-and-effect are intrinsic to notation or record. The story of the meeting at Thebes crossroads belongs to category C3. Is there any essential difference between the record C3 and the signification of constant conjunction by C1 (definitory hypotheses)? A term "cat" (C1) signifies a constant conjunction. So does the crossroads episode I have placed in C3. There is no narrative and no causation theory in "cat". The crossroads narrative has power to represent murderous feeling as part of the constant conjunction. C1 differs from C3 in that the crossroads narrative, if placed correctly in C1, would indicate the

[1] The narrative, by introducing cause and effect as a means of binding *its* elements, *mis*-represents the constant conjunction relationship. Cause and effect is proper to the *narrative* but has no corresponding link between one element and another in the realization. In the realization the elements are merely conjoined.

boundary within which the problem was to be completed. C3 would indicate that the story represented an element, part of a record, of a problem stated but incompletely. H1 would be a category in which only those elements would find a place which implied closure, e.g. the primitive counterparts of a circle cut by a line in two points, actual and separate. H3, however, would require that there was no limiting boundary. If the category of the episode were H3 it would represent an emotional experience outside the personality but cutting it at two points quite different from the point pair of H1. Alternatively, the two straight lines, representing the no-penis, would not be limited by any boundary and the frame of reference would have to be provided by something that could fulfil the functions of two axes and a system of co-ordinates. The system of co-ordinates, by making possible a transformation from the visual imagery of geometry to the manipulations of algebraic symbols confers greater freedom of investigation and in this respect differs from the frame of reference provided by a state of being inside or outside the state represented by a circle. That state is centred on a no-breast (or point) and is therefore analogous to the geometrical circle, "centred on" its centre (or point).

Column 1 categories are limiting since the definitory hypothesis is to mark a constant conjunction and the exclusion of all previously recorded constant conjunctions (the "negative" quality of definition). The column 3 categories bind a constant conjunction, but the meaning of the constant conjunction does not have to be sought within the domain of the conjoined elements: it must be assumed that the recording aspect of notation is related to the need to find other constant conjunctions which, taken with conjunctions already bound and recorded, yield meanings (that is, relatedness and coherence) hitherto unrecorded. The recording aspect of 3 is related to the function of attention that inheres in all column 4 elements.

Freud speaks[1] of the capacity for thinking as affording relief from frustration, in that thought can fill the gap

[1] Freud, S.: *Two Principles of Mental Functioning*. Standard Edition, Vol. XII.

between the time when an impulse is born and its satisfaction. He is referring to action taken by the organism, under the influence of pain, to change its environment. I propose to class the transformation that takes place when thought is expressed in speech as action. Before this transformation thought is restricted to the domain of β-elements, α-elements, and dreams before they are verbalized. But as thought can be used to inhibit action, so definition can be used to inhibit thought. If persecutory feelings are strong the constant conjunction of elements can lead to a naming of the conjunction with intent to contain it, rather than to mark it for investigation. Such motivation, represented by D, approximates to the production of β-elements; but in its less severe forms shows as speech in which nothing can be taken for granted; the term "cat" has no undertones and overtones, whether it is heard or uttered. In talking to a person in whom such a state is active it appears to be impossible to avoid misunderstanding unless words are used with their exact signification. The negative aspect of the definitory hypothesis is strengthened so that the exclusive function of the hypothesis is not a barrier against irrelevance but a denial of the domain to which the hypothesis belongs. For example, the term "cat" would not bind a constant conjunction that excludes "dogginess", but binds a constant conjunction so restrictively that it excludes all animal characteristics. Carried to extremes, the term "cat" is merely a sign analogous to the "point" as the "place where the breast used to be"[1] and should mean the "no-cat". Further denudation leads ultimately to the point which is merely a position without any trace of what used to occupy that position.

There would seem to be no reason why the point or the line should not be regarded as "an abstraction" or an "unknown" in the mathematical sense. It will, or will not, be so regarded according to the use to which it is put (the horizontal axis of the grid). Where I think it is useful to

[1] Although I shall continue to speak of the place where something "used to be" I mean it to be understood that the tense is a matter of indifference because, as I said earlier (Chapter 5) the point is also a "now" which has no past or future.

differ from the philosophical or mathematical view is in regarding "abstraction" or "unknown" as designations of stages on the genetic axis.

The point (·) or the line (———) and all substantival terms may, in the view put forward in *Learning from Experience*, *Elements of Psycho-Analysis*, and this book, be regarded as unknowns having two values: one, a sign for a constant conjunction and the other, a sign for the position, unoccupied, of the object.

Now the object, the constant conjunction, or the position it does *not* occupy, lend themselves to different treatment in that they differ from each other. If the difference can be recognized it becomes possible to elaborate procedures which will turn to good account the properties of the two objects. For convenience I shall distinguish the object from the "position it does not occupy" by signifying the latter by minus signs.

The rules for the manipulation of · and ——— lead to formulations, first through geometrical configurations and then through algebraic transformations of those configurations, that are analogous to pre-conceptions (row D) but belong to row H. These formulations may then be used in accordance with the categories I have set out on the vertical axis; such elaborations depend upon the genetic history of · and ———. This is a dimension of · and ———. They must represent where the · and the ——— used to be or where they will be at some future date. This is denied if time is reduced to a "now" alone with a "future" (that is, where a future used to be, a not-present) and a "past" (that is, where a past used to be and is now a not-present) that are both representations of the wreckage left by splitting attacks on the present. We must next consider the relationship of the no-thing to ideas of space and the no-present to ideas of time.

The — · and — ——— retain meaning, as does the no-thing (because at least there is a trace of whatever it is that does not occupy the position) so long as time itself is not reduced to the moment without a past or a future. But if · represents only a position without duration, it and the corresponding line have become meaningless. In the situation represented by the meaningless · and meaningless ——— the patient can attempt to manipulate the analyst to give interpretations so that the session is used to deny complete meaninglessness and thus to provide reassurance against the dread that all meaning, all source of meaning, has been annihilated. This dread is associated with belief in the breast as the source of meaning as, physically, it is felt to be the source of milk.[1]

The point or line of the geometer may seem indistinguishable from the − · or − ———. In that case the failure to use or develop these objects or − would have to be sought in the relationship of the personality to the · or ——— part of itself. − · and + · are two values of · and the same is true of + and − ———. The transformation is from · or ——— to + or − · and + or − ———. If we use the grid we may replace − · and − ——— by $\underset{\cdot}{\leftarrow}\uparrow$ and $\underline{\leftarrow}\uparrow$. Such signs represent objects which are devoid of characteristics, lack duration, or position, and, therefore, existence. But the sign $\leftarrow\uparrow$ indicates that the object is not static. $\leftarrow\uparrow$ represents a force[2] that continues after · has been annihilated and it destroys existence, time and space.

The state represented by $\underset{\cdot}{\leftarrow}\uparrow$ is different from that represented by · or ———. If these signs merely represent the place where the object was or could be there is nothing inherently difficult in supposing that they could be used for thinking about objects *in their absence*. I can make the mark · where I like and I can make another so —— and these marks may then be manipulated into a design according to my predispositions. They may be combined to form a geometrical configuration, or letters of a script, or a drawing. In the latter instance, the recognizable artistic product and the subject it is supposed to portray have features in common that may be called invariants. There may be other invariants common to the artistic production and the no-thing, the thing represented by a · where the thing is not, and

[1] See Chapter 6.

[2] I do not wish to commit myself to the theory that there is a realization approximating to this force.

these invariants are the points and lines actually represented by marks on paper or "seen" (the mental counterpart) with the inward eye.[1] Some suspicion of the existence of this component probably lies in the search to find golden sections and other geometrical figures in, or to impose them on, artistic productions.

The need for rules by which · and ——— are to be regulated if they are to communicate, say, an impression of a landscape, is recognized. The same is true of every form of expression: it is accepted that there must be rules that are to be obeyed in verbal communication, or music, or painting, if the transformation of O is to combine the invariants in such a way that communication with others is effectual. These rules must be such that the no-thing is adequately communicated by a proper combination of the invariants. A work of art should satisfy by a proper disposition of the invariants to O, the no-thing (· or ———) and T β.

The problem posed by ← ↑ can be stated by analogy with *existing* objects. ← ↑ is violent, greedy and envious, ruthless, murderous and predatory, without respect for the truth, persons or things. It is, as it were, what Pirandello might have called a Character in Search of an Author.[2] In so far as it has found a "character" it appears to be a completely immoral conscience. This force is dominated by an envious determination to possess everything that objects that exist possess including existence itself.

The premiss that the object does not exist would rule out the *existence* of the characteristics I have adumbrated except in the mind of the patient who appears to entertain the phantasy of such a self-contradictory object. But the patient may identify himself with such an object and the contradiction then lies in his existing sufficiently to feel that he does not exist. The rule that a thing cannot both be and not be is inadequate.

The problem is simplified by a rule that "a thing can never

[1] See Milton: *Paradise Lost*, Bk. III, "and the mind through all her powers irradiate, there plant eyes. . . ." (lines 51–55).

[2] Pirandello: *Six Characters in Search of an Author*.

be unless it both is and is not". Stating the rule in other forms: "a thing cannot exist in the mind alone: nor can a thing exist unless at the same time there is a corresponding no-thing." The rules that apply to the thing do not apply to the no-thing. Contradiction is not an invariant under psycho-analysis though it may exist in the domain of psycho-analytic objects (which *must* both be and not be).

If there is a "no-thing" the "thing" must exist. By analogy, if Falstaff is a no-thing Falstaff also exists: if it can be said that Falstaff, Shakespeare's character who had no real existence, has more "reality" than people who existed in fact, it is because an actual Falstaff exists: the invariant under psycho-analysis is the ratio of no-thing to thing. But + · and — · can coincide; in this case the patient who displays a state of mind approximating to this representation regards the analyst who is actually present as also the *place* where the analyst is not. Conversely, the analyst who is actually absent is regarded as a space which is occupied by the absent analyst.[1]

The above description is an approximation. Its relationship with the description that follows is analogical. Using the geometrical visual image I can represent the frame of mind to which I wish to draw attention by the point-pair that is actual and coincident (contrasted with the point-pair that is actual and separate and the point-pair that is conjugate complex). The line on which the coincident pair is situated is tangential to the circle which represents a situation in which "inside" and "outside" exist. The visual image, of the tangent to a circle, can represent a contact with a personality that has an inside and an outside in a manner that makes the + · and the — · coincident; there is no distinction between the thing and the no-thing though both exist. The personality has contact only at one point: since the point-pair are coincident the contact represents the tenuous relationship seen in patients with disturbances of thought.

The line and circle cut at coincident points can also be

[1] See Hallucinosis, Chapter 5, where I discuss transformations in hallucinosis.

used to represent the relationship between ♀ and ♂ described by me in *Learning from Experience*. If ♂ is replaced by the visual image of the line (———) and ♀ by the visual image of the point (·) the relationship between the two objects, linear and circular (inside and outside), can be expressed by the relative positions of the two points without direct appeal to line or circle. The two points, thing and no-thing, are determined by the fact that they lie on the point of intersection of line and circle.

From what I have said of ← ↑ the ultimate non-existent "object", the "space" and "time" annihilated object and its all-consuming greed for, and envy of, anything that exists, because it exists, is associated with fear of being the victim of this "space" either as an object that would be devoured by it, or as the servant compelled to provide the ← ↑ (space) with the means with which to satisfy its demand for all that exists. The individual feels himself to be occupying property that belongs to "space". "Space" and the psyche are not felt to be capable of co-existence. Such fears can be seen in analysis of psychotic and claustrophobic patients. The Mad Hatter's tea party in *Alice in Wonderland* is a representation to which this timeless and spaceless "space" approximates.

The analogies which I have sought for the breast and no-breast may be employed again with regard to the space and no-space. Space may be regarded as pure, violent emotion, dominated by greed: no-space as the place where space was. Or, to find another analogy, + space is high pressure, − space or no-space, is low pressure: low pressure devours high pressure, high pressure occupies low pressure.

The relationship of Euclidean geometry to what is ordinarily called space has often been remarked upon and it has been supposed that in ordinary space, so-called, could be found the realizations that approximate to the theoretical constructions of Euclidean geometry and from thence, at a further remove, the transformation leading to algebraic geometry. In my description I have remarked on certain states in which thought itself has been attacked as being indistinguishable from a no-thing. From this I have proceeded to $\underset{\cdot}{\leftarrow}$, $\underset{\cdot}{\leftarrow}$ ↑, and finally to what I have represented by $\leftarrow \uparrow$ or emotion + no-emotion, high pressure and low pressure. Geometrical constructions have shown their value in representing the realizations found in geographical space. By proceeding $\underset{\cdot}{\leftarrow} \uparrow$ I have sought to show that geometrical constructions related to, and strove originally to represent, biological realities such as emotions. The progression represented by $\underset{\cdot}{\leftarrow} \uparrow$ leads to the possibility that mathematical space may represent emotion, anxiety of psychotic intensity, or repose also of psychotic intensity—a repose more psychiatrically described as stupor. In every case the emotion is to be part of the progression, breast → emotion (or place where breast was) → place where emotion was. I hope that in time the base will be laid for a mathematical approach to biology, founded on the biological origins of mathematics, and not on an attempt to fasten on biology a mathematical structure[1] which owes its existence to the mathematician's ability to find realizations, that approximate to his constructs, amongst the characteristics of the inanimate.

I propose to devote a little time to the relationship of the elements of mathematics to the biological realizations to which they approximate.

[1] See remarks on the golden section, p. 102.

CHAPTER EIGHT

THE domain of thought may be conceived of as a space occupied by no-things; the space occupied by a particular no-thing is marked by a sign such as the words "chair", or "cat" or "point" or "dog". The attempt to free this domain from associations of space perception is supported by use of concepts such as "thought" or "thinking" or "in the mind", but a thought continues to have the penumbra of associations proper to "the place where . . ." the no-thing is. This is also true of feelings and emotions however expressed.

The "objects" with which psycho-analysis deals include the *relationship* of the no-thing and the thing. The personality that is capable of tolerating a no-thing can make use of the no-thing, and so is able to make use of what we can now call thoughts. Since he can do so he can seek to fill the "space" occupied by the thought; this makes it possible for the "thought" of space, line, point to be matched with a realization that is felt to approximate to it. In this respect $\underset{\cdot}{\rightarrow}$ contrasts with $\underset{\cdot}{\leftarrow}$ and new uses can be found for $\underset{\cdot}{\rightarrow}$ that cannot be found for $\underset{\cdot}{\leftarrow}$. The search for, and discovery of, elements perceived in space is part of the procedure by which elements of category 1 begin to acquire meaning; the negative quality of the definitory hypothesis is discarded or replaced by new elements that saturate the (ξ) elements of $\psi(\xi)$.[1] It is convenient to postulate the existence of a mind represented entirely by points, positions of objects, places where something used to be, or would be at some future date. Objects perceived in space contribute to the transformation of these elements (analogous to ξ) into specific no-things.[2]

On the interplay between the no-thing and the realization that is felt to approximate to it depends the development of thought, and by thought I mean, in this context, that which

[1] *Learning from Experience.*

[2] Similar to the meeting of pre-conception with realization to give rise to conception, but different from it by its closer approximation to the concept of Platonic forms of which the personality is "reminded" by contact with a real object.

enables problems to be solved in the absence of the object. Indeed unless the object is absent there is no problem. The problem is associated with the sense that the realization only approximates to the pre-conception (D1) (or A1, B1, C1). Whether the realization approximates, and if so how closely, depends on a number of factors with which I shall not deal here; with the psychotic personality the approximation has to be extremely close. Consequently (ξ) often remains unsaturated even though the realization does, to ordinary eyes, exist and appears to achieve an adequate degree of approximation to D1. No matter what the reason for the "absence" may be the active no-thing, without a corresponding thing, is associated with dis-satisfaction in the domain of alimentation when hunger exists, but there is no food.

The following may be distinguished from each other: the no-thing and no corresponding realization, the realization, but no corresponding no-thing, the co-incidence of no-thing and thing (the sense-perceived object); this last is inseparable from contact at one point only between a personality (a series of points) and an inside-outside personality ($\therefore$ with a surface) represented by a circle. We shall have to consider shortly the problems of geometrical representation when detached from its genetic developmental association with sense-perceived space and return it to represent the mental domain from which it sprang.[1]

First I consider $\hookleftarrow\!\uparrow$ "in search of existence". What this sign represents must be determined by discovery of realizations approximating to it; it is both mental, and susceptible of sense-perception. (Sense-perception must here be contrasted with, and distinguished from, Freud's "consciousness[2] as a sense-organ of psychic quality".)

Having allocated a sign $\hookleftarrow\!\uparrow$ which, according to theory, means that there is a constant conjunction that requires to be bound I need to know what the constant conjunction thus represented means. I might as well say that it is because I think there is a constant conjunction that I think there is a meaning. Further, my belief that there is a meaning is itself

[1] See Agoraphobia, Chapter 9.

[2] Freud, S.: *Interpretation of Dreams*, Chap. VII. Standard Edition, Vol. V.

one element that is constantly conjoined with other elements in any situation in which a constant conjunction is felt to occur.

It is necessary to suppose that there is awareness of a constant conjunction. Since I have already allocated a meaning to ↲↑ I could attribute awareness of the constant conjunction to it. I shall not however do so. I shall keep it unaltered as a β-element. It may however improve the efficacy of ↲↑ as a form of notation if I, who think that stupor and violent greedy ambition to possess all the qualities of existence have the same configuration, re-write ↲↑ as $\pm$ ↲↑.

To return to "awareness". By analogy I would like as a temporary measure to use Cs as a sign for "awareness". It might be useful to attribute this to $\pm$ ↲↑, but Cs and $-$ ↲↑ appear to be inconceivable. As I do not wish to be deterred from discussing the point merely because it is inconceivable, I shall assume a Cs that is a β-element (grid category A1), and further that Cs (A1) is or is not inseparable from $\pm$ ↲↑ according to the needs of my inquiry. A wish to communicate with others involves consideration of the limitations imposed by that desire.

If I postulate Cs belonging to the category A1 I am assuming it is possible to conceive of a β-element and so to use the *concept* of a β-element although it is impossible to use a β-element itself. Therefore my *concept* of a β-element (category D1, D3, D4) is used as if it were "about" something, that is, as if it had a meaning; that implies that there is, or that I can conceive that there is, a constant conjunction corresponding to my statement "β-element", or, more particularly in this context, Cs (A1).

By analogy with more sophisticated inquiries I can ask what are the properties of Cs (A1); it has none of the qualities ordinarily believed to inhere in the idea of properties. The "properties" of Cs (A1) are analogous to the "properties" of zinc when they are said to be such that zinc combined with sulphuric acid produces zinc sulphate + water. In short, Cs (A1) represents a constant conjunction of relationships.

Cs (A1) is of the nature of a tropism. It involves $\psi(\xi)$ in which (ξ) seeks saturation. This "consciousness" is an awareness of a lack of existence that demands an existence, a thought in search of a meaning, a definitory hypothesis in search of a realization approximating to it, a psyche seeking for a physical habitation to give it existence, ♀ seeking ♂. By analogy with mathematics one may then say that psycho-analysis is concerned with establishing the laws governing relationships of psycho-analytic objects. To express this in a variety of terms: any constant conjunction that *is* apparent, *becomes* apparent; any constant conjunction that is apparent, is; any constant conjunction is a function of the relationships described (broadly) as a conjunction. The quality of any constant conjunction (its properties) is a function of the relationships "within" the conjunction together with the function of its relationship with other constant conjunctions.

If I re-read one of my own notes, knowing it embodies what to me was knowledge when I wrote it, it can seem tautological or to express a meaning so inadequately that if an interval of time separates me from the state of mind in which I wrote it it fails to communicate its message even to myself. Yet its capacity to record is enough to make it possible for me to contrast two different views[1] and thereby see its defects both as a record (column 3) and as a precursor to further investigation (column 4).

A visual impression, as used by Euclid when he relies on deducation from visual representations, would offer some prospect of gain in communicability even if at the loss of logical rigour.[2] I gain something by using ↲↑ instead of a host of analogies, but this must be balanced against the advantages of using analogies instead of ↲↑. Logic, common sense, induction, deduction are terms that often

[1] This statement is itself an instance of splitting in time, as a method of achieving correlation.

[2] Logical rigour is an attribute of a particular form of manipulation. Every element, according to its grid category, has its appropriate and most nearly rewarding technique of manipulation. Logicians tend to believe that logical rigour is a *sine qua non*. Hence complete neglect of Newton's theological and mystical pre-occupations as if they had no part in the genesis of, for instance, *Opticks*.

represent mechanisms for bringing an intuition within reach of a realization should one exist. But intuition itself is a function of $\pm \hookleftarrow\!\uparrow$.

By regarding $\hookleftarrow\!\uparrow$ as a β-element and replacing Cs by something akin to a tropism I can include in $\hookleftarrow\!\uparrow$ the counterpart of Cs in an element that is not defined by me as an element of thought.

The importance of such a manoeuvre is that it makes it possible to view consciousness as an element for which, at any of its stages of development, an appropriate grid category can be found.

Hitherto I have used the grid for the categorization of elements which have qualities usually associated with substantives; except for ease of exposition this is not necessary. For example, "consciousness" may be categorized in such a way that the use is emphasized. The grid categories have been left so that the horizontal axis can be extended. Thus: suppose the link to be H and the category D4. Consciousness categorized as link H (D4) would represent a state of hostile (H) scrutiny (D or pre-conception) for the purpose of destructive investigation (column 4). Suppose some method of notation by which the column 4 component is strengthened then consciousness would be categorized to show less substantival and more operator quality.

I have chosen to discuss consciousness deliberately. From the present instance, and from previous discussion of awareness associated with tropism, it is evident that a term is needed which may represent the invariant function of consciousness in all grid categories in which it can appear or be placed. I propose to resort to the visual representation afforded by geometrical figures.

First I shall equate the object that I have described as analogous to consciousness with "a point of view". Since I do not wish to identify it with any particular point of view, or indeed with any sense, I shall not consider it to be a point "of view" or "of smell" or "of touch" or "of hearing" but simply as a point. The answer to the question, "point of what?" is then left to be determined by clinical experience; the geometrical point used to indicate the point of central projection in projective geometry will serve as a model. The geometer has succeeded, by transformation of Euclidean geometry and its visual representation into algebraic projective geometry, in freeing his investigations from some of the restrictions imposed by the genetic history of the procedures he uses; so psycho-analysis must be freed from the restrictions imposed by the associations with space and sight by which I look to geometry to simplify exposition. The difficulty is one that has to be resolved whenever past meaning, essential to communication or the rendering of private communication into public communication, has to be made suitable for further investigation. Repeating the present example in grid terms, the problem lies in the change that has to take place when column 3 elements are to be made suitable for functions appropriate to columns 4 and 5, and row H elements must provide models for row C.

Visual representations, sprung from the realm of emotional life, e.g. "Shall I compare thee to a summer's day?" and applied to the realm of realization in space have undergone transformation to make them suitable to their investigatory function, whether for discovery of mathematical objects or suitable husbands or wives and recording them when so discovered: I need to return these procedures to the investigation of what I suspect to be their own origins. The argument is, I think, circular: I am relying on the adequacy of the circle's diameter.

The state I have represented by — ↲↑ is one I can also represent in terms classifiable as C3, thus: — ↲↑ may be personified by a non-existent "person" whose hatred and envy is such that "it" is determined to remove and destroy every scrap of "existence" from any object which might be considered to "have" any existence to remove. Such a non-existent object can be so terrifying that its "existence" is denied, leaving only the "place where it was". This does not solve the problem because the place where it was, the no-thing, is even more terrifying because it has, as it were, been further denied existence instead of being allowed to glut itself with any existence it has been able enviously to find. Denial of the existence of the "place where it was" only makes matters worse because now the "point", marking the position of the no-thing, cannot be located.

In accordance with Kleinian theory such an object can be within the personality of either analyst or analysand. Furthermore it can be regarded as being projected out "into" (this point will be reconsidered in a moment) some other object. Equally it may be the ejecting force, that is, it may enter into an "existing" object in order to eject the "existingness".

— ↲↑ may be anywhere. Its position, if known, may be represented by a point, or, it may be represented by "space". Space is therefore indistinguishable from feeling + or —. ↲↑ may represent stupor ("le silence de ces espaces infinies m'effraie") or violence.

To consider the state I have just described from another "point of view"; for reasons already given I do not wish to commit myself to a "point of" anything. I require an element (category column 3 and 4 and $C \leftrightarrow G$) that is *unsaturated.* It would be useful to postulate unlimited "points of . . .". I shall use points on the circumference of a circle to represent unlimited "positions" (formerly points of view) since it may be useful to be able to indicate direction "inward" or "outward". Any point or number of points may then be regarded as vertices of projection. Any point, including that representing the centre of the circle, may represent the vertex of projection.

I shall illustrate the clinical use of this scheme by supposing that the extreme — ↲↑ is the vertex of a central projection. The clinical realization corresponding to this would be a patient dominated by bad internal objects with characteristics that I have described approximately above. The "symptoms" as observed clinically can be represented "spatially" in this geometric scheme by points that belong to the projected transformation. Before we can suppose that this geometric representation is appropriate to the realization there must be some evidence to justify the supposition that the transformation is projected to a distance and in a manner that would make the points on the circumference of a circle a reasonable representation of symptoms other than those at the vertex. For example, if the patient showed that he felt that he was identified with the breast and that the transformed elements had been projected on to the inner source of the limiting breast, this might reasonably be regarded by the analyst as an occasion for supposing that this geometric representation was apposite. If my description seems strange to the reader it may help if I remind him that I have chosen an illustration from amongst what I have called projective transformations and that I have distinguished these from rigid transformations in which transference manifestations as usually understood in classical analytic theory appear.

In the example I have given it would be unlikely that — ↲↑ at a central vertex would project a transformation in a way that made anything so well organized as a circle or a sphere an appropriate representation of the receptor or field for the transformation. It is therefore necessary to consider further the ground of the transformation. What I mean by "receptor" or "field" or "ground" can be most simply grasped by analogy with painting in which the ground for the transformation would be the canvas on to which the transformation was projected. First the analytic situation has been devised to provide conditions in which the patient has a ground on to which he can project, either in the manner of projective transformation, or in the manner of rigid motion. For various reasons, the commonest being disturbances in the analyst, the "analytic situation" can at best only approximate to the desirable.[1] Increasing analytic sophistication in the environment from which patients come will introduce further variations in the nature of analytic situations. Even rigid motion transformations cannot always find an appropriate ground on which transference (in the classical sense) may be detected. I do not propose to discuss this further than to indicate that the ground (or analytic situation) will need more study so as to include

[1] Other reasons will probably be discovered when the geometrical approach will demonstrate the "paranoid-schizoid position" of Melanie Klein and the geometer's vector space to be in a relation to each other analogous to the two views of a reversible perspective.

these changes and make it possible to detect transformations into different types of "analytic situation". I propose to discuss the problem of the ground for projective and rigid motion transformations as if it were stable and corresponded to what is regarded in classical analysis as the analytic situation.

So far I have expressed the idea of an analytic situation in column 1 category terms, say D1 or E1. There is rightly an aversion from formulations that seem to indicate a higher degree of scientific sophistication than is possible. Nor is it my intention to do more than explore the possibility of advance.

The idea implicit in the theory of transference is that the analyst is the person on to whom the analysand transfers his images. The theories of Malanie Klein already show that such a medium is not adequate for Tp β in what I have called projective transformations. In particular it does not help the analyst to recognize the elements of projective identification as they appear amidst clinical symptoms and material. The analyst must be able to detect signs of projective identification in a field which, relative to that which obtains in classical theory, is, as it were, multi-dimensional.[1] The analytic situation requires greater width and depth than can be provided by a model from Euclidean space. A patient who, in my view, is displaying projective transformations and requires the use of Kleinian theories for comprehension, also uses a field which is not simply the analyst, or his own personality, or even the relationship between himself and the analyst, but all those and more. He will say ". . . this woman" ". . . this dream" and use other similarly undefined (to the analyst) expressions. As this vagueness is an expression of β-element "thinking" the vagueness is not due to loss of definition but can obtrude because the analyst is in a position analogous to that of a listener to the description of a work of art that has been implemented in materials and on a scale that is not known to him. It is as if he heard the description of a painting, was searching on a canvas for the details represented to him,

[1] Vector space, as a mathematical concept, comes as near as possible to representing multi-dimensional objects.

whereas the object had been executed in a material with which he is unfamiliar. Such a patient can talk of a "penis black with rage" or an "eye green with envy" as being visible in a painting. These objects may not be visible to the analyst: he may think the patient is hallucinating them. But such an idea, perhaps sound to the view of a psychiatrist, is not penetrating enough for his work as an analyst. Hallucination may be more profitably seen as a dimension of the analytic situation in which, together with the remaining "dimensions", these objects are sense-able (if we include analytic intuition or consciousness, taking a lead from Freud, as a sense-organ of psychic quality).[1]

To make a step towards definition of this space we consider it to be a —K "space" and contrast it with K "space"—the space in which what is normally regarded as classical analysis takes place and classical transference manifestations become "sense-able". Using once more the analogies (C3 elements) I have already employed, —K "space" may be described as the place where space used to be. It is filled with no-objects which are violently and enviously greedy of any and every quality, thing, or object, for its "possession" (so to speak) of existence. I do not propose to carry my analogies further than to indicate that —K "space", is the material in which, with which, on which (etc.) the "artist" in projective transformation works. As an analogy with space may easily distort I propose to drop the term and speak of transformation in —K.[2]

Can the psycho-analyst find signs that will represent —K? They must be such that he is able to work with them and provide the rules for doing so.

It is obviously extremely clumsy to have to repeat terms such as "no-thing", "place where the thing was", "·", "point" and so on. Unless each term can be defined and used with accuracy misunderstandings multiply. Rigid definition would defeat the aim to provide an element unsaturated, but awaiting saturation, in the clinical experience (a D4 element). It is therefore desirable to use grid

[1] Freud, S.: *Interpretation of Dreams.* Chap. VII. Standard Edition, Vol. V.

[2] See below: Platonic forms, Christian Incarnation and Hyperbole.

categories to distinguish between different no-things and to relate them to the grid categories already proposed. This can be done by assigning a grid category to a statement and then assigning a grid category to the category already determined. Thus a second cycle of categorization is initiated. The process can be continued provided the differences in cycle are recognized.

CHAPTER NINE

THE visual images and terms employed in the following model are chosen without regard to the sources from which they have been derived.

Two people are present: myself and a patient. I am detached and so is he, though for both of us the experience is important. As he lies on the couch and I sit I imagine that a cloud begins to form rather in the way that clouds can sometimes be seen to form above a hot-point on a summer's day. It seems to be above him. A similar cloud may be visible to him, but he will see it arising from me. These are probability clouds.

Soon other clouds form: some of these are new clouds, some formed from old ones, probability clouds that have changed into possibility clouds. The situation must be conceived of as tense however little appears to be happening. I extend the scope of my model by doing away with the restriction implicit in the term "visual" imagery. "Olfactory image", "auditory image", "tactile image" are absurd terms which however can indicate the direction and scope of freedom I want. To abolish any restriction on absurdity, implicit in the analogies drawn from sense impressions, I shall describe the model as composed of C category elements and assume that tension, like "possibility" and "probability", is apparent[1] even if it is not apparent to any known sense. C category elements are described as visual because it enables me to draw on analogy from the sense of sight to communicate my meaning. The tension which is an essential part of the model is perceptible as are clouds. The clouds have increased; possibility clouds become clouds of doubt. Certainty clouds also appear; clouds of depression, guilt, hope and fear likewise. To every cloud there corresponds its hot point, but the cloud, like its analogue in nature, may have wandered far from it.

I associate pressure with both tension and clouds. The

[1] Metaphor? or does tension "appear" visually?

total situation I have tried to describe pictorially I would like to be able to describe odoriferously—as a dog might smell it, and, if he were sufficiently gifted, might delineate it odoriferously. And similarly with all other sensuous media available. Since I wish to find a system of representation that would serve for all these systems, and some of whose existence I am unaware, I seek a system of representation that is unsaturated ($\psi(\xi)$) and will permit of saturation.

Now it will be remembered that in a system in which β-elements dominate, "thoughts" are "things", and I pointed out that β-elements do not lend themselves to use as column 4 elements do because they are already saturated; there can be no pre-conception (row D) that can be *used* as a pre-conception, awaiting the realization that produces a conception, because the β-element is already saturated. We can now see that the defects of the no-thing are precisely these —the "absent" or "non-existent" object occupies the space that should be vacant. The analyst can represent the "no-thing" by a sign that *can* be saturated though the object represented *cannot*.

Using clinical experience to represent the situation just described I may describe it thus: The patient occupies the couch because he is determined that no one else should. His aim is to "saturate" the session so that I cannot work and no one can take *his* place. He employs terms (words, etc.) which are occupied by the meaning that they used to have *but* the meaning has been destroyed (or the term has been denuded of its meaning) so that the terms mark the place where the meaning used to be. This absent meaning (that is nevertheless present), will not permit any meaning to take its place. The verbal communication is therefore one that cannot represent O by virtue of the accepted meaning of the sign employed nor can it represent O by access of meaning through saturation.

Therefore in my search for a system that would represent the chief systems that can be seen to exist in the analytic situation (as I have described it in grid category C1 terms) I must replace the C1 elements, visual images of clouds, analyst, analysand, etc., and replace them by elements approximating to $\psi(\xi)$. It is clear that the C1 elements must not be denuded because were that to occur they would be replaced by β-elements.

I can do this by using the point (·) to represent the "place where" a some-thing (as contrasted with no-thing) could be, and the line (———) as the locus of a point or the place where a point is going. The analogy is defective because it is saturated by a meaning of movement. I shall try to make it more suitable for thought by considering point (·) and line (———) to represent a relationship thus: the point, (·), "place where", stage, must be conceived of as pertaining to the genetic axis: the line (———) must be conceived of as pertaining to the horizontal axis. A pre-conception, represented by · is a stage of development (a seed, so to speak, is a tree at particular stage of its development: so is a tree). A pre-conception represented by a line (———) is a use (such as D4).

The changes I have had to make throughout this book from analogy to more precise formulation, and from more precise formulation to analogy again, illustrate some of the difficulties with which I am attempting to deal. All these changes are examples of transformation. It may be as well to consider what the value of these transformations can be. With regard to transformation into terms of row C categories one advantage is that the sensuous model has a reality, and that reality an invariant quality, that aids communication. A "circle" expresses a meaning that is at once understood by the person to whom it is addressed. If I mean to use (·) to represent "the place where" or "time when" or "stage of growth" to which an object has attained (so that I am freed of limitations imposed by saturation) it is also true that I assume the existence of invariants under the particular transformation to which I resort. For example: I spoke in my model (row C) of clouds. I replace a cloud by · because I may want to replace this by the idea represented by the term "breast" or "penis", or "flatus" or "sanity" or by a no-thing.

I have spoken of a non-existent malignant, hostile, greedy breast. We may regard these characteristics as, so to speak, inborn, primary, essential: or we may regard them as secondary; or indifferently as primary or secondary, but possessing those qualities by virtue of the accident that that is the point at which we start our story. Bearing in mind that narrative and causation are peculiarities of a mode of communication and may therefore be regarded as T α, the qualities attributed to the breast are quite likely to be a function of the relationship between observer and observed. Consideration of in-born or primary or secondary in this context must not interfere with the possibility that the qualities of any object are a function of its relationships.

Thus, to resort again to C category, one cloud in my model may represent greed, hostility, envy and the hot-point may be the genital (of analyst, of analysand, etc.). This view may depend on a narrative approach and be a function of the fact that the analyst has just observed the object. Or it may be a function of "tension". By this I mean that the total analytic situation may be regarded as a system of energy, such as Freud postulated in his attempt towards a neuro-physiological scientific psychology, in which the sum total remains the same within the system but that the instability of any given part of the system can be seen in rises of "pressure". Using this description as my model (row C) the terms greed, hostile, malignant, may be regarded as T β of an O that is a pressure increase associated with relationships. If so, it is important to find rules for the manipulation of the signs, geometric and other, to be used. The rules for manipulation might be such that the signs, when manipulated in accordance with them, preserve a relationship to each other that represents the pressure changes and other supposed "qualities" of the objects (cloud, etc.).[1] We may also consider to what extent the rules for the manipulation of the signs may themselves find a realization, in the rules governing the relationship of personalities, that approximates to them.

If the qualities represented by point or line are a function

[1] The reader may compare the rules of grammatical construction used in a description of anxiety produced by a domestic crisis with the "laws of nature" governing the production of anxiety by a domestic crisis.

of the relationship between the point and line; if the point is representing a genetic stage and the line the category of use, it is clear that the rules governing the manipulations of point and lines are really governing the relationships between two aspects of the same object—the point. But the use of the term "aspect" in the above sentence and the meaning of the term "use" has now become so obscure that it is better to replace both by the point.

To return to the model on p. 117: the model (represented by verbal signs of C category) of analyst and patient served to communicate by virtue of the rigidity (invariant quality) of the images. This same rigidity meant the model was saturated and therefore unsuitable for use as a pre-conception (column 4 element). The combination of terms such as "hot-point" with other terms such as "cloud" and "probability" denied the model any variety of applicability but restricted its usefulness to one context. Terms such as "probability" and "cloud" are not homogeneous. Can they be replaced by signs that are? Yes: if they are replaced by points.

I am assuming that points were originally the space that had been occupied by a feeling, but had become a "no-feeling" or the space where a feeling used to be. Furthermore I assume that instead of having this "space" occupied by a "no-thing" a "point of view" (vertex of projection) can be found if the "space" may be used as an unsaturated element. Systems of geometry significant in scientific development can be regarded as such unsaturated elements. Euclidean geometry has been found to have many approximations in realizations of space. It is supposed that Euclidean geometry was derived from experience of space. My suggestion is that its *intra-psychic* origin is experience of "the space" where a feeling, emotion, or other mental experience "was".

The rules governing points and lines which have been elaborated by geometers may be reconsidered by reference back to the emotional phenomena that were replaced by "the place (or space) where the mental phenomena were". Such a procedure would establish an abstract deductive system based on a geometric foundation with intuitive psycho-analytic theory as its concrete realization. The statements (i) the resumption by the psyche of an emotional experience that has been detoxicated by a sojourn in the good breast (Melanie Klein) and (ii) the transformation of the emotional experience into a geometrical formulation and the use of this geometrical formulation as the counterpart of a concrete realization for a geometrically based, rigorously formulated, deductive system (possibly algebraic), may now be regarded as the (i) intuitive psycho-analytic and (ii) axiomatic deductive representations of the same process. Both statements are verbal representations of a realization and neither of them is satisfactory; nor is much improvement likely by mastery of the medium of verbal expression. The intuitive statement lends itself to the representation of genetic stages: the axiomatic formulation lends itself to the representation of a use.

This distinction points to a similarity between the weakness of the element suitable for representing a genetic stage to the weakness of the β-element. The element that represents genetic stages appears to have or to require a capacity for saturation, for becoming pregnant. I have phrased my last sentence in terms that illustrate the difficulty that arises when a term that in some contexts gains by its metaphorical quality (a "pregnant statement") loses communicative quality if it is employed in a context where its metaphorical quality ceases to be metaphorical because its context has approximated it to a β-element—it is, relative to its context, saturated. Some psychotic patients show skill in manipulating the analytic situation to bring this about. Therefore the element employed requires to have a high saturation point in its context.

The psychotic patient will show fear of an element with a high saturation point because a high capacity for saturation is felt as indistinguishable from greed in the element. That is, if I speak to him using terms in what I consider to be an ordinary conversational sense, and he thinks, perhaps rightly, that I am wishing to elicit information, he will react as if he thought I was trying to take away, not information but his sanity. His reply will be what sounds to me nonsense but is his method of parting with rubbish, or making splitting attacks on my speech. If the latter, his sentences are felt by him to be split into words but each word then becomes a greedy, unsaturated (that is, meaningless and schizophrenogenetic) element in return. The presenting objects are further attacked and become more malignant and minute till finally they qualify to be represented by my sign — ← ↑ for non-existent existence-greedy objects. Can this example from experience provide a starting point for transforming the model into something more scientific?

Agoraphobia is a psychiatric term for a state of mind found in some patients. In my terms it is a name "binding" a constant conjunction. If a patient presenting such symptoms is investigated psycho-analytically we find an extremely complex personality; this in itself is of no significance but for the fact, relevant to this discussion, that I am soon unable to use the term agoraphobia in a way that is meaningful: the conjunction is not of the elements that first appeared to compose it nor are they constant. I need to continue using this term, and with it the term "claustrophobia". I therefore assume that, both for the reader and myself, the term binds a constant conjunction.

In analysis it appears that the patient has terrible feelings when he is in open spaces or if he feels shut in.

I propose to use some of the ideas I have been putting forward in this book, as follows: The patient is coming to me for help and one reason for his distress is that his formulation does not afford scope for solution of his problem. With an actual case I would not attach importance to this, but in this discussion I shall suppose he is stating *his* experience inadequately for *my* purpose which is to know what he is talking about and to meditate upon it. (What he is talking about = O.) I therefore transform his statement thus: the patient, experiencing "terrible" feelings with the intensity of emotion of an infant having painful feelings, supposes them to be some bad object, perhaps part of himself, if he thinks he has a self, perhaps not. Mobilizing his adult armoury of speech he says he cannot possibly describe his feelings and then proceeds to do so. Since they are indescribable that itself indicates that the feelings described cannot be the ones that were felt. The patient may continue his description: "lost", "shut in", "panic", etc. I can match his diversity of terms with a diversity of my own: "depersonalized", "internal object", etc. For my purposes I want terms which will always be right in all situations in which the problems have the same configuration. Patients and analysts are constantly using different terms to describe situations that appear to have the same configuration. I want to find invariants, under psycho-analysis, to all of them. This condition is almost filled by the term "place where the thing was" or "space". Almost, but not quite. Its virtue can be seen in the fact that it will do equally well for agoraphobia or claustrophobia, and to that extent avoids two terms for configurations that are only apparently different. What is needed is a solution that will dispose finally of the diversity of terms, at present required to describe the experience called "claustro- or agoraphobia", and the far more serious defect associated with it, namely, the elaboration of as many theories as there are sufferers, matched by almost as many theories as there are therapists, when it is acknowledged that the configurations are probably the same. The solution required will cover more than claustrophobia and agoraphobia which I have chosen as a starting point. I choose "space" to represent, on the one hand, emotions which are felt to be indistinguishable from the "place where something was", and on the other, space akin to the geometric realization from which Euclidean geometry is believed to derive.

Certain peculiarities of the problem I am attempting to state are inherent in the problem. Thus I state, as part of an intuitive psycho-analytic theory, that the patient has an experience, such as an infant might have when the breast is withdrawn, of facing emotions that are unknown, unrecognized as belonging to himself, and confused with an object which he but recently possessed. Further descriptions only add to the multiplicity of which I already complain as the reader will see if he consults any analytic descriptions of infantile behaviour. The relationship of these representations with the realizations approximating to them may be compared with the axiomatic geometric deductive space that I wish to introduce as a step towards formulations that are precise, communicable without distortion, and more nearly adequate to cover all situations that are basically the same. I suggest the following comparisons: (i) "Unknown", in the model afforded by the intuitive psycho-analytical theory, with "unknown", in the mathematical sense in which I wish to use "geometric space". (ii) "Variable", as applied to the sense of instability and insecurity in the model of infantile anxiety, with "variable", as I wish to apply it to geometric space. Thus geometric space may represent and be replaced by constant values for any particular universe of discourse. The relationship of geometric space to the psycho-analytic intuitive theory that I propose as *its* realization; the further relationship of the psycho-analytical intuitive theory to the clinical experience which I consider is *its* realization; together these represent a progression such as that in the transformation of an experience into a poem—"emotion recollected in tranquillity." The geometric transformation may be regarded as a representation, "detoxicated" (that is, with the painful emotion made bearable) of the same realization as that represented (but with the painful emotion expressed), by the intuitive psycho-analytical theory. This implies that any individual capable of making the transformation from O, when O is a psychic reality, to T β is capable of doing for himself something analogous to projective identification into the good breast, he being identified with himself and the breast.

There are further similarities to which I want to draw attention: if it is accepted that geometric space affords a link between unsophisticated emotional problems, their unsophisticated solutions and the possibility of their restatement in sophisticated terms admitting of sophisticated solutions, then it may be that musical and other artistic methods afford a similar link. These must not be regarded as replacements of the geometric approach. The investigation must be directed to the elucidation of point and line as elements imbedded in the material of transformations in the media of all arts and sciences. In the poem it may be found in the long–short of rhythm; in painting it may be found, not as Vitruvius sought to find it, in a golden section or other geometric plan, as the method of construction, but in the matter from which the construct is formed. In music it may be looked for not in musical notation, but music itself. In science it may be seen in the atomic theories of Democritus of Abdera.

The grid provides a scheme whereby visual images of category C may be seen to have counterpart in H category, and vice versa. The categories reserved for mathematical representations only may be open to sophisticated versions of auditory, visual, or other forms of C category representation. Thus certain paintings, or musical compositions, could properly be considered to fall in H categories together with certain algebraic formulations, if their invariants were recognized and their relationships seen to conform to rule.

This discussion is concerned with such representations, whatever the discipline, as having disposed within them the invariants of point and line; intuitive psycho-analytical theory is its corresponding realization.

CHAPTER TEN

THIS chapter is a review and summary. I begin with a model of transformation: suppose a number of marbles of different colours and sizes, $\frac{1}{2}''$, $\frac{3}{4}''$ and 1″ in diameter, lying in a tray. The colours and sizes are "dimensions". Make a rule that in another tray must be placed as many marbles of 1″ diameter as there are green marbles in the first tray. When the operation has been completed the marbles in the second tray will represent a transformation of the "space" represented by the marbles of different size and colour in the first tray. The collection on the first tray represents the "space" I have denoted O. The rule regulating the disposition of marbles on the second tray represents the mental activity I have denoted by T α (or T aα if it governs the behaviour of the analyst). The marbles on the second tray represent the transformation I have denoted T β (or T aβ if effected by the analyst).

I may now use the marbles on the second tray as the O for further transformation. I can denote this by writing O (2nd cycle) = T aβ (1st cycle). I make a rule that on another tray are to be placed as many marbles of 1″ diameter as there are blue marbles on the second tray. This rule may accordingly be denoted T aα (2nd cycle) and when the operation is complete the marbles on the third tray represent a state I denote by the sign T aβ (2nd cycle). This can now be made the starting point of a further operation which is similar to the two preceding but is now the third cycle of transformation.

The foregoing model I shall replace by one that comes nearer to representing an analytic experience, thus: suppose the patient makes a complex statement, in the sense I have given the term, which may have consisted of anything from a solitary ejaculation to a session of free associations. I shall suppose that the statement is so complex that it would only be adequately represented by being categorized in every grid category. The categories, like the sizes and colours of the marbles, may be regarded as "dimensions" of the statement. In practice, the patient's behaviour can fairly easily be seen to fall into two or three categories and analysts are familiar with the problem of trying to decide what aspect of the material should be regarded as immediately significant and interpreted accordingly. Use of the grid makes it possible to scan the analytic material methodically. At first it is wise to use it retrospectively so that nothing should interfere with the analyst's absorption of the evidence. Practice in review of analytic work by this method leads quite soon to facility in unconscious and immediate assessment of evidence as it unfolds in the session. The hypothetical statement of my model has facets qualifying it for every grid category. I have previously said[1] that it is important to play psycho-analytic games as a part of the daily review of analytic work, and one valuable game consists in supposing what the interpretations would have been and what course the analyst might have taken if, instead of the actual conjectures and interpretations, the material had been categorized quite differently. Stating this in terms of transformation theory the statement is regarded as a field of diverse dimensions with which we are required to deal. We may choose column 2 elements as most significant and ignore all other categories that are present. The interpretation which we base on the dimension thus isolated will be denoted T $a\beta$. O, corresponding to the first tray of marbles in model 1, will be the total statement. The decision to choose column 2 elements, as more significant than all others, corresponds to the rule determining how the marbles were to be disposed on the second tray; it is accordingly denoted by T $a\alpha$. The interpretation is the transformed statement and corresponds to the marbles on tray 2.

At first this rule appears arbitrary compared to the rule in model 1 because it can be argued that T $a\alpha$, in model 2, is merely a decision to ignore one set of facts in favour of another. Yet the rule in model 1 is no less arbitrary although an appearance of legality is conferred by an appeal to the

[1] In *Elements of Psycho-Analysis*.

contents of tray 1 as decisive in determining the contents of tray 2.

The difference in the two models consists in the fact that in model 2 the rule makes the point of arbitrary change explicit. The fact that there are so many green marbles in tray 1 is used to decide the number of marbles of 1″ diameter in the second. No more explanation is given for this than for ignoring all dimensions save column 2 in the second model.

In model 2 the interpretation (T aβ) should be associated with a K link; the analyst is concerned to understand the associations and to communicate that understanding to the patient. The patient in accordance with our postulate is the source of an L, H or —K link. But, since he comes voluntarily it must be assumed that his associations are also intended to be part of a K link.

The conclusion must be that we must make assumptions about assumptions about . . . *ad infinitum.* No conclusion is possible about the arbitrary nature of the rule. The rule may be seen however to be a special case of the pre-conception. It is a formulation representing a pre-conception and it is used in accordance with column 4. The provisional category for the rule is D4. If we suppose that the rule is intended to *do* something we attribute to it the quality of an act and the category would be more correctly D6.

T aα is a private process limited to the analyst's mind: the categorization of T aα impinges on the domain of counter-transference and the analyst's own analysis. The matter is relevant to discussion of the nature of the relationship of interpretations to the matter interpreted. The assumption underlying loyalty to the K link is that the personality of analyst and analysand can survive the loss of its protective coat of lies, subterfuge, evasion and hallucination and may even be fortified and enriched by the loss. It is an assumption strongly disputed by the psychotic and *a fortiori* by the group, which relies on psychotic mechanisms for its coherence and sense of well-being. Discussion of this assumption will lie on the periphery of the theme of transformations which I take next.

Treating my hypothetical statement, with dimensions represented by all grid categories, as the subject for the psycho-analytical game, I wish to consider the implications of ignoring all aspects (dimensions) of the statement save those that fall in category A6. I shall assume that it is not obligatory to do this and that many correct interpretations could be seen to be available from an ordinary scansion of the other grid dimensions, the dimensions I propose to ignore. I wish it to be supposed that if a layman could hear the patient he would not feel completely at a loss to understand though he might easily be aware that there was something he did *not* understand and be puzzled to know why. I also wish it to be supposed that the only reason for questioning the soundness of an analysis based on classical analytic theories would be the bizarre response to interpretations which would appear to be quite correct. By bizarre I mean that the patient's response does not saturate the analyst's pre-conceptions but appears itself to require saturation. In conditions such as these, postulated to facilitate psychological preparation for the theories that follow, the psycho-analytical game may develop the analyst's intuition (as a musician's exercises facilitate his capacity to perform an actual musical creation though not themselves being more than scales and other manual exercises) in preparation for the work required of it in analysis.

My aim is to illustrate a particular form of transformation and to approach it by consideration of the elements of a statement and its dimensions, notably the dimension bound by me by the term β-element, as manipulated in a mental domain where thoughts are not distinguished from things and the mind is felt to operate as if it were a muscle.

As I am assuming the grid category is A6 I shall not consider the significance of what is said to reside predominantly in the meanings of the words and sentences as it would do if I regarded the communication made by the patient as part of a rigid motion transformation. I expect it to be significant that the patient in the course of speaking expels air from his lungs. His failure to distinguish thoughts from things contributes to a sense that the actual meaning of the words, as that would be understood in a rigid motion transformation, is expelled as air from his lungs is expelled. Conformably with this the patient seems to feel that his mind is an expelling organ like a lung in act of expiration. Were I regarding his communication as part of a rigid motion transformation I should hear him say something like this: "Whatever has happened to my key? It can't be six unless the milkman came early. The rounds are impeccable as a rule though my friend said it was quite different her way. You think you are wonderful but you are just a thief."

As I am supposing that his communication is part of a projective transformation composed of A6 elements, I consider that some "thing" is being evacuated. The "thing" may be the scene in the consulting room. In that case the patient is using his eyes, and the mental counterpart of his capacity for vision, as evacuatory musculature. What to me appears to him to be the product of a visual evacuation.

The "thing" may be something adumbrated by his words —if I may assume I am correct in allowing myself to gain an impression based on what *I* think his words should mean if he were talking conversational English. Such an impression is based on long experience of the patient's communications and on acceptance of them as row A formulations of a highly idiosyncratic type. What my assumptions amount to is that the communication is a mixture in which a meaning, grasped by ordinary modes of understanding, has been treated by the patient as if it were a thing, and evacuated phonetically and mentally as if by an apparatus whose characteristics are those usually associated with muscles.

I cannot attempt a detailed description of how or why I arrive at the qualities which I am about to attribute to the evacuated object. The F category meanings can be expressed approximately as follows: "the key, that which gives potency and is itself capacity or potency, has gone. The coming of the milkman could tell me the time—six o'clock. The time, six o'clock, could tell me the milkman was coming. The milkman's ejaculation (coming) could tell me the time and feed me. But none of these things happens. The key has been lost; they have been denuded of their meaning. I know this is because I am self-supporting because I can hallucinate a meal, time, an ejaculation and whatever else I need. Then, from these evacuated objects (hallucinations in the analyst's opinion) I can gain all the mental and physical sustenance I require. But I am unable to get such sustenance. Obviously, therefore, what you, the analyst, call psycho-analysis is simply your method of stealing the sustenance from my hallucinations, leaving me without a key, while you are able to feel how superior your psycho-analysis is and how clever you are. But psycho-analysis is not superior to my hallucinations. You only make it appear so by stealing the goodness from hallucinations so they seem bad mental faeces and psycho-analysis is made good."

My account of these events cannot be made plausible to anyone who has not had the analyst's experience. I shall not attempt to make the description convincing but shall pass on to consider implications of this and similar ineffable experiences.

Although I have said I proposed to play my psycho-analytical game on the assumption that all elements were A6 my introduction of the mixed association in which F row elements were being treated as if they belonged to A row shows, as anyone might reasonably expect, that nothing in the practice of psycho-analysis ever fits into neat and rigid categorizations. Nevertheless the grid categories do make it possible to draw attention to find shades of difference in meaning in a way which would be difficult or impossible without them—as in this instance where relatively sophisticated elements are being treated in a manner much more suited to the primitive and immature.

As a result of treating the elements of the statement as A6 certain factors peripheral to A6 elements can be seen to be activated and can be detected in analysis.

(i) Hallucination is seen as a method of achieving independence which the patient considers to be superior to psycho-analysis.

(ii) Its failure, in so far as it is seen as a failure, is attributed to the rivalry, envy and thieving propensities of the analyst.

(iii) Rivalry, envy, greed, thieving, together with his

sense of being blameless, deserve consideration as invariants under hallucinosis.

(iv) The concept of hallucinosis needs to be widened to fit a number of configurations which are at present not recognized as being the same.

(v) Transformation, in rigid motion or projection, must be seen to have hallucinosis as one of its media.

(vi) The rules of transformation in hallucinosis must be established through clinical observation. I have no doubt that they exist and can be delineated by observation of the operation envy, greed, rivalry, "moral" and scientific superiority in hallucinosis. I offer the following suggestions provisionally as an example of such "rules".

A. If an object is "top" it dictates "action"; it is superior in all respects to all other objects and is self-sufficient and independent of them.

B. Objects that can occupy such a position include (*a*) Father, (*b*) Mother, (*c*) Analyst, (*d*) Aim, object or ambition, (*e*) Interpretation, (*f*) Ideas, whether moral or scientific.

C. The only relationship between two objects is that of superior to inferior.

D. To receive is better than to give.

Similarly it is possible to formulate a mathematics of hallucinosis. I offer the following suggestions formulated to give first a description of the emotional background and second the arithmetical statement. In rigid motion transformation:

a^1 The infant feels it is being satisfied by the breast: the breast disappears and the satisfaction with it.

a^2 1 breast + 0 breast = 0 breast

a^3 $1 + 0 = 0$

Suppose now that the personality cannot tolerate frustration. This is associated with "that state of mind in which ideas may be supposed to assume the force of sensations through the confusion of thought with the objects of thought, and the excess of passion animating the creations of imagination"[1]

[1] Shelley, P. B.: Hellas. His sixth note on the poem.

(I use Shelley's formulation of his poetic intuition to provide the background realization for the statement "hallucinosis"). Memory of the satisfaction is used to deny the absence of satisfaction. Denial of time is used to deny that the breast is the place where the breast used to be and to maintain that it is where the breast now is. The mathematical transformation in hallucinosis may be stated thus (b^2 taking the place of a^2, etc.):

b^2 1 breast + 0 breast = 1 breast
b^3 1 + 0 = 1.

There may be good reasons for supposing that 1 + 0 = 1, for example that there is a realization that may approximate to it and the formulation 1 + 0 = 1 may help to establish a K link with such a realization. But b^3 is intended to demonstrate the relationship between 0 and 1 in a domain where it is possible to remove the "noughtness" from 0 and so produce 1. Therefore in the domain of hallucinosis 0 − 0 = 1. It is natural to wonder what would be the result of adding nought to nought. It is $0 + 0 = 0^0$. That is to say that if noughtness is added to noughtness the noughtness is multiplied by itself. The emotional state that might provide a background realization approximating to this is the state of complete freedom from the restriction imposed by contact with realizations of any kind. The ability of 0 to increase thus by parthogenesis corresponds to the characteristics of greed which is also able to grow and flourish exceedingly by supplying itself with unrestricted supplies of nothing.

These mathematical manipulations serve a purpose in the domain of hallucinosis analogous to that served by mathematics in D4 and 5 investigations where frustration exists. In hallucinosis nought denuded of its noughtness is hostile envious and greedy and does not even exist as it is denuded of its existence.

The realizations which form the background of hallucinosis differ from those that form the background in the domain of accepted frustration. (To save time I shall denote the latter by *f* and the former by *h*.) In *f*, 1 breast +

0 breast + 1 breast + 0 breast + 1 breast + 0 breast + 1 breast + 0 breast = −4 breasts. Or: 1 + 0 + 1 + 0 + 1 + 0 + 1 + 0 = −4. In *h*, 1 breast + 0 breast = "one breast denuded of existence" and "a place where the breast was, also denuded of existence" = a raging inferno of greedy non-existence.

If we compare 1 in *f* mathematics with 1 in *h* mathematics, it can be seen in *f* to be a dimension of a statement even though the statement of which it is a dimension is not known and may be a realization whose existence is revealed only by the existence of this one dimension. In *h*, 1 is a column 2 element and is intended and understood to mean that an object is devoid of dimensions because it has dimensions that are to be rendered incapable of transformation. To be incapable of transformation the statement must be denuded of dimensions, rules must be made incapable of regulation (in other words denuded of any dimensions that qualify rules to be regarded as rules) and vertices must be destroyed. For analytic practice this means that any efforts that the analyst makes towards establishing dimensions, rules or vertices, or establishing that such dimensions, rules and vertices exist, will be under attack. Amongst such procedures will be projective identification placed in a vertex so that it will be inoperable; thus a part of the patient's personality will occupy "the place of" the analyst to deny that vertex to the analyst. This leads me to reconsider some aspects of that particular form of transformation known to analysts as the interpretation.

For a greater part of its history it has been assumed that a psycho-analytic interpretation had as its function the rendering conscious of that which is unconscious. The relatively simple division of elements into conscious and unconscious has proved extremely fruitful, but it no longer provides a satisfactory criterion of an interpretation to regard it as either making or failing to make that which is unconscious conscious. With the grid it is possible to categorize a statement, its interpretation, and the statement that is a resultant of the two. Can the relationship between the categories to which statements are assigned provide a more illuminating approach than the relationship conscious:unconscious?

In the three models of transformation that I have sketched out in this chapter (A1, B1 and B2) O, T aα and T pα, T aβ and T pβ, can be distinguished. The medium in the first is provided by marbles and trays, in the second by the relationship between analyst and analysand (as subject to manipulation by the patient to make it fit in the framework of hallucinosis) and in the third by the relationship between analyst and analysand as subject to representation so that the representation could be manipulated as part of a K link.

The difference between B1 and B2 makes it likely that the statements of the analysand will differ in category from those of the analyst, for the medium of the analysand's transformation lies in the sphere of action, that of the analyst in the sphere of thought and its verbal representations.

The patient whose transformations are effected in the medium of hallucinosis might almost have as his motto "actions speak louder than words" with its hint of rivalry as an essential feature of the relationship. The analyst appears to be offered the choice of abandoning his technique, which is an admission of surrender to the superior wisdom and technique of the analysand, or, keeping to analysis and thereby showing by *his* actions that *he* considers *his* technique superior; either course would fit in with an acting out of rivalry.

The statement "acting out of rivalry" in my last sentence will serve as an example of the distorting effect produced by the approach to a configuration through one of its parts. Rivalry is an important element but its significance depends on the particular constant conjunction or configuration of which it is a part. "Rivalry" signifies a constant conjunction but the constant conjunction it signifies is not the relevant one in this context. It is common to find some feature, such as the cruelty of the super-ego, and to suppose that one has discovered the key to a baffling situation only to find that the same feature occurs in other situations which bear no marked resemblance to the situation to which one hoped the key had been discovered. In my experience this difficulty arises because the *key* has been detected in the elements of a second, third or subsequent cycle of psycho-analytic (that is, analyst's) transformations when it should be sought in the nature of the transformations effected by the analysand. What matters in the present context is not rivalry so much as rivalry under transformations in hallucinosis. I shall therefore devote further attention to expanding what I mean by this term without troubling over-much to make the description rigorous. The general picture the patient presents is that of a person anxious to demonstrate his independence of anything other than his own creations. These creations are the results of his supposed ability to use his senses as organs of evacuation which are able to surround him with a universe that has been generated by himself: the function of the senses and their mental counterpart is to create the patient's perfect world. Evidence of imperfection is *ipso facto* evidence for the intervention of hostile envious forces. Thanks to the patient's capacity for satisfying all his needs from his own creations he is entirely independent of anyone or anything other than his products and therefore is beyond rivalry, envy, greed, meanness, love or hate; but the evidence of his senses belies his pre-determinations; he is *not* satisfied.

We may now reconsider the term "hallucination". It must be distinguished from an illusion or delusion because both these terms are required to represent other phenomena, namely those that are associated with pre-conceptions that turn to conceptions because they mate with realizations that do not approximate to the pre-conceptions closely enough to saturate the pre-conception, but closely enough to give rise to a conception or mis-conception. The pre-conception requires saturation by a realization that is *not* an evacuation of the senses but has an existence independent of the personality. The hallucination arises from a pre-determination and requires satisfaction from (*a*) an evacuation from the personality and (*b*) from conviction that the element *is* its own evacuation. Confusion occurs if due weight is not given to the fact that the total conjunction bound by the term hallucination is associated with two different points of view, or, as I prefer to call it, with two different vertices, one represented by the patient, the other by the analyst.

To understand the nature of the difference between the two vertices it will be necessary to review phenomena that I class as D1, D2, D3. The intuitive psycho-analytic background is that which I have "bound" by terms such as preconception, definition, notation, attention. My object in using grid categories is to escape from the trammels imposed by the penumbra of associations that these terms possess; in the course of this digression I shall say something more of the term pre-determination which I introduced to represent a phenomenon of hallucinosis. I shall borrow freely any material that is likely to simplify my task, starting with Plato's theories of Forms. As I understand the term, various phenomena, such as the appearance of a beautiful object, are significant not because they are beautiful or good but because they serve to "remind" the beholder of the beauty or the good which was once, but no longer is, known. This object, of which the phenomenon serves as a reminder, is a Form. I claim Plato as a supporter for the pre-conception, the Kleinian internal object, the inborn anticipation. Melanie Klein objected in conversation with me to the idea that the infant had an inborn pre-conception of the breast, but though it may be difficult to produce evidence for the existence of a realization that approximates to this theory, the theory itself seems to me to be useful as a contribution to a vertex I want to establish. Phenomena, the term being used as Kant might use it, are transformed into representations, T β. T β may then be regarded as a representation of the individual's experience O, but the significance of O derives from and inheres in the Platonic Form.

The object represented by the term Platonic Form may also be represented in mystical terms such as "One is one and all alone and ever more shall be so", and those of canto xxxiii of the Paradiso. (Barbara Reynolds's translation.)

> "Eternal Light, that in Thyself alone
> Dwelling, alone dost know Thyself, and smile
> On Thy self-love, so knowing and so known!"

The emphasis is altered by Christian Platonism so that the balance between the elements of the configuration is altered; this may be seen most clearly expressed in the doctrine of the Incarnation. The particular representation which is significant for this discussion has been formulated by Meister Eckhart and the Blessed John Ruysbroeck who distinguish the Godhead from God; thus in Tractate XI "God in the Godhead is spiritual substance, so elemental that we can say nothing about it."

It is evident that in this view God is regarded as a Person independent of the human mind. The phenomenon of Good or Beauty would not then be that which "reminds" the personality of a Form (pre-conception) but is an incarnation of a part of an independent Person, wholly outside the personality, to whom the phenomena are "given". The phenomenon does not "remind" the individual of the Form but enables the person to achieve union with an incarnation of the Godhead, or the thing-in-itself (or Person-in-Himself).

For convenience I shall refer to these two configurations as "Forms" and "Incarnation". In both there is a suggestion that there is an ultimate reality with which it is possible to have direct contact although in both it appears that each direct contact is possible only after submission to an exacting discipline of relationships with phenomena, in one configuration, and incarnate Godhead in the other. In neither is there discussion of establishing a direct contact with the reality of absolute evil, though it is possible that some of the "repellant" quality attributed to St John of the Cross may be an unconscious tribute to his identification of absolute real evil with absolute real good.

The object of this digression, as of the previous discussions in this chapter and book, is to arrive at a postulate. The postulate is that already designated by O. To qualify O for inclusion amongst the column 1 categories by defining its definitory qualities I list the following negatives: Its existence as indwelling has no significance whether it is supposed to dwell in an individual person or in God or Devil; it is not good or evil; it cannot be known, loved or hated. It can be represented by terms such as ultimate reality or truth. The most, and the least that the individual person can do is to be it. Being identified with it is a measure of distance from it. The beauty of a rose is a phenomenon betraying the ugliness of O just as ugliness betrays or reveals the existence of O. L, H, K are links and by virtue of that fact are substitutes for the ultimate relationship with O which is not a relationship or an identification or an atonement or a reunion. The qualities attributed to O, the links with O, are all transformations of O and *being* O. The rose *is* itself whatever it may be *said* to be. The human person *is* himself and by "is" I mean in both instances a positive act of being for which L, H, K are only substitutes and approximations.

Any formulation, including this one, is a representation and all representations are transformations, often of transformations. Any analytic statement can be represented by the sign T $\alpha\beta$ (cycle n) or T $p\beta$ (cycle n).

O, representing the unknowable ultimate reality can be represented by any formulation of a transformation—such as "unknowable ultimate reality" which I have just formulated. It may therefore seem unnecessary to multiply representations of it; indeed from the psycho-analytic vertex that is true. But I wish to make it clear that my reason for saying O is unknowable is not that I consider human capacity unequal to the task but because K, L, or H are inappropriate to O. They are appropriate to transformations of O but not to O. To recapitulate:

Transformations may be scientific, aesthetic, religious, mystical, psycho-analytical. They may be described as psychotic and neurotic also, but though all these classifications have a value it does not appear to me that the value that they have is psycho-analytically adequate. I have chosen to write, though briefly, of transformation in hallucinosis because the description may serve to explain why I consider existing methods of observation, notation, attention and curiosity are inadequate, why a theory of transformations may aid in making these methods more nearly adequate and why the theory of transformations itself must be freed from existing associations if it is to be fitted for its psycho-analytic tasks. The suggestion of projective transformations differentiated from rigid motion transformations is but one step to indicate the possibilities. The subject cannot be pursued further without considering the relationship between categories of patient's transformations and categories of analyst's transformations. These last I have said must be transformations in K and this leads me to a peculiarity of transformations in K.

It is a commonplace that any attempt at scientific inquiry involves distortion through the exaggeration of certain elements in order to display their significance. This characteristic is present in L and H as much as in K. In order to link its phenomenological counterpart in analytic practice, with the penumbra of associations that I regard as significant, I shall call this characteristic hyperbole. I mean the term to convey an impression of exaggeration, of rivalry and, by retention of its original significance, throwing and outdistancing. The appearance of hyperbole in any form must be regarded as significant of a transformation in which rivalry, envy and evacuation are operating. There is a profound difference between "being" O and rivalry with O. The latter is characterized by envy, hate, love, megalomania and the state known to analysts as acting out, which must be sharply differentiated from acting; which is characteristic of "being" O.

Just as exaggeration is helpful in clarifying a problem so it can be felt to be important to exaggerate in order to gain the attention necessary to have a problem clarified. Now the "clarification" of a primitive emotion depends on its being contained by a container which will detoxicate it.[1] In order to enlist the aid of the container the emotion must be exaggerated. The "container" may be a "good breast", internal or external, which is able to detoxicate the emotion. Or the container may not be able to tolerate the emotion and the contained emotion may not be able to tolerate neglect. The result is hyperbole. That is to say, the emotion that cannot tolerate neglect grows in intensity, is exaggerated to ensure attention and the container reacts by more, and

[1] See Bion, W. R.: *Elements of Psycho-Analysis*, p. 27.

still more, violent evacuation. By using the term "hyperbole" I mean to bind the constant conjunction of increasing force of emotion with increasing force of evacuation. It is immaterial to hyperbole what the emotion is; but on the emotion will depend whether the hyperbolic expression is idealizing or denigrating.

When the presenting problem in analysis is the hallucinations of the patient a crux has been reached. In addition to the problem that the patient is attempting to solve by transformation in hallucinosis is the secondary problem presented by his method of solution. This secondary problem appears in analysis as a conflict between the method employed by the analyst and the method employed by the patient. The conflict can be described as a disagreement on the respective virtues of a transformation in hallucinosis and a transformation in psycho-analysis. The disagreement is coloured by the patient's feeling that the disagreement between patient and analyst is a disagreement between rivals and that it concerns rival methods of approach. Unless this point is made clear no progress can be made. When it has been made clear the disagreement still continues but it becomes endo-psychic: the rival methods struggle for supremacy within the patient. The characteristics of the conflict are easier to discern when externalized as a conflict between analyst and patient and this can lead to a collusion between the two for the patient finds it more tolerable and the analyst easier. As the conflict involves the nature of the contributions made by both, I shall use the grid to elucidate the difference between the two.

As I have said the patient's contributions are A6. The "rules" according to which he manipulates these elements are (i) He needs no analyst because he provides the material for his own cure and knows how to obtain the cure from it. (ii) The material is evacuated by the mental counterpart (as the analyst would believe) of his sensory equipment. (iii) Painful experience is not cure, any more than pleasure, but both are methods of scoring points in a rivalry relationship. (iv) The relationship between the contestants is designed to prove the superiority of the patient and hallucinosis over the analyst and psycho-analysis. (v) "Cure" is identical with "winning".

Following from these "rules" certain anomalies arise: Any benefit achieved as a result of analytic cure is vitiated by its being indistinguishable from "defect" of the analysand. Any victory of the analysand is vitiated by perpetuating the painful status quo. The painful element is due to the obtrusion of the analyst—"the analyst's fault". The analyst's "fault" in the eyes of the analysand is attributable to a two-fold source: (i) All his "interpretations" are A6 elements evacuated by him as a part of his resort to the patient's methods and employment of transformation in hallucinosis; (ii) All his interpretations are psycho-analytic elements designed to prove the superiority of himself and psycho-analysis. In so far as he is guilty of (i) his actions as a psycho-analyst are "acting out"; and of (ii) his actions as a psycho-analyst are acts (as opposed to "acting out") and are expressions of a capacity for compassion. But a capacity for compassion is a source of admiration and therefore envy in an analysand who feels incapable of mature compassion.

It follows that it is a matter of difficulty for the analyst to conduct himself in such a manner that his association with the analysand is beneficial to the analysand. The exercise, in the patient's view, is the establishment of the superiority of rivalry, envy and hate over compassion, complementation and generosity. The crux to which I referred is found in the character of the co-operation between two people and not in the problem for which the co-operation is required. The nature of the co-operation may be determined by the disturbances in the personality of the patient, but that situation may be presumed to be amenable to psycho-analysis; it differs from the situation produced by the inborn disposition of the patient. If analysis has been successful in restoring the personality of the patient he will approximate to being the person he was when his development became compromised. His disturbed state may be the outcome of an inadequate solution of his problem, but when that situation has been psycho-analytically reconstructed the need arises to solve the problem more adequately. If rivalry, envy and hate are secondary the chance of an adequate solution would seem to be greater than would be the case if the patient's endowment of rivalry, envy and hate is intrinsic, inborn, the very stuff of his personality.

The more the problem relates to the patient's inborn character the more difficult it is for him to modify his adherence to transformation in hallucinosis as *the* superior approach. If his solution were determined by a false belief that no real solution exists it would be easier for him to admit his mistake than it is when his solution is dictated by an inborn need to be "top". This would be unimportant were it not for the belief that certain disorders, notably schizophrenia, are physical and originate in pathological physical states. Their nature would be easier to grasp if seen to originate in a *normal* physical state and to spring from the very health and virility of the patient's endowment of ambition, intolerance of frustration, envy, aggression and his belief that there is, or ought to be, or will be (even if it has to be created by himself) an ideal object that exists to fulfil itself. The impression such patients give of suffering from a character disorder derives from the sense that their well-being and vitality spring from the same characteristics which give trouble. The sense that loss of the bad parts of his personality is inseparable from loss of that part in which all his mental health resides, contributes to the acuity of the patient's fears. This acute fear is inseparable from any attempt to resolve the crux. Is the patient going to repeat the former error by becoming confirmed in his adherence to transformation in hallucinosis or will he turn to transformation in psycho-analysis?

The generally accepted view amongst psycho-analysts is that interpretations are expressed verbally, that they should be terse and to the point, namely to make the patient aware of his unconscious motivations. The orthodox view can be expressed in my terms thus: the medium of transformation is conversational English. The analyst's statements should belong to categories F1, 3, 4. The link with analysand should be K, not H or L. He should not express himself in any terms other than those used by an adult; theoretically this excludes certain categories (notably column 2) but, as I have shown, it is possible to regard the patient's statement in different ways, so that sometimes one dimension is thrown into relief, at other times another, and it is equally open to the patient to do just that. It is because he does so that his response to an interpretation may appear anomalous. Therefore although the analyst is under an obligation to speak with as little ambiguity as possible, in fact his aims are limited by the analysand who is free to receive interpretations in whatever way he chooses. In a sense it can seem that the analyst is hoist with his own petard: he is free to interpret the statements of the analysand how he will; the analysand retorts in kind. The analyst is not free except in the sense that when the patient comes to him for analysis he is obliged to speak in a way which would not be tolerable in any other frame of reference and then only from a particular vertex.

The patient's response would also be intolerable if there were no psycho-analytic indulgence to excuse it, or, if it were not for a psycho-analytic vertex.

If the reader will reconsider the last page he will see a number of statements whose relationship to each other, and therefore meaning, is illuminated if we employ the concept of vertex thus:

"The generally accepted view amongst psycho-analysts . . ."—vertex 1

"The orthodox view . . ."—vertex 2

"Terms used by an adult . . ."—vertex 3

". . . analyst under an obligation . . ."—vertex 4 (implied, not stated)

". . . free to receive . . . he chooses . . ."—vertex 5 (receptor vertex)

". . . in a sense it can be seen . . ."—vertex 6

". . . the analyst . . . is obliged . . ."—vertex 7

". . . not be tolerable . . . in any other frame of reference . . ."—vertex 8.

All these vertices represent views with which I am identified. With myself as the vertex all these vertices represent "other-people-as-seen-by-me." Any view with which I am identified is, as I explained discussing O, a vertex from which I have separated myself or with which I have attempted to become-at-one; the direction of the link is immaterial in this context. "Other-people-as-seen-by-me" are phenomena. I can know phenomena: I can know various aspects of my personality with which I am identified. I can identify myself with aspects of myself which I can know. Any such identification or knowledge is formulated and thereby becomes a statement and, like every other statement in whatever medium, can be classified in a grid category. It is a transformation T $x\beta$. ($x =$ the personality in whom T $x\alpha$ has taken place.)

CHAPTER ELEVEN

In none of this have I spoken of O except in so far as the horizontal axis of the grid implies the existence of an object that "uses" and the vertical axis implies the existence of an object that "possesses" something to use.

My theory would seem to imply a gap between phenomena and the thing-in-itself and all that I have said is not incompatible with Plato, Kant, Berkeley, Freud and Klein, to name a few, who show the extent to which they believe that a curtain of illusion separates us from reality. Some consciously believe the curtain of illusion to be a protection against truth which is essential to the survival of humanity; the remainder of us believe it unconsciously but no less tenaciously for that. Even those who consider such a view mistaken and truth essential consider that the gap cannot be bridged because the nature of the human being precludes knowledge of anything beyond phenomena save conjecture. From this conviction of the inaccessibility of absolute reality the mystics must be exempted. Their inability to express themselves through the medium of ordinary language, art or music is related to the fact that all such methods of communication are transformations and transformations deal with phenomena and are dealt with by being known, loved or hated—K, L or H. Transformation then is intermediate between O and T $x\beta$. We must therefore consider further the gap between O and knowledge of phenomena and transformations of O.

The gap between reality and the personality, or, as I prefer to call it, the inaccessibility of O, is an aspect of life with which analysts are familiar under the guise of resistance. Resistance is only manifest when the threat is contact with what is believed to be real. There is no resistance to anything because it is believed to be false. Resistance operates because it is feared that the reality of the object is imminent. O represents this dimension of anything whatever—its reality.

It is not knowledge of reality that is at stake, nor yet the human equipment for knowing. The belief that reality is or could be known is mistaken because reality is not something which lends itself to being known. It is impossible to know reality for the same reason that makes it impossible to sing potatoes; they may be grown, or pulled, or eaten, but not sung. Reality has to be "been": there should be a transitive verb "to be" expressly for use with the term "reality".

When, as psycho-analysts, we are concerned with the reality of the personality there is more at stake than an exhortation to "know thyself, accept thyself, be thyself", because implicit in psycho-analytic procedure is the idea that this exhortation cannot be put into practice without the psycho-analytic experience. The point at issue is how to pass from "knowing" "phenomena" to "being" that which is "real".

To recapitulate: It is possible through phenomena to be reminded of the "form". It is possible through "incarnation" to be united with a part, the incarnate part, of the Godhead. It is possible through hyperbole for the individual to deal with the real individual. Is it possible through psycho-analytic interpretation to effect a transition from knowing the phenomena of the real self to being the real self?

If I am right in suggesting that phenomena are known but reality is "become" the interpretation must do more than increase knowledge. It can be argued that this is not a matter for the analyst and that he can only increase knowledge; that the further steps required to bridge the gap must come from the analysand; or from a particular part of the analysand, namely his "godhead", which must consent to incarnation in the person of the analysand.

Here there seems to be a matter of "direction": it is not the same for the "godhead" to consent to incarnation in the person of the analysand as for the analysand to consent to "becoming" god or the "godhead" of which "god" is the phenomenological counterpart. The latter, at any rate, would seem to be closer to insanity than mental health.

The problem, psycho-analytically, is easier to grasp if O

represents ultimate reality, good and evil. Becoming O would then seem to be easier to associate with cure than becoming ultimate good or ultimate evil by splitting. Moreover, health may be more easily associated with being passive, *vis-à-vis* ultimate good and evil, rather than with being active.

The gap between "knowing phenomena" and "being reality" resembles the gap between "Knowing about psycho-analysis" and "Being psycho-analysed". The transition from "knowing phenomena" to "being reality" would seem certain to involve experience of modifying adherence to column 2 statements. It would appear to involve abandonment of making statements known to be false to form a barrier against statements believed to be true. If so, further consideration of column 2 categories offers a promising approach. In terms of resistance theory the aim of resistance is to preserve unconsciousness of thoughts, feelings and "facts", presumably because that is felt to be the best method, *in the circumstances*, of dealing with the problem presented by those thoughts, feelings and "facts". Resistance cannot however be evoked unless there is in operation the contrary feeling that consciousness is the best approach. A widely inclusive example of such conflict is provided by the personality who feels unable to improve defects whose existence he suspects and resorts to being unaware of what he feels unable to change. There are occasions in the life of everyone when it is felt to be wise, not pathological, to turn a "blind eye". Such situations become pathological when the "cure" achieved by these means is felt to be more painful that the original dis-ease. It is not always a matter of finding the "cure" more painful: if the exclusion of unwelcome elements is effected with a view to keeping thoughts relevant to the problem and free from distraction, then dissatisfaction is felt because the result of the exclusion is to prejudice the usefulness of the train of thought. In analysis the problem is not necessarily associated with any particular instance of column 2 operation but is associated with the habit of mind that resorts to column 2 mechanisms with such frequency that the state of "being" O is indefinitely postponed.

The first requisite is to detect the column 2 dimension of the statements that are being made. It may not be a significant dimension and in that case the analyst must use his judgment to decide what statement or statements he is going to treat in this way. In transforming the patient's statement he is ignoring its other dimensions just as, in the model with which I start this chapter, the rule for forming the second tray of marbles ignores all dimensions save the green glass of the marbles on the first tray; all dimensions except for one very important one—the *number* of green glass marbles. To this important exception I shall now turn.

Mathematicians are aware that the progress of arithmetic is obstructed probably through some unsolved problem with regard to the nature of the discipline. Psycho-analytically the problem can be approached in the manner I have laid down in this book. "Numbers" such as "many", "three", "one", "too much" are attempts to bind a constant conjunction, preparatory to understanding the conjunction. Numbers are signs denoting a constant conjunction and are an attempt to bind the constant conjunction, but the constant conjunction is itself a constant conjunction—a group of elements that are felt to be constantly conjoined. Number is an attempt to seize upon a system, so to speak, of a group and by naming it take the first step towards understanding, or finding a meaning for, the group. One, true to the negative quality of the definitory hypothesis (col. 1) is a denial of the group. All other numbers are likewise attempts, first to bind, then to understand, the group. It is an over-simplification to describe the object as a group: it is perhaps too mathematical to call it infinity, too mystical to call it the infinite, too religious to call it the Godhead.

Psychologically the problem commences with the impingement on the individual of an object containing in itself the potentiality of all distinctions as yet undeveloped, a group, a conjunction and the need to bind the "groupishness" of the group by a name, a column 1 element. If the initiative is felt to lie with the object its "distinctions" develop till such point as a "distinction" impinges on the individual; in so far as it is felt to lie with the individual his awareness develops to a point where some "distinction", or dimension as I have called it, appears to him to demand binding.

Verbal expressions intended to represent the ultimate object often appear to be contradictory within themselves, but there is a surprising degree of agreement, despite differences of background, time and space, in the descriptions offered by mystics who feel they have experienced the ultimate reality. Sometimes the agreement seems close even when, as with Milton, the individual seems to know of it rather than to have experienced it.

> "The rising world of waters dark and deep
> Won from the void and formless infinite."[1]

I am not interpreting what Milton says but using it to represent O. The process of binding is a part of the procedure by which something is "won from the void and formless infinite"; it is K and must be distinguished from the process by which O is "become". The sense of inside and outside, internal and external objects, introjection and projection, container and contained, all are associated with K.

Distinction between the "geometric" and "arithmetic" developments can be made thus: the geometric developments of points and line are primarily associated with the presence or absence, existence or non-existence, of an object. The arithmetic development is associated with the state of the object, whether it is whole or fragmented, whole object or part object.

The geometric development is associated with depression, absence or presence of the object: the arithmetic development with feelings of persecution, the Kleinian theory of a paranoid-schizoid position.

When the dimensions of a statement are the presenting feature in analysis it is a matter of importance to observe whether the object is considered to have dimensions as a part of synthesis (K) or because the dimensions are seen as fragments unrelated to each other, the debris, as it were, of a splitting process (H).

[1] Milton, J.: *Paradise Lost*, Bk. III.

It may at first seem strange to suggest that groups or the infinite should be regarded as epistemologically prior to all else, but less so if we consider that only when a problem is intractable, or seems to be so, will it be felt to engage, and demand, our most powerful efforts. Reciprocally the more we feel ourselves deeply engaged the more likely we are to suppose that the problem *must* be intractable and that it is so intrinsically.

We may now reconsider some of the problems associated with ideas of causation. T β is a formulated transformation, whatever the medium in which the transformation is expressed. T α is the process, employing α-elements, by which the individual arrives at T β. In thinking about transformation we may arrest the process, at whatever point we wish, to give ourselves the conditions in which to make our inspection. If carried to extremes the process of arrest can amount to a denial of the passage of time as in the instances I have cited of the disturbed state where time itself is destroyed by being reduced to a point and then denied altogether. Ignoring this extreme, but taking advantage of the freedom conferred by thought we may interrupt what in fact is a continuous process by inspecting T α, T β or O in as far as it can be possible to know, or be curious, *about* O. We can only have a K link with *transformations* of O. One dimension of O is expressed by terms such as "cause", or a "first cause".

The "cause" O may be felt to be present or absent, single or multiple, independent of the personality or hallucinated. O, in its "caused" dimension, as in all others, may be located in the Platonic Form, of which people and things are "reminders"; in a deity, of which people and things are "incarnations"; in hyperbole, of which people and things are containers. "Causation", as a dimension of O, has the characteristics of all other dimensions of O that are subjected to the various processes of transformation and inspected at various stages in the process.

Any statement should be assessed according to its grid category, re-assessed as T β in accordance with its position in the Reality scale, that is Form and reminder, deity and incarnation, hyperbole and evacuation. The interpretation should be such that the transition from *knowing about* reality to *becoming real* is furthered. This transition depends on matching the analysand's statement with an interpretation which is such that the circular argument remains circular but has an adequate diameter. If it is too small the circular argument becomes a point; if too great it becomes a straight line. The point and straight line together with numbers are representatives of states of mind which are primitive and unassociated with mature experience. The profitable circular argument depends on a sufficiency of experience to provide an orbit in which to circulate. To re-state this in terms of greater sophistication, the analytic experience must consist of knowing and being successively many elementary statements, discerning their orbital or circular or spherical relationship and establishing the statements which are complementary. The interpretations that effect the transition from knowing about O to becoming O are those establishing complementarity: all others are concerned with establishing the material through which the argument circulates.

The transition from "knowing about" to "becoming" O can be seen as a particular instance of the development of the conception from the pre-conception (row E from row D). I have described that process as one of saturation of an unsaturated element $\psi(\xi)$, to become $\psi(\psi)(\xi)$. That is to say, a pre-conception becomes a conception and retains its dimension of "usability" as a pre-conception. The transition, in terms of transformation, may be formulated as $T\alpha \rightarrow T\beta$ (cycle 1), $T\beta$ (cycle 1) $\rightarrow T\alpha$ (cycle 2). The psycho-analytic conception of cure should include the idea of a transformation whereby an element is saturated and thereby made ready for further saturation. Yet a distinction must be made between this dimension of "cure" or "growth" and greed. To this I shall revert after considering "arithmetic" further. I should say, if it is not already clear, that the domain of mathematics with which I am concerned is the "Dodgsonian" or "Alice Through the Looking-Glass" variety.

I have said numbers are a means of binding (col. 1) a constant conjunction. By definition this means that the conjunction is unknown or devoid of meaning. O is not known, but for ease in exposition I am supposing that the conjunction, or part of a conjunction, which is to be bound with a view to investigation, is the "group". The number signified by 1 is a way of denoting a whole object which is not a group. The group is infinite, whether it is a group of people, things or "causes". From this we may proceed to emotional mathematics (or the mathematics of emotion) thus: 1 = "one is one and all alone and evermore shall be so". $\frac{1}{1}$ = a relationship with "the whole of an object that is a whole object, that is unrelated to any other objects and therefore has no properties; since properties are a dimension of relationships." With religion as vertex this sign can represent the O represented by the term "Godhead". With a Miltonic vertex it is represented by the "void and formless infinite" from which is "won" the object that is known. With a Dantesque vertex it is represented by the 33rd canto of the Paradise. With a mathematical vertex, and regarding it in its negative aspect of definition, it can be represented by the term "not infinity".

Similarly $\frac{1}{2}$ can represent, in its column 1 dimension, a relationship with a part of a part of a group. In its negative dimension it denies that there are more than, or less than, two in the group and affirms that the relationship is with one of them.

When formulated these numbers can be used in the process of transformation. They can be combined with other numbers as and when other numbers are formulated. The development is therefore two-fold: the group can be denoted by a new number whenever a constant conjunction is felt to require binding, as for example if a number "two" is felt to be necessary because O is not felt to be represented by 1. Thus development can proceed according to a plan of enumeration. Or, curiosity about the relationship of 1 to $\frac{1}{1}$ or $\frac{1}{2}$ to O, and from that to the relationship that each has to the other, leads to manipulation and combination of the numbers. A religious counterpart can be seen in St Augustine's formulation in *The City of God* that only when the individual has regulated his relationship with God (O, or more precisely 1, for the relationship with God is possible, but not with the Godhead because the latter is Darkness and Formlessness, potentially containing all distinctions but yet undeveloped), can he regulate his relationship with his fellow men.

The combination and manipulation of numbers is stimulated by the same force as stimulates their formulation—the awareness of a constant conjunction that requires to be bound.

Manipulation and combination of numbers lead to mathematical formulation as it is ordinarily understood; these formulations (or formulae) may be regarded as D category and used as elements in column 3 and 4 categories are used (or, of course, as elements in any other columns are used). In their category 3 and 4 dimensions they may then be used in the exploration of the world as it is ordinarily supposed by scientists to exist. The spur to the investigation is still the same spur that led to the binding of the constant conjunctions in the first instance. The domain investigated, whether it be called Platonic memories, or religious incarnations, or hyperbole (in the sense in which I have used the term) containers and contained, supplies further stimulation in that each D3 and D4 statement requires further saturation. Evidently the impulse to achieve saturation is unlikely to be fulfilled because in addition to the limitations of human capacity there is the factor of "the void and formless infinite" which, whether thought of as in the mind of man or outside it, cannot be known but must be "become," that is, saturated in a particular way.

Psycho-analysts may find what I have said about theories of causation in the context of Transformation, as it exists in *knowing about* and *becoming* O, more familiar if they remember how big a part is played in analysis by the need to blame other people and the difficulties of maturation because maturation involves *being* responsible.

The function of T α is to lead to T β, which in turn must lead to growth, and therefore must be capable of categorization in D3 or D4. In K, a domain in which it is sufficient to know *about* something, the apparatus of pre-conception and transformation leads to repetition but in a new cycle. We need to know what kind of transformation ($T\alpha \rightarrow T\beta$) is required to effect the transition from K to "becoming" or "being". The discovery of the Differential Calculus by Gallileo, Newton and Descartes produced a weapon adequate to deal with K phenomena in their inanimate dimension. But it does not produce growth, only permits accretions of knowledge about growth. The differential calculus may be described as D3 and D4 category in K and must therefore be seen as an instrument furthering K, but not O. It is *conducive* to becoming, or being O, but has nothing to say about its place in that transformation. We do not learn from it what part it plays, or what the process is in which it plays a part, by which $T\,\alpha \rightarrow T\,\beta = K \rightarrow O$.

To rigid motion transformations, projective transformations, transformations in hallucinosis, I shall now add transformations in O. That is to say I propose to extend the significance O to cover the domain of reality and "becoming". Transformations in O contrast with other transformations in that the former are related to growth in becoming and the latter to growth in "knowing about" growth; they resemble each other in that "growth" is common to both.

Transformation in K has, contrary to the common view, been less adequately expressed by mathematical formulation than by religious formulations. Both are defective when required to express growth, and therefore transformation, in O. Even so, religious formulations come nearer to meeting the requirements of transformations in O than mathematical formulations. I shall illustrate my meaning by discussing first, Berkeley's objection to Halley and Newton's formulation in his "Opticks of the Differential Calculus", which Halley sponsored, and second, the phenomenon known to analysts as Resistance.

CHAPTER TWELVE

Bishop Berkeley, prompted by the irreligion of Newton and his sponsor Edmund Halley, attacked certain illogicalities, notably circular argument, in Newton's presentation of the differential calculus; his criticisms exercised mathematicians for over a century. The following quotation is from *The Analyst* (published in 1734):

> "It must, indeed, be acknowledged that he used fluxions, like the scaffold of a building, as things to be laid aside or got rid of as soon as finite lines were found proportional to them. But then these finite exponents are found by the help of fluxions. Whatever therefore is got by such exponents and proportions is to be ascribed to fluxions: which must therefore be previously understood. And what are these fluxions? The velocities of evanescent increments. And what are these same evanescent increments? They are neither finite quantities, nor quantities infinitely small, nor yet nothing. May we not call them the ghosts of departed quantities?"

Newton's formulation of the differential calculus is a transformation in K. "The ghosts of departed quantities" expresses the negative of the column 1 dimension of his formulation. The transformation in K is effected by discarding the "scaffolding" of fluxions, "the ghosts of departed quantities". The discarding of the scaffolding may be regarded as a step to achieve finite lines "proportional to them", a category H3 formulation; or, "the finite lines . . . proportional to them" may be regarded as an F3 formulation used as a column 2 formulation to prevent emergence of the "ghosts of departed quantities" and the psychological turbulence that such an emergence would precipitate; Newton did have what we would today regard as a psychotic breakdown in which, in his own words, he lost "the former consistency of his mind" and from which he emerged, according to J. M. Keynes, "slightly 'gaga' ". Keynes's paper, which was read by his brother at the Centenary Celebrations held in July 1946, contains material which will repay study for its penetrating insights though I cannot enter into it here.

Berkeley's formulation may be regarded as an F3 contribution. The polemical tone gives it a column 2 category, denying, though he acknowledges the truth of Newton's result, the validity of the method: the ironic tone denies the reality of "the ghosts of departed quantities". The pamphlet as a whole is thus an example of an F3 formulation used, in its second cycle, as column 2 to deny both the "ghosts" component and the H3 component in his and Newton's confrontation. From a psycho-analytic vertex both formulations, Newton's and Berkeley's, can be seen as T β col. 3 (intended to produce a formulation T β (col. 3) (cycle 2)), or, T β col. 2 (intended to deny emergence of β-elements).

T Newton β H3 furthers mathematic inquiry: T Newton β col. 2 denies the "ghosts". T Berkeley β col. 2 denies, by irony, "ghosts" and, by polemic, the scientific approach. In both instances the col. 2 dimension is directed against psychological turbulence; why? for fear of the turbulence and its associated "becoming". Put in other terms, transformations in K are feared when they threaten the emergence of transformations in O. This can be restated as fear when $T\alpha \rightarrow T\beta = K \rightarrow O$. Resistance to an interpretation is resistance against change from K to O. Change from K to O is a special case of Transformation; it is of particular concern to the analyst in his function of aiding maturation of the personalities of his patients.

My term "psychological turbulence" needs elucidation. By it I mean a state of mind the painful quality of which may be expressed in terms borrowed from St John of the Cross. I quote:[1]

> "The first (night of the soul) has to do with the point from which the soul goes forth, for it has gradually to deprive itself of desire for all the worldly things which it possessed, by denying them to itself; the which denial and

[1] *The Ascent of Mount Carmel*, 1, 1 and 2.

deprivation are, as it were, night to all the senses of man. The second reason has to do with the mean, or the road along which the soul must travel to this union—that is, faith, which is likewise as dark as night to the understanding. The third has to do with the point to which it travels—namely, God, Who, equally, is dark night to the soul in this life."

I use these formulations to express, in exaggerated form, the pain which is involved in achieving the state of naivety inseparable from binding or definition (col. 1). Any naming of a constant conjunction involves admission of the negative dimension and is opposed by the fear of ignorance. Therefore at the outset there is a tendency to precocious advance, that is, to a formulation which is a col. 2 formulation intended to deny ignorance—the dark night of the senses. The relevance of this to psychological phenomena springs from the fact that they are not amenable to apprehension by the senses; this tends to precipitate transformation into such objects as *are* and so contributes to Transformation in hypochondriasis. The "col. 1" elements thus formed are liable to be second cycle col. 2—transformations which are $T\beta$ col. 1 $\rightarrow$ $T\beta$ (second cycle) col. 2.

Similarly the intuitive approach is obstructed because the "faith" involved is associated with absence of inquiry, or "dark night" to K.

The third "dark night" is associated with the transformation in O, that is from $K \rightarrow O$. The transformation that involves "becoming" is felt as inseparable from becoming God, ultimate reality, the First Cause. The "dark night" pain is fear of megalomania. This fear inhibits acceptance of being responsible, that is mature, because it appears to involve *being* God, being the First Cause, being ultimate reality with a pain that can be, though inadequately, expressed by "megalomania".

The same tensions are involved in all transformations in O and these I shall now discuss.

Interpretations are part of K. The anxiety lest transformation in K leads to transformations in O is responsible for the form of resistance in which interpretations appear to be accepted but in fact the acceptance is with the intention of "knowing about" rather than "becoming". In other terms, it is an acceptance to preserve the K link as a col. 2 element against transformation in O. By agreeing with the interpretation it is hoped that the analyst will be inveigled into a collusive relationship to preserve K without being aware that he is doing so. If the manoeuvre is successful transformations in K fulfil an F2 role preventing the inception of $T\alpha \rightarrow T\beta = K \rightarrow O$.

For the next step in this discussion I shall regard the Kleinian theory of Projective Identification as a psycho-analytic formulation (row F categories) based on a background of realizations encountered in analytic practice and in every-day life: these realizations I shall name "hyperbole". "Hyperbole" is a term belonging to the system of Theories of Observation in contrast to the theory of Projective Identification which I regard as a term belonging to the system of Psycho-Analytical Theory. I do not propose to discuss the system of Psycho-Analytical Theory. For that I refer the reader to the work of Bowlby and the Research Committee of the British Psycho-Analytical Society of which he is Chairman, Sandler and his co-workers, Segal and her introduction to Melanie Klein and Wisdom on the theories of Klein and Fairbairn. The domains of Theories of Observation and Theories of Psycho-Analysis overlap but the problem is simplified if a distinction is made and can be preserved. The workers on the Theories of Psycho-Analysis, to whom I have referred, are engaged on a task which should lead to precise determination and formulation of psycho-analytic theory and eventually to a corpus which belongs uniformly to the category row F. "Hyperbole" is the term I give, in theories of observation, to the realizations that correspond to the theory of projective identification.

The following is a series of statements used as illustrations:

1. I have always believed you are a very good analyst.
2. I knew a woman in Peru, when I was a child, who had second sight.

3. It seems to me psycho-analysts would do better if they believed in God: God *can* cure.
4. There ought not to be so much pain and suffering in the world. What can a mere human being do?

The interpretation of these statements would depend on circumstances which I cannot report here; the suggestions I make must be seen as related to exposition and not clinical experience.

Comment:

1. (*a*) The goodness of the analyst stops short, as it were, in my person. I am "it".

(*b*) The goodness of the analyst is incarnate in me. I am the embodiment of analytic goodness.

(*c*) The goodness of the analyst is incorporated in me. Either I have obtained possession of the goodness of the analyst by "taking it into" myself or some force has "put it into" me.

Which of these statements represents the facts most closely depends on the judgment the analyst forms in the emotional experience itself.

2. (*a*) The goodness of the analyst has been projected a long way in time and place. This is hyperbole; there is something in the experience with the analysand that makes this term suitable for binding the particular conjunction, and none other (the negative dimension of the definition), which I want to examine. The term already marks a conjunction (the positive dimension of the definitory hypothesis) which is present in the conjunction to which I want to draw attention, namely the early meaning of hyperbole as a "throwing beyond" someone else, signifying rivalry.

(*b*) The goodness of the analyst has been thrown "into" the woman, or Peru, or the past.

The analyst will have to decide according to the experience what further qualities are conjoined with the qualities represented by the term "hyperbole". For example, is the goodness incarnate in the woman or incorporated by her, or projected into her, and if so by whom? And who or where is the rival?

These questions, often answered implicitly, require a

means for making them explicit; this is aided by the grid and the Theory of Transformations. The term "hyperbole" has a history which fits it for compact representation of a number of clinical statements which (i) occur frequently, (ii) are easily recognizable as instances of hyperbole and (iii) are almost certainly symptomatic of a constant conjunction which has significance for the personality being analysed and for the main body of psycho-analytic theories of idealization, splitting, projective identification, rivalry and envy. In grid categorical terms it can be classified as row A (β-elements), row C (the visual or pictorial dimension), row D and row E. It has therefore a wide spectrum, is flexible and lends itself easily for use by the analyst as a "selected fact" to aid in displaying coherence which, without it, may not be apparent. "Hyperbole" can be regarded as representing hyperbole and hyperbole is projection conjoined with rivalry, ambition, vigour which can amount to violence and hence to "distance" to which an object is projected. By "distance" I mean something which is the "ghost of a departed quantity" or, to put it in another way, distance $= \psi(\xi)$ where $(\xi) =$ a non-existent quantity. It could be where quantity was or where it will be but not where it *is*; it represents an unsaturated element, an evanescent increment or "departed quantity". I shall reconsider O with the help of (ξ), Platonic Forms and their "reminders" (phenomena); "godhead", "god" and "his" incarnations; Ultimate Reality or Truth and the phenomena which are all that human beings can know of the thing-in-itself: all three possess a similar configuration. Milton can invoke light which at the voice of God invested

> "The rising world of waters dark and deep
> Won from the void and formless infinite."

Eckhart considers Godhead to contain all distinctions as yet undeveloped and to be Darkness and Formlessness. It cannot be the object of Knowledge until there flows out from it Trinity and the Trinity *can* be known. According to Kant the thing-in-itself cannot be known but secondary and primary qualities can be. Examples of similar configurations can be multiplied but for my purposes these are sufficient to indicate, without I hope distorting the historical meanings that the authors wished to formulate, what I mean to signify by O. According to need it may be supposed that (i) from O undeveloped distinctions evolve, or, that (ii) from O, the "void and formless infinite", the individual (sense) and group (common sense) win secondary and primary qualities (in Kant's sense). The "winning" of qualities is part of K. In so far as potentialities and distinctions "evolve" from O it is a part of becoming or Transformation in O. Transformations in K may be described loosely as akin to "knowing about" something whereas Transformations in O are related to becoming or being O or to being "become" by O. The "distance" (ξ) between O and Tβ may be artificially described in a series of stages. Assuming a direction O $\rightarrow$ Tβ, O can be said to "evolve" by (*a*) becoming manifest (or "knowable") Tβ K $\rightarrow$ (*b*) by becoming a "reminder", an "incarnation" or "embodiment" or an "incorporation". $\rightarrow$ (*c*) by becoming Tβ O or, "at-one-ment". Assuming the reverse direction Tβ $\rightarrow$ O, the individual proceeds (Tα K) $\rightarrow$ (*a*) Tβ K, (col. 1) definition, $\rightarrow$ (*b*) Tβ K (cycle 1) = Tα K (cycle 2) $\rightarrow$ Tβ K (cycle 2) (col. 3) memory or notation "reminder", "incarnation", or "incorporation" $\rightarrow$ (*c*) Tβ (cycle n − 1) = Tα K (cycle n) $\rightarrow$ Tβ O.

As I have said resistances, though apparently K phenomena, derive from Transformations in O. Hatred and fear derive from the fact that transformations in K threaten the further transformation represented by T β (cycle n − 2) $\rightarrow$ T β (cycle n − 1) = T α (cycle n) K $\rightarrow$ Tβ O.

The resistance based on hatred and fear of T K $\rightarrow$ T O manifests itself as preference for knowing about something to becoming something. The photograph representing Monet's Les Coquelicots (or any other artistic representation) is preferred to exposure to the painting itself: exposure to the painting is restricted to perceiving that it is "about" a field of poppies. No matter what the domain may be the resistance by "knowing about" against "becoming" is sure to be in evidence and is by no means restricted to psycho-analysis. Nevertheless in analysis, where analyst and patient must hope for growth in a capacity for maturation, this aspect of T K → T O is important and must be considered further. Any interpretation may be accepted in K but rejected in O; acceptance in O means that acceptance of an interpretation enabling the patient to "know" that part of himself to which attention has been drawn is felt to involve "being" or "becoming" that person. For many interpretations this price is paid. But some are felt to involve too high a price, notably those which the patient regards as involving him in "going mad" or committing murder of himself or someone else, or becoming "responsible" and therefore guilty. There is one class of interpretations, which seems to illuminate good qualities, to which the objection is not so easy to understand. The extreme example, interpretations which involve "becoming O" are dreaded as inseparable from megalomania, or what the psychiatrists or public might name delusions of grandeur or other diagnosis implying grave pathological disorder. The public or psychiatric view is more important than might appear as it introduces the social or group component in mental disorder and its treatment. To this I shall now turn.

A patient will manipulate his analysis and his environment in a manner which is consistent, determined, bearing the impress of a plan which is set but of which the pattern remains obscure. With most patients it is easy to understand that his disabilities are a trial to himself and his associates but with a few his pain, obvious enough, seems to matter far less to him than it does to everyone else, including the analyst. Relatives and associates are frightened by his irresponsibility into accepting, however powerless they may be, the responsibility he will not accept himself: he who has the power won't exercise it, they, who have not, are forced to do so. His company, so painful to himself, is nurtured and developed so that it will be even more painful to others. Granted the necessary endurance and a capacity to combine observation with it, certain characteristics begin to emerge; here are some:

1. Whenever the patient arouses pity or compassion he associates it with "statements" that leave the analyst a

choice between hating the patient or feeling that he has been guilty of inexperience of the world as it is.

2. Associated with 1. above the analysand exudes a sense of his superiority, an aloofness from humanity and the particular specimen that is his analyst. How he does this must be experienced in detail by the analyst and demonstrated to the analysand.

3. The patient's statements give an impression, sharp enough to evoke forebodings in the analyst yet vague enough to evoke forebodings about the forebodings. The qualities of 1. and 2. above are thus in evidence, "splitting" the analyst by leaving him evenly balanced on the horns of a dilemma, unable to remain indecisive and unable to decide on one interpretation without misgivings that the other was correct, thus contributing to the establishment of the superiority of the analysand. The additional feature is the forebodings. They derive from the patient's transformations, composed of category A3 and C3 elements, which are again transformed (cycle 2) into col. 6 elements for corrective purposes. The analyst finds himself in the following dilemma: the patient's statements (hints, clues, innuendos) give every reason to suppose that some grave threat to analyst and analysis is impending, the patient himself being all unaware of any cause for anxiety. These same statements are also made to carry an innuendo that if the analyst thinks the patient is "all unaware" of what is happening the analyst must be as inferior as the analysand thinks. If the analyst gives an interpretation the patient will make a new statement showing that he is unaware of what the analyst has said but that, according to the interpretation the analyst has given, either (*a*) the analyst is unaware of the feelings that all men of common sense would be bound to entertain about his conduct of the case, or, (*b*) the analyst is, without cause, feeling persecuted. The total experience, typical of many, demonstrates the crudity of expression and of the ideas expressed by the analyst as contrasted with the subtlety and evocative potency[1] of the analysand's ideas and methods of expression. Further the analysand has demonstrated the

[1] Cf. Bion, W. R.: *Learning from Experience*—beta-screen.

superiority of the aim to exacerbate pain over the aim to alleviate it.

From observation in the consulting-room the analyst is left to deduce the patient's skilful use of psychological insight in manipulation of the individual (the analyst) and the group (the patient's associates outside the consulting-room).

To sum up briefly: The theories of splitting, projective identification, persecution by the projected (evacuated) split-off elements have their approximate realization in the personality of the analysand. These realizations in the domain of the analysand's personality have been transformed (projective transformation), Tp β, the elements of which belong to row A (2nd cycle B $\leftrightarrow$ H) and col. 6 (second cycle 1, 2, 3, 4, 5, all $-$K). This transformation is then used in the consulting-room to destroy the analyst's psycho-analytic capacity and the psycho-analytic intercourse between analysand and analyst. To sum up in still more general terms, the analysis has been changed into a contest between (*a*) thought against action, (*b*) therapeutic use of insight against insight used to exacerbate, (*c*) pairing and dependent group against flight-fight group, (*d*) individual against group.

The patient's dilemma, in so far as he too is trying to be co-operative, reparative and creative, lies in his having to choose between "sanity" which is powerful, destructive and devoted to exacerbation, on the one hand, and creativeness which is impotent and "insane" on the other. If he wishes to be destructive his choice is between sanity which is creative and destructiveness which is insane. Strength of the desire is the determining factor. It has to be observed that this attempt at simplification by summary is vulnerable through its crudity. In the treatment of such cases there is no signification that is not over-simplification and no subtlety of discrimination that is not over-subtlety.

The complexity of a statement whether made by analyst of analysand imposes choice on the analyst; he must decide what dimension of the patient's statement he is to interpret and in what terms he will interpret it. To a great extent the choice is already determined by the analyst's personality and historical development and with those factors I do not intend to deal; I am concerned more with the immediate circumstances and those factors which are under the analyst's conscious control. He must beware of interpretation for no better reason than that the interpretation is one he can make. He cannot "win" it "from the void and formless infinite" of the analysand's personality, but only from the elements of the statement that the analysand has won from his own "void and formless infinite". Nothing is to be gained from telling the patient what he already knows unless what he "knows" is being used to exclude what he "is" (K opposed to O). Such an interpretation is part of the circular argument of which the "diameter" is too small: similarly the interpretation can be too abstruse and belong to a circular argument of which the "diameter" is too great. How is the "diameter" to be measured? If the interpretation is made mainly because it is available it is a col. 2 statement intended to prevent "turbulence" in the analyst. The abstruse interpretation relates to desire in the analyst, a wish to feel that he can see further than his analysand or some other who serves as a rival. It belongs to the domain of hyperbole. Too small and too large diameters indicate defence against and projection of hyperbole: defence is against hyperbole originated by the analysand.

Any statement may be supposed to include dimensions represented by every grid category. Not all dimensions have evolved (or been won) from the formlessness in which the potentiality for all distinctions exists. Therefore a statement can lack a varying number of classifiable dimensions because they remain undifferentiated potentialities. Epistemologically a statement may be regarded as evolved when any dimension can have a grid category assigned to it. For purposes of interpretation the statement is insufficiently evolved until its column 2 dimension is apparent. When the column 2 dimension has evolved, the statement can be said to be ripe for interpretation; its development as material for interpretation has reached maturity.

It is to be noted that a statement may be true in the context to which the analysand considers it to be relevant and yet have a column 2 dimension; it has a context to which its relevance is its column 2 dimension. A simple example of this is provided by statements which are recitals of common sense facts intended to deny expression to phantasy; the "fact" in this context is a theory known to be false.

A distinction must be made between the genesis of thought in the patient's life history and the genesis of expressions of thought in a given contingency. The emergence of the column 2 dimension may be observed in the contingency of the analysis as a step in the evolution of the statement and from it the analyst can judge that the conditions for interpretation have arrived; but it does not mean that an interpretation must be made; for the analyst's thought also must reach maturation. When he can see the column 2 element in his thoughts the conditions for interpretation are complete: an interpretation should be made. In terms of analytic theory it is approximately correct, but only approximately, to say that the conditions for an interpretation have arrived when the patient's statements provide evidence that resistance is operating: the conditions are complete when the analyst feels aware of resistance in himself—not counter-transference which must be dealt with by analysis of the analyst, but resistance to the reaction he anticipates from the analysand if he gives the interpretation. Note the similarity of the analyst's resistance to the response he anticipates from the patient to his interpretation and the patient's resistance to the analyst's interpretation: the response anticipated by the analyst is coloured by his α-element version of the interpretation of his interpretation.

So far the "distance" between the analysand's statement (association) and the analyst's statement (interpretation) has been stated in terms of time required for the emergence of the column 2 element in the statement of the analysand and "proto-resistance", to coin a phrase, in the analyst to a response that has not yet been made. The analyst's proto-resistance must be projection of his own resistance to one dimension of his proposed interpretation. The interpretation he does give is a theory, known to be false, *vis-à-vis* an unknown contingent circumstance, but maintained as a barrier against turbulence expected to occur were it not so maintained; no statement is without a realization to which it stands in a col. 2 relationship. Thus a religious statement known to be false is used to exclude an aesthetic or scientific or other statement and vice versa.

In O the falsity of the statement is secondary to the fact that it is known to be so for it is the latter that inhibits growth whereas the former is part of human inadequacy. In K the fact that the statement is known to be false is secondary to the fact that it is so for it is the latter that inhibits the establishment of meaning whereas the former is part of individual maladjustment. Since the analyst is concerned with development of the personality it follows that the falsity of the statement will vary in significance according to its grid category and the transformation of which it is a part. To illustrate: suppose the statement is "the sun will rise tomorrow". If the patient is summarizing a weather forecast his statement is a form of notation or forecast. It is false because the sun does not rise but its employment is not to deny a fact but to explore possibilities. The category would be D3 or 4 according to the judgment of the person to whom the statement is made. If the statement has been made in analysis and is an expression of optimism it may be his transformation of feelings engendered by an interpretation he has just been given. If so it is transformation denoted by Tp β in O. But if he means he is going out with his girl friend its category is C3; it is an instance of hyperbole and the configuration of which it is a part is quite different from that of which the previous interpretation is a part. The words are the same, but the first example is D3 and 4 and the second C3. There is no intrinsic merit in establishing the category, but the attempt to do so forces clarification in the analyst's mind of what it is he is actually observing. For example: assuming the category to be C3 and that the girl *is* his friend it would follow that the link is L, the hyperbole an element in L (approximating to psycho-analytic theories of idealization) and the transformation a rigid motion transformation (approximating to psycho-analytic theories of transference).

Granting that the above is an adequate description of the analyst's transformation (Ta β) he may then enter on a second cycle of transformation in which the total statement is felt to be a denial of hostility. Ta β (cycle 1) then becomes Ta α (cycle 2). In the second cycle = Tp β = T α (cycle 2) = C3 cycle 2 = D2 and the statement, apparently loving idealization, is a denial of hostility to the analyst. The hyperbole is then a projection of the patient's hostility. This entirely alters the configuration, for the patient's transformation Tp β now appears to be a projective transformation, intended to rid himself of his hostility to the analyst, and approximates to the Kleinian theory of projective identification.

It is said that a discipline cannot properly be regarded as scientific until it has been mathematized and I may have given the impression, by adumbrating a Lewis Carol mathematics for analysis, that I support this view and in doing so risk the proposal of a premature mathematization of a subject which is not sufficiently mature for such a procedure. I shall therefore draw attention to some features of mathematical development which have not hitherto been adequately considered psycho-analytically. As an illustration I shall use the description, earlier in this chapter, of the transition from the dark and formless Godhead of Meister Eckhart to the "knowable" Trinity. My suggestion is that an intrinsic feature of the transition from the "unknowability" of infinite Godhead to the "knowable" Trinity is the introduction of the number "three". The Godhead has become, or been, mathematized. The configuration which can be recognized as common to all developmental processes whether religious, aesthetic, scientific or psycho-analytical is a progression from the "void and formless infinite" to a "saturated" formulation which is finite and associated with number, e.g. "three" or geometric, e.g. the triangle, point, line or circle. Associated with this is the need for a geometric or numerological component in effecting a transformation, e.g. in the model of the transformation of marbles on one tray to the marbles on the second tray. To what extent does this represent an essential link in the ability to effect transformations from experience of reality into knowledge of its manifestations from K to O? The transition from sensibility to awareness, of a kind suitable to be the foundation of action, cannot take place unless the process of change, T α, is mathematical though perhaps in a form that has not been recognized as such.[1]

I shall not discuss the topic here except in the resemblance of numeration to pre-conception (row D). It differs in that the problem seems to spring from a sense of "infinite" space, time, number which is then made finite. Confronted with the unknown, "the void and formless infinite", the personality of whatever age fills the void (saturates the element), provides a form (names and binds a constant conjunction) and gives boundaries to the infinite (number and position). Pascal's phrase "Le silence de ces espaces infines m'effraie" can serve as an expression of intolerance and fear of the "unknowable" and hence of the unconscious in the sense of the undiscovered or the unevolved.

The bearing on psycho-analysis and interpretation of what I have said may seem obscure; it is this: The beginning of a session has the configuration already formulated in the concept of the Godhead. From this there evolves a pattern and at the same time the analyst seeks to establish contact with the evolving pattern. This is subject to his Transformation and culminates in his interpretation Ta β. I am aware of the problems I have left without attempting an approach to their solution; some of these I hope to attempt later. In this book I draw attention to a few of the problems which present themselves in analytic material and offer suggestions for clarifying first, observation and then, assessment of what has been observed.

[1] A simple example of this is seen when an attempt is made to communicate, by means other than a full analysis, what a psycho-analysis is so that rules for its practice can be formulated: "five times" a week and for "50" minutes are readily "won" from the ineffable experience.

INDEX

ATTENTION AND INTERPRETATION

There are two ways, and can only be two, of seeking and finding truth. The one, from senses and particulars, takes a flight to the most general axioms, and from those principles and their truths, settled once for all, invents and judges of intermediate axioms. The other method collects axioms from senses and particulars, ascending continuously and by degrees, so that in the end it arrives at the more general axioms; this latter way is the true one, but hitherto untried.

—Francis Bacon, *Novum Organum*

Contents

1 · *Introduction*

I doubt if anyone but a practising psycho-analyst can understand this book although I have done my best to make it simple. Any psycho-analyst who is *practising* can grasp my meaning because he, unlike those who only read or hear *about* psycho-analysis, has the opportunity to experience for himself what I in this book can only represent by words and verbal formulations designed for a different task. They were developed from a background of sensuous experience. Reason is emotion's slave and exists to rationalize emotional experience. Sometimes the function of speech is to communicate experience to another; sometimes it is to miscommunicate experience to another. Sometimes the object is to achieve access to, and permit access from, a good spirit; conversely, to deny access to a bad spirit. The vocabulary forged from such material serves, though inadequately, when, as in psycho-analytic practice, the object being studied is present. In mathematics, calculations can be made without the presence of the objects about which calculation is necessary, but in psycho-analytic practice it is essential for the psycho-analyst to be able to demonstrate as he formulates. This is not possible the moment the conditions for psycho-analysis, in the narrow technical sense, do not exist. Some of us have sought to extend psycho-analytic method so that it can be employed in a group setting. Such a development, if it can be done without mutilation of the fundamental character of psycho-analytic method, would initiate the change from private to public communication. Language does just that in the domain of sensible experience. Poetic and religious expressions have made possible a degree of 'public-ation' in that formulations exist which have achieved durability and extensibility. To say the same thing differently, the carrying power of the statement has been extended in time and in space. *Vixere fortes ante Agamemnona multi* and 'Not marble, nor the guilded monuments / Of princes, shall outlive this powerful rhyme' are expressions of that belief; they are interpretations of human experience. In his sphere the psycho-analyst's attention is arrested by a particular experience to which he would draw the attention of the analysand. To do this he must employ the Language of Achievement. That is to say, he must employ methods which have the counterpart of durability or extension in a domain where there is no time or space as those terms are used in the world of sense.

What I have said with regard to this book also applies to the psycho-analytic session; it is certainly my impression that the experience of psycho-analysis is supposed or intended to have an enduring effect. Unlike this book the session affords me and others an opportunity for drawing attention to the actual phenomena to which I think the analysand should attend and this might reinforce the effect of my communication. A similar advantage seems to me to be available in a psycho-analytic approach to groups; it is possible to hope that the capacity of the artist, though useful, may not be essential to the psycho-analyst. Indeed, it may be a disadvantage in so far as the artist's capacity may enable him to provide, as Plato feared, a *substitute* for the truth.

In this book I have made a few tentative approaches to a matter which I think has not received proper attention in psycho-analysis, namely, lying. The disposition to lie may be regarded as a sympton of a severely disordered personality. It certainly contributes many difficulties to any attempt at a psycho-analytic approach, but on the other hand my experience of psycho-analysis makes me feel that the aptitude for lying, so universal that only a liar could disregard its all-pervading nature, has its own place as an object for study and is ignored at a dangerous cost to analyst and analysand. In short, I agree that it is often a symptom of a disordered personality but submit that it is not necessarily a contraindication for analysis. Here I can only indicate one or two aspects.

It is too often forgotten that the gift of speech, so centrally employed, has been elaborated as much for the purpose of concealing thought by dissimulation and lying as for the purpose of elucidating or communicating thought. Therefore, the Language of Achievement, if it is to be employed for elucidating the truth, must be recognized as deriving not only from sensuous experience but also from impulses and dispositions far from those ordinarily associated with scientific discussion. Freud, like others before him, felt the need to isolate himself – insulate himself? – from the group in order to work. This would mean insulating ourselves against the very material we should study. We should, therefore, reorientate our views on such matters as rationalization and the employment of reason generally. The patient says, 'Suddenly, just as I finished lunch he threw a mug of beer in my face without any warning. I kept my head and showed no resentment at all remembering what you had said about psycho-analysis. So it passed off without anyone noticing.' Is he lying? Is he verbalizing a present hallucination? Matters of this kind are occurring throughout a psycho-analysis and demand correct assessment by the psycho-analyst. Yet we have not elaborated instruments – I have tried to do so with the grid [1] – for making the assessment. I am not speaking of making the *interpretation* or of the many theories that facilitate the making of an interpretation; the grid is of a different category altogether, analogous to a ruler in physical science, formed from a matrix of theories to aid observation and not as a substitute for observation. I commend to others a proper study of the lie and its differential diagnosis from phenomena which appear similar. The psycho-analyst must employ the Language of Achievement, but he must remember that the language was elaborated as much for the achievement of deception and evasion as for truth. This

[1] See frontispiece, and *Elements of psycho-analysis* (Bion, 1963), where the grid system is more fully discussed.

aspect is particularly clear when the prevalent emotional field is one of rivalry and hostility such as I have described, in group situations, as peculiar to the fight–flight basic assumption (Bion, 1961). The individual is similarly affected by the *group* emotional situation. It is, therefore, impossible to give correct interpretations, save by accident, unless that *situation* is assessed. For example, drug addiction is exploited as a cover for psychosis, lying is often excused as an aspect of drug addiction, and vice versa.

Psycho-analysts should determine whether they are talking of means of communication, including verbal communications, as things-in-themselves or whether they are talking of other things-in-themselves which these communication elements, gestures, actions, silences, and verbal formulations, are being used to represent. The grid is intended to remind the psycho-analyst that it is necessary to discriminate one element in his psycho-analytic experience from another and, in particular, to recognize that what matters is both the communication and the use to which it is being put. He must observe whether the presenting feature (or the feature to the obtrusion of which he wants to draw attention) is intended to further illumination or deception, and where in the genetic spectrum it belongs (primitive communication or sophisticated).

Although the grid is unsatisfactory in its present form, it will not, I hope, mislead but lead to an improved version. I have used the following signs:[1]

T – transformation
$T\alpha$ – the point from which the transformation starts
$T\beta$ – the point at which the transformation is presumed to be complete
Ta – the psycho-analyst's transformation
Tp – the analysand's transformation
O – the experience (thing-in-itself)

Analogies are frequently used. The things used and what those things represent are dissimilar. It is supposed that a

[1] Originally in *Transformations* (Bion, 1965).

rifle and a penis are similar. But what should be exact is the *relationship* between the particular objects in the particular analogy and not the objects themselves. Thus: as the breast is to the baby's mouth so the surgeon's knife is to the X. In any particular instance the inexactitude of the *relationship* merits criticism and appraisal. The objects are faulty and to be condemned if they *are* similar. For example, 'The knife is to the fork as the knife is to the fork' is a 'non-analogy'. 'The eyes are to the mind as the mouth is to the food' is a correct analogy and draws attention to the matter that is to be observed, namely, the relationship between the two.

2 · *Medicine as a Model*

Most people think of psycho-analysis, as Freud did, as a method of treatment for a complaint. The complaint was regarded as similar to a physical ailment which, when you know what it is, has to be treated in accordance with the rules of medicine. The parallel with medicine was, and still is, useful. But as psycho-analysis has grown so it has been seen to differ from physical medicine until the gap between them has passed from the obvious to the unbridgeable. For most purposes the similarity yields illuminating comparisons and models that facilitate discussion. But the more we see of psycho-analysis the more the models become inadequate to define, report, or apply psycho-analysis. Differentiation has meant that models which were illuminating have become opaque and often misleading even to psycho analysts. Let us see why. We may start by discussing the obvious and simple reasons, though they will not remain either for long.

In physical medicine the patient may have a pain in his chest for which he can go to his doctor. To him he can explain its nature and its history and from him he can receive instructions to undergo further examination, say, by X-rays or microscopy, or certain forms of treatment. Or so it appears; later we may have reason to question this account. For the present it will serve to point the divergence of physical medicine and psycho-analysis.

Suppose the patient complained not of physical but of mental pain; no one doubts the existence of anxiety or sees any incongruity in seeking help to cure it. We find it necessary to differentiate between the pain of a broken leg and the pain, say, of bereavement; sometimes we prefer not to, but exchange mental for physical pain and vice versa. Physician and psycho-analyst are alike in considering that the disease should be recognized by the physician; in psycho-analysis recognition must be by the sufferer too. The physician considers recognition of the pain subordinate to its cure; the psycho-analyst's view is expressed by Doctor Johnson's letter to Bennet Langton: 'Whether to see life as it is, will give us much consolation, I know not; but the consolation which is drawn from truth, if any there be, is solid and durable; that which may be derived from errour must be, like its original, fallacious and fugitive.'

The point that demonstrates the divergence most clearly is that the physician is dependent on realization of sensuous experience in contrast with the psycho-analyst whose dependence is on experience that is not sensuous. The physician can see and touch and smell. The realizations with which a psycho-analyst deals cannot be seen or touched; anxiety has no shape or colour, smell or sound. For convenience, I propose to use the term 'intuit' as a parallel in the psycho-analyst's domain to the physician's use of 'see', 'touch', 'smell', and 'hear'.

I shall now give three different formulations of the same episode occurring in the psycho-analysis of a woman. More could easily be given to demonstrate the problem of communication and publication that faces the psycho-analyst.

The patient produced an association to express, though in a disguised manner, her hostility to parents whose relationship to each other she represented as that between pander and whore. She intended also to evoke a response from the analyst such that he would be wrong whatever facet of a multi-dimensional association he selected for interpretation. Choice of dimension and interpretation could be 'proved' to reflect the analyst, not the analysand; he could hesitate impotently before the wealth of alternatives presented to him.

A version employing more analytically recondite Kleinian intuitional formulations: the patient was directing an attack on the analyst's psycho-analytic potency; the 'missile' was the association – which therefore is to be regarded as an object of grid category A6. The characteristics of the association are either that it subjects the analyst's intuition to splitting because of his inability to formulate simultaneous expressions of diverse and possibly incompatible interpretations, or that it has the ability to compel the analyst, through the need to act, to adopt a moral standpoint for interpretation because the scientific standpoint involves being 'split' between alternative interpretations. The close relationship between moral attitudes and action, as contrasted with thought or meditation, will be investigated later. The first problem is to choose what interpretation to give. Any one of many facets of the patient's statement may be noticed rather than any other. It can be considered as a statement or as a transformation; as multi-dimensional or multi-faceted; it could be represented by a visual image of a figure in which many planes meet or lines pass through a common point. I can represent it to myself by a visual image of a geometric solid with an infinite number of surfaces. It depends on a realization, derived from space, of sensuous experience. The attempt to externalize the visual image is restricted as if the representation by points and lines was itself a 'space' too restricted to 'contain' the visual image; thus, —— has breadth whereas the *mental* visual image of a line or a point has not.

Projective identification has hitherto been formulated in terms derived from a realization of the ordinary man's (or woman's) idea of three-dimensional space. The usual Kleinian formulations depend on a visual image of a space containing all kinds of objects. Into these objects in this space it is supposed that the patients project parts of their personality that they have split off. Melanie Klein, who discovered this mechanism, considered it to be observable in psychotic and borderline psychotic patients. Later, she and her co-workers considered that the theory had a more extended application and that realizations approximating to it could be detected in neurotic and normal personalities. She stressed the degree of fragmentation and the distance to which the fragments were projected as a determining factor in the degree of mental disturbance the patient displayed in his contact with reality. With this view I agree; as my practice with disturbed patients increased it became evident that more rigorous formulation of the theory was needed if the gap between representation and realization was to be bridged by the analyst's interpretation. This was brought home to me in circumstances adumbrated in *Learning from experience* and *Elements of psycho-analysis*. I shall recapitulate briefly some of what I wrote then and later in *Transformations*.

There are patients whose contact with reality presents most difficulty when that reality is their own mental state. For example, a baby discovers its hand; it might as well have discovered its stomach-ache, or its feeling of dread or anxiety, or mental pain. In most ordinary personalities this is true, but people exist who are so intolerant of pain or frustration (or in whom pain or frustration is so intolerable) that they feel the pain but will not suffer it and so cannot be said to discover it. *What* it is that they will not suffer or discover we have to conjecture from what we learn from patients who *do* allow themselves to suffer. The patient who will not suffer pain fails to 'suffer' pleasure and this denies the patient the encouragement he might otherwise receive from accidental or intrinsic relief. Where one patient would understand a word to mark a constant conjunction this patient experiences it as a thing that is not there, and the thing that is not there, like the thing that *is* there, is indistinguishable from an hallucination. Since the term 'hallucination' has a penumbra of associations which would be inappropriate I have named these objects beta-elements.

These descriptions of how these objects appear to the patient and how they appear to me are intended to aid the reader's understanding, but are not sufficiently rigorous for use in practice. The formulations have the status of elements in grid category C.

Suppose the patient is capable of tolerating frustration and pain: his story will differ in important respects from the above. To him the name represents a 'no-thing', but his capacity for toleration enables him to observe a constant conjunction, to bind it with a name or to use it when it has already been named. Patient A, for I shall now call the intolerant patient so, has then at his disposal beta-elements or bizarre objects and his case differs in this respect from patient B, as I now designate the second patient, who can tolerate and therefore name (even if the name is no more than a grunt or a yell) a constant conjunction and so investigate its meaning. Whether the beta-element or the bizarre object is to be classified as thought or not is a matter of scientific convenience which may be determined later. I suggest provisionally that all beta-elements are distinguished from elements that pervade the mental processes of patient B by considering the latter to be thoughts and the former not. The most genetically primitive elements of thought I shall group together as alpha-elements, in distinction to beta-elements.

I shall now use the geometrical concepts of lines, points, and space (as derived originally not from a realization of three-dimensional space but from the realizations of the emotional mental life) as returnable to the realm from which they appear to me to spring. That is, if the geometer's concept of space derives from an experience of 'the place where something was' it is to be returned to illuminate the domain where it is in my experience meaningful to say that 'a feeling of depression' is 'the place where a breast or other lost object was' and that 'space' is 'where depression, or some other emotion, used to be'.

I have pointed out that this space, these points, and these lines differ in one important respect, namely, that in the domain of mental visual images an infinite number of lines may pass through one point but, were I to attempt to represent such a visual image by point and lines on a piece of paper, there would be a finite number of lines. This limiting quality inheres in all realizations of three-dimensional space that approximate to the points, lines, and space of the geometer. It does not inhere in mental space until an attempt is made to represent mental space by verbal thought. I am thus postulating mental space as a thing-in-itself that is unknowable, but that can be represented by thoughts. In thought I include all that is primitive, including alpha-elements as I have so far described them. I exclude, arbitrarily by definition, beta-elements. Thoughts may be classed with the realizations of all objects approximating to the representations of three-dimensional space in this particular: they are intolerable to patient A because they share the frustrating quality of all realizations. Yet to the 'ordinary man' thoughts do not have this restrictive character until it is necessary to apply them to pre-verbal material. Material may be pre-verbal because the individual who seeks to verbalize it has not had sufficient experience of the material to observe a constant conjunction. He is in a state analogous to that seen in a number of similar configurations such as: having pain without suffering it; not understanding planetary movement because the differential calculus has not been invented; not being conscious of a mental phenomenon because it has been repressed; not knowing an event because the event has not occurred.

In all these situations the associated problems require thought for their solution. In all of them thought is restrictive and can be directly experienced as such as soon as an intuition demands representation for private communication. Since thought liberates the intuition there is conflict between the impulse to leave the intuition unexpressed and the impulse to express it. The restrictive element of representation therefore obtrudes in transformation $T\alpha \rightarrow T\beta$ of pre-verbal material. One man achieves the transformation; the other, who cannot tolerate restriction, does not. He therefore forfeits the relief from frustration that thought, were he able to tolerate it, would give. The onset of the reality principle is thus imperilled. In my definition of thought, he will not generate alpha-elements and will not be capable of thought. Whatever substitute he finds for thought is not to be classified as thought. When I discuss psychotic verbalization this point will be considered again.

The failure of alpha-function, which should produce alpha-elements, involves the absence of mental visual images of points, lines, and space. Patient A therefore lacks equipment that would help him to map the realization of mental space. His position is analogous to that of the geometer who had to await the invention of Cartesian co-ordinates before he could elaborate algebraic geometry.

Now consider patient A confronted with an experience in which B would resort to projective identification as adumbrated by Melanie Klein. The restrictive character of reality and the dependence of projective identification on recognition of objects preclude projection of parts of the personality because there is no conception of containers into which the projection could take place. The explosive projection is therefore felt to take place in what is, to the analyst, the *realization* of mental space: a mental space that has no visual images to fulfil the functions of a co-ordinate system, either the 'faceted solid' or the multi-dimensional, multi-linear figure of lines intersecting at a point. The mental realization of space is therefore felt as an immensity so great that it cannot be represented even by astronomical space because it cannot be represented at all.

Paradoxically this explosion is so violent and is accompanied by such immense fear – hereafter referred to as psychotic fear or psychotic panic – that the patient may express it by sudden and complete silence (as if to go to an extreme as far from a devastating explosion as possible).

The ensuing state can be most easily expressed by using surgical shock as a model: in this the dilatation of the capillaries throughout the body so increases the space in which blood can circulate that the patient may bleed to death in his own tissues. Mental space is so vast compared with any realization of three-dimensional space that the patient's capacity for emotion is felt to be lost because emotion itself is felt to drain away and be lost in the immensity. What may then appear to the observer as thoughts, visual images, and verbalizations must be regarded by him as debris, remnants or scraps of imitated speech and histrionic synthetic emotion, floating in a space so vast that its confines, temporal as well as spatial, are without definition. The events of an analysis, spread out over what to the analyst are many years, are to A but the fragments of a moment dispersed in space. The distance in time separating one statement from another can be taken as a measure of the distance in space of one element from another in which all are contemporary. Thus A says he could buy no ice-cream. Six months later he says he cannot even buy ice-cream. Three days later he mentions his being too late to buy ice-cream: there was no ice-cream left. Two years later he says he supposes there was no ice-cream. Had I known, when the topic was mentioned first, what I know now I might have noted the time and place of the reference, but I did not know and therefore could not attend to this statement or note it. When I did, it was because of the obtrusive 'I scream' theme. It was later still that I grasped the significance of 'no – I scream'. By this time, I could make only the vaguest reference to previous appearances of the material. As it turned out this difficulty did not appear to matter and my interpretation was taken. Yet I would feel happier if I thought that my gain in experience could lead to earlier observation and use of the material. I now know that a violent attack had been delivered on a relationship in which the link between the two personalities had been 'I scream'. This had been destroyed and the place of the link 'I scream' had been taken by a 'no – I scream'. The 'I scream' link had itself previously been food, 'ice-cream', a 'breast', until envy and destructiveness had turned the good breast into an 'I scream'. In narrative form: he had been linked to his object by a good breast (he liked ice-cream). This he had attacked, possibly bitten it in actuality. The place of the breast as link was then taken by an 'I scream'. Further attacks made it a 'no – I scream'. The destruction of the link by explosion now took place in the domain of mental realization. Mental space being infinite, the fragments of the link are dispersed instantaneously over infinite space. The 'distance' between one piece and another is measured in time.[1]

The patient should be shown the evidence on which the interpretation is based; if the evidence is scattered sparsely over a period of years of acting-out, the problem of interpretation assumes serious proportions, because the medium in which the patient is effecting his transformation is not predominantly conversational English, but acting-out. The analysis may be regarded as one moment in time stretched out so that it becomes a line or surface spread out over a period of years – an extremely thin membrane of a moment. Regarded thus, the total analysis can be seen as a transformation in which an intense catastrophic emotional explosion O has occurred (elements of personality, link, and second personality having been instantaneously expelled to vast distances from their point of origin and from each other). This explosive event O is then transformed, in the medium of acting-out and by virtue of beta-elements, to T$p\beta$, in which space, being restrictive and not amenable to adequate formulation of distance between beta-elements, is replaced by the realization corresponding to time. Though there is no representation of mental space available to the patient and though the realization of three-dimensional space is too restrictive for a temperament intolerant of frustration, the realization of mental space, being unbounded, permits of a continuous and continuing expansion and separation of beta-elements. For the investigation of this mental state the patient cannot, but the analyst can, employ points, lines, and space. The geometer has used them for the investigation of three-dimensional space and, by the substitution of algebraic geometry for the figurative geometry of Euclid, has been

[1] The account I have just given is an example of taking T$p\beta$ as my TaO, and by T$a\alpha$ proceeding to T$a\beta$. T$a\beta$ is my attempt at a reconstruction of TpO, T$p\alpha$, T$p\beta$. When this degree of private communication has been attained, the problem becomes one of publishing it – formulating it in conversational English that the patient can understand (see Bion, 1965).

able to extend his investigation to multi-dimensional space and leave Euclidean space to be used for psychological preparation for the non-Euclidean geometries now available. Can we similarly use the concepts of Euclidean geometry to get back to the emotional realizations from which I believe it originally sprang? The need is for a formulation so general that a multiplication of theories to meet a diversity of realizations bearing the same configuration is obviated, yet so precise that it will not cover configurations whose similarity is only apparent, or whose appearance of similarity is due to irrelevant C category visual imagery.

The impossibility of communication without frustration is so familiar that the nature of the frustration is forgotten. Most people are aware of it as a transient phenomenon experienced on relatively few occasions. In psycho-analytic work the problems are more obtrusive than usual because the subject is novel and its difficulties are uncharted; difficulties become more marked still when the material to be communicated is pre- or non-verbal. The psycho-analyst can employ silences; he, like the painter or musician, can communicate non-verbal material. Similarly, the painter can communicate material that is non-visual and the musician material that is inaudible. The pre-verbal matter the psycho-analyst must discuss is certain to be an illustration of the difficulty in communication that he himself is experiencing. Ability to use points, lines, and space becomes important for understanding 'emotional space', for the continuance of the work and avoidance of a situation in which two inarticulate personalities are unable to release themselves from the bondage of inarticulation. This mutually sterile relationship provides a model for some relationships of the self with itself. When the relationship of the self with itself is of this kind, either the container or the contained must be destroyed. Finally, the individual cannot contain the impulses proper to a pair and the pair cannot contain the impulses proper to a group. The psycho-analytic problem is the problem of growth and its harmonious resolution in the relationship between the container and the contained, repeated in individual, pair, and finally group (intra and extra psychically).

Any definitory hypothesis, be it exclamation, name, theoretical system, or extended statement such as a book, has, and has always been recognized to have, a negative function. It must always imply that something is; equally it implies that something is not. It is therefore open to the recipient to infer one or other according to his temper. If the personality is incapable of tolerating frustration there seems to be no reason why he should not develop on the assumption that the definitory hypothesis means that something is. The statement is then allowed to become a pre-conception and the way is open for the unsaturated element to become saturated. But suppose that the inability to tolerate frustration is 'excessive': the personality may react against the statement, seeing only its negative implications and, in the extreme case, refusing to allow the statement, to him a 'nothing', even to exist. The attempt then is to annihilate the statement in its function of definitory hypothesis. A model would be the infant who cannot tolerate weaning because it is dominated by the *loss* of the breast and who therefore cannot accept what it might have instead. The patient cannot tolerate the definitory hypothesis and therefore does not achieve the pre-conception (D4).

Knowledge of loss, of the negative aspect of the definition, of the 'thought' as a 'no-thing', is immediate; knowledge of gain, if any, has to wait upon the fruits of permitting the thought, or other statement, to be a pre-conception (ψ (ξ)). Therefore 'excessive' inability to tolerate frustration is likely to obstruct development of pre-conception (D4 functions). 'Excessive' intolerance is likely to obstruct awareness of realizations. The 'no-thing' with its corresponding realization (of some object not present) will be liable to destruction whereas 'hallucination' will be favoured for its immediacy. Another formulation of this is to say that the domain of realizations and all that might represent realizations is felt not to afford enough 'space' for freedom whereas the domain of hallucination does. In passing, I must draw attention to the fact that the sense of loss in the definitory hypothesis and the sense of gratification in hallucination both depend on a restricted mental range. In both instances the reaction, of intolerance in one and gratification in the other, might be said to be associated with a short-sighted 'view'. Thought consequently is not seen as offering freedom for development, but is felt as a restriction; by contrast, 'acting-out' is felt to yield a sense of freedom. *A fortiori* an hallucination is designed through its quality as the-thing-itself (not the thought of a breast but the breast itself) to be indistinguishable from freedom. The patient then may be seen as facing a choice: either he may allow his intolerance of frustration to use what might otherwise be a 'no-thing' to become a thought and so achieve the freedom Freud (1911) describes, or he may use what might be a 'no-thing' to be the foundation for a system of hallucinosis.

From this last will spring the set of transformations in hallucinosis which it will be necessary to differentiate from transformations in painting, music, mathematics, and the domain of verbal communication. The importance of making this last distinction is enhanced by the fact that words are used both in the expression of verbal communication and in transformations in hallucinosis. Yet consideration of the nature of the differing reaction to the 'no-thing' will show that the word representing a thought is not the same as the identical word when it is representing an hallucination. Since the similarity may be extremely close in the words employed in both systems and sometimes in the method by which they appear to be combined, it is important to discover in what the difference lies. The difference between philosophy (and even theoretical psycho-analysis) and the practice of psycho-analysis can be seen by considering what the detection of this difference means for the philosopher or theoretician and what it means for the practising psycho-analyst who has to decide in the emotional situation itself whether the patient's statements represent an hallucination or a fact of external reality. It is for this reason that the psycho-analyst must be experienced in non-sensuous realities and able to ignore sensuously derived experience as it appears formalized in memory. The word 'dog' represents different realizations in scientific inquiry and hallucinosis; but the word 'dog' is itself not the same when it is representing a realization in scientific inquiry and an element belonging to the domain of hallucinatory transformations. It is sometimes useful to regard it as analogous to the visual image in a reversible perspective. In the visual image the marks of a drawing on paper remain unchanged but 'mean' two faces or a vase; similarly, 'dog' may mean dog or God (to take but one example). In non-psychotic transformations the invariant is insignificant: the resemblance to ordinary speech, the fact that the word is identical in psychotic and non-psychotic transformation, is accidental.

Verbal, musical, artistic modes of communication all meet with realizations that they appear to represent only very approximately. Hallucination may be regarded, wrongly, as a representation and therefore as unsuited to some activities. As verbal, musical, and artistic transformations have compensating values arising from their being *transformations* of O, it is natural to consider the like possibility with hallucinosis. But hallucinations are *not* representations: they are things-in-themselves born of intolerance of frustration and desire. Their defects are due not to their failure to represent but to their failure to *be*. Thus we need to consider the difference between psychic and external reality.

As I am primarily concerned with the formulation of theory, the illustrations I am about to give are by way of C formulations, not records of clinical experience. The intention is to approach to more rigorous theoretical presentation, that is, presentation less open to misunderstanding through logical defect, or over-flexibility in an attempt to represent different configurations of the same fundamental structures and functions, or failure to represent, through over-rigidity, realizations in which the fundamentals are invariant but the accidentals diverse. The illustrations are C category elements used as preparation for theoretical formulations that can stand by themselves: the reader should regard the 'illustrations' as psychological aids to understanding the theories proper. From this point to the end of the chapter emotional experiences will be represented by C formulations.

1. The patients, for the treatment of whom I wish to formulate theories, experience pain but not suffering. They may be suffering in the eyes of the analyst because the analyst can, and indeed must, suffer. The patient may say he suffers but this is only because he does not know what suffering is and mistakes feeling pain for suffering it. The theory will need to be such that it represents the realization in which this is possible and shows how it comes about. The *intensity* of the patient's pain contributes to his fear of suffering pain.

2. Suffering pain involves respect for the fact of pain, his own or another's. This respect he does not have and therefore he has no respect for any procedure, such as psychoanalysis, which is concerned with the existence of pain.

3. Frustration and intense pain are equated.

4. Pain is sexualized; it is therefore inflicted or accepted but is not suffered – except in the view of the analyst or other observer.

5. For purposes of this exposition the following conjunction is described in narrative form, the elements being sequential and bound in a chain of causation. The realization of the constant conjunction does not have any element that approximates to the sequential or causal elements of the narrative representing it. These features belong only to the C category representation, not to the realization they represent. The patient feels the pain of an absence of fulfilment of his desires. The absent fulfilment is experienced as a 'no-thing'. The emotion aroused by the 'no-thing' is felt as indistinguishable from the 'no-thing'. The emotion is replaced

by a 'no-emotion'. In practice this can mean no feeling at all, or an emotion, such as rage, which is a column 2 emotion, that is, an emotion of which the fundamental function is denial of another emotion.

6. As a column 2 element all felt emotion is a 'no-emotion'. In this respect it is analogous to 'past' or 'future' as representing the 'place where the present used to be' before all time was annihilated.

7. The 'place' where time was (or a feeling was, or a 'no-thing' of any kind was) is then similarly annihilated. There is thus created a domain of the non-existent. I have not come across any realization that corresponds to such a state though I can imagine a stupor so intense that it might seem to do so. It is nevertheless useful to postulate it partly because there are occasions when it is convenient to suppose that the patient holds such a belief, and partly because it is convenient for the analyst. As will be seen, meanings other than sophisticated meanings creep back into the relatively meaningless state of the term 'non-existent' as E1 category. Some patients with whom I am familiar achieve a state, to which I wish to apply the term 'non-existence', for a few moments at most; this is followed by an externalization or evacuation of 'non-existence'. 'Non-existence' immediately becomes an object that is immensely hostile and filled with murderous envy towards the quality or function of existence wherever it is to be found. 'Space', either as a representation, or the realization the term derives from or represents, becomes terrifying or terror itself: 'Le silence de ces espaces infinies m'effraie.' The space of the ordinary man, the astronomer, or the physicist, becomes confounded with 'mental space', and its objects with the objects of 'mental space'.

8. The scientific or sophisticated approach tends to become confounded with the realizations its formulations are intended to represent. The point (.) and the line (—) are regarded as if they were analogous to representations of

reversible perspective. Their significance therefore varies according to the point of view (or vertex) with which they are associated. Vertices may have as their approximate realizations various recognized disciplines such as religion, mathematics, physics, music, painting, and other arts. The formulations associated with a particular vertex may be categorized in accordance with the grid.

9. The following illustration is to facilitate an approach to a more rigorous representation of 'points of view' or vertices. The patient corresponds to the A personality, the analyst to B. The analytic exchange described is at an advanced stage in the analysis, in the sense that what was an extremely disturbed patient has become better adjusted to what the psycho-analyst regards as reality. The psycho-analyst similarly has become better adjusted to what the patient regards as reality. 'Somewhere' there is present a 'super-ego' that is cruel, denuded of all the characteristics usually associated with the super-ego, and, finally, of 'existence' itself. It therefore has the characteristics of 'non-existence' described in 7 above. I use the term 'super-ego' as a psycho-analytical intuitive theory, now with the status of a realization, which I want to reformulate in terms of another intuitive theory.

The patient talks freely, but his communications are disjointed sentences which would, anywhere but in analysis, be described as 'incoherent'. Such a term is insufficiently illuminating to lead to a psycho-analytical interpretation, but the 'vertex' (the 'point of view' provided by regarding an analysis as an ordinary conversation) gives me a descriptive term suitable for the immediate purpose. As it is not suitable for continuing the psycho-analytic discussion the term 'incoherence' must be observed more critically.

As time passes, and it may require many months of observation, 'incoherence' displays many characteristics and they are changing constantly. The patient may, in a fit of impatience, describe them as pointless; and so they may prove to be, for sentences can indeed communicate everything but the point. The sentences were mutilated. Personal pronouns were used without indication of the person to whom they might relate. Important parts of speech were missing; and so on. The mutilations varied in form and in effect; they did not always make sentences pointless though sometimes 'pointlessness' was the 'point'. This type of peculiarity is but one manifestation of attacks on linking, the technique of psycho-analysis and indeed articulate speech itself being the link. My immediate concern is not with attacks on linking but with an aspect of transformation (Bion, 1965). The patient, having delivered himself of a series of statements, listens to the interpretation and then continues, to all outward appearance, in much the same way. Further observation reveals that there has in fact been a change. If my interpretation was intended to show him that he was speaking to conceal, rather than to reveal, something about his sexual life, he will identify himself with a 'point of view', a vertex, such that only certain elements in my interpretation are illumined. Thus he emulates the mathematician whose formula effects a transformation in vector space. What takes place I shall represent by a slow-motion model:

The patient grasps the gist of what I say. The totality of the statement, including the implication that I am the analyst, is evacuated (the mechanism represented by the theory of projective identification). He identifies himself with the analyst and by virtue of his intuition is able to 'see' the meaning of my interpretation. The meaning that he thus 'sees' is that I am annoyed, jealous, envious at my exclusion from participation in, or understanding of, his sexual life. He then exclaims, 'Oh that frightful noise!'

His remark, without the interpolated story, appears to be a *non sequitur*; if the account given is assumed to represent the mental events, unexpressed in the interval between interpretation and rejoinder, incoherence disappears. Many assumptions can be made about the link between interpretation and response. One set assumes that it should be compatible with respect for the truth; another that it should conform to respect for omniscience; yet another that it should be compatible with both. The role of desire, in pre-conception, is determinant.

In this episode there are some of the unsatisfactory features to which I would draw attention. There is no evidence to support the particular assumption made. To produce it would involve the impossible task of explaining the history of my mental development, or even that limited part of it shared with the patient, that has led to accretions of 'desires' to original beliefs (grid category C1) that my analysand was my patient.

Furthermore, I have used terms, 'omniscient' is one of them, that represent similar developments of meaning in order that the term should become the premiss of further developments. 'Omniscient' is therefore an element categorized as $\overleftarrow{C}3$ and $\overrightarrow{D}4$.

The patient may categorize the same statements in an entirely different way, as is apparent from the description I have given of his interpretation of my interpretation. To meet this difficulty I propose to construct a figure that will serve to represent the invariants of an ever-changing situation.

By way of psychological preparation for the reception of a system that is independent of the particular situations it is intended to serve, I shall use descriptions that lack rigour but have definition. This makes for a lack of flexibility in the final formulation which is intended to combine flexibility with rigour. The system may be regarded as being contained within an emotional space within itself – an 'exo-skeleton' or an 'endo-skeleton'.

To construct this I differentiate an awareness of reality from a denial, or ignoring, or ignorance, of reality. A will ignore reality; B will accept it. With vertex A, reality will be restrictive and frustrating; with vertex B, reality will be liberating and conducive to growth.

Further, I assume an axiomatic approach in all theoretical

formulations; axiomatic statements are not differentiated from postulates and premisses: they are treated as indistinguishable from each other and from definitory hypotheses. Definitory hypotheses are statements marking the binding of a constant conjunction whatever the content of the formulation may be. Any theorem I regard as capable of one of the uses of the horizontal axis. But when a column 1 → columns 3 and 4, it means the category has changed to row D. Any theorem may illuminate facts it was not designed to display, but, conversely, any deductive system will be seen, as soon as it is used, to accumulate meaning in a manner analogous to that of the pre-conception and, in doing so, to require axioms that have not been necessary for the completion of the system.

Any deductive system may appear to be consistent within itself provided it remains definitory, that is to say, with characteristics that qualify it for column 1. The deductions may appear to be consistent and logically necessary so long as it is not asked 'necessary to what?' or 'to whom?' But if they are said to be logically necessary this is itself a statement about the system and this statement cannot be refuted unless it is used. But if it *is* allowed to become saturated, that is to say *used* as a pre-conception, then the pre-conception mates with the realization to produce a conception (E) and again to produce a concept (F). The conception (E) has the characteristic not only that it records by implication (a realization exists which approximates to the pre-conception) but that a realization exists which approximates to the conception although its existence was not known when the pre-conception was formulated. As soon as the deductive system proves its value as an exploratory tool, the self-consistency, which appeared to exist when the domain in which the system applied was limited, is imperilled because readjustments become necessary to fit the theorem to its extended domain. As the system illuminates facts whose significance was unknown before (the elements of the paranoid–schizoid position) and thus imperils its self-consistency, it throws off the limitations of the domain in which it applies. It approximates to illimitability and universality. The dilemma can be stated thus: the system, if consistent within itself, is limited; if not limited, then it cannot be regarded as self-consistent because its self-consistency is contingent. Furthermore, its statements can be seen to depend on an axiomatic statement whose existence was not even suspected, let alone regarded as logically necessary, when the system was formulated and had the status common to column 1 categories.

3 · *Reality Sensuous and Psychic*

The illustrations in the previous chapter are not satisfactory and I propose to consider some reasons for this.

Psycho-analytical events cannot be stated directly, indubitably, or incorrigibly any more than can those of other scientific research. I shall use the sign O to denote that which is the ultimate reality represented by terms such as ultimate reality, absolute truth, the godhead, the infinite, the thing-in-itself. O does not fall in the domain of knowledge or learning save incidentally; it can be 'become', but it cannot be 'known'. It is darkness and formlessness but it enters the domain K when it has evolved to a point where it can be known, through knowledge gained by experience, and formulated in terms derived from sensuous experience; its existence is conjectured phenomenologically.

The events of the psycho-analytic experience are transformed and formulated. The value of these formulations can be assessed according to the conditions under which the transformations are effected. Formulations of the events of analysis made in the course of analysis must possess value different from that of formulations made extra-sessionally. Their value therapeutically is greater if they are conducive to transformations in O; less if conducive to transformations in K.

The experience of psycho-analysis affords material impossible to equal from any other source. It follows that this material should be available in full to the psycho-analyst. The analysis that every psycho-analyst is obliged to undergo as part of his training is necessary because it removes obstacles to participation in the psycho-analytic experience; it has many facets, but for the psycho-analyst none can compare in importance with this; what I have to say is ancillary to this.

It is impossible to undergo an analysis without learning about psycho-analysis as practised by one particular psycho-analyst; this is a misfortune rather than an advantage. Furthermore, established beliefs and conventions, hardened habits of thought, unless subjected to vigilance, re-establish themselves and encroach upon the freedom the psycho-analyst has won by being psycho-analysed and lead to deterioration of his efficiency.

In the course of analysis it is inevitable that the analysand imparts a great deal of information *about* himself just as the analyst imparts information *about* analysis. This information is worthless at best and, at worst, harmful because every analysis is unique; talk about analysis is not.

The analyst must focus his attention on O, the unknown and unknowable. The success of psycho-analysis depends on the maintenance of a psycho-analytic point of view; the point of view is the psycho-analytic vertex; the psycho-analytic vertex is O. With this the analyst cannot be identified: he must *be* it.

Every object known or knowable by man, including himself, must be an evolution of O. It is O when it has evolved sufficiently to be met by K capacities in the psycho-analyst. He does not know the 'ultimate reality' of a chair or anxiety or time or space, but he knows a chair, anxiety, time, and space. In so far as the analyst becomes O he is able to know the events that are *evolutions* of O.

Restating this in terms of psycho-analytic experience, the psycho-analyst can know what the patient says, does, and appears to be, but cannot know the O of which the patient is an evolution: he can only 'be' it. He knows phenomena by virtue of his senses but, since his concern is with O, events must be regarded as possessing either the defects of irrelevancies obstructing, or the merits of pointers initiating, the process of 'becoming' O. Yet interpretations depend on 'becoming' (since he cannot know O). The interpretation is an actual event in an evolution of O that is common to analyst and analysand.

A fallacious but helpful description in A is that the practising analyst must wait for the analytic session to 'evolve'. He must wait not for the analysand to talk or to be silent or to gesture, or for any other occurrence that is an actual event, but for an evolution to take place so that O becomes manifest in K through the emergence of actual events. Similarly, the reader must disregard what I say until the O of the experience of reading has evolved to a point where the actual events of reading issue in his interpretation of the experiences. Too great a regard for what I have written obstructs the process I represent by the terms 'he becomes the O that is common to himself and myself'.

The reasons for this are as follows: There can be no genuine outcome that is based on falsity. Therefore the outcome depends on the closeness with which the interpretative appraisal approximates to truth. The psycho-analyst and his analysand are alike dependent on the senses, but psychic qualities, with which psycho-analysis deals, are not perceived by the senses but, as Freud says, by some mental counterpart of the sense organs, a function that he attributed to consciousness. Without wishing to discard this possibility I prefer to consider it as an open question and substitute a more general postulate which I represent by O. To put it in more popular terms, I would say the more 'real' the psycho-analyst is the more he can be at one with the reality of the patient. Conversely, the more he depends on actual events the more he relies on thinking that depends on a background of sense impression.

In the primitive phase, which Freud regards as dominated by the pleasure principle and from which he excludes the operation of memory, this last being dependent on the prior development of a capacity for thought, the prototype of memory appears to reside in one of the aspects of projective identification. This mechanism, employed to fulfil the duties of thought until thought takes over, appears as an interchange first between mouth and breast and then between introjected mouth and introjected breast. This I regard as reaction between container ♀ and contained ♂. ♀ seems to be the element which is nearest in this phase to the memory. The terms I use must be regarded as verbal representations of visual images; the whole description will be in these C category terms because I find them easier to employ and more likely to be understood. Later, I may attempt more sophisticated formulations.

♂ evacuates unpleasure in order to get rid of it, to have it transformed into something that is, or feels, pleasurable, for the pleasure of evacuation, for the pleasure of being contained. ♀ takes in the evacuations for the same motives. The nature of the relationship needs investigation. ♀, which may evacuate or retain, is the prototype of a forgetful or retentive memory. Pleasure may be retained if possession is the dominant concern; grievance if a store of ammunition is the main concern. Evacuation may be forcible as if to convert the evacuated object into a missile; introjection likewise as fulfilment of greed. Developments of memory that are inevitable to the psycho-analyst are C category elements, the dominance of ♀♂, the primacy of pleasure–pain (in contrast with reality or truth), and 'possession' with its reciprocal, fear of loss; all have been acquired in close association with the senses.

The impulse to be rid of painful stimuli gives the 'content' of the memory (♀) an unsatisfactory quality when one is engaged in the pursuit of truth O. The more successful the memory is in its accumulations the more nearly it approximates to resembling a saturated element saturated with saturated elements. An analyst with such a mind is one who is incapable of learning because he is satisfied. Furthermore, because of its primitive nature, his memory is believed to be filled only with objects giving rise to feelings of pleasure and to be empty of unpleasure components, or vice versa. The attitude towards the 'memory' or 'unconscious' depends on the idea that it is a container for the 'evacuations' of projective identification. Such a 'memory' is no equipment for an analyst whose aim is O, as may be seen by considering what is represented by this sign.

It stands for the absolute truth in and of any object; it is assumed that this cannot be known by any human being; it can be known about, its presence can be recognized and felt, but it cannot be known. It is possible to be at one with it. That it exists is an essential postulate of science but it cannot be scientifically discovered. No psycho-analytic discovery is possible without recognition of its existence, at-one-ment with it and evolution. The religious mystics have probably approximated most closely to expression of experience of it. Its existence is as essential to science as to religion. Conversely, the scientific approach is as essential to religion as it is to science and is as ineffectual until a transformation from $K \rightarrow O$ takes place.

In order to know about the analysand the analyst has recourse to K. Memory is a part of K. Notation (Freud, 1911), in the wide sense of the term, is its servant. But memory depends on the senses. It is limited by the limitations of the senses and their subordination to the pleasure–pain principle; memories are therefore fallacious and memory has the defects of its origin in functions of possessiveness and evacuation.

The psycho-analyst is concerned with O, which is incommunicable save through K activity. O may appear to be attainable by K through phenomena, but in fact that is not so. K depends on the evolution of $O \rightarrow K$. At-one-ment with O would seem to be possible through the transformation $K \rightarrow O$, but it is not so. The transformation $O \rightarrow K$ depends on ridding K of memory and desire. I turn accordingly to consider 'desire'.

It may not seem necessary to postulate desire as well as memory: if memory could be dispensed with, desire would likewise disappear and vice versa. But this would involve loss of meaning which I wish to retain. So, in addition to memories, I wish to consider thoughts, which are formulations of desire, and probably, but not certainly, objects we represent by the term 'desire'. They are not verbal formulations merely, or even verbal formulations of elements of C category. The desires that can be represented verbally are relatively simple to deal with. For example, the thought occurs that one would like to go abroad for the annual holiday; this can be followed by further ideas, more or less detailed elaborations of the main theme. These thoughts are typical 'desires'; they are extremely common and can be harboured almost unaware; they may be reminiscences or anticipations.

The 'memories' and 'desires' to which I wish to draw attention have the following elements in common: they are ready formulated and therefore require no formulation; they derive from experience gained through the senses; they are evocations of feelings of pleasure or pain; they are formulations 'containing' pleasure or pain. In so far as they are column 2 statements their function is to prevent transformation of the K → O order.

The above characteristics cannot be indulged by the psycho-analyst without impairment of analytic capacity. For any who have been used to remembering what patients say and to desiring their welfare, it will be hard to entertain the harm to analytic intuition that is inseparable from *any* memories and *any* desires.

The first point is for the analyst to impose on himself a positive discipline of eschewing memory and desire. I do not mean that 'forgetting' is enough: what is required is a positive act of refraining from memory and desire.

It may be wondered what state of mind is welcome if desires and memories are not. A term that would express approximately what I need to express is 'faith' – faith that there is an ultimate reality and truth – the unknown, unknowable, 'formless infinite'. This must be believed of every object of which the personality can be aware: the evolution of ultimate reality (signified by O) has issued in objects of which the individual can be aware. The objects of awareness are aspects of the 'evolved' O and are such that the sensuously derived mental functions are adequate to apprehend them. For them faith is not required; for O it is. The analyst is not concerned with such sensuously apprehended objects or with knowledge of such objects. Memories and desires are worthless but inevitable features that he encounters in himself as he works. He *is* concerned with these objects in his analysand because he is concerned with the working of the analysand's mind. His analysand will express his awareness of O in people and things by formulations representing the intersection of evolutions of O with the evolution of his awareness.

It is not possible to say that such formulations by the analysand are not to be interpreted: no such rule can be laid down far from the situation in which it is to be applied because the criteria for it do not exist. Nor can the criteria be established in the situation of the analysis, for they are part of an ineffable experience. There can be no rules about the nature of the emotional experience that will show that the emotional experience is ripe for interpretation. Instead I can only suggest rules for the analyst that will help him to achieve the frame of mind in which he is receptive to O of the analytic experience. If he is able to be receptive to O, then he may feel impelled to deal with the intersection of the evolution of O with the domain of objects of sense or of formulations based on the senses. Whether he does so or not cannot depend on *rules* for O, or O → K, but only on his ability to be at one with O.

My last sentence represents an 'act' of what I have called 'faith'. It is in my view a scientific statement because for me 'faith' is a scientific state of mind and should be recognized as such. But it must be 'faith' unstained by any element of memory or desire. If it reveals an aspect of O which has to be formulated, then the *transformation* will require the operation of memory and desire; even so the formulation will require the negative characteristics of column 1 elements – that is to say that the statements must affirm implicitly that the object defined is *not* any of the elements whose names are used in the definitory hypothesis, but is a constant conjunction whose meaning will declare itself only when all traces of memory and desire have been removed from the elements invoked to produce the new formulation. Failure to observe the nature of transformation O → K (that is, the use of objects of memory and desire to mark a new constant conjunction, and the need to discard the evocative characteristics of memory and desire so that the formulation representing the new constant conjunction is unsaturated) has obscured the only sense in which the term 'abstraction' has any useful meaning. A formulation has the quality of an abstraction only in so far as it is divorced from the sensuous background inherent in and essential to memory and desire. The abstract statement must not stimulate memory and desire though memory and desire have contributed elements to its formulation.

Memory and desire are essential elements in the composition of the new formulation, but a distinction must be made between two classes of mental event. One is an evocation of memory and desire with impulses of possessiveness and sensuous greed: the impulses generate memory and desire; memory and desire generate sensuous greed. The other is the evocation of memories and desires because the experience of at-one-ment *resembles* possession and sensuous fulfilment. The classes differ because the mode of selection differs, and since the classes differ the interpretation (the formulation by the analyst) will differ. The evocation of that which provided a container for possessions, and of the sensuous gratifications with which to fill it, will differ from an evocation stimulated by at-one-ment. The exercises in discarding memory and desire must be seen as preparatory to a state of mind in which O can evolve. The facilitation of 'constellation'[1] must in turn be seen as a step in the process of at-one-ment (the transformation O → K). In practice this means not that the analyst recalls some relevant memory but that a relevant constellation will be evoked during the process of at-one-ment with O, the process denoted by transformation O → K.

[1] I use the term 'constellation' to represent the process precipitating a constant conjunction.

To what then *is* the analyst's memory relevant and why can there not be a constellation that has a relevance other than relevance to analysis?

It is difficult to conceive of an analysis having a satisfactory outcome without the analysand's becoming reconciled to, or at one with, himself. It is tempting to suppose that such an outcome, or the desire for such an outcome, might provide a criterion for relevance. Conversely, it would be convenient if the analyst's memories, as reminiscences of sensuous experience, could be disregarded as column 2 phenomena mobilized to keep at bay the experience inseparable from the transformations in O. If the objection to memory can be sustained because all memory is a special case of keeping (possessing) a theory known to be (or suspected of being) false in order to prevent the psychological upheavel inseparable from mental growth, it will have the advantage of decreasing the number of theories required to extend, as I propose to do, the theories of resistance. It is sometimes said that a particular interpretation is inadvisable because it increases resistances, but any approach produces its proper resistances and it is as possible to identify an approach by its resistances as it is to judge a tree by its fruit. Resistance to growth is endo-psychic and endo-gregious; it is associated with turbulence in the individual and in the group to which the growing individual belongs.

C category elements, developed from experience gained by the senses, all have gratificatory quality associated with dominance of the pleasure–pain principle. Objections to 'memories' and 'desires' are therefore objections to C3 and C3(2) statements. Later it will be necessary when we deal with hallucinations to distinguish between C elements having a background of visual sensation and those with other sense backgrounds.

The discipline that I propose for the analyst, namely avoidance of memory and desire, in the sense in which I have used those terms, increases his ability to exercise 'acts of faith'. An 'act of faith' is peculiar to scientific procedure and must be distinguished from the religious meaning with which it is invested in conversational usage; it becomes apprehensible when it can be represented in and by thought. It must 'evolve' before it can be apprehended and it is apprehended when it is a thought just as the artist's O is apprehensible when it has been transformed into a work of art.

But the 'act of faith' is not a statement, not even a column 6 statement, though it has resemblances to column 6 elements. All grid elements have a background of O from which they have evolved and it is only when O has evolved sufficiently to be apprehended that it can be represented by a grid element. It is only when it has evolved to the point where it can be represented by a grid element that it can be apprehended. When it is apprehended the element can be represented by a grid category.

The 'act of faith' has no association with memory or desire or sensation. It has a relationship to thought analogous to the relationship of *a priori* knowledge to knowledge. It does not belong to the ±K system but to the O system. It does not by itself lead to knowledge 'about' something, but knowledge 'about' something may be the outcome of a defence against the consequences of an 'act of faith'. A thought has as its realization a no-thing. An 'act of faith' has as its background something that is unconscious and unknown because it has not happened. Thoughts have as their background realizations that are sensible: anxiety, fear, sex can be thought about only when O has evolved to a point where it is apprehensible in sense and has become amenable to transformations in K. Anxiety is 'known' by its secondary qualities. Yet no one has any doubt about anxiety or about 'feeling' the reality, though what is felt is sensations associated with anxiety and not anxiety itself. Similarly, no one who denudes himself of memory and desire, and of all those elements of sense impression ordinarily present, can have any doubt of the reality of the psycho-analytical experience which remains ineffable.

Receptiveness achieved by denudation of memory and

desire (which is essential to the operation of 'acts of faith') is essential to the operation of psycho-analysis and other scientific proceedings. It is essential for experiencing hallucination or the state of hallucinosis.

This state I do not regard as an exaggeration of a pathological or even natural condition: I consider it rather to be a state always present, but overlaid by other phenomena, which screen it. If these other elements can be moderated or suspended hallucinosis becomes demonstrable; its full depth and richness are accessible only to 'acts of faith'. Elements of hallucinosis of which it is possible to be sensible are the grosser manifestations and are of secondary importance; to appreciate hallucination the analyst must participate in the state of hallucinosis. From what I have said it will be clear that this is so, for I have postulated that a K link can operate only on a background of the senses, is capable of yielding only knowledge 'about' something, and must be differentiated from the O link essential to transformations in O. Before interpretations of hallucination can be given, which are themselves transformations $O \rightarrow K$, it is necessary that the analyst undergoes in his own personality the transformation $O \rightarrow K$. By eschewing memories, desires, and the operations of memory he can approach the domain of hallucinosis and of the 'acts of faith' by which alone he can become at one with his patients' hallucinations and so effect transformations $O \rightarrow K$.

A type of hallucination worthy of study is that which one may describe provisionally as visual. I have described a patient who seemed to think that my words flew over his head and could be detected in what to me were the patterns on a cushion. I have since found that the pattern on the cushion was seen by him to travel, as it were, in the opposite direction. That is, he was able, in a state of hallucinosis, to see that the patterns were really my words travelling, through his eyes, to him. Furthermore the 'meaning', which could not be grasped outside the conditions of hallucinosis, was perfectly clear in a state of hallucinosis. The 'meaning' of a statement in hallucinosis is not, however, the same as its meaning in the domain of rational thought. Ordinarily, constellation, constant conjunction, and binding (by nomenation) are a prelude to exploration of meaning. In the domain of hallucinosis the mental event is transformed into a sense impression and sense impressions in this domain do not have meaning; they provide pleasure or pain. In this way the unsense-able mental phenomenon is transformed into a beta-element which can be evacuated and reintroduced so that the act yields, not a meaning, but pleasure or pain.

The analysand in a state of hallucinosis experiences visual hallucinations which tend to be self-perpetuating. They yield pleasure and pain, both being valued, and fail to yield meaning in the sense in which that term is understood in the domain of rational thought. He tends therefore to demand, and provide, more hallucination to compensate for the missing gratification. He feels the pleasure and pain to be inadequate; the 'meaning' is likewise inadequate. The less gratification he achieves the more greedy he becomes; the more greedy, the more hallucinated. The visual element is expected to be exempt from the disabilities inherent in those senses that depend for their efficacy on proximity to the object of gratification. Meaning is lost, pain and pleasure are gained, from a state that is independent of proximity to an object and of the frustration peculiar to thoughts and their genetic association with the 'no-thing'.[1]

I suspect that what I have said of visual hallucinations is true of hallucinations with a background of senses other than visual, but other senses lack the quality of independence of close contact with objects.

A patient who feared guilt substituted punishment. It was achieved by hallucinosis. His circumstances were comfortable and he did not manipulate events by acting out, which he might have done, to produce a penitential life. He could

[1] It is worth contrasting this type of independence of objects, conferred by hallucinosis and the advantages of 'visual' impression, with the independence of the physical presence of objects peculiar to 'maths' and 'thinking'. Note, too, the distraction caused by the *presence* of objects.

presumably have forced the police to take action by committing some variety of sexual offence – sexual offences often appeared in his statements – but instead he complained incessantly though inarticulately of what he ultimately came to recognize as sexual visions, which he admitted were present throughout the sessions. For months during which I had interpreted that he was seeing visions he denied them, but they were maintained tenaciously. After their presence had been admitted he feared to lose them though their dominance was painful. The pain yielded pleasure, and therefore there was cause for him to cherish the state of which he complained. His complaints, his flow of statements, produced a painful state in analysis and then were made into a sexual link between him and me. At the stage of which I write this was a gratification and also a protection against behaviour which might yield pleasure in a more expansive way – by his becoming involved with the police, for example. But his fear of any change was so acute that it was impossible to say with any plausibility what he expected to take the place of his hallucinations were they to cease. In time, however, certain fears could be discussed. Acting-out limited the amount of experience and its extent because the reality component involved frustration and delay, and real pain and pleasure seemed deficient in power to satisfy.[1] This, however, was his complaint against hallucinatory gratification. Hallucinations of dreams seemed to be deficient in associations and unsuited to perform the functions of dreams, and to be felt as unrewarding. Yet he reported what he said were dreams.

In this period hallucination supplied him with punishment as it might in other circumstances have supplied him with sexual pleasure, food, or any other sensual gratification. His analysis indeed showed that the usefulness of hallucination was absolutely limited to elements with a background of sense-able realizations: this was their virtue and their defect.

[1] In this respect real objects, real pain and pleasure, are felt as distraction. It is worth comparing *this* type of distraction with the frustration experienced by a calculator who has to think out mathematical problems only in the presence of objects which are the essence of his calculation.

Their moral value seemed to be that they punished him by providing him with ill-deserved pain to compensate for having been once used as the source of ill-deserved pleasure. In the analytic session they seemed as a barrier against any appreciation of the realities of the session. Yet some interpretations were grasped sometimes. I found it difficult to establish any rule that would govern the time at which interpretations could be understood but I did note that the interpretation had to be exact. He could not correct or adjust an inexactitude so as to bring the interpretation into line with the realization it was intended to illumine. It had to remain uncorrected and unabsorbed because it was wrong.

The sessions were occupied in verbalization of his visual images. His verbalizations were peppered with locutions such as 'tomorrow', 'yesterday', 'last week', all of which could be taken to mean 'not now'. Splitting in time was very common and psycho-analytic objects were scattered over a range of years. Corresponding to this was a denial of the present which amounted to a denial of the passage of time. It was as if a moment of time had been stretched out to cover an enormous area as if it were a piece of elastic.

There had been an occasion when he smelled coffee in the house where I was working. He had once seen me caught in a rain shower without a coat or umbrella. Both these facts appeared in fragments spread out over many years. It would be an exaggeration to say they were expressed unmistakably. I have no doubt, or, more accurately, by an 'act of faith' I am confident, that the scraps of sentences and intonations when put together were signs that he had had both these experiences as I have described them. Were it possible for him to witness my having coffee and being caught in the rain, to 'take it in' and then fragment what he had thus taken in, to evacuate these fragments and leave them scattered over a wide space of time, then that would be what he was doing. The two facts appear in the analysis as if they have been embedded in the elastic moment of time that has been stretched out to cover an enormous area. How far is it safe to use such descriptions as a valid basis for conjecture? I can imagine that this patient's grasp of fact is so slight that he has not enough with which to provide a cover for his psychotic mechanisms. Further, I can suppose that the obtrusion of psychotic mechanisms is such that the 'skin' or 'sanity' is stretched to breaking-point. Either description is likely to be so limited as to lead to a multiplicity of theories to serve a single configuration. But an illumination for the psycho-analyst does not necessarily provide illumination for someone not sharing the experience or illuminate for the patient who shares the experience but who transforms it under hallucinosis.

This problem prompts comparison of interpretation with the matter interpreted, or comparison of the category of associations with the category of the interpretation; the grid is an instrument by which this can be effected. If some relationship between the categories could be established it might be possible to discover the nature of the relationship between psychotic association and the appropriate interpretation. This involves a further look at projective transformation.

The views expressed about memory and desire and the need for their regulation as the psycho-analyst's preparation for his work provide a starting-point for reconsidering the nature of the projective transformation. Hallucinosis, which can be *observed* by divesting oneself of memory and desire, must have had some corresponding mechanism in the events that led to its inception. If the analyst can take certain steps that enable him to 'see' what the patient sees, it is reasonable to suppose that the patient has likewise 'taken steps', though not necessarily the same ones, to enable him to 'see' what he sees.

4 · *Opacity of Memory and Desire*

The 'act of faith' (*F*) depends on disciplined denial of memory and desire. A bad memory is not enough: what is ordinarily called forgetting is as bad as remembering. It is necessary to inhibit dwelling on memories and desires. They are two facets of the same thing: both are composed of elements based on sense impressions; both imply the absence of immediate sensual satisfaction; one supposes a store of sensual objects, the memory being the container, and the other a conjunction of sensually satisfying objects. The invariants are an inside and an outside composed of objects which are sensible. The more the psycho-analyst occupies himself with memory and desire the more his facility for harbouring them increases and the nearer he comes to undermining his capacity for F. For consider: if his mind is preoccupied with what is or is not said, or with what he does or does not hope, it must mean that he cannot allow the experience to obtrude, particularly that aspect of it which is more than the sound of the patient's voice or the sight of his postures. What sounds the patient makes, or what spectacle he presents, relates to O only in so far as O has evolved into the K domain.

Uninhibited exercise of memories and desires is indistinguishable from, inseparable from, and analogous to, making pre-conception impossible by virtue of leaving no unsaturated element (the desire or the memory precludes pre-conception if it occupies the 'space' that should remain unsaturated). If the mind is preoccupied with elements perceptible to sense it will be that much less able to perceive elements that cannot be sensed. Yet obviously anxiety cannot be said, except by analogy, to be smelled or touched or felt. Even so, anxiety comes nearer to being 'sensed' than many more subtle aspects of the personality which do nevertheless exist. It is important that the analyst should avoid mental activity, memory and desire, which is as harmful to his mental fitness as some forms of physical activity are to physical fitness.

'Past' and 'future' represent a realization related to another realization represented by the terms 'internal' and 'external'. The past is something contained 'within' the 'memory', and the 'future' something that cannot be so contained. 'Memories' can be regarded as possessions; desires, though just as much 'in' the mind as are memories, and therefore just as much 'possessions', are spoken of as if they 'possessed' the mind. A certain class of patient feels 'possessed' by or imprisoned 'in' the mind of the analyst if he considers the analyst desires something relative to him – his presence, or his cure, or his welfare. I have said if the patient 'considers' the analyst desires something, but in fact to say in this context that the patient 'considers' is to use an approximation that may be misleading because its penumbra of association conceals more than it reveals of the state of mind of the patient. The patient is in a state of mind for which there is no verbal apparatus and the psycho-analyst is constantly faced by the need to produce his own apparatus for investigation while he is carrying on the investigation. If the psycho-analyst has not deliberately divested himself of memory and desire the patient can 'feel' this and is dominated by the 'feeling' that he is possessed by and contained in the analyst's state of mind, namely, the state represented by the term 'desire'.

A means of representing mental phenomena without words (which are unsuitable because of their background of sensible experience) is required. The patient uses words that represent visual images, or he may be mute for long periods, or use words that are evocations of emotion, sometimes powerful emotions, but challenge the psycho-analyst to detect a content and express it in ordinary English. Evocations of anger, anxiety, fear, pity, hate, and loyalty to himself often include words that give the total a particular coloration: wreath, upset, cemetery, may be words scattered through the flow in such a way as to suggest bereavement; or solicitors, damages, illness, to suggest legal proceedings.

In this way he appears to be having an experience that he is not able to represent in terms of ordinary speech. He could be described therefore as suffering from a speech disorder were it not that the disturbance would appear to be inadequately or eccentrically described in such terms; reciprocally, to ordinary view, it seems eccentric to say that a stammerer suffers from a psychosis. But in fact the descriptions of the psychotic patient as having a speech disorder and the stammerer as being psychotic both have substance, and in both eccentricity depends on the vertex. 'Stammer' and 'psychosis' are vertices displaying the same configuration in a manner that illuminates characteristics just as binocular vision demonstrates qualities that require stereoscopy to make them manifest.

Freud, in a letter to Lou Andreas-Salome, suggested his method of achieving a state of mind which would give advantages that would compensate for obscurity when the object investigated was peculiarly obscure. He speaks of blinding himself artificially. As a method of achieving this artificial blinding I have indicated the importance of eschewing memory and desire. Continuing and extending the process, I include understanding and sense perception with the properties to be eschewed. The suspension of memory, desire, understanding, and sense impressions may seem to be impossible without a complete denial of reality; but the psycho-analyst is seeking something that differs from what is normally known as reality; a criticism that applies to what is ordinarily meant by reality does not indicate undesirability for the purpose of achieving contact with psychic reality, namely, the evolved characteristics of O. This procedure is valid in psycho-analysis and other sciences; F, likewise, is an essential component of scientific procedure however rigorous.

There is the possibility of suppressing one or all of these functions of memory, desire, understanding, and sense either together or in turn. Practice in suppression of these faculties may lead to an ability to suppress one or other according to need, so that suspension of one might enhance the effect of domination by the other in a manner analogous to the use of alternate eyes.

Before considering the distinction to be made between total suppression, sleep or other recognized states we must consider in more detail what is meant by understanding or memory or desire. I accept Freud's view of memory and its relationship with notation (Freud, 1911). Since all memory has a background of sense impressions, the appropriate category is row C. As there are a number of respects in which memory and desire seem to have a similar configuration I propose to consider only the C3 function of memory. What of a 'memory' of a gratification that was *missed*? – an unfulfilled desire must be classed as a desire.[1] If the constellation of thought to which it belongs is associated with feelings of grievance, regret, or remorse, such a desire may have to be regarded by the psycho-analyst as dominating or possessing the memory. A practising psycho-analyst has to decide whether he is psycho-analytically witnessing the operation of a *particular* internal object or not. Does the patient feel like that, or does what he feels like approximate to the formulations of Melanie Klein? I am concerned with developing a mode of thought which is such that a correct clinical observation can be made, for if *that* is achieved there is always hope of evolution of the appropriate theory. Defective observation means that a correct interpretation is an accident. The memory can become possessed by a desire; it can cease to be felt as a possession but itself becomes a possessor of the personality that harbours it. The category is no longer C3. What then is it? The unwelcome answer is that so long as progress, growth, is taking place, no one knows.

The probability is that either a process of rationalization

[1] To be a desire the idea must be felt to be unfulfilled.

leads to its conversion to categories D → F and columns 2, 4, 5, 6, n − 1, n 1, or it becomes fixed in row C and column 2. The need to resist the impact of changing circumstances requires that the C2 memory should become more and more independent of, and impervious to, the world of reality (sensible). These are developments in the category C3(2) and are, according to intensity, memories of sense impressions designed to act as a barrier *against* sense impressions; it would seem likely to lead to a development akin to hallucinations. The solution of the problem is made nearer by giving 'projective identification' a direction and greatly increasing the vertices and destinations. Not enough attention is paid to the unconscious as itself a destination of the projected object nor yet to the evacuation from the mental world into the sensible world and so out of the mental system.

Desire is similar to memory in that both have a background of sense impressions. But desire relates to that which is felt not to be possessed; it is 'unsaturated'. There is therefore a correspondence between desire as an unsaturated term and the evolution of O it represents. The problem in discussing O is that the discussion can only be about evolved characteristics of O (K) whereas F is related to O itself.

The problem of differentiating desire from memory lies in the fact that it is 'located' in a 'place' which cannot be determined any more than can the 'place' where parallel lines of a railway-track meet. 'Where' is a term with a background of sense impressions. The difference between desire and memory has no background of sense impressions and cannot be discussed adequately in terms that have such a background. Nevertheless, in psycho-analytic practice it is possible to decide when memory is being experienced by the patient and when desire: one is the 'past' tense and the other the 'future'. The decision depends on the fact that the experience the analyst has of the patient's experience is different from the patient's experience. Investigation of the problems involved depends on F. This means that the understanding of the patient and the identification with him that have been regarded as sufficient hitherto must be replaced by something quite different. The transformation in K must be replaced by the transformation in O, and K must be replaced by F. Now in transformations in K, the point on which attention is focused lies on the line of intersection of the evolution of O with $T\alpha$ to produce $T\beta$. In transformation in O, the attention is focused beyond the intersection and in O. $T\alpha$ and $T\beta$ are therefore projections onto a surface from a point at O (infinity), and although O (infinity) is inaccessible to K it is perfectly accessible to T in O. The analyst has to *become infinite* by the suspension of memory, desire, understanding. The emotional state of transformations in O is akin to dread as it is represented by the formulation:

Like one that on a lonesome road
Doth walk in fear and dread;
And having once turned round walks on,
And turns no more his head;
Because he knows a frightful fiend
Doth close behind him tread.

The 'frightful fiend' represents indifferently the quest for truth or the active defences against it, depending on the vertex.

The menace to 'reality' is felt to derive from: (1) the suppression of memory, desire, and understanding, for such suppression undermines sense-based experience which is the reality with which the individual is familiar; (2) the increase of power of F, which reveals and makes possible experiences that are often painful and difficult for the individual analyst and analysand to tolerate; and (3) the peculiar type of relationship between one element and another in the O domain. Included in this is a relationship that is indifferently expressed as spatial or temporal. Thus, in my quotation, the walker is being 'overtaken' by dread; he walks a 'lonesome road'. It may seem improbable that dread should be associated with analytic progress towards a more realistic outlook. I shall therefore discuss the phenomenon at greater length.

First it is to be noted that the submergence of memory, desire, and understanding appears not only to run flat contrary to accepted procedure but also to be close to what occurs spontaneously in the severely regressed patient.[1] The analyst who tries this disciplinary activity will find it disturbing despite his own analysis, however thorough and prolonged it might have been. It is necessary to consider why this should be so.

Desire, memory, and understanding are based on sensuous experience, expressed in terms whose background is precisely the same experience and which are designed for use related to that experience. They are vitiated by the same defect as are formulations based on a background of inanimate reality when they are applied to biological reality. Anxiety, depression, persecution are not *sensed* (though common usage sanctions an analogical use of the term 'sensed' in a context in which it is not appropriate). The nearer the analyst comes to achieving suppression of desire, memory, and understanding, the more likely he is to slip into a sleep akin to stupor. Though different, the difference is hard to define. The sharpening of contact with O cannot be separated from an increase of perception, in particular of elements of K; this sensuous sharpening is painful although partial and mitigated by the general obliteration of sensory perception. The residual sensory perception, often auditory and restricted to particular kinds of sound, is responsible for inducing a sharp and painful reaction (similar to the startle reaction seen in babies).

Furthermore, the sacrifice of pleasure and pain is a deprivation that is not easily tolerated in prospect and is disliked by the analysand when he senses it in the analyst. The deprivation corresponds to displacement of the pleasure–

[1] There are real dangers associated with the appearance; this is why the procedure here adumbrated is advocated only for the psycho-analyst whose own analysis has been carried at least far enough for the recognition of paranoid–schizoid and depressive positions.

pain principle from its dominant position. This would not matter were it not for a simultaneous apparent deposition of the reality principle, for that is based on a background of realizations which are perceptible to the psyche through the mediation of the senses. The disciplined increase of F by suppression of K, or subordination of transformations in K to transformations in O, is therefore felt as a very serious attack on the ego until F has become established. If psychoanalytic method is narrowly conceived of as consisting in the accumulation of knowledge (possessiveness), in harmony with the reality principle, and divorced from the processes of maturation and growth (either because growth is not recognized or because it is recognized but felt to be unattainable and beyond the control of the individual), it becomes a potent stimulus of envy. A further source of distortion is the tendency to link F with the supernatural because of lack of experience of the 'natural' to which it relates. The tendency is to introduce a god or devil that F is to reveal (or that is to 'evolve' from O). The element F, which should remain unsaturated, becomes saturated and unfitted for its purpose. The progressive stages in the disciplinary exercise proposed for the analyst are repellent rather than attractive. The more the analyst becomes expert in excluding memory, desire, and understanding from his mental activity, the more he is likely, at least in the early stages, to experience painful emotions that are usually excluded or screened by the conventional apparatus of 'memory' of the session, analytical theories, often disguised desires or denials of ignorance, and 'understanding' (which consists more often than not of column 2 elements). I exclude consideration of painful experiences in so far as they lie in unresolved conflicts in the analyst, for these do not differ from similar experiences in the practice of accepted methods; I have nothing to add to what is already known of counter-transference and the complications to which it may give rise. But it may be as well to glance at some of the more common experiences if only as a warning to anyone disposed to practise the approach I advocate.

In the first place, the analyst will soon find that he appears to be ignorant of knowledge which he has hitherto regarded as the hallmark of scrupulous medical responsibility. It is disconcerting to find that one is without an idea, say, that the patient has been married, or has children, or of certain events deemed by the analysand to have been of great significance. If the patient has paranoid trends and displays a tendency towards litigation it may seem to be running an unwarranted risk to be ignorant of matters that could, in a court of law, be regarded as significant and as evidence of ordinary medical care for detail. This would indeed be the case if there were not cogent reasons for *not* 'remembering' such detail. As it is, I think that whatever the risks may be the obligation is for the analyst to conduct the case in accordance with his lights – and not in accordance with the supposed risks to himself. In this method the experience the analyst gains bears little resemblance to the files and case-histories with which psychiatry is familiar. It may appear to differ from what would be expected in the light of accepted analytic theory. Thus an analyst may feel, to take a common example, that his married patient is unmarried; if so, it means that psycho-analytically his patient *is* unmarried: the emotional reality and the reality based on the supposition of the marriage contract are discrepant. If this seems to suggest the analyst must preserve his capacity for memory, I maintain that he always does (as does the patient, however regressed), but error is more likely to arise through inability to *divest* oneself of memory than through forgetfulness. If the analyst does not remember that his patient is married, the fact that he *is* is irrelevant until the patient says something that reminds the analyst of this fact.

I have spoken of the 'fact' that the patient is married. Sooner or later it will be necessary to abandon locutions which, though helpful when adumbrated (i.e. used to bind a constant conjunction), become unable to fulfil the function for which they are intended. To take the present instance as an example: provided one does not consider too deeply what is meant, no difficulty is experienced in using the phrase, or the idea that is represented by the phrase, 'the patient is married'. But in psycho-analysis such matters as the patient's marriage have to be considered deeply. Is an overt practising homosexual with several children and a wife with whom he has entered into the marriage contract married? In psycho-analysis the answer does not depend only on what is meant by marriage, because marriage is but one 'element' among many: for example, the 'meaning' of having several children, or a wife or husband with whom a legal marriage has been contracted. In such a context the value can be seen of regarding both the term 'marriage' (the verbal expression) and the fact of several children, and a wife or husband, as 'statements' whose grid category can be determined. If one considers the 'fact' of marriage it soon becomes necessary to suppose a number of different kinds of fact, such as a fact of 'external reality' or a fact of 'psychic reality'. Such terms are useful but they are themselves statements, and the belief that an event belongs to a category of 'events of external reality' leads to confusion and contradiction. It is simpler to regard the patient's statements as having a category in the vertex of the analyst and to observe that they do not, in the analyst's view, 'mean' that the patient is married (i.e. they are not column 3 elements) but that they have a particular category and that it is from the analyst's assessment of the category that the 'meaning' derives. *His* unsaturated elements are saturated. What the patient *thinks* he means is, as far as the analyst is concerned, irrelevant, but what the statement *is*, and to what use it is put, *is* relevant. What matters is that to statements of a particular category the patient begins to add statements of a different category. The patient whose statements have at no time suggested to the analyst that he, the patient, is married, now, at a particular point in his analysis, introduces statements that indicate that he *is*; that is to say, he behaves in a way that makes the analyst regard his statements as belonging to new categories including column 6 (he is asserting that he has actually *done* something, resorted to the kind of statement that consists in actually doing something, e.g. getting married).

Now it is clear that if the psycho-analyst has allowed himself the unfettered play of memory, desire, and understanding, his pre-conceptions will be habitually saturated and his 'habits' will lead him to resort to instantaneous and well-practised saturation from 'meaning' rather than from O.

When the psycho-analyst anticipates some crisis, and especially if he has, or thinks he has, good grounds for anxiety, his tendency is to resort to memory and understanding to satisfy his desire for security (or to resort to 'saturation' to avoid 'unsaturation'). If he gives in to this tendency he is proceeding in a direction calculated to preclude any possibility of union with O. This is understood by the psychotic patient, who does not resort to resistances but relies on being able to evoke the resistance-proliferating elements in his analyst; in other words, to stimulate the analyst's desires (notably for a successful outcome of the analysis), his memories, and his understanding, thereby intending that his analyst's state of mind will not be open to the experience of which he might otherwise be a witness.

This digression brings us back to the question of what is to be regarded as a fact. It appears to mean that the analysis should reinforce doubts of 'facts' which are part of 'memory'. The tendency to try to recall some supposed 'cause' of the crisis and to desire some different and more pleasing situation must be resisted. At best it can only recall some episode supposed to be the 'cause'. The 'recalled memory' saturates the psycho-analyst's pre-conceptions and obscures the issues at the one point where clarity of judgement and scope for its exercise are able to coincide – the current session.

To repeat: the capacity to forget, the ability to eschew desire and understanding, must be regarded as essential discipline for the psycho-analyst. Failure to practise this discipline will lead to a steady deterioration in the powers of observation whose maintenance is essential. The vigilant submission to such discipline will by degrees strengthen the analyst's mental powers just in proportion as lapses in this discipline will debilitate them. This view departs from commonly accepted practice and it may be as well, therefore, to consider the theoretical basis implicit in accepted practice.

The idea that patient A comes five times a week and has been doing so for months or years is based on a background of sense impressions and a view of the individual's continuity as an individual which is primitive and crude. It is the emergence of primitive number as a method of asserting 'constant conjunction', of asserting that the object is recurrent, that the 'breast' is something that reappears. We are not concerned with the patient's anatomy; a belief that no cellular changes take place in twenty-four hours is unwarranted on any but a crudely macroscopic view. The mental phenomena with which we are confronted cannot possibly have remained unaltered even if no analysis had been done. The mental phenomena should reveal invariance and it should be possible to observe the invariants embedded in these phenomena, but an invariant is a characteristic not of permanence but of transformation. It must be sought for in transformation. A psycho-analyst who remembers that A is the same person as A was yesterday indulges a column 2 element. Nor is there any reason for the analysand to believe that the analyst is the same person as the analyst of the previous day. Such belief is suspect as the sign of a collusive relationship intended to prevent emergence of an unknown, incoherent, formless void and an associated sense of persecution by the elements of an evolving O.

Desire, memory, understanding thus have the column 2 function of keeping F at bay and preventing the transformation in K from becoming transformation in O. Ostensibly they represent a compromise, for not only do they preclude F and transformations in O but they substitute transformations in K which give a similitude of transformation in O and make the pre-conception (D) in K serve as a saturation rather than as a means to a saturation. 'How I wish I had the chance to swim!' expresses the idea that a particular state of completion (wishing to swim) has been achieved and precludes the unsaturation that would be felt were the individual to *wish* to swim. Of all the hateful possibilities, growth and maturation are feared and detested most frequently. This hostility to the process of maturation becomes most marked when maturation seems to involve the subordination of the pleasure principle and the emergence of the reality principle. The change cannot be regarded as hated because it involves loss of pleasure, for the activity of the pleasure principle means activity of pain. Similarly, the continuation of pleasure when the dominance of the pleasure principle is in abeyance is not precluded by the dominance of the reality principle. But the change from pleasure principle to reality principle does mean abandonment of control over the proportion of pain to pleasure and leaves it to forces that are outside the personality. At-one-ment or unity with O is in prospect fearful. No experience challenging this preconception prevails because it is embodied in memory and desire, belongs to K, and does not transform into, though it may mark the inception of, O.

The central point appears to be the painful nature of change in the direction of maturation. It is probably idle to ask why it should be painful, why intensity of pain bears so little relationship to intensity of recognizable danger, and why pain is so feared. There is no doubt that mental pain in particular is feared in a way that would be appropriate if it corresponded directly with mental danger. The relationship of pain to danger is, however, obscure. In this it is not peculiar, for any relationship of one element of the personality with another seems difficult to determine. A science of relationships has yet to be established and one would look to find some discipline analogous to mathematics to represent the relationship of one element in the structure of the psychic personality with another. It is possible to argue that mathematical formulations can be fully appreciated because there is always some more concrete background to which they can be seen to relate, *even though that background may itself be only mathematical.* Something similar may be possible in the relationship of elements of the structure of personality. Envy is typical of other elements of the personality in that everyone would be prepared to admit its existence. Yet it does not smell; it is invisible, inaudible, intangible. It has no shape. It must have invariance, or it could not be so widely and surely recognized; and if it has invariants it must be invariant with regard to some kind of operation and therefore there must be an underlying group of such operations.

5 · *Theories: Particular Instance or General Configuration*

Controversy is the growing-point from which development springs but it must be a genuine confrontation and not an impotent beating of the air by opponents whose differences of view never meet. What follows is a contribution to bringing different psycho-analytic views together in agreement or disagreement.

Hearing psycho-analytic controversy I have felt that the same configuration was being described and that the apparent differences were more often accidental than intrinsic; different points of view are believed to be significant of membership of a group, not of a scientific experience. Yet everyone knows that what is important is not the supposed use of a particular theory but whether the theory has been understood properly and then whether the application has been sound.

It may be objected that to establish this would involve consideration of every individual analyst and of the circumstances of every individual interpretation. Even so, many difficulties could be obviated by more precise definition of the point of view (vertex). It is permissible for an observer to say that he has no evidence of infantile sexuality provided he also adds that he is an aeronautical engineer and does not take anything but a cursory view of children. What is *not* permissible is that he should say that he has no evidence of infantile sexuality without mentioning his vertex. I hope that there will be evolved a method of designating the vertex with brevity and precision. The following is a loose description, by way of a prelude to something more scientific.

To attain to the state of mind essential for the practice of psycho-analysis I avoid any exercise of memory; I make no notes. When I am tempted to remember the events of any particular session I resist the temptation. If I find myself wandering mentally into the domain of memory I desist. In this my practice is at variance with the view that notes should be kept or that psycho-analysts should find some method by which they can record their sessions mechanically or should train themselves to have a good memory. If I find that I am without any clue to what the patient is doing and am tempted to feel that the secret lies hidden in something I have forgotten, I resist any impulse to remember what happened or how I interpreted what happened on some previous occasion. If I find that some half-memory is beginning to obtrude I resist its recall no matter how pressing or desirable its recall may seem to be.

A similar procedure is followed with regard to desires: I avoid entertaining desires and attempt to dismiss them from my mind. (It is not enough to try to do this in the session because that is too late: the habit of desiring must not be allowed to grow.) For example, I think it a serious defect to allow oneself to desire the end of a session, or week, or term; it interferes with analytic work to permit desires for the patient's cure, or well-being, or future to enter the mind. Such desires erode the analyst's power to analyse and lead to progressive deterioration of his intuition. Introspection will show how widespread and frequent memories and desires are. They are constantly present in the mind and to follow the advice I am giving is a difficult discipline. There are exceptions, all of a simple and obvious kind.

Some matters can be easily recorded and need not burden the mind, as, for example, the times of sessions. It would be absurd if the analyst forgot to keep them and they are easily recorded on a timetable. The same may be true of age, members of the family, past illnesses, and other such facts as fancy might dictate. But these are to be recorded, together with addresses and telephone numbers, because they can then be forgotten and because they lend themselves to record. While it can be precisely stated that the patient is married and has four children it is not easily stated that his state of mind is that of a married man with four children because there is no such state of mind. Furthermore, such a 'memory', and the remembrancer that such a note would provide, would greatly obscure observation of the patient's state of mind suppose it were to be more nearly what one might expect of a bachelor.

Matters that can be recorded with the means at present at our disposal, including mental means, are sensuous experiences, and the transformations they undergo issue in formulations which have all, mathematical formulations included, a sensuous background. The central phenomena of psycho-analysis have no background in sense data. Even the signs that accompany anxiety, for example increased respiration, would be more appropriate to smelling a danger, if that danger had a scent and our olfactory powers were well developed, than to detecting an endo-psychic phenomenon. An apparatus that might be useful where a danger is sensible is useless or obstructive when the danger derives from a background that is mental and not sensible. Therefore, keep records for events whose background is sensible, such as the time at which a patient is to appear, but not for phenomena of central concern to the psycho-analyst, since their background is not sensible.

How, then, are we to 'observe' and 'record' the patient's state of mind? Since I wish to discuss this but do not know the answer, I shall say 'by F'.

Freud said that he had to 'blind myself artificially to focus all the light on one dark spot'.[1] This provides a useful formulation for describing the area I wish to cover by F. By rendering oneself 'artificially blind' through the exclusion of memory and desire, one achieves F; the piercing shaft of darkness can be directed on the dark features of the analytic situation. Through F one can 'see', 'hear', and 'feel' the mental phenomena of whose reality no practising psycho-

[1] In the letter referred to on p. 43 above.

analyst has any doubt though he cannot with any accuracy represent them by existing formulations.

The vertex I have thus far attempted to represent in this description may later be more accurately defined. Even as it is, I hope that my description will serve to make certain advantages clear. For example, it is easier for another psycho-analyst to appreciate my work if he knows the vertex and can thus anticipate what he thinks are its merits and defects. He does not have to engage in a barren argument about the theories I use (in a context of which he can know nothing) if he is given some idea of the state of mind in which I apply them.

It can be seen that with one vertex theories might be useful that are not useful with another; that if the vertex were altered other theories would be required to illuminate the phenomena discussed. Conversely, another psycho-analyst could understand that I might 'see' the oedipal situation in a context in which he might not.

The rules are relatively easy for a psycho-analyst to obey, and if they are obeyed dissimilar people with dissimilar patients may yet have a similar experience and so tend less often to mistake for general laws what are in fact only particular instances of old ones.

The experience to which I refer is the contact with the evolved aspects of O, the realization that I have variously described as ultimate reality, the thing-in-itself, or truth. Logically, in so far as logic affords a model for the approach I am making, the absence of memory and desire should free the analyst of those peculiarities that make him a creature of his circumstances and leave him with those functions that are invariant, the functions that make up the irreducible ultimate man. In fact this cannot be. Yet upon his ability to approximate to this will depend his ability to achieve the 'blindness' that is a prerequisite for 'seeing' the evolved elements of O.

Reciprocally, his freedom from being 'blinded' by the qualities (or his perception of them) that belong to the domain of the senses should enable the analyst to 'see' those evolved aspects of O that are invariant in the analysand. The further the analysis progresses the more the psycho-analyst and the analysand achieve a state in which both contemplate the irreducible minimum that is the patient. (This irreducible minimum is incurable because what is seen is that without which the patient would not be the patient.)

Suppose the patient proliferates endless stories, coherent, plausible, and apparently true. After some analysis it becomes evident that something is wrong: the associations vary from accounts of episodes alleged to have happened and quite likely to have happened, to accounts that sound no less convincing but that reveal flaws. From internal evidence it is clear that the event could not have happened. But for incongruities, the tone of assurance of the narrative would have lulled all suspicion. If the narration is challenged the patient admits the fault and at once begins to proliferate further fabrications which invite the analyst either to withdraw his comments and acknowledge the truth of the patient's assertions or to say openly that he is lying.

It is not relevant to describe details of this case. By regarding the patient's statements as transformations and categorizing them by means of the grid, one can do something towards understanding what is taking place. I have advocated (in *Elements of psycho-analysis*) exercises of this kind but it must not be supposed that understanding of this nature is required. On the contrary, such 'understanding' can be seen to have as its background memory and desire and should therefore be avoided. The importance of the exercise is to facilitate the analyst's capacity for conjecture, not to intrude upon an analytic session. If the analysis is conducted as I advocate, the 'evolution of O' becomes manifest in the chains of fabrications such as I have described. It should be possible to observe a wide spectrum of categories of lies and what they represent. The flow of associations demands a high degree of inventiveness and speed (especially in sealing off any breach in the fabrications), and a measure of verbal facility that may give an impression of intelligence, especially if memory and desire distort judgement of the category. I am concerned here not with the diagnosis, prognosis, treatment, or cure, but with the O of psycho-analysis.

From one vertex it might seem that the analysand was 'blinding' the analyst in that the analyst was flooded with illumination – so many facts that the 'obscure' point could not be 'seen'. Is this statement distinguishable from the state produced if the analyst is not successful in ridding himself of memory and desire? Only the psycho-analytic session can provide the answer. Extra-analytic activity stimulates doubt and curiosity in the analyst. Such a patient stimulates memory and desire by appearing to satisfy but without doing so; the analyst is tacitly invited to 'remember' all he is told.

A number of questions, of which the following are a few, are posed by this behaviour:

1. Are the patient's statements lies? Is 'lie' the most appropriate term to use? If not, what is the correct formulation?

2. Why does the patient transform in fabrications and what does he thus transform?

3. Does the fabrication differ from myth? It is often a plausible and coherent narrative, but it seems to declare itself to be category 3 when in fact it would appear to be C2. What, then, are the emotional experiences that are to be covered up and not allowed to emerge?

4. How do the patient's statements differ from other false statements? Respect for the truth appears to have low value compared with other vertices. What, then, is the vertex? –K? How does this compare with Plato's objections to the poet in society? With regard to other false statements it is usually supposed that there is either a mistaken idea that the lie is correct, or a belief that some reward attaches to being able to mislead. Some statements appear to be without reward to either party but perhaps there is a pleasure in creation even though creation can be achieved only by a lie. Is it a *folie à deux* – a

collaboration? Certainly with F it could be a sado-masochistic collusion to 'poison' or be 'poisoned'.

These questions can be answered only in analytic contact with the patient. The grid, or some improved version of it, facilitates mental gymnastics in preparation for it.

6 · *The Mystic and the Group*

It seems absurd that a psycho-analyst should be unable to assess the quality of his work. In attempting an assessment he has available popular repute (notoriously fickle and unreliable, and unsuited for use as a foundation for any judgement), anxiety, or a sense of satisfaction and well-being about a piece of work that appears to him to be well done. This last is probably as reliable a foundation as any, but is subject to doubt and misgiving. The only other person well placed to have an opinion is the analysand. His opinion is likewise a matter for scrutiny. The friendly or hostile feelings revealed converge towards a point where there should be a wise and compassionate, though critical, judgement. Instead there is an intuition, 'That is truth, accept it.' Such formulations are not regarded as scientifically adequate and one craves something better. The craving cannot be satisfied unless it is recognized that standpoints such as religion, art, science, as we understand them today, are as unsatisfactory as the formulations truth, beauty, god, or future life.

The formulation is the end-product of a transformation; all transformations are associated with a particular vertex. The psycho-analyst is faced at an early date in his own development and at an early stage in the development of psycho-analysis itself with problems that arise because no vertex at present recognized is adequate. It is as absurd to criticize a piece of psycho-analytic work on the ground that it is 'not scientific' as it is to criticize it because it is 'not religious' or 'not artistic'. It is not any of these things. Its failure to be so is a criticism; but its 'success' at being any of them would not remove the reproach. The critical formulation for which there is no substitute is that it is 'not psycho-analysis'.

It would seem that we are as far as ever from a positive result to the discussion; 'psycho-analysis' must be regarded as a term binding a constant conjunction. Years must pass before we understand what are conjoined and what the conjunction means. Can it be done in verbal terms? Are there any other terms?

It has been said in criticism of psycho-analysis that it cannot be regarded as a science because it cannot be mathematized. Available mathematics do not provide the psycho-analyst with appropriate formulations. The same is true of available verbalizations, but this has been obscured because ordinary conversation has served fairly well for the analysands who have come for analysis hitherto. This situation has been altered by the advent of so-called severe cases on the one hand, and by the needs of communication between psycho-analytic colleagues on the other. It is clear that a development is required that will help psycho-analysis in a manner analogous to that in which modern mathematics has helped the development of physics. In the meantime we are thrown back on existing verbal, mathematical, and artistic formulations and the exceptional individuals capable of employing them. Genius has been said to be akin to madness. It would be more true to say that psychotic mechanisms require a genius to manipulate them in a manner adequate to promote growth or life (which is synonymous with growth).

The group needs to preserve its coherence and identity; efforts to do so are manifested in conventions, laws, culture, and language. It also needs the exceptional individual and therefore needs to make provision for the exceptional individual. This might be simple if exceptional individuals declared themselves in unexceptionable terms and if the nature of their impact on the group, its laws and conventions, could be judged as life-giving or the reverse. The possibility of such discrimination is doubtful and, centuries after, it may still be debated whether an individual of this kind exerted a beneficial or deleterious effect. The same is true of ideas; furthermore, groups are hostile or friendly, favourable or unfriendly, to the development of the new person or idea.

The 'exceptional individual' may be variously described as a genius, a messiah, a mystic, and his following may be large or small. The negative group declares itself an enemy of promise in a manner that may not be discernible to ordinary individuals, but is apparently clear to the gifted individual who seeks an atmosphere more congenial to the exercise of his gifts. For convenience, I shall use the term 'mystic' to describe these exceptional individuals. I include scientists, and Newton is the outstanding example of such a man: his mystical and religious preoccupations have been dismissed as an aberration when they should be considered as the matrix from which his mathematical formulations evolved.

The mystic may declare himself as revolutionary or he may claim that his function is to fulfil the laws, conventions, and destiny of his group. It would be surprising if any true mystic were not regarded by the group as a mystical nihilist at some stage of his career and by a greater or less proportion of the group. It would be equally surprising if he were not in fact nihilistic to some group if for no other reason than that the nature of his contribution is certain to be destructive of the laws, conventions, culture, and therefore coherence, of a group within the group, if not of the whole group. In this it is evident that the character of the group, which I do not discuss, cannot be excluded from the facts of the evolution of a mystic in a group. The disruptive force of the mystical nihilist, or of the mystic whose impact on a particular group is of a disruptive or nihilist character, extends to and depends on the Language of Achievement, be it expressed in action, speech, writing, or aesthetic. Usually the spread of the disruptive force is limited by the vehicle of communication. The phenomena of destruction remain the same but reception of their message varies, often being restricted to relatively few.

Melanie Klein writes of symbol formation as if it were a particular function that could distintegrate or be disordered and give rise to deep disturbance in a personality; there are realizations that correspond to this theory, but I think the area of disturbance should be regarded as greater than her theory implies. For example, the psychotic patient does not always behave as if he is incapable of symbol formation. Indeed, he often talks or behaves as if he is convinced that certain actions, which to me are innocent of any symbolic significance, are obviously symbolic. They mean, apparently obviously, some message which is of personal and particular concern to him. This 'meaning' is quite different from the meaning one assumes to lie behind a constant conjunction that is public and not private to one individual. The former is, and appears to belong to, a private communication made by God (or Devil or Fate); when the psychotic symbol is met with in practice its significance seems to be less that it symbolizes something, more that it indicates that the patient is in private rapport with a deity or demon. The symbol, as it is usually understood, represents a conjunction which is recognized by a group to be constant; as encountered in psychosis it represents a conjunction between a patient and his deity which the patient feels to be constant.

The 'symbol' can be an attempt of the personality to use its experience to formulate a theory, which may then be used when the appropriate realization presents itself, or an attempt to use an external event, e.g. a meeting with an acquaintance, to yield an interpretation *as if it were* a symbol. Thus an adverse circumstance can be used as a 'symbol' (not 'sign') of God's wrath, or past experiences can be represented by symbols whose genetic base is in their *sensuous* background. The emotional experience is thus made manageable by being symbolized, whether it is in origin felt to be a response to a painful external stimulus, or whether the external experience is felt to be the confirmation of a painful internal psychic experience.

The inescapable bestiality of the human animal is the

quality from which our cherished and admired characteristics spring. 'Man is a political animal' means that he has the mental counterpart of the physical characteristics of a herd animal. As psycho-analysts, we are concerned with the mental counterpart of such physical characteristics as can be discerned in the individual when in semi-isolation from his group, but closely involved in a situation likely to stimulate his 'pair' characteristics. Birth, dependence, pairing, and warfare – these are the basic situations to which the basic emotional drives correspond.

This summary of the human condition adds nothing new to what is already familiar, in greater detail, to every psycho-analyst. The summary is intended as a reminder that the analytic situation itself, and then the psycho-analytic occupation or task itself, are bound to stimulate primitive and basic feeling in analyst and analysand. Therefore, if the technique I propose for ensuring vivid appreciation of the emotional facts is as sound as I think it, these fundamental characteristics, love, hate, dread, are sharpened to a point where the participating pair may feel them to be almost unbearable: it is the price that has to be paid for the transformation of an activity that is *about* psycho-analysis into an activity that *is* psycho-analysis. The activity that is psycho-analysis evokes desires to know how the group is reacting to the pair relationship; this desire often masquerades as a wish for validation, popular repute, or approval.

We thus return to the original problem (p. 6f. above) and the impulse to repudiate the approach I have adumbrated. The more reminiscence is indulged, the farther one is removed from a form of anxiety: one's historical identity is asserted, one was such and such and had certain recognized and remembered associates; one has done as well as, or less well than, so and so. It is doubtful whether these 'historical' reminiscences would be corroborated by any of the characters who figure in one's own story, but they serve to deny the painfulness of the actual predicament that is the source of embarrassment. It is difficult, short of hallucination, to do anything about the present predicament: reminiscence becomes a C2 category orgy to keep out the painful insights that follow on denial of sensuous experience.

There is one form of denial of sensuous experience that has been a commonplace since Freud pointed out that analysis must be conducted in an atmosphere of deprivation.[1] It has not been recognized that to achieve this it is not enough to hope that analysis of the analyst and denial of the patient's wishes will serve. Anyone who considers it possible to achieve a suitable frame of mind by a few minutes of psychological tidying up before starting work cannot have grasped the nature of the discipline necessary to be an analyst or the nature of the insights that become available to the analysed analyst if he brings 'artificial blindness' to bear on his dark spots. It may well be that analysts who attempt the approach advocated in Chapter 4 on 'Memory and Desire' will find that the intuitions achieved by it cause them to feel the need for further analysis. It is possible that the test of sensuous deprivation involved in eschewing memory and desire will bring to light a need for analysis that exists because the analytic experience has not been sufficient, or it may be that it indicates an *additional* demand that would not have occurred had the analyst remained content with the 'atmosphere of deprivation' as it has been understood hitherto. The point is of moment because, if the abandonment of memory and desire brings a need for increased stamina, analysts may have to accept that advances in insight have to be matched by further analysis. Such a contingency imposes revision of training and maintenance of capacity for a psycho-analytic career.

Though it is easy to envisage the need for further analysis, it is not certain that the further analysis must be similar to analysis as experienced and understood when we undergo our first analysis. The importance of the unconscious must not blind us to the fact that in addition to our unconscious memories and desires, dealt with psycho-analytically, there

[1] Discussed in detail in a paper by Dr Samuel Futterman of Los Angeles.

is a problem to solve in the handling of our conscious memories and desires. What kind of 'psycho-analysis' is required for the conscious?

The psychotic *is* conscious of what we feel requires analysis; to approach this problem it will be necessary to discuss memory and desire relative to loss of contact with reality. It has been supposed that the psychotic severs links with reality as a step to a sexual life in phantasy, but it is equally intended to establish freedom from sexual and allied stimulation. He appears to achieve a result resembling the neurotic patient's contact with the unconscious as it is known in classical analysis. The psychotic seems to have the same relationship and attitude to what he has *not* been able to repress, and what therefore remains conscious, that other patients have to the unconscious. The neurotic patient is concerned to show that neurotic elements in his behaviour are rational and does his best to rationalize them. The psychotic can 'see' that any action has a symbolic meaning and that the conjunction of the elements is not fortuitous but has a meaning which is clear *to him*. This is possible provided he has severed all links with anything that shows the conjunction to be fortuitous and devoid of meaning, that is, in my terminology, unsaturated – a D category element. The premature saturation involved in this has the paradoxical effect that all acts are symbolic and yet the patient is incapable of symbol formation in the way open to the normal personality who can allow his elements to remain unsaturated. Contact with reality is unwelcome because it tends not only to show that an element is unsaturated but also to saturate the element in ways that are painful to the personality. As all his 'symbols' have an obvious meaning they can hardly be regarded as symbols at all and nothing is left that can fulfil the function that symbols fill for the non-psychotic personality.

How does this differ from the state produced by the elimination of memory and desire?

First, I am advocating only a partial severance with

reality. Second, it is a deliberate, conscious act of discipline. Third, it has a purpose that would appear to differ from the purpose of the psychotic manoeuvre. He wishes to destroy contact; I wish to establish it. Furthermore, he is primarily concerned with destruction of sensuous contact and its concomitant saturation whereas I am anxious to diminish sensuous contact to bring psychic reality into focus. The psychotic fears and hates that result; it is an extension of reality.

The domain of personality is so extensive that it cannot be investigated with thoroughness. The power of psycho-analysis demonstrates to any practising psycho-analyst that adjectives like 'complete' or 'full' have no place in qualifying 'analysis'. The more nearly thorough the investigation, the clearer it becomes that however prolonged a psycho-analysis may be it represents only the start of an investigation. It stimulates growth of the domain it investigates. This difficulty I mean to exploit in this way: if it is true that the proportion of the known to the unknown is so small at the *end* of analysis, it must be even smaller *during* analysis. Therefore to spend time on what has been discovered is to concentrate on an irrelevance. What matters is the unknown and on this the psycho-analyst must focus his attention. Therefore 'memory' is a dwelling on the unimportant to the exclusion of the important. Similarly, 'desire' is an intrusion into the analyst's state of mind which covers up, disguises, and blinds him to, the point at issue: that aspect of O that is currently presenting the unknown and unknowable though it is manifested to the two people present in its evolved character. This is the 'dark spot' that must be illuminated by 'blindness'. Memory and desire are 'illuminations' that destroy the value of the analyst's capacity for observation as a leakage of light into a camera might destroy the value of the film being exposed.

To consider objections to the elimination of memory: it may seem impossible to have a link with a patient without remembering who he or she is; but such recognition does not depend on memory, nor does psycho-analysis. It depends on a background of an experience the peculiarity of which I shall indicate by a series of approximations. We are familiar with the experience of *remembering* a dream; this must be contrasted with dreams that float into the mind unbidden and unsought and float away again as mysteriously. The emotional tone of this experience is not peculiar to the dream: thoughts also come unbidden, sharply, distinctly, with what appears to be unforgettable clarity, and then disappear leaving no trace by which they can be recaptured. I wish to reserve the term 'memory' for experience related to conscious attempts at recall. These are expressions of a fear that some element, 'uncertainties, mysteries, doubts',[1] will obtrude.

Dream-like memory is the memory of psychic reality and is the stuff of analysis. That which is related to a background of sensuous experience is not suitable to the phenomena of mental life which are shapeless, untouchable, invisible, odourless, tasteless. These psychically real (in the sense of belonging to psychic reality) elements are what the analyst has to work with.

It may appear that this contradicts the psycho-analytic theory of dreams unless it is remembered that the dream is the *evolution* of O where O has evolved sufficiently to be represented by sensuous experience. The sensuous elements of a psychotic dream do not represent anything. They *are* a sensuous experience.[2]

Anyone who has made careful notes of what he considers to be the facts of a session must be familiar with the experience in which such notes will, on occasion, seem to be drained of all reality: they might be notes of dreams made to ensure that he will not forget them on waking. To me it suggests that the experience of the session relates to material akin to the dream, not in the sense that dreams might be part

[1] John Keats, 'Letter to George and Thomas Keats', 21 December 1817.

[2] The use of the sensuous experience to represent a psychic reality differentiates the neurotic dream and its symbolic quality from the psychotic dream.

of the preoccupation of the session but that the dream and the psycho-analyst's working material both share dream-like quality.

The *reality* of the psychic experience – the O in the human personality – is such that the more the analyst is in contact, the more real will be that part of it that he has been able to interpret. It will be clear to him that he is formulating only one aspect of a multi-dimensional experience. What will dwell in his mind will be the multi-dimensional experience. Once he has interpreted it the facet that he has interpreted ceases to be of moment. The psycho-analyst reads his notes with a sense of an emotional experience powerfully present in his mind, but it is of an experience of the as-yet unknown. It is against this powerful sense that he reads the note of an event which ceased to be of importance when it was formulated. The attempt to remember or record destroys the capacity for, and interrupts the exercise of, observation of the psycho-analytically significant events.

Conversely, the sacrifice of memory and desire is conducive to the growth of dream-like 'memory' which is a part of the experience of psycho-analytical reality. The transformation of the emotional experience into mental growth of analyst and analysand contributes to the difficulty of both to 'remember' what took place; in so far as the experience contributes to growth it ceases to be recognizable; if it does not become assimilated it adds to those elements that are remembered and forgotten. Desire obstructs the transformation from knowing and understanding to being, $K \rightarrow O$.

7 · *Container and Contained*

An advantage of believing that observations are the foundation of scientific method is that the conditions in which they are made can be stated and then produced. The simplicity of this has its appeal for the psycho-analyst: an analytic situation is presumed to exist and interpretations of the observations made in that situation are then reported. It is possible to believe that the analysis has a location in time and space: for example, the hours arranged for the sessions and the four walls of the consulting-room; that at such times and in such a place the analyst can make observations which he cannot do if the domain has not these limitations, or if 'psycho-analytic observations' do not conform to the conventional view of an observation. If I pictorialize the statement 'the conventional view of an observation' to be a container, like a sphere, and the 'psycho-analytic observation' as something that cannot be contained within it, I have a model that will do very well not only for the 'conventional view', to represent my feelings about a 'psycho-analytic situation', but also for the 'psycho-analysis' that it cannot contain. It will also serve as a model for my feelings about certain patients: I cannot observe Mr X because he will not remain 'inside' the analytic situation or even 'within' Mr X himself.

I have found theories of acting-out enlightening, but not enlightening enough; none of the theories known to me 'contains' the 'facts' by which I seek to be enlightened. My 'facts' gird against the framework of definition and theory which I seek to erect around them. The patient who is acting out cannot be 'contained' within existing formulations.

This is a characteristic of the mental domain: it cannot be contained within the framework of psycho-analytic theory. Is this a sign of defective theory, or a sign that psycho-analysts do not understand that psycho-analysis cannot be contained permanently within the definitions they use? It would be a valid observation to say that psycho-analysis cannot 'contain' the mental domain because it is not a 'container' but a 'probe'; the formulation that I have tried to further by using the symbols ♀ and ♂ minimizes this difficulty by leaving ♀ and ♂ as unknowns whose value is to be determined.

I would pursue this train of thought further by discussing something more practical and particular. It is a matter where action[1] seems to be called for, namely, the institutionalization of psycho-analysis comprising publication, selection, training, and qualification.

In recent years there has grown up the use of the term Establishment; it seems to refer to that body of persons in the State who may be expected usually to exercise power and responsibility by virtue of their social position, wealth, and intellectual and emotional endowment. (This list is not an order of priority of attainments.) I propose to borrow this term to denote everything from the penumbra of associations generally evoked, to the predominating and ruling characteristics of an individual, and the characteristics of a ruling caste in a group (such as a psycho-analytical institute, or a nation or group of nations). Because of my choice of subject it will usually be used for talking about the ruling 'caste' in psycho-analytical institutes.

The Establishment has to find and provide a substitute for genius. One of its more controversial activities is to promulgate rules (known in religious activities as dogmas, in scientific groups as 'laws', e.g. of nature or perspective) for the benefit of those who are not by nature fitted to have direct experience of *being* psycho-analytic (or religious, or scientific, or artistic) so that they may, as it were by proxy, have and impart knowledge of psycho-analysis. Group members will not through incapacity be denied a sense of participation

[1] I shall include psycho-analysis itself in the category of 'action' for reasons given under the heading of Language of Achievement in Chapter 13.

in an experience from which they would otherwise feel for ever excluded. At the same time these rules (or dogmas) must be such that they attract rather than repel, help rather than hinder, the membership of genius, which is essential to the group's continued existence and vitality. A Freud can discover and establish psycho-analysis, but it must be maintained by a continued supply of 'genius'. This cannot be ordered; but if it comes the Establishment must be able to stand the shock. Failing genius, and clearly it may not materialize for a very long period, the group must have its rules and a structure to preserve them. Thus an environment exists ready, as Nietzsche said of the nation, to fulfil its proper function, namely, to produce a genius. Similarly, it may be said of the individual that he should be ready to produce a 'flash of genius'. Let us therefore consider this phenomenon.

The term 'genius' does not carry the associations I want, so I propose to use the term 'mystic', leaving it to be supposed that the mystic has characteristics usually associated with genius and that the person represented by the term 'genius' or 'mystic' may with equal propriety be described by the term 'messiah'.

The mystic is both creative and destructive. I make a distinction between two extremes that coexist in the same person. The extreme formulations represent two types: the 'creative' mystic, who formally claims to conform to or even fulfil the conventions of the Establishment that governs his group; and the mystic nihilist, who appears to destroy his own creations. I mean the terms to be used only when there is outstanding creativeness or destructiveness, and the terms 'mystic', 'genius', 'messiah' could be interchangeable.

The problem posed by the relationship between the mystic and the institution has an emotional pattern that repeats itself in history and in a variety of forms. The pattern may appear in the relationship of a new phenomenon to the formulation that has to represent it. It appears in the relationship of widely dissimilar groups to their mystics; it reveals itself in the history of the Christian heresies, the heliocentric theories, the relationship of the rabbinical directorate of the Kabbalah to revolutionary mystics such as Isaac Luria, the political reformer, and the Establishment.

My object is to show that certain elements in the development of psycho-analysis are not new or peculiar to analysis, but have in fact a history that suggests that they transcend barriers of race, time, and discipline, and are inherent in the relationship of the mystic to the group. The Establishment cannot be dispensed with (though this may appear to be approximately achieved in Sufism and in the theory of Marxism) because the institutionalized group, the Work group (see Bion, 1961), is as essential to the development of the individual, including the mystic, as he is to it. Homeric psychology indicates a stage of mental development in which the distinction between man and god is ill defined; in the individual psyche, little distinction between ego and super-ego is recognized. The Work group, under the religious vertex, must differentiate between man and god. Institutionalized religion must make man conscious of this gulf in himself and in the counterparts of himself in the group of which he is a member.

The institutionalization of psycho-analysis requires a psycho-analytic group which has 'Establishment' as one of its functions. It is itself a replica, in the external world, of an object in which the desired separation has been effected. But its function is then to effect this separation in the personalities of its members. It is thus both a model of a state that is desired and an institution whose function it is to make the individual aware of the gap between himself (his idealized, super-egoized self) and himself (his unregenerate, un-psycho-analysed self).

One result of separation is no direct access of the individual to the god with whom he used formerly to be on familiar terms. But the god has undergone a change as a part of the process of discrimination. The god with whom he was familiar was finite; the god from whom he is now separated is transcendent and infinite.

To restate the above in terms appropriate to a background of human experience: Freud and his associates mix on terms of equality such as exist between any human colleagues in a common venture. Freud, merely by being a person of outstanding stature, stimulates the tensions and emotional drives appropriate to a primitive group and stimulates them still further by his work. The primitive stages of the analytic group contribute to the obtrusion of tensions and emotional drives appropriate to the primitive group, as Freud observed through his study of the individual. I doubt that he appreciated the force of the messianic hopes aroused. The primitive stage makes way for the stage of discrimination described in the religious group: a distinction is made, otherwise there will not be recognition of the real distinction that exists between a mystic (in my sense) and ordinary human beings.

This distinction cannot be achieved adequately by saying that it is inseparable from idealization. Idealization in the group is a reality-based activity which is essential for the growth of discrimination in the individual. The individual himself must be able to distinguish between himself as an ordinary person and his view that he is omniscient and omnipotent. It is a step towards recognition of a distinction between the group as it really is and its idealization as an embodiment of the omnipotence of the individuals who compose it. Sometimes the separation fails and the group is not only seen to be ideally omnipotent and omniscient but believed to be so in actuality. The individual's realization of a gulf between his view of himself as omnipotent and his view of himself as an ordinary human being must be achieved as the result of a task of the group itself as well as in individual analysis. Otherwise there is a danger that a state of mind is transferred (by projective identification) to the group and *acted out* there – not altered. Some details of this situation must be described.

In the first stage there is no real confrontation between the god and the man because there is really no such distinction. In the second stage the infinite and transcendent god is confronted by the finite man. When the function of the group is to *establish* the separation there is no question of reunion. In the third stage the individual, or at least a particular individual – the mystic – needs to reassert a direct experience of god of which he has been, and is, deprived by the institutionalized group. Before I turn to this it is necessary to glance at some peculiarities of the group that has been institutionalized and of life in it.

The individuals show signs of their divine origin (just as the gods of the previous stage show signs of human origin). The individuals may be regarded as being incarnations of the deity; each individual retains an inalienable element which is a part of the deity himself that resides in the individual. He can be regarded as constantly attempting to achieve union with the deity, or he can be regarded as divine in a somewhat low-grade way. This last shows signs of being related genetically to the stage where no real distinction exists between god-like human beings on the one hand and very human gods on the other. Finally, the individual strives for reunion with the god from whom he feels consciously separated. This is reflected in the actualities of the human relationship and contributes to the hatred of the group for a state in which individuals cannot have direct access, or even a sense of direct access, to the great man (as they might once have had to Freud). Individuals cannot reconcile themselves to a discrimination that means conscious separation of themselves from a belief in their Freud-like qualities and recognition that Freud, a genius (mystic), no longer exists. Another Freud cannot be created no matter how essential he may be.

The group and mystic are essential to each other; it is therefore important to consider how or why the group can destroy the mystic on whom its future depends and how or why the mystic may destroy the group. I shall indicate the nature of the questions at issue since it is vital that the problem should be seen to exist. It is inherent both in the nature of man as a political animal and in the nature of psycho-analysis as the explosive force.

The relationship between group and mystic may belong to one of three categories. It may be commensal, symbiotic, or parasitic. The same categorization may be applied to the relationship of one group with another. I shall not trouble with the commensal relationship: the two sides coexist and the existence of each can be seen to be harmless to the other. In the symbiotic relationship there is a confrontation and the result is growth-producing though that growth may not be discerned without some difficulty. In the parasitic relationship the product of the association is something that destroys both parties to the association. The realization that approximates most closely to my formulation is the group–individual setting dominated by envy. Envy begets envy, and this self-perpetuating emotion finally destroys host and parasite alike. The envy cannot be satisfactorily ascribed to one or other party; in fact it is a function of the relationship.

In a symbiotic relationship the group is capable of hostility and benevolence and the mystic contribution is subject to close scrutiny. From this scrutiny the group grows in stature and the mystic likewise. In the parasitic association even friendliness is deadly. An easily seen example of this is the group's promotion of the individual to a position in the Establishment where his energies are deflected from his creative–destructive role and absorbed in administrative functions. He epitaph might be 'He was loaded with honours and sank without a trace'. Eissler (1965), without mentioning the general principle involved, shows the dangers of the invitation to group or individual to become respectable, to be medically qualified, to be a university department, to be a therapeutic group, to be anything in short, but *not* explosive. The reciprocal attitude in the mystic is that the group should thrive or disintegrate but must *not* be indifferent. The attitudes are not conscious and deliberate; they are essential. Without them the group is not a group nor the 'mystic' a mystic. An analytic parallel is the psycho-analytic interpretation which is death to the existing state of mind, the state of mind that is being interpreted. Worse than being right or wrong is the failure of an interpretation to be significant, though to be significant is not enough; it merely ensures that it exists. It must also be true. The parasitic group can be primarily concerned to destroy the mystic, or mystic (messianic) ideas, but if it fails to do so it must 'establish' his or their truth.

Eissler discusses 'applied' psycho-analysis. I suspect that applied psycho-analysis, even if 'applied' to curing people, is a method of bringing psycho-analysis under control and rendering it harmless to the Establishment. I have expressed this in another context and in a different approach by a rule that the analyst should not permit himself to harbour desires, even the desire to cure, since to do so is inimical to psycho-analytical development. Development itself is not an object that can be 'desired'. The painful nature of the dilemma is essential.

The recurrent configuration is of an explosive force with a restraining framework. For example, the mystic in conflict with the Establishment; the new idea constrained within a formulation not intended to express it; the art form outmoded by new forces requiring representation.

It is essential that the language should be preserved. To this end, rules are produced under which words and definitions are to be used. The *Oxford dictionary*, linguistic philosophy, mathematical logic, are tributes to the work that is incessantly proceeding for this purpose. On this work ordinary men and women with ordinary ability depend to do work that otherwise would be done only by exceptional people. Thanks to Faraday and other scientists ordinary people can illuminate a room by the touch of a switch; thanks to Freud and his co-workers ordinary people hope by psycho-analysis to be able to illuminate the mind. The fact that the world's work has to be done by ordinary people makes this work of scientification (or vulgarization, or simplification, or communication, or all together) imperative. There are not enough mystics and those that there are must not be wasted.

The more successfully the word and its use can be 'established', the more its precision becomes an obstructive rigidity; the more imprecise it is, the more it is a stumbling-block to comprehension. The new idea 'explodes' the formulation designed to express it. Sometimes the emotion is powerful but the idea weak. If the formulation survives it can be repeated. If it can be repeated under severe conditions it becomes stronger until it communicates meaning without distintegration. Conversely, the formulation may destroy its content. In his play *Major Barbara*, George Bernard Shaw describes the apotheosis of the dictum 'No man is good enough to be another man's master' as a method of rendering the emotional content ineffectual.

It may be that the distinction between creative and nihilistic mystic is no more than a temporary expedient depending on the need to express one view of the mystic rather than the other. The most powerful emotional explosion known so far, spreading to many cultures and over many centuries, has been that produced by the formulations of Jesus. The effects are still felt and present grave problems of containment even now, though some measure of control has been established. Jesus at first expressly disavowed any aim other than fulfilment of the laws of his group. The rabbinical directorate failed to solve the problem of containment, a failure associated with disastrous consequences for the Jewish group. The disaster attributed to Christian teachings did not terminate at any finite point, as for example at the crucifixion; after Alaric had sacked Rome four hundred years later St Augustine felt the reproaches against the Christians to be sufficiently serious to require refutation in his 'City of God'.

The problems of mystical revelation that centre on having, or claiming to have, a direct relationship with the deity remain. The need for the Establishment to do what the rabbinical directorate had failed to do soon became evident. Complaints by the disciples that miracles were being done by unauthorized or, as we might say, 'lay', people, suggest awareness that we expect to find associated with an Establishment. That, and evidence of a need to establish a structured hierarchy ('who shall sit at the right hand'), is too slender to be more than a starting-point for conjecture. Something must have contributed to the efflorescence of structure, hierarchy, and institution. The institution is evidence of the need for the function that the rabbinical directorate had failed to provide. Although in many respects the Church was more successful, the long history of heresy (see Knox, 1950) shows that the structure required to contain the teaching of Jesus was, and still is, subjected to a great strain. It has not, however, been without its successes, and even today complaints can be heard, which are really a tribute to the success of the institutionalizing process, of the lack of enthusiasm, drive, and 'spirituality' of the Church.

Though we may contrast the success of the Church favourably with the failure of the rabbinical directorate, the force of the mystical revelation has not yet spent itself. There are signs that the Oedipus myth, and the elements that in the Christian religion touch on paternity and sonship, both have a configuration suggesting an underlying group of which these elements are representative. I have used the sign O to denote this 'ultimate reality'. Any formulation felt to approximate to illumination of O is certain to produce an institutionalizing reaction. The institution may flourish at the expense of the mystic or idea, or it may be so feeble that it fails to contain the mystical revelation.

A formulation may approximate to 'illumination' of O. Many mystics express their experience of direct access to the deity in terms of light, but light is not the only model used. Jewish mystics in particular find the voice a telling representation of the experience. St Paul found light *and* voice necessary to represent the experience. It is significant that psycho-analysts seeking direct access to an aspect of O, though it is not only to that part of O that informs god-like characteristics, conduct their affairs through language. To be confined to one medium of communication only is too restrictive even if it has the flexibility and capacity for development of language. Psycho-analytical observation certainly cannot afford to be confined to perception of what is verbalized only: what of more primitive uses of the tongue?

The suspension of memory and desire promotes exercise of aspects of the psyche that have no background of sensuous experiences. Paradoxically, the release of these aspects of the psyche enables them to reveal elements such as the non-verbal muscular movements of the tongue, as in stammer. The dominance of sensuous experience promotes expressions such as 'seeing' or 'hearing'; the falseness introduced by such formulation contributes to those differences that seem so significant but are in fact unimportant. Intuitive power cannot develop because it is hindered by such obtrusions of 'sense'. The institutionalizing of words, religions, psycho-analysis, – all are special instances of institutionalizing memory so that it may 'contain' the mystic revelation and its creative and destructive force. The function of the group is to produce a genius; the function of the Establishment is to take up and absorb the consequences so that the group is not destroyed.

8 · *Vertices: Evolution*

Some psycho-analytic tensions appear in a simpler, less disguised form if we use as a model the impact of the thought of Jesus on the Jewish group and on later religious institutions. The stress on miracles of healing represented an urge to 'medicalize' the institution intended to serve the teaching of Jesus. Healing retains its dominance in Christian Science, Lourdes, faith-healing. An example in the early Christian group of a problem of institutionalizing is the query put to Jesus by the disciples who wanted to have a ruling on recognition of those who cast out devils in Jesus' name. His attitude appears to have been against rigid qualification for membership of the group – 'those that are not against me are for me'. Although this reply cannot now be interpreted with sureness and may have been referable to the favourable (for Christianity) effect of turpitude in the opponents of Christianity, it shows the recurrent configuration of the problem of selection (lay versus professional, or outgroup versus ingroup). These conjectures illustrate the configuration to which I want to draw attention.

Psycho-analysis cannot escape ideas of cure, treatment, illness, in psycho-analysts and patients alike. Eissler warns against a structure that is too rigid and too limited to permit development. At the opposite extreme the Sufis have no rigid institution yet have endured; their solution would open the way for an 'expanding universe' of psycho-analysis but it would not be long before members of the psycho-analytic movement could not understand each other.

The importance of unconscious motivation has tended to screen the importance of conscious motivation. An analyst or a particular group of analysts may stress a medical view possessing, in my terms, a common vertex; an observer of the group would expect to find that its vertex is recognized by certain invariants such as ideas of disease, treatment, prognosis, pathology, and cure. The unconscious counterparts of such a vertex will have been laid bare in the psychoanalysis of the individuals, but this should not blind us to the conscious aspects of this vertex.

Suppose a group in whom the need or desire to make money is obtrusive. The unconscious counterpart of this will likewise have been laid bare in the analysis of the individuals. The greater the need or the 'desire', the easier it would be to detect a particular application of psycho-analytic theory (what Eissler calls 'applied' psycho-analysis as opposed to 'anthropic').

Other groups may display similarly obtrusive vertices: a wish for power, influence, propaganda, education, research, or poverty. It is evident that, in our present stage of development, if we achieve 'psycho-analytic' psycho-analysis, the vertex of the group will make a difference to the findings of the group. So far, analysts have seemed to act on the assumption that motives should be analysed and may, therefore, be safely left without further consideration. This view ignores the varieties of development opened up by the analytic experience.

The oedipal situation, or its even more primitive roots, would have a different configuration according to whether the vertex of the group was psycho-analytic, religious, financial, legal, or some other. This itself increases the variety of experiences opened up within the limits of even rigid psychoanalysis. The messianic expectation, formulated and institutionalized in the Christian religion, may represent the evolved aspect of an element which is represented also at its evolved stage by the Oedipus myth.

Similarities in the configurations suggest a common origin and common disorders associated with the problem of containing the mystic and institutionalizing his work. The emotional impact of ♀♂ will be proportionately greater the more closely it is related to the forces represented by the messianic hope, the Oedipus myth, the Babel myth, and the Eden myth; the greater the emotional impulse the greater the problem. These myths are evolved states of O and *represent* the evolution of O. They represent the state of mind achieved by the human being at his intersection with the evolving O.

Where Eissler speaks of applied psycho-analysis I shall speak of psycho-analysis conducted from a particular vertex. If an analyst or group of analysts regards the making of money as an essential part of psycho-analytic practice, that is to say that they regard it as an essential part of practice which is an equally essential part of cure, then I think that the vertex should be described as money-making and the discoveries that are made in such analysis will bear the stamp of the financial vertex.

If the vertex is religious I should expect the discoveries to bear the stamp of that vertex. In time, the configurations associated with the various vertices would evolve to a point where they could be formulated. I should then expect the rigidity conferred by the formulation to be resisted by the fluidity of the O represented by the formulation. Just as there is at present an unbridged gap between the animate and the inanimate, which makes the transformation of the inanimate into the animate impossible, so there is a gap between the formulation of the configuration and the underlying realization approximating to it. The configuration that represents the relationship between the mystic and the institution can be recognized in, and be the representation of, the relationship between the emotional experience and the representative formulation (words, music, painting, etc.) designed to contain it. The same configuration can be seen in the relationship between the Dionysian emotional experience and the Apollonian representation. Direct access to the O of the mystic and the O of the Dionysian orgy is both contained and restrained by the religious dogmas substituted for them in the minds of 'ordinary' people.

Most analysts have felt at some time that the 'universe of discussion' in psycho-analysis is expanding so fast that we no longer maintain what a soldier calls 'lateral communication'. To take one instance about which I am able to have an opinion: the gap between what some regard as analysis and what I, as a Kleinian, regard as analysis is very wide and widening. This is attributed to differences in theory. I do not believe that what separates scientists is their difference in theory. I have not always felt 'separated' from someone who differs from me in the theories he holds; that does not seem to me to afford a standard of measurement by which the gap can be measured. Conversely, I have felt very far separated from some who, apparently, hold the same theories. Therefore, if the 'gap' is to be 'measured' it will have to be in some domain other than that of theory. The differences in theory are symptoms of differences in vertex and not a measure of the differences.

9 · *Ultimate Reality*

So far this book has been concerned with the formulation of a theory, the few 'facts' mentioned being illustrative models intended to give body to what might otherwise be an exercise in the manipulation of abstractions. It leads up to the formulation of a theory which has as its realization a background of psycho-analytic practice. The theory formulates a recurrent pattern of emotional experience of wide distribution. It does not replace any existing psycho-analytical theory, but is intended to display relationships which have not been remarked.

However thorough an analysis is, the person undergoing it will be only partially revealed; at any point in the analysis the proportion of what is known to what is unknown is small. Therefore the dominant feature of a session is the unknown personality and not what the analysand or analyst thinks he knows.

All psycho-analytic progress exposes a need for further investigation. There is a 'thing-in-itself', which can never be known; by contrast, the religious mystic claims direct access to the deity with whom he aspires to be at one. Since this experience is often expressed in terms that I find it useful to borrow, I shall do so, but with a difference that brings them closer to my purpose. The penumbra of associations is intended to help those who look for my meaning.

In any object, material or immaterial, resides the unknowable ultimate reality, the 'thing-in-itself'. Objects have emanations or emergent qualities or evolving characteristics that impinge upon the human personality as phenomena. Of these qualities the personality may be consciously or unconsciously aware; they differ from the ultimate reality.

'Ultimate reality' is a term with a penumbra of associations, which makes it psychologically helpful, but this fact makes it unsuitable to represent something that by definition is unknowable. The same objection applies to the term 'godhead'. Meister Eckhart expresses his sense that the godhead evolves to a point where it becomes apprehensible by man as the Trinity.

By contrast the godhead is formless and infinite. Milton expresses a similar idea in the description of the world of waters dark and deep which has been 'won from the void and formless infinite', though here the emphasis is less on the evolution characteristic of the godhead and more on the capacity of the apprehending object to apprehend.

The religious approach postulates an emanation of the deity and an incarnation of the deity. Both formulations are needed to represent states of mind in which there is an interaction between states of an object that is sometimes whole, sometimes split into fragments dispersed within a multiplicity of objects. For the analyst, the doctrine of the incarnation yields the rewarding model so I shall concentrate on it first.

The psycho-analyst witnesses the behaviour of a being who is usually, but not always, lying on a couch and talking. The analyst may take in the scene as a whole or any part of it. 'Whole' or 'part' is an aspect of an ultimate reality that has evolved until it intersects the personality of the observer (see Chapter 3 above).

The scientific approach, associated with a background of sense impressions, for example the presence of the psycho-analyst and his patient in the same room, may be regarded as having a base. In so far as it is associated with the ultimate reality of the personality, O, it is baseless. This does not mean that the psycho-analytic method is unscientific, but that the term 'science', as it has been commonly used hitherto to describe an attitude to objects of sense, is not adequate to represent an approach to those realities with which 'psycho-analytical science' has to deal. Nor is it adequate to represent that aspect of the human personality that is concerned with the unknown and ultimately unknowable – with O.

The criticism applies to every vertex, be it musical, religious, aesthetic, political; all are inadequate when related to O because, with the possible exception of the religion of the mystic, these and similar vertices are not adapted to the sensually baseless. The realities with which psycho-analysis deals, for example fear, panic, love, anxiety, passion, have no sensuous background, though there is a sensuous background (respiratory rate, pain, touch, etc.) that is often identified with them and then treated, supposedly scientifically. What is required is not a base for psycho-analysis and its theories but a science that is not restricted by its genesis in knowledge and sensuous background. It must be a science of at-one-ment. It must have a mathematics of at-one-ment, not identification. There can be no geometry of 'similar', 'identical', 'equal'; only of analogy.

The Platonic theory of Forms and the Christian dogma of the Incarnation imply absolute essence which I wish to postulate as a universal quality of phenomena such as 'panic', 'anxiety', 'fear', 'love'. In brief, I use O to represent this central feature of every situation that the psycho-analyst has to meet. With this he must be at one; with the *evolution* of this he must identify so that he can formulate it in an interpretation. Certain states of mind obstruct this and of them I shall say more later.

An aspect of O that evolves is signified by number. Participating in the evolution can be the object, which may multiply or decrease, and the observer, who feels that the object multiplies or decreases. Ignoring the object so as to discuss only the observer one may say that he *feels* that the object increases or decreases. The constant conjunction signified by number excites curiosity to know which, what, when, why, or how. 'The need to know' (whether the change ($\pm$) is in the objects observed or in the 'feeling') may be activated. The 'number' is assumed to relate to an aspect of the object observed, but it may with equal propriety be regarded as relating to the feeling. I shall be discussing mostly the 'number' as being the name of the feeling, but to avoid confusion I shall distinguish between, say, R3 (external reality) and ψ3 (psychic reality), the latter being the sign for a feeling of 'threeness' which may or may not be contemporaneous with 'threeness' as an aspect of the observed object.

When I speak of 'number', in the context of feelings, the term has too many associations that I do not require. I shall therefore use (ξ) to denote the name of a 'mathematical object'[1] which I am using as the name of a 'feeling'.

The following illustrations, taken from religion, politics, conversational intercourse, and so on, may act as an introduction to 'psychical' mathematics:

'The majority of people . . .'
'Thousands (millions) all over the world . . .'
'The Trinity'
'Four or five people . . .'
'For weeks (months, years) they waited for . . .'

In these examples, numbers, used to represent a feeling in the observer, may be categorized in accordance with the principles of the grid as intended to evoke curiosity (category 4) or as a barrier against statements that might evoke a psychological disturbance (category 2).

These 'numbers' have been transformed from ψ (ξ) to R (ξ), so that they represent realizations which approximate to them. These realizations can become extremely complex. Thus Euclidean geometry has been regarded as a representation to which space, as ordinary people know it, is the approximate realization. Euclidean geometry then becomes the background realization that approximates to axiomatic algebra, which represents *it*.

Axiomatic algebra appears to be entirely independent of its background and can be developed accordingly; on the theory developed here, although it may start by representing feelings that provide the background, axiomatic algebra, the example I have taken, becomes entirely independent of that

[1] Borrowed from Frege (1950).

background of feelings. The H formulations (grid category) begin to lack 'body'. What does it mean that these formulations lose 'body', cease to represent a 'feeling'? The number 'three' or 'ten' can easily represent a 'feeling' that there are three or ten objects present. The names three and ten do not seem to represent constant conjunctions in the way that 'cat' does. 'Cat' has a sensuous background; so has $R(\xi)$; but $\psi(\xi)$ has not unless we reverse a process of transformation through Euclidean geometry back to ordinary space.

Non-sensuous phenomena form the totality of what is commonly regarded as mental or spiritual experience. $\psi(\xi)$, which represents non-sensuous realizations, seems to be relatively easily adapted for manipulations to represent *sensuous* realizations, but not for manipulations to represent non-sensuous realizations. If 'three' represents a non-sensuous realization of 'threeness', why can it not, in combination with 'ten', 'five', etc., be made to represent anxiety or love or hate?

Certain problems can be handled by mathematics, others by economics, others by religion. It should be possible to transfer a problem, that fails to yield to the discipline to which it appears to belong, to a discipline that can handle it. If Euclidean geometry cannot handle multi-dimensional problems they can be transferred to algebraic geometry which can handle them. In this way certain problems can be transferred within their own discipline so that their solution can be attempted. The mathematics evolved by the manipulation of 'numbers' has so far proved very successful in matching the formulation with the realization it represents. But the numbers representing feelings have not evolved so that they can handle the realizations of the domain from which they appear to have sprung.

Before we consider the transference of problems from one discipline to another, or of the procedures proper to one discipline to procedures proper to another discipline, we shall examine the peculiarities of catastrophic change.

10 · *Visual Images and Invariants*

From the material discussed it should now be possible to detect a pattern that remains unaltered in apparently widely differing contexts. It would be useful to isolate and formulate the invariants of that pattern so that it could be communicated.

Freud's formulations do just that. Thinking, developed through psycho-analysis, has led to discoveries that were not made by Freud, but that reveal configurations resembling those in discoveries he *did* make. Can his formulations be replaced by others that reveal as nearly as possible *all* the configurations that are similar and not merely those instances that his formulations were intended to illuminate?

If his Oedipus theory is used in conjunction with the Eden myth, the Babel myth, and a version of messianic expectation, it can continue to illuminate the mind's workings as it does now and to display elements of an underlying configuration that widen significantly the area illuminated. The deity's hostility to curiosity remarked by Milton's Satan (Book IV, *Paradise Lost*) can be matched in Babel by the attack on speech (the infliction of confusion of tongues); in Oedipus by Tiresias and his warning; in the messianic story by the attack on the son by the father. The same pattern is reflected in the self-inflicted punishments of the Sphinx and Oedipus. Each version emphasizes a different facet; together they suggest a common configuration. The attempt to differentiate emotional elements is curiously unsuccessful. Thus 'omnipotent good', 'evil', 'pursuit of knowledge through curiosity', 'impending disaster', 'arrogance', and so on, each attempt seems to weaken the impact that the elements have when they are part of the narrative as a whole; they undergo a transformation similar to that undergone by the dream upon being consciously recalled, or by a work of art when it is replaced by a reproduction. The transformation depends on a change of vertex. The vertex of the myth-maker is not mine as I attempt this reformulation; the vertex of the dreamer is not that of the dreamer awake; the vertex of the artist is not that of the interpreter of the work of art. Similarly, the vertex of the psycho-analyst, and changes of vertex corresponding to moment-to-moment changes in a session, effect the transformations made manifest in associations and interpretations.

First, there must be a difference of vertex to make correlation possible. It must ultimately take place in the individual. (For the moment I assume that correlation is a necessary part of confrontation and that confrontation is a necessary part of analysis.) Schizophrenic defences are mobilized against confrontation; violence makes confrontation impossible because both sides of a confrontation are annihilated.

Second, the vertex must not be too distant or too near, otherwise correlation becomes impossible. How is 'distance' measured between the vertex of the analysand and the vertex of the analyst? If the analyst wants to make a living and the analysand wants to be 'cured', how is the 'distance' between these vertices to be 'measured'? A man and a woman can have such different outlooks that their temperaments are described as incompatible; or views so similar that they cannot stimulate each other. Is there any sense in which their views can be so 'far apart' that the distance can be 'measured', that a phrase used metaphorically can be treated so that the metaphorical sense is replaced by a literal sense?

Under this vertex the views of patient and analyst are separated; the 'gap' separating them is bridged by something that I call linear or planar, or a line or film. Very different is the gap that is bridged by a relationship between container and contained. The following will serve as a model for a theoretical formulation of this kind of link: a man speaking of an emotional experience in which he was closely involved began to stammer badly as the memory became increasingly vivid to him. The aspects of the model that are significant are these: the man was trying to contain his experience in a form of words; he was trying to contain himself, as one sometimes says of someone about to lose control of himself; he was trying to 'contain' his emotions within a form of words, as one might speak of a general attempting to 'contain' enemy forces within a given zone.

The words that should have represented the meaning the man wanted to express were fragmented by the emotional forces to which he wished to give only verbal expression; the verbal formulation could not 'contain' his emotions, which broke through and dispersed it as enemy forces might break through the forces that strove to contain them.

The stammerer, in his attempt to avoid the contingency I have described, resorted to modes of expression so boring that they failed to express the meaning he wished to convey; he was thus no nearer to his goal. His verbal formulation could be described as like to the military forces that are worn by the attrition to which they are subjected by the contained forces. The meaning he was striving to express was denuded of meaning. His attempt to use his tongue for verbal expression failed to 'contain' his wish to use his tongue for masturbatory movement in his mouth.

Sometimes the stammerer could be reduced to silence. This situation can be represented by a visual image of a man who talked so much that any meaning he wished to express was drowned by his flood of words.

I hope that I have conveyed my meaning to the reader by virtue of the verbal transformations of visual images that I have used. However, the communication is not satisfactory. The visual images are too concrete to be suitable for expressing the relationship of the mystic to the group. They are too evocative of a penumbra of associations which they already carry. In short, the situation is similar to that of the stammerer whose words, or lack of them, contain rather than communicate his meaning. Alternatively, the meaning is too powerful for the verbal formulation; the expression is lost in an 'explosion' in which the verbal formulation is destroyed.

To consider the essentials: the communication is about a relationship between meaning and its expression, between emotion and its expression. But I am aware that it is not a relationship between any things; it is a pattern of relationships in the way that mathematicians speak of mathematics as expressing relationships. I have in the past used the symbols ♀ and ♂ to express a relationship between container and contained; for the present I shall continue to do so.

The theory is that an object is placed into a container in such a way that either the container or the contained object is destroyed. In pictorial terms the container is represented by a mouth or vagina, the contained by breast or penis. The relationship between these objects, which I shall represent by the male and female signs ♂ and ♀, may be commensal, symbiotic, or parasitic.

By 'commensal' I mean a relationship in which two objects share a third to the advantage of all three. By 'symbiotic' I understand a relationship in which one depends on another to mutual advantage. By 'parasitic' I mean to represent a relationship in which one depends on another to produce a third, which is destructive of all three.

Take another simple visual model: a man wishing to communicate his annoyance is so overwhelmed by emotion that he stammers and becomes incoherent. The invariants under the theory I wish to formulate are the forms of speech that the man uses to convey his meaning; these I regard as being intended to 'contain' what he has to say and therefore to correspond to the sign ♀. The annoyance he strives to communicate I regard as being what should be contained in his speech, and therefore it is appropriately represented by ♂. If the man remained coherent, this could correspond to an overwhelming of the content by the container: his speech would in this case be so restrained that it could not express his feelings. But suppose he expressed himself 'perfectly':

one could then imagine that his emotions had served to develop his ability for well-chosen speech and that his capacity for speech had helped his emotional development. This contrasts with development leading to incoherence. Such a failure is the outcome of a 'parasitic' relationship between the contained (or rather, *not* contained) material and the speech devised to contain it: 'container' and 'contained' have produced a third 'object' – incoherence – which makes expression and the means of expression impossible. In so far as the imaginary episode led to a development of powers of expression and of the personality that strove to express itself, the relationship could be described as symbiotic. 'Commensal' is illustrated by supposing that the episode occurred in an age and society (as in Elizabethan England) in which language had reached a point of development where the ordinary man was inspired to speak it well: that which was to be expressed and the vehicle for its expression profited from the culture to which they belonged.

11 · *Lies and the Thinker*

The distinction between truth and lie constantly confronts the psycho-analyst who has to apply in a rough and ready practical way ideas that have been the centre of discussion over the centuries. The rough and ready application may be too crude to do the work required of it. The psycho-analyst seeks ideas sufficiently accurate and robust to survive the emotional storms they should illuminate.

To the problems of understanding I have said that the psycho-analyst can bring something that is unknown to the philosopher of science because the psycho-analyst has experience of the dynamics of *misunderstanding*; the psycho-analyst is concerned *practically* with a problem that the philosopher approaches *theoretically*. Investigations of understanding and misunderstanding impinge on problems associated with truth and untruth. The reality of the problem becomes apparent when the psycho-analyst must ask himself, can a liar be psycho-analysed?

The problem can be formulated in grid terms without moral overtones. Category 2 (reserved for formulations known by the initiator to be false but maintained as a barrier against statements that lead to a psychological upheaval) would seem provisionally to offer a home to the lie. Such a categorization supposes that an experience has been permitted to continue to a point where the patient thinks he knows his formulation to be untrue, but is it true that he maintains it because it would be disturbing to his development not to do so? The lie could be uttered because in the view of the liar it would be profitable to him or injurious to another: is it correct in such a case to say it would be true, and if true significant, that inability to profit himself or injure another would lead to his having a psychological upheaval?

As I think it would be true, I must indicate why and in what way it is reasonable to categorize the lie in 2. First I am concerned with patients who come for analysis and not with those who do not. To such a patient it is clear that he risks exposure of the lie. He must either have great confidence in his capacity (or lack of it in the analyst) or feel some dissatisfaction with the lie. These are random conjectures, however, and beg the question at issue, which must be answered in the course of an analysis the very practicability of which is under debate. The extreme case would seem to offer the best chance of being able to observe the essential characteristics, or, as I prefer to call them, the invariants, of the liar. Present considerations make it unlikely that the psychoanalyst would treat such a case by choice. The supposition that he was going to cure such a patient would lead him to hesitate about accepting him. Therefore the probability is that the lying is so well concealed that he stumbles into such a collaboration unwittingly. This makes it possible that the same may be true of the patient; so at the outset one must be prepared to find that the supposition that the patient thinks he risks exposure, or minds it if he does, is not in fact the case.

The need for a category for statements known by the patient to be untrue arises when, for example, a patient, who has been shown in the course of analysis that there are a number of explanations of the fact that he is late, continues to repeat apologies. The analyst is challenged to accept them, at the risk of showing himself unmindful of the truth, or to reject them and assume the role of being the patient's conscience. A statement may be made not to mislead but to fill the function of evocation. Thus a lying report may be evocative or provocative, accusatory or defensive, to name only a few of the more obvious uses. In such a case category 2 is not the correct category because the statement is intended to lead to emotional upheaval. In short, the lying statement is not category 2 but category 6. Its nature must be indicated by some usage such as minus L (−L) or minus K (−K).

The term 'lie' thus has limited value for use in the course

of psycho-analysis. It focuses attention on something that is not invariant; on the other hand, −L or −K, together with the appropriate grid category, leaves it open to saturation by appropriate 'meanings' should realizations that approximate present themselves to the psycho-analyst and analysand.

If we suppose now that the emotional upheaval against which the lie is mobilized is identical with catastrophic change it becomes easier to understand why investigation uncovers an ambiguous position which is capable of arousing strong feelings. These feelings relate to an outraged moral system; their strength derives from risk of change in the psyche. As the episode that I describe occurs frequently and can be resolved only in a way that seems to set the pattern for the resolution of subsequent recurrences, it is necessary to dwell on certain features which have an importance that may escape notice.

The patient can be seen to make a decision between the lie and the truth. The frequency with which this 'decision' is automatically made in favour of the statement known to be untrue will determine the nature of the case. I focus attention on the position that now arises for the analyst.

By definition and by the tradition of all scientific discipline, the psycho-analytic movement is committed to the truth as the central aim. If the patient constantly formulates −L and −K statements, he and the analyst are, in theory at least, in conflict. In practice, however, the situation does not present itself so simply. The patient, especially if intelligent and sophisticated, offers every inducement to bring the analyst to interpretations that leave the defence intact and, ultimately, to acceptance of the lie as a working principle of superior efficacy. In the last resort he will make consistent progress towards a 'cure' which will be flattering to analyst and patient alike. The alternative he offers is bleak: progressive deterioration, loss of mutual esteem both private and public, hostility, and, in extreme cases, threats of legal action. Against this the analyst has to balance a hope of retaining his integrity.

Some forms of lying appear to be closely related to experiencing desire. Long stories, with every appearance of truth, are spun out extempore as if the virtuosity of the exercise gave pleasure. One would expect such fabrications to be idealizations, and some are, but the liar's state of mind is not ordinary and the divergence from the usual is screened by the plausibility of his lies. They are usually C category formulations and may present more difficulty to an analyst whose mind is built on sensuous experience than to one who is used to discounting memory. As the problems of the psycho-analysis of the liar differ so much from those of the psycho-analysis of one whose outlook is scientific, it is worth considering shortly what is meant by the scientific approach. In ordinary speech it is taken to mean an assumption that the truth is of overriding importance and that reason should be harnessed to its elucidation. As a preliminary to attempting a more sophisticated formulation the opposite view may be stated in terms of fable, thus:

> The liars showed courage and resolution in their opposition to the scientists who with their pernicious doctrines bid fair to strip every shred of self-deception from their dupes leaving them without any of the natural protection necessary for the preservation of their mental health against the impact of truth. Some, knowing full well the risks that they ran, nevertheless laid down their lives in affirmations of lies so that the weak and doubtful would be convinced by the ardour of their conviction of the truth of even the most preposterous statements. It is not too much to say that the human race owes its salvation to that small band of gifted liars who were prepared even in the face of indubitable facts to maintain the truth of their falsehoods. Even death was denied and the most ingenious arguments were educed to support obviously ridiculous statements that the dead lived on in bliss. These martyrs to untruth were often of humble origin whose very names have perished. But for them and the witness borne by their obvious sincerity the sanity of the race must have perished under the load placed on it. By laying down their lives they carry the morals of the world on their shoulders. Their lives and the lives of their followers were devoted to

the elaboration of systems of great intricacy and beauty in which the logical structure was preserved by the exercise of a powerful intellect and faultless reasoning. By contrast the feeble processes by which the scientists again and again attempted to support their hypotheses made it easy for the liars to show the hollowness of the pretensions of the upstarts and thus to delay, if not to prevent, the spread of doctrines whose effect could only have been to induce a sense of helplessness and unimportance in the liars and their beneficiaries.

It is not necessary to elaborate this phantasy further; this sample should indicate the vertex I wish to establish, but in so far as it does so it throws up difficulties. It is easy to imagine that there are such things as facts independent of the mind. A belief that led a man to throw himself off a cliff in confidence that his capacity to fly would preserve him from injury would contribute to his injury because the reality of his belief, the O of his belief, is, from the vertex of survival, of less consequence than the O of throwing himself from a cliff. But O, without such a vertex, is an absolute, inhering in ('incarnate' in) everything and unknowable by man. The belief that he would fly off uninjured can be compared with the belief that he would break his neck. Depending on the vertex, the two beliefs can be regarded as valuable and precedence accorded to one of them. But to what scale of values is the value of the belief related? Ruskin defined 'valuable' as life-giving. This may do in that the oedipal theory and primal scene afford a link (as does the theorem of Pythagoras, by the use of Cartesian co-ordinates, for the conversion of geometry to algebraic formulation) between life instincts and death instincts and that which is valuable or life-giving and its opposite.

If value is to be the criterion, difficulty arises because there is no *absolute* value: the individual does not necessarily believe it is better to create than to destroy; a suicidal patient may seem to embrace the opposite view.

The determination of the system of beliefs, the vertices, aims, complaints, and 'cures', is often mistaken by the patient for an attempt to establish a correct system. The investigation of category 2 is to see in what respect its pains compare with those of other systems and in what way the relationships differ. Such insights laid at the disposal of the patient seem to give him the opportunity to correct errors. The contemplation of various systems enables the analyst to reconsider and correct his own system. Category 2 involves conflict with impressions of reality; sometimes these may not matter but beyond a certain point the conflict between the need to know and the need to deny becomes acute and may usher in attacks on linking to stop stimulation which leads to conflict. But this presupposes an aim on the part of the liar, and therefore a pattern that can be detected. This is not the case with some liars. Hence it is not possible to rely on picking up a symptom, such as a wish to please the analyst, that will betray the pattern.

For satisfaction, the liar needs an audience; this makes him vulnerable, since his audience must set a value on his fabrications. It is therefore necessary that the analyst-victim should attach importance to the patient's statements as formulations of a truth. It must be possible to observe incoherent elements and to detect a pattern that brings together the disparate elements, showing a coherence and a meaning that they had not without it. So far, this description does not differ from that of the transformation from the paranoid–schizoid to the depressive position. It is superior to a narrative formulation which betrays the lying element of the story only by the weakness of the causative links. The $Ps \leftrightarrow D$ reaction reveals a whole situation which seems to belong to a reality that pre-exists the individual who has discovered it. The lying discovery lacks the spontaneous bleakness of the genuine $Ps \leftrightarrow D$. The lie requires a thinker to think. The truth, or true thought, does not require a thinker – he is not logically necessary.

Provisionally, we may consider that the difference between a true thought and a lie consists in the fact that a thinker is logically necessary for the lie but not for the true thought. Nobody need think the true thought: it awaits the advent of the thinker who achieves significance through the true thought. The lie and its thinker are inseparable. The thinker is of no consequence to the truth, but the truth is logically necessary to the thinker. His significance depends on whether or not he will entertain the thought, but the thought remains unaltered.

In contrast, the lie gains existence by virtue of the epistemologically prior existence of the liar. The only thoughts to which a thinker is absolutely essential are lies. Descartes's tacit assumption that thoughts presuppose a thinker is valid only for the lie.

The paranoid–schizoid state may then be seen as peculiar to the thinker who is in a state of persecution by thoughts that belong to a non-human system, the O domain. The O domain may be said to be, *vis-à-vis* the thinker, in a state of evolution. This evolving system intersects with the personality of the individual thinker. The impact of the evolving O domain on the domain of the thinker is signalized by persecutory feelings of the paranoid–schizoid position. Whether the thoughts are entertained or not is of significance to the thinker but not to the truth. If entertained, they are conducive to mental health; if not, they initiate disturbance. The lie depends on the thinker and gains significance through him. It is the link between host and parasite in the parasitic relationship.

The relationship between the lie, the thought, the thinker, and the group is complex. The thinker may express the truth in a lying group; the group may not want its ideas disturbed and will be dominated by category 2 mechanisms and formulations. The relationship between such a group and such a thinker will be one of envy and hate. If the thinker is expressing lies, the relationship of the thinker to his lies will be parasitic, and lies and thinker will destroy each other. If the lie is of the 'sun rises at dawn' type, the relationship between lie and thinker is commensal – such a thought *requires* a thinker and the thinker is essential. But the relationship, at least in our present age, is commensal. The thought that the world will endure may be a lie but it may be essential to keep at bay ideas that the world is on the verge of coming to an end. Such a relationship between lie and thinker is symbiotic.

The link between one mind and another that leads to destruction of both is the lie. The term 'link' gives an inadequate idea of the realization it is intended to represent. The lie is not restricted, as the word 'lie' would ordinarily imply, to the domain of thought, but has its counterpart in the domain of being; it is possible to be a lie and being so precludes at-one-ment in O.

In psycho-analysis the liar is a significant fact and gains significance from the lying nature of what he says. The parasitic relationship between liar and environment, corresponding to the parasitic relationship between the thinker and the lie, denudes the environment of significance. The analyst who accepts such lies is acting as host; if he does not he contributes to the feelings of persecution by 'being' an unthought thought, a thought without a thinker. The thought to which a thinker is not necessary is also a thought that the thinker would not regard as likely to contribute to *his* significance. On the contrary, once he has expressed a truth the thinker is redundant.

To summarize, I formulate two definitions:

1. True thought requires neither formulation nor thinker.
2. The lie is a thought to which a formulation and a thinker are essential.

The lie is peculiar to a relationship between the host mind and the parasitic mind and destroys both. The thinker can harbour thoughts if he does not need thoughts to contribute to his significance and can tolerate thoughts that do not do so. If essential to the thought, the thinker conflicts with other thinkers who feel themselves to be essential to the thought. The envy, jealousy, and possessiveness aroused are the mental counterparts of toxic elements in physical parasitism.

They contribute to the destructive nature of the culture that develops from the development of the lie. The need for each individual to claim his contribution to the thought as unique and essential differentiates the emotional climate from that in which the inevitability of the thought and the unimportance of the individual who harbours it do not gratify the narcissism of the individual and therefore lack emotional appeal. Work that corroborates the discovery of others has a lack of appeal. Even if it requires a thinker it does not require a *particular* thinker and in this resembles truths – thoughts that require no thinker.

Since the analyst's concern is with the evolved elements of O and their formulation, formulations can be judged by considering how necessary his existence is to the thoughts he expresses. The more his interpretations can be judged as showing how necessary *his* knowledge, *his* experience, *his* character are to the thought as formulated, the more reason there is to suppose that the interpretation is psychoanalytically worthless, that is, alien to the domain O.

12 · *Container and Contained Transformed*

In this chapter I repeat the configuration in formulations that appear to be descriptions of events in psycho-analysis or history but have not the status of historical narrative. They are C category elements, images derived from a background of experience or reported experience, reassembled for my purpose.

Description 1: The signs ♂ and ♀ I call the contained and the container. The use of the male and female symbols is deliberate but must not be taken to mean that other than sexual implications are excluded. These signs designate a relationship between ♀ and ♂. The link may be commensal, symbiotic, or parasitic.

Description 2: A word contains a meaning; conversely, a meaning can contain a word – which may or may not be discovered. The relationship is established by the nature of the link. A constant conjunction of elements in a psycho-analysis can be 'bound' by the attribution to it of a word, a theory, or other formulation. The word by which it is bound can have such a powerful pre-existing penumbra of associations that it squeezes the meaning out of the constant conjunction it is supposed to mark. Conversely, the constant conjunction can destroy the word, theory, or other formulation that the formulation is intended to 'contain'. For example, a man is attempting to express such powerful feelings that his capacity for verbal expression disintegrates into a stammer or a meaningless, incoherent babble of words.

Description 3: The container (♀) extracts so much from the contained (♂) that the contained is left without substance. A psycho-analysis is so long continued that the patient can get no further meaning from it. A converse example would be the continuation until the patient had no more patience, tolerance, fortitude, or money left. The container can squeeze everything 'out of' the contained; or the 'pressure' may be exerted by the contained so that the container disintegrates. An illustration would be the word used as a metaphor until the background is lost and the word loses its meaning.[1]

Description 4: The marriage *in* which the sexual relationship ♀♂ plays such a part that there is *no room* for any of the other activities in which the married couple might engage. Conversely, the other (i.e. 'other than sexual') activities play such a part that there is *no room* for sexual fulfilment. (The metaphors used in this description exemplify the outside–inside, container–contained, ♀♂ pattern.)

♀ or ♂ may represent memory. The container ♀ is filled with 'memories' derived from sensuous experience. The sensuous background is dominant and 'memories' with such a background are tenacious. The ♀ memory is saturated accordingly. The analyst who comes to a session with an active memory is therefore in no position to make 'observations' of unknown mental phenomena because these are not sensuously apprehended. There is something that has often been called 'remembering' and that is essential to psychoanalytic work; this must be sharply distinguished from what I have been calling memory. I want to make a distinction between (1) remembering a dream or having a memory of a dream and (2) the experience of the dream which seems to cohere as if it were a whole, at one moment absent, at the next present. This experience, which I consider to be essential to evolution of the emotional reality of the session, is often called a memory, but it is to be distinguished from the experience of remembering. In memory, time is of the essence. Time has often been regarded as being of the

[1] See H. W. Fowler's *Dictionary of modern English usage,* 2nd edition, 'Metaphor' 2D.

essence of psycho-analysis; in the growth process it has no part. Mental evolution or growth is catastrophic and timeless. I shall use 'memory' with its ordinary conversational meaning; it represents something that is out of place in the psycho-analyst's conduct of a psycho-analysis. A patient's close relatives are burdened with memories which make them unreliable judges of the patient's personality and unfit to be the patient's analyst.

So far, I have examined the configuration as it appears in the limits of words themselves; its appearance in more complex formulation indicates the degree of its persistence. The psycho-analytic situation provides and evokes examples of the configuration; it pervades difficulties which analysand and analyst find in communication. There are emotional experiences to be conveyed or represented, some of great intensity. Therefore, we find instances of the configuration in the subject-matter and in the psycho-analytic procedure designed to deal with it.

Description 5: The patient will be at a loss to convey his meaning, or the meaning he wishes to convey will be too intense for him to express properly, or the formulation will be so rigid that he feels that the meaning conveyed is devoid of any interest or vitality. Similarly, the interpretations given by the analyst, ♂, will meet with the apparently co-operative response of being repeated for confirmation, which deprives ♂ of meaning either by compression or by denudation. Failure to observe or demonstrate the point may produce an outwardly progressive but factually sterile analysis. The clue lies in the observation of the fluctuations which make the analyst at one moment ♀ and the analysand ♂, and at the next reverse the roles. When this pattern is observed the links (commensal, symbiotic, or parasitic) within the pattern must also be observed.

The more familiar the analyst becomes with the configuration ♀ and ♂, and with events in the session that approximate to these two representations, the better. The essential experience is not the reading of this volume but the matching of the real event in the psycho-analysis that approximates to these formulations. The frequent references made to events that occur 'in analysis' or 'in the past' or 'inside' or 'outside' should aid recognition of the realizations to which these signs relate. The recognition of the category of link that is operating may be more difficult unless a lead-in can be obtained by considering the kind of event that takes the place of ♀ or ♂. Thus an extremely greedy patient may want to obtain as much as he can from his analysis while giving as little as possible; we should expect this to show itself by frequent events in which the container was denuding the contained object, and vice versa. The patient might show that he made enormous demands on his family but resented doing anything for it. Many patients might show behaviour of this kind on relatively rare occasions, but some might show it in many activities and in striking degree as, for example, by habitual incoherence while demanding great precision of interpretation from the analyst. This kind of patient cannot well be described in terms of narrative recording actual events, first, because any such formulation is suspect for reasons I have given in discussing memory, and, second, because it is impossible to predict what form his greed will take. Therefore the psycho-analyst who may have such a patient, or a patient showing such patterns of behaviour relatively rarely, or anything between these extremes, needs formulations of theory that enable him to have as wide a spectrum of observation as possible so that these configurations do not pass unnoticed. If these formulations are too abstract they lack body. Accordingly I give them body by using C category descriptions, but these are liable to produce so great a penumbra of associations that the formulations become saturated and narrow the psycho-analyst's perspicacity.

Descriptions 1–5 could include claustrophobia, agoraphobia, and acting-out as illustrations of the configuration.

Acting-out, as it is ordinarily understood, takes place 'in' the analysis and the analysis is then itself a part of acting-out. The claustrophobic-agoraphobic patient identifies himself with an object which is inside or outside a container. An ability to see the configuration reveals relationships within the patient's personality that otherwise would remain unknown. When a patient can be said to be acting out the analysis is 'in' a situation of which the boundaries are unknown. If the behaviour characterized as 'acting-out' is brought to the analysis it can be accompanied by claustrophobic symptoms in the patient. The coherence of these symptoms may not be detected if the underlying configuration is not realized. As this last point touches on group behaviour I shall make my next description a formulation in terms of history. The description will appear to be complex because I intend to broaden the scope of the configuration but its complexity will be less if it is borne in mind that the description has the same fundamental configuration even if at first sight it appears that this is not so. It may help if I explain that new ideas may appear to be presented in this description; their novelty or otherwise is a function of the reader's personality and must not be supposed to inhere in the communication.

Description 6: This section is mostly recapitulation and expansion of the model of mystic and group. Some mystics attract notice but others do not because the conditions are not propitious. The same is true of ideas. The idea which I consider to be the counterpart of the mystic or genius I call the 'messianic idea'. The idea that is messianic may be confused with the person; he may believe he is the messiah. The person I call 'the mystic'; the idea I call the 'messianic idea'. The terms 'mystic' and 'genius' are interchangeable. Mystics appear in any religion, science, time, or place. Such persons 'contain' the 'messianic idea' or the 'messianic idea' may 'contain' the person who is sought to incarnate, represent, or manifest the messiah in a manner analogous to the meaning that is felt to 'contain' the word that is to represent it.

The society in which the mystic appears has been described by Nietzsche as a body whose function it is to produce a genius. It is also the function of the society to make the mystic or messianic idea available to the members of the group. This is effected by laws (in society), dogma (in religion), rules or laws (in mathematics or science). The governing body of the society I call the Establishment; the counterpart in the domain of thought would be the pre-existing disposition or pre-conception.

The mystic makes direct contact with, or is 'at one' with, God. This capacity is not attributed to the ordinary member of the group. The Establishment must pronounce dogmatically, make laws or rules, so that the advantages of the mystic's communion with God or ultimate truth or reality may be shared at one remove by the ordinary members. This the Establishment may fail to do through lack of discrimination, leading to the furtherance of false views, or through rigid adherence to an existing framework, so that a parasitic link is set up between mystic and group, ♂ and ♀. The life is then squeezed out of the mystic or messianic idea or the society is disrupted.

Description 7: The conflict between the mystic and his group is exhibited in its most exaggerated, and therefore most easily studied, form in the account of Jesus and his relationship with the group. He himself claimed, in a manner typical of many mystics, that his teachings were in conformity with the existing Establishment: 'Think not that I am come to destroy the law or the prophets: I am not come to destroy but to fulfil' (Matthew 5 : 17, A.V.). This claim is often associated with an awareness of the disruptive force that is being brought to bear upon the group from within. The mystic does not always claim to conform to the group. He may appear in the guise of a destroyer from within or without. He does not claim peaceable intentions or methods. A distinction is sometimes made between the nihilistic mystic, who disrupts the community, and the creative mystic, who denies violent methods particularly against his own group. I wish to stress the disruptive quality of the mystic, whether he claims to be disruptive or not, for it is this disruptive quality that is associated with the group's hostility to the mystic, and vice versa. It is, furthermore, the quality that I wish to emphasize in this description.

The reaction of the Establishment is to prevent the disruption, and this it does by incorporating the mystic within itself. This is expressed in the biblical illustration by the temptation in the wilderness where the rewards of conformity are clearly stated. Conformity can be renunciation of the messianic idea or acceptance of the role of the messiah. Alternatively, the mystic can be destroyed and an attempt made to ensure the same fate for his ideas.

The functions of containment – I use the word with its military implication of one force containing another – had to be assumed by the split factions of the group, one ostensibly against and the other for Jesus. Gradually a fresh group was formed and a fresh Establishment to contain the mystic or rather the messianic idea. The Jewish group learned to handle the mystic with consequences that were less disastrous for itself. The Christian group, though finding a different solution of the problem, achieved a similarly satisfactory result. Neither system was free from recurrences of the problem. One Christian Establishment restored the disrupted structure and ensured its continuity by taking over the festivals of paganism and thus mollifying the hostility that might otherwise have followed the loss of holidays and feasts that were beloved and valued. The theme could be stated as bigger and brighter paganism, with gods refurbished and rejuvenated as saints and devils. (Milton expresses this very clearly in his representation of Pandemonium in Books I and III of *Paradise Lost.*)

The problems of the Christian Establishment developed in the lifetime of Jesus. They were: delineation of the borders of the group, selection and training, and stabilization of the hierarchy.

To take the last point first. In the account in Mark's Gospel (10:35–45), the problem was clearly posed by James and John with their request for status. In his reply Jesus seems to suggest a kind of initiation or test, but the alacrity with which the two accept the conditions makes it hard to know what the initiation was, though it is clear that Jesus regarded its performance as beyond them. He also adumbrates a change in the function of the Establishment as it existed among the Gentiles of that time. The proposal put forward by James and John seems to be for status, and status appears to be a substitute for qualification. Their desires were to be satisfied as it were *ex officio*. The reply given by James seems to indicate that the 'position' achieved *ex officio* was an alternative preferred by the pair to undergoing the experience of the mystic himself. In this respect the rejected solution meets one of the requirements of society, namely, to make the fruits of the mystic's work available to ordinary members who have not the mystic's qualifications for at-one-ment with the deity.

The problem of membership of the group and how to decide whether or not a man was to call himself a Christian [1] also arose early. Characteristically, it hinged on the question of the therapeutic efficiency of the Christian and his brand of Christianity. The problem was brought to a head through the apparently successful therapeutic effects obtained by persons not qualified members of the group (Mark 9:38). In the instance quoted, the criterion proposed by Jesus seems to be the successful cure and its attribution by the therapist to Jesus. The issues involved are: membership of the group as itself being a symbol of status; status, expressed by the locution 'in Thy name' as a therapeutic agent; therapeutic result as a criterion of membership of the group. The solution was empirical but it accepted the criterion of therapeutic

[1] The modern Israeli state has met the same problem of deciding who is, or is not, a Jew.

efficiency. For the time being the test of membership seems to be twofold, namely, medical or therapeutic, and capacity for achieving results. This last requirement has been a problem throughout history. It might be described as a demand that the group leader should be able to forestall the future, confer adequacy on someone already supposed to be suitable, and guarantee his adequacy in future contingencies.

The Christian hierarchy soon found itself faced by the same problems that had defeated the rabbinical directorate. The same forces were involved: on the one side, the need to control the messianic idea and make it available to ordinary people through dogmatic formulation; on the other side, the messianic idea or its incarnation perpetually breaking through the barriers intended to control it and threatening to disrupt the society in which it became manifest. The Reformation was a spectacular example of this (see Knox, 1950).

I have used for descriptions 6 and 7 material familiar to all, for a configuration that is repeated in many forms and at many times. It is not limited to religious societies, or therapeutic societies, or artistic societies, or scientific societies, but is discernible in many societies. My intention is, however, not to express any opinion upon the nature of diverse groups. I am not purporting to write history but to formulate a pattern in picturesque C category terms; that is to say, to represent a configuration in terms that will give body to an idea that might otherwise seem to be a meaningless elaboration of abstractions. Naturally, I suppose that people other than psycho-analysts would profit from a recognition of the configuration and the underlying group to which one suspects that it belongs. But here I am concerned only as an analyst with the configuration as it might be discerned by other analysts. Descriptions 6 and 7 must not, therefore, be supposed to have a sociological or political application but to be by way of fables or mythological constructs (C category) which, if formulated with greater precision and sophistication, represent a pattern to which the human personality would be found to approximate. The fable, constructed in terms of the group, must be regarded as a pictorialization of man's inner world (Money-Kyrle, 1961). For those familiar with Kleinian theory my description can be seen as a dramatized, personified, socialized, and pictorialized representation of the human personality. It may clarify the procedure to contrast this pictorial view with the accepted morphology of classical analysis. The theory formulated in terms of ego, super-ego, and id differs in two respects. First, it is an F category formulation whereas the pictorialized formulation I am representing verbally is a C category formulation, primitive and based on sensuously derived terminology. Second, it is a theory of which the realization that approximates to it is to be found in psychopathology and psychomorphology. The realization approximating to the C category formulation is to be found in material that is superficial and easily accessible to the conscious. Its unconscious roots are to be discovered through psycho-analytic investigation.

The nature of the messianic idea can be only very approximately represented by the C category formulations I have been using. Jesus, Meister Eckhart, and Isaac Luria represent in different ways the problem of reconciling the messianic idea and the Establishment. The rabbinical directorate learned caution, so that when it had to adjust to the Lurianic doctrine, and to the injuries that Lurianic doctrine was alleged by its opponents to have inflicted on Judaism, it did not contribute to an explosion. Luria for his part insisted on his conservatism and related all he said to older authorities. Significantly, he left no writings and, when questioned by a disciple about his reasons for not setting out his teaching in book form, he replied: 'It is impossible because all things are interrelated. I can hardly open my mouth to speak without feeling as though the sea burst its dams and overflowed. How then shall I express what my soul has received, and how can I put it down in a book?' (Scholem,

1955, p. 254). Meister Eckhart wrote extensively, but the obscurity of his writing and perhaps the matter led to the condemnation as heretical of some twenty-eight propositions from his later writings. The main question seems to centre on his forthright statements of identity with the deity – 'we are transformed and changed into God'. The fate of Jesus himself has been crucifixion as a criminal on the one hand, and deification on the other. Both Isaac Luria and Jesus were alike in being followed by a proliferation of hagiographical biography; much of it, in the instance of Jesus, not being included in the canon. The common features are: containment of the messianic idea in the individual; containment of the messianic individual in the group; the problem for the Establishment that is concerned with the group on the one hand and the messianic idea and individual on the other. It is now necessary to return to the word.

Description 2 (cycle 2): If it were necessary to express descriptions 6 and 7 by one word, a choice could be made from terms such as 'religion' or 'Christianity' or 'God'. If none of these terms is considered suitable, an attempt could be made to find the suitable term by introspection. This attempt is a search in the mind for the term supposed to exist or it is a search in the meaning for the term; the latter is an instance of the meaning containing the word. The difficulties attendant on finding the word are described in the terms used by Poincaré, searching for a mathematical formula, or by Luria in the passage quoted above (p. 115). A better idea of the problem is obtained by substituting the term 'statement' for 'word' and including in its definition any act of expression whatever. In C category terms the problem is analogous to that of the sculptor finding his form in the block of his material, of the musician finding the formula of musical notation within the sounds he hears, of the man of action finding the actions that represent his thoughts. One of the peculiarities of this discussion lies in its being an example of the problem being discussed. It is an attempt to find a verbal formulation to which psycho-analytic realizations approximate. I restate the problem thus: psycho-analysis, the thing-in-itself, existed. It remained for Freud to reveal the formulation embedded in it. Conversely, once formulated by Freud it remains for others (including Freud himself) to discover the meaning of the conjunction bound by his formulation.

It is necessary to postulate 'thinking' without supposing a thinker to be essential. I shall not at this point try to explain why. All thinking and all thoughts are true when there is no thinker. In contrast to this, for lies and falsities a thinker is absolutely necessary. In any situation where a thinker is present the thoughts when formulated are expressions of falsities and lies. The only true thought is one that has never found an individual to 'contain' it.

The messianic idea may be supposed to have a counterpart, the absolute truth, O, for which a thinker is not necessary. Falsity is the characteristic of thought within an individual, or thought within a container. It follows that all thought as it is ordinarily known, that is, as an attribute of the human being, is false, the problem associated with it being the degree and nature of the falsity. The lie is a falsity associated with 'morals'.

The messianic idea is a term representing O at the point at which its evolution and the evolution of a thinker intersect. The mystic, as seen in descriptions 6 and 7, is a thinker who claims the capacity for direct contact with O. The degree of falsity depends on whether the relationship with O is commensal, symbiotic, or parasitic. It is not often enough recognized that a patient in whom resistance is active can be reacting against what he feels to be a thought in search of a thinker. It is supposedly his own thought (classical resistance theory), but it does not have to be so.

The thought O and the thinker exist independently of each other. There is no reaction, or, as we should ordinarily say, identifying ourselves with the thinker, the truth has not been discovered though it 'exists'. In symbiosis the thought and the thinker correspond, and modify each other through the correspondence. The thought proliferates and the thinker develops. In a parasitic relationship between thought and thinker there is a correspondence but the correspondence is category 2, meaning that the formulation is known to be false but is retained as a barrier against truth which is feared as annihilating to the container or vice versa. The falsity proliferates until it becomes the lie. The barrier of the lie increases the need for the truth and vice versa.

The commensal position changes when thought and thinker approximate. In more usual terms, a critical situation arises when a 'discovery' threatens. It is commonly said that messianic hopes were more than usually active at the birth of Jesus and it is a matter for remark that more than one investigator often seems to be approaching a discovery at the time when a discovery is made. The resistance of the thinker to the unthought thought is characteristic of category 2 thinking. The crucial problem appears to be the relative strength of the messianic idea and the personality who is to 'contain' it. We must therefore reconsider the personality. To do this I shall use descriptions 6 and 7 as pictorial representations (C category) of the parts composing the totality of the individual, not the group. I am assuming that the reader keeps in mind existing theories of personality structure. It is not to be supposed that they are to be abandoned or even modified by what follows. Existing theories are F category formulations; what takes place in the consulting-room is an emotional situation which is itself the intersection of an evolving O with another evolving O. The description I am giving is, as it has been throughout this chapter, a C category formulation intended to bridge the gap between a unique event on the one hand and a generalized F category formulation on the other.

Description 3 (cycle 2): The messianic idea clothes itself in a variety of forms. Though it may take any form there appears to be difficulty for form and idea to achieve a symbiotic or commensal relationship. Therefore it is difficult to find a formulation by which I can convey my meaning to the reader, but I can point to the consulting-room or group where he may intuit it for himself. Similarly, I can direct him to observe the word 'cure' when he hears it; for 'within' this word he may be able to intuit the messianic idea. His attention should dwell on formulations in which he is described in positive terms; for 'within' these statements he may be able to intuit the 'contained' messianic idea. Whether the statement appears outwardly to be representing a summer holiday or a car or a person or a state in time, he should be able by degrees to intuit the frequent occurrence of the messianic idea and be persuaded of its reality and his ability to feel its presence.

When I say the reader might search the consulting-room or group, I am restricting the field of search to provide a 'container' wherein the search may be pursued without difficulty and relatively quickly. Yet it is doubtful whether intuition of a constant conjunction in the domain of psychic reality can be attainable quickly or easily. Therefore there can be no short cut for the psycho-analyst; he can hope that experience may enable him to intuit the messianic idea or recognize that this hope is itself a formulation containing it.

The idea that the messianic idea is contained within the analysis, or that descriptions 6 and 7 can be used as C category statements or formulations of the individual personality, implies that the personality can be represented by a ♂♀ relationship and that the personality has a ♀♂ relationship with a psycho-analysis. Such a formulation assists the psycho-analyst to intuit a personality, external to the psycho-analysis, which is present in the psycho-analysis only by 'hearsay'; the patient becomes a voice reporting that the messianic idea is abroad. A typical complexity of the ♀♂ relation, significant for its bearing on 'acting-out', relates to beta-elements lying outside the domain of thought proper but appearing to belong to it because they are represented 'in' the psycho-analysis by C3 statements made by the analysand. The psycho-analyst and his analysand appear, therefore, to be excluded from the domain of action and 'confined within' the domain of thought in such a way that they are not in a position to 'psycho-analyse' but only to substitute 'psycho-analysis' for psycho-analytic thinking, which is a prelude to interpretations – the psycho-analytic counterpart of action.

Psycho-analytic practice shows that the motives for any human activity are numerous and complex. They are derived from a background of sensuous desires; as fast as one is demonstrated it is apparent that further desires lie unknown. The aims of the psycho-analytic couple are arrived at by conjecture and are formulated, at least as far as the analysand is concerned, in terms representative of sensuous experience. Even the objects of curiosity are formulated in terms suitable to a sensuous background. In so far as desires can be stated they will be sensuous desires and sensuous aims, the overriding aim being to keep alive. Without exception these aims and desires are not relevant to psycho-analysis. Nor have they proved relevant in either Judaism or Christianity. Their place has not yet been taken by any formulations that are more satisfactory. So long as thinking is regarded as subordinate to the senses there is no difficulty. If thinking is a primary activity, the *aims* of contemplation or meditation are presumed to exist because thinking is tied to its genetic history as subordinate to muscular activity; similarly, muscular activity is presumed to have an aim in accord with the dominance of the pleasure principle.

It is possible that the vacuity produced by the subordination of sensuous aims to growth of a capacity for contemplation or meditation was filled, in the course of his teaching, by Jesus. But as his teaching was subjected to the twin pressures I have described, namely, annihilation by physical destruction on the one hand and divine honours on the other, we do not know what such a solution might have been. In practice the problem is shelved; thinking remains subordinate to the satisfaction of sensuous desires.

In consequence, psycho-analysis is saddled with an aim that, according to their various desires, is attributed to it by both analyst and analysand. Both are debarred from fulfilling their aim when the aim is pursued in the domain of action and the psycho-analysis is confined to the domain of thought in which thought is the only means of fulfilment. The 'conflict' is between action and thought, the counterpart, in descriptions 6 and 7, being the conflict expressed in St Augustine's refutation of the responsibility of Christianity for the fall of Rome. In the individual, demands for action and sensuous gratifications associated with physical survival conflict with the demand for mental 'activity'. The latter cannot justify itself in terms comprehensible to the former. The former cannot justify itself to the latter, for its apparatus of sensuous fulfilment is irrelevant to the domain of thought.

I have used the term 'conflict', in describing action and thought, as a reminder of the accepted view. The object of using ♀♂ is to differentiate the states of containment which, as with thought and action, prevent conflict by containing thought and containing action in a mutually exclusive commensal state. In this condition thought and action do not modify each other but persist commensally in the same personality. Actions that appear to be compulsive are in reality beta-elements confined to the domain of action and thus insulated against thoughts, which are confined to the domain of thought – which includes psycho-analysis. Similarly, thoughts are within the domain of thought and cannot be influenced by beta-elements confined within the domain of action. An apparent exception, not real, is provided by C3 elements in thoughts that appear to bring A category into the realm of thought but are only C category *records* of action; there is no conflict.

The domains of thought and action are so close, when the musculature used in talking is involved with beta-elements, that the distinction between them becomes confused. The same confusion arises if intolerance of frustration leads to a substitution of thought for action. The associated omnipotence of thought obstructs the proper use of the musculature, as a feeling of helplessness stimulated by ineffectual muscular action is often the genetic base of omnipotence: when one is active the other is present.

In the previous paragraphs I have given examples of ♀♂ associated with outside and inside. They have a psychological value in giving body to a formulation that might otherwise lack it, but the reader should seek further instances from his practice. According to his background a patient will describe various objects as containers, such as his mind, the unconscious, the nation; others as contained, such as his money, his ideas. The objects are many but the relationships are not.

The individual always displays some aspect of his personality that is stable and constant even though it may sometimes be very difficult to detect in the welter of evidence for instability; it may appear only in the regularity with which the patient attends his sessions. In this stability will be found the counterpart of what, in descriptions 6 and 7, I have called the Establishment. It will be maintained with great tenacity as the only force likely to contain the counterpart of the messianic idea. Reciprocally, the messianic idea is the only force likely to withstand the pressures of the counterpart of the Establishment in the individual. Fears of megalomanic identification with the messianic idea are associated with an inability to be at one with the omnipotent Father. The counterpart of the Establishment in the individual is not related to father or mother but can be related to fragments of both.

In the ♀♂ configuration decision is synonymous with selection for inclusion or exclusion. Thus the psycho-analyst has to decide whether to include himself in or exclude himself from various groups; to include or exclude given associations, ideas, experiences, and so on. The Establishment of the group has to decide to include or exclude certain individuals. The personality decides to include or exclude certain characteristics or, failing that, to include or exclude awareness of their existence. Dislike of the onus of decision, or awareness of responsibility for the decision, contributes to the formulation of selection procedures by which selection, like dogma and laws of science, is made to act as a substitute for judgement or a scapegoat for the guilt attendant on overtly acknowledged exercise of responsibility.

The configuration to which I have drawn attention can be seen to have a penumbra of associations which retain an illuminating function in the circumstances on which they are brought to bear. At times the light they shed distorts by over-emphasis of the irrelevant past and occlusion of the unknown (and therefore relevant) present and future. Once the constancy of the configuration is recognized its nature can be assessed and related to psycho-analytic theory. Reciprocally, theory can be reformulated when it requires readjustment.

The primitive formulation of ♀♂ in C category terms of breast and mouth, penis and vagina, has the simplicity of all C category formulations. Although descriptions 6 and 7 appear more complex, they too share the stamp of all C category formulations. Both appear to differ from the configurations represented by the Kleinian theory of paranoid–schizoid and depressive position interplay. I am unwilling to accept this apparent cleavage. The most satisfactory formulation that displays the underlying harmony relates to the practice of psycho-analysis.

The discussion of the configuration of container and contained has occupied a considerable space in this book. It may, therefore, seem surprising if, at this stage and in relatively few sentences, I describe what is perhaps the most important mechanism employed by the practising psycho-analyst. It requires less description and is relatively more easily grasped. It is for these reasons only that it occupies what may appear to be an insignificant place in this book. It is derived from Melanie Klein's descriptions of the paranoid–

schizoid and depressive positions, and to these the reader should refer.

Here, briefly, is my formulation of this matter as it concerns the practising analyst:

In every session the psycho-analyst should be able, if he has followed what I have said in this book, particularly with regard to memory and desire, to be aware of the aspects of the material that, however familiar they may seem to be, relate to what is unknown both to him and to the analysand. Any attempt to cling to what he knows must be resisted for the sake of achieving a state of mind analogous to the paranoid–schizoid position. For this state I have coined the term 'patience' to distinguish it from 'paranoid–schizoid position', which should be left to describe the pathological state for which Melanie Klein used it. I mean the term to retain its association with suffering and tolerance of frustration.

'Patience' should be retained without 'irritable reaching after fact and reason' until a pattern 'evolves'. This state is the analogue to what Melanie Klein has called the depressive position. For this state I use the term 'security'. This I mean to leave with its association of safety and diminished anxiety. I consider that no analyst is entitled to believe that he has done the work required to give an interpretation unless he has passed through both phases – 'patience' and 'security'. The passage from the one to the other may be very short, as in the terminal stages of analysis, or it may be long. Few, if any, psycho-analysts should believe that they are likely to escape the feelings of persecution and depression commonly associated with the pathological states known as the paranoid–schizoid and depressive positions. In short, a sense of achievement of a correct interpretation will be commonly found to be followed almost immediately by a sense of depression. I consider the experience of oscillation between 'patience' and 'security' to be an indication that valuable work is being achieved.

13 · *Prelude to or Substitute for Achievement*

'I had not a dispute but a disquisition with Dilke on various subjects; several things dove-tailed in my mind, and at once it struck me what quality went to form a Man of Achievement, especially in Literature, and which Shakespeare possessed so enormously – I mean Negative Capability, that is, when a man is capable of being in uncertainties, mysteries, doubts, without any irritable reaching after fact and reason' – John Keats.[1]

A number of aspects of the practice of psycho-analysis must now be discussed; I group them under the Language of Achievement. The quotation from Keats will serve as an introduction to the area to be covered. Language is loosely and widely defined to include behaviour of which it is sometimes said 'actions speak louder than words'. Set over against and in contrast with the Language of Achievement I consider the language that is a substitute for, and not a prelude to, action. Language of Achievement includes language that is both prelude to action and itself a kind of action; the meeting of psycho-analyst and analysand is itself an example of this language. This discussion is centred on the problem of bringing attention to bear on the realizations to which Freud's theories approximate.

Any session should be judged by comparison with the Keats formulation so as to guard against one commonly unobserved fault leading to analysis 'interminable'. The fault lies in the failure to observe and is intensified by the inability to appreciate the significance of observation. I have rarely failed to experience hatred of psycho-analysis and its

[1] 'Letter to George and Thomas Keats', 21 December 1817.

reciprocal, sexualization of psycho-analysis. These are part of a 'constant conjunction'. In C category terms: the human animal has not ceased to be persecuted by his mind and the thoughts usually associated with it – whatever their origin may be. Therefore I do not expect any psycho-analysis properly done to escape the odium inseparable from the mind. Refuge is sure to be sought in mindlessness, sexualization, acting-out, and degrees of stupor. The psycho-analyst's attention must not wander from areas of material characterized either by the Language of Substitution or by the Language of Achievement; he must remain sensitive to both. I do not claim that sensitivity can be achieved easily: the mental space available to the analysand and the material observed are subject to so many transformations that such a claim suggests inexperience of the practice of psycho-analysis. The experienced analysand finds dreams a useful stand-by because psycho-analysts are rightly expected to want to hear them. Current events can be transformed to expression in sado-masochistic terms or near psychopathological jargon; there is no limit to the forms of transformation. Experience leads to an extension of the area over which the Language of Achievement operates and therefore an extension of the area in which its operation can be recognized. We must now consider the extension of the concept of vertices in relation to both individuals in the psycho-analytical couple.

It will be remembered that the term 'vertex' can be understood as similar to 'point of view' except in certain special instances. There is a psychological or mental specificity analogous to the specificity associated with the relationship of sense organs to sense impressions. To allow for this specificity it is necessary to discard the term 'point of view' and replace it by a more abstract term such as 'vertex'. Language of Achievement is always related to a vertex whether that vertex has been determined (or evolved) or not. Since we shall consider both psycho-analyst and analysand we shall have to approach our problem by moving *outside* the field usually thought of as belonging to psycho-analysis. The states of mind with which psycho-analysts deal comprise many that are generally the hunting-ground of other than psycho-analysts; for example, thieves, burglars, sexual perverts, murderers, blackmailers. Their mental world is matched by a world of external reality which caters for their states of mind by an established organization of international and commercial spying, police forces, religious organizations; the one group is matched by the other. A process of selection in Church or police force is carried out by examiners (in the instance of delinquents, by varieties of courts of law). It is intended to separate the good from the bad. Who or what is to exercise the power and what voice is to utter the Language of Achievement is a matter of consequence and has been accepted as such whether the field in which the struggle is carried on is the individual or agglomerations of individuals. Psycho-analysts accept their field to be the individual. The supposition that inhibitions should be decreased seems to be based on a view of the individual analogous to a view of the group in which democracy is a bad form of government but none the less the best.

The psycho-analyst and the analysand each have a vertex (or vertices) which, if it were known, would indicate the organization each regarded as best. Freud's scheme of id, ego, super-ego suggests one view of the organization of the personality, though there is nothing to suggest that the scheme represents a preference and not an observation.

The idea that is nourished by love develops from matrix to function in Language of Achievement; from which it can be transformed into achievement. But if the idea is subjected to splitting it may split again repeatedly, each split growing and having to be split again. Thus one gets not development but division and multiplication – cancerous, not qualitative, increase. There appears to be a great increase in ideation, but there is not, because all the ideas turn out, on inspection, to be the same one. The emotional matrix from which this springs is not envy and gratitude, but envy and greed. The idea is split over and over again and is felt to produce a quantity of splits – 'mental faeces'. Envy and gratitude, on the other hand, stimulate a desire for gain, but enable the individual to establish a good relation between what has been gained and that which has enabled him to gain it. The repudiation of the debt owed to his 'predatory' personality, and the need to continue repudiating it, exclude other parts of the personality from activity. The greed of the super-ego leads to the usurpation of the domain of reality (scientific facts) by the 'moral' outlook, and of 'scientific' laws by 'moral' laws.

The model for cancerous growth is not splitting of the object but splitting of the envy, each 'bit' then growing independently of every other 'bit'. Ostensibly these 'bits' appear as 'different' ideas. In fact they are a cover: ideas → impulses → ONE impulse. In this respect sessions can be regarded as repeating themselves, and the unchanging quality of the sessions should betray itself despite the multitudinous changes in disguise. Sometimes this state is described as a negative therapeutic reaction when it would be more accurately described as 'proliferation of fragmented envy'. If the envy were to assume an aspect of whole object it could be seen as envy of the personality capable of maturation and of the object stimulating maturation. The stimulating object is the breast (♀) or mouth (♂). They replace each other. The stimulating quality in turn replaces the stimulating object. A series of transformations is thus initiated, each a substitution for the previous one and each subject to splitting. Berkeley's criticism of Newton's mathematics is psychologically well based because it is NOT the mathematics of growth that is represented by the infinitesimal calculus and its use of concepts of infinitely small positive and negative increments – 'the ghosts of departed quantities'. It is psychologically more nearly true to regard Newton's formulation as *measurement* of restoration of whole objects than as measurement of growth. Is mathematics the Language of Achievement or of Restoration? What is required is not the decrease of inhibition but a decrease of the impulse to inhibit; the impulse to inhibit is fundamentally envy of the growth-stimulating objects. What is to be sought is an activity that is both the restoration of god (the Mother) and the evolution of god (the formless, infinite, ineffable, non-existent), which can be found only in the state in which there is NO memory, desire, understanding.

REFERENCES

BION, W. R. (1961). *Experiences in groups*. London: Tavistock.

— (1962). *Learning from experience*. London: Heinemann.

— (1963). *Elements of psycho-analysis*. London: Heinemann.

— (1965). *Transformations*. London: Heinemann.

EISSLER, K. R. (1965). *Medical orthodoxy and the future of psychoanalysis*. New York: International Universities Press.

FREGE, G. (1950). *The foundations of arithmetic*. Oxford: Blackwell.

FREUD, S. (1911). Formulations on the two principles of mental functioning. *Standard Edition* **12**.

KEATS, JOHN (1952). *Letters,* edited by M. B. Forman. 4th edition. London: Oxford University Press.

KNOX, R. A. (1950). *Enthusiasm*. London: Oxford University Press.

MONEY-KYRLE, R. E. (1961). *Man's picture of his world.* London: Duckworth.

SCHOLEM, G. (1955). *Major trends in Jewish mysticism*. London: Thames & Hudson.

Index

This index, like the rest of the book, is the outcome of an attempt at precision. The failure of the attempt will be clear; what may not be clear is the following dilemma: 'precision' is too often a distortion of the reality, 'imprecision' too often indistinguishable from confusion.